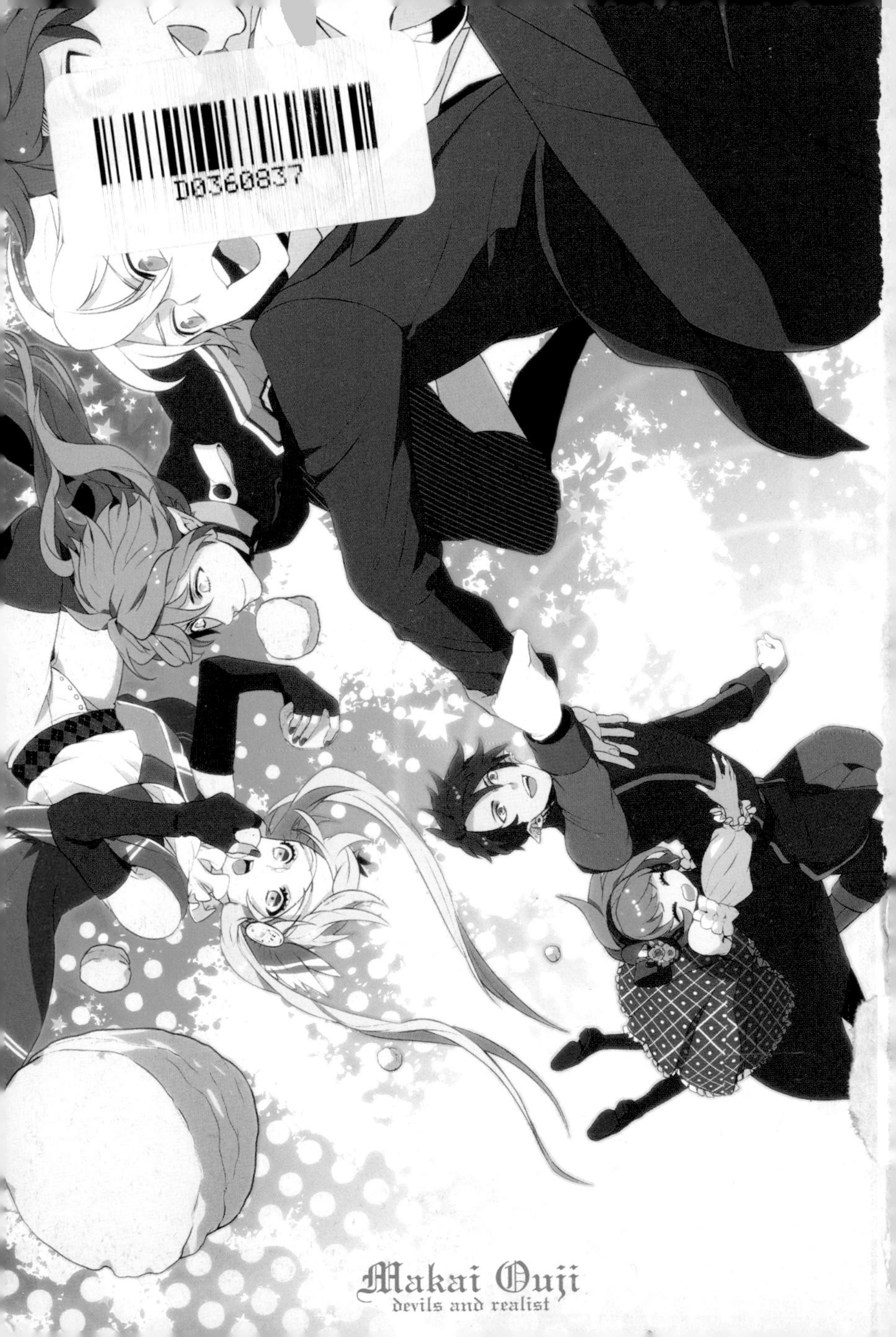

Makai Ouji
devils and realist

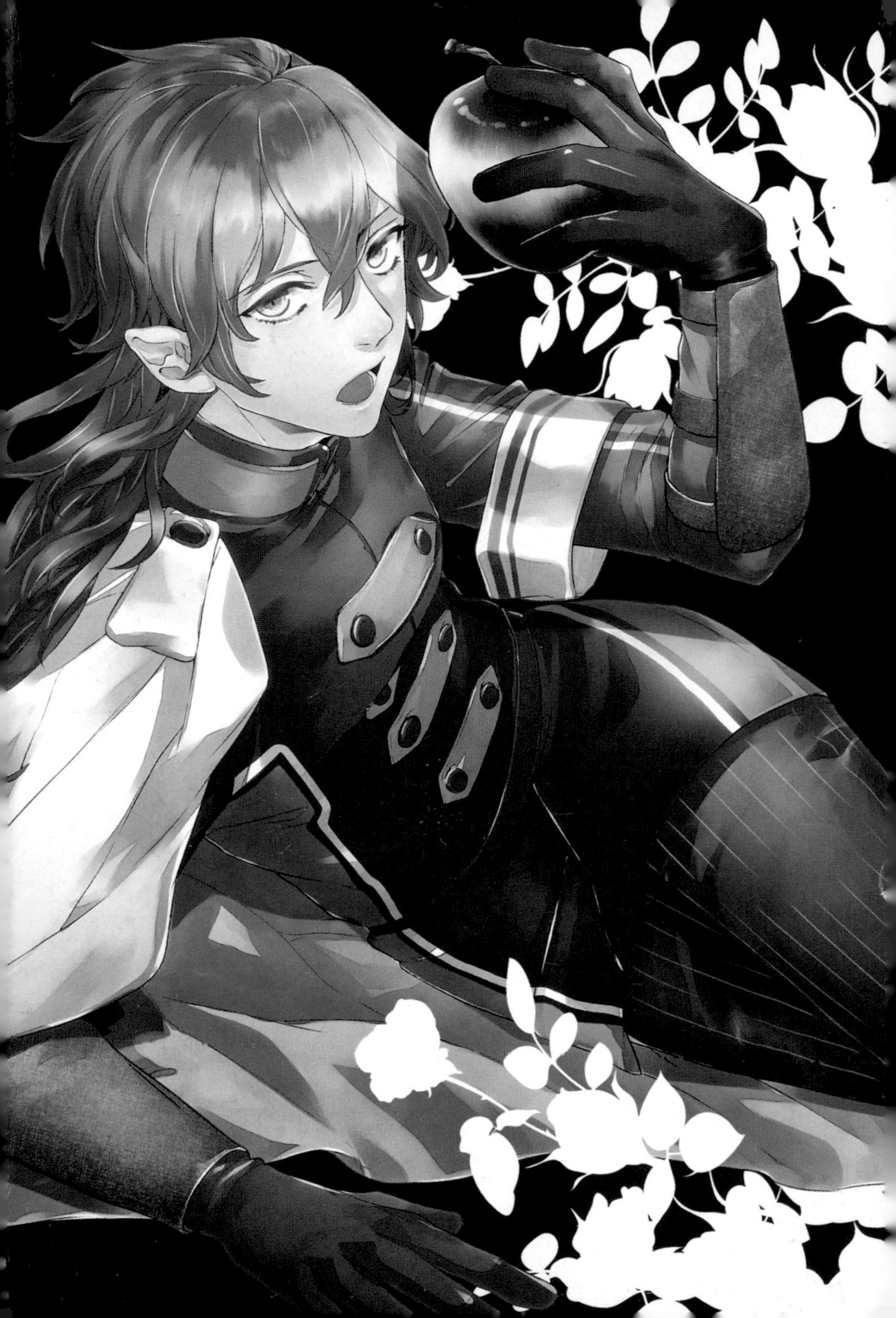

SEVEN SEAS ENTERTAINMENT PRESENTS

Devils

art by **UTAKO YUKIHIRO** / story by **MADOKA TAKADONO**   VOLUME 6

TRANSLATION
Jocelyne Allen

ADAPTATION
Danielle King

LETTERING
Roland Amago

LAYOUT
Bambi Eloriaga-Amago

COVER DESIGN
Nicky Lim

PROOFREADER
Lee Otter

ASSISTANT EDITOR
Lissa Pattillo

MANAGING EDITOR
Adam Arnold

PUBLISHER
Jason DeAngelis

MAKAI OUJI: DEVILS AND REALIST VOL. 6
© Utako Yukihiro/Madoka Takadono 2013
First published in Japan in 2013 by ICHIJINSHA Inc., Tokyo.
English translation rights arranged with ICHIJINSHA Inc., Tokyo, Japan.

Seven Seas books may be purchased in bulk for educational, business, or promotional use. For information on bulk purchases, please contact Macmillan Corporate & Premium Sales Department at 1-800-221-7945 (ext 5442) or write specialmarkets@macmillan.com.

Seven Seas and the Seven Seas logo are trademarks of Seven Seas Entertainment, LLC. All rights reserved.

ISBN: 978-1-626921-66-5

Printed in Canada

First Printing: August 2015

10 9 8 7 6 5 4 3 2 1

FOLLOW US ONLINE: *www.gomanga.com*

READING DIRECTIONS

This book reads from *right to left*, Japanese style. If this is your first time reading manga, you start reading from the top right panel on each page and take it from there. If you get lost, just follow the numbered diagram here. It may seem backwards at first, but you'll get the hang of it! Have fun!!

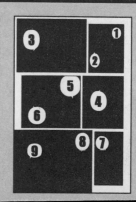

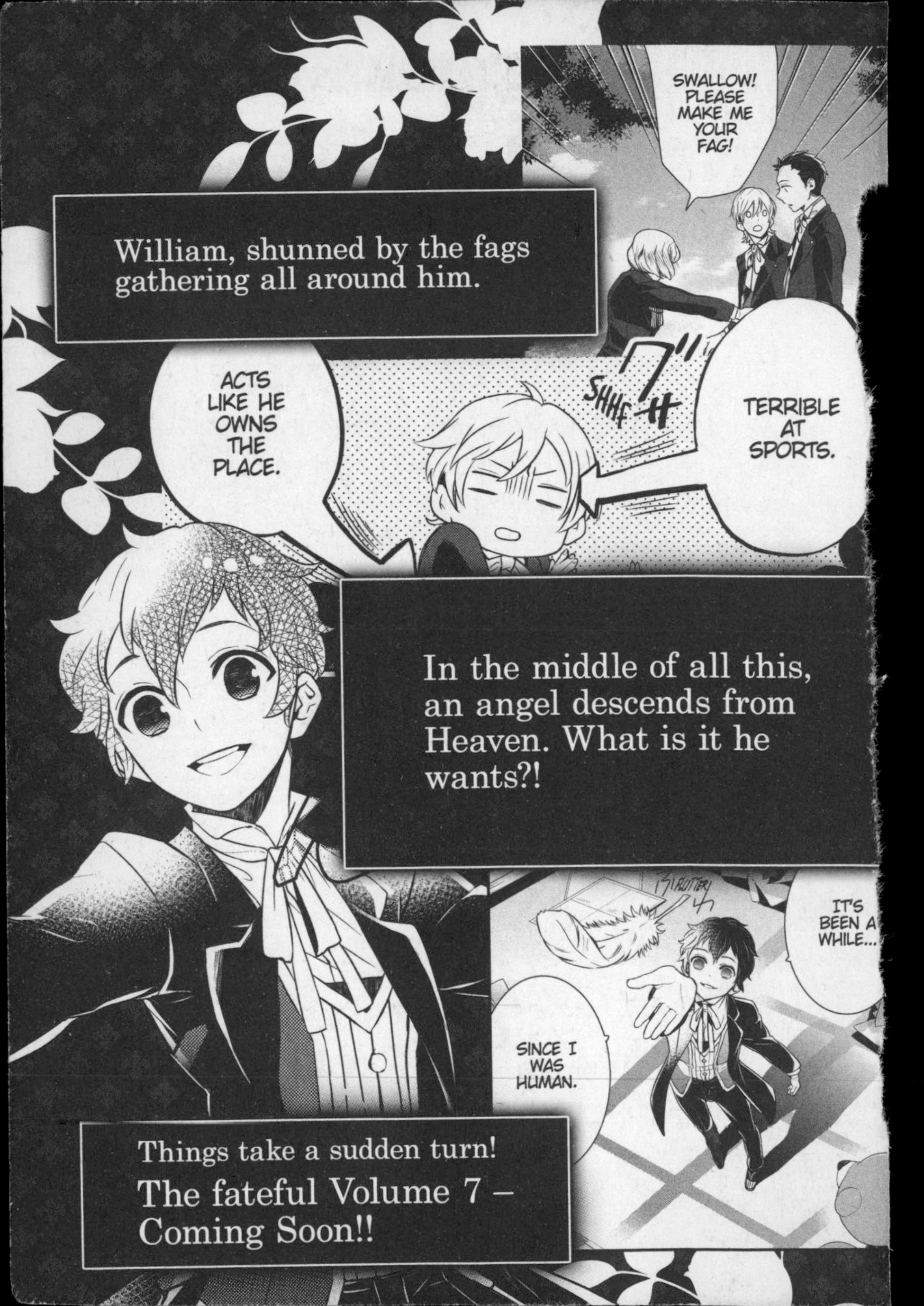
SWALLOW! PLEASE MAKE ME YOUR FAG!
William, shunned by the fags gathering all around him.
TERRIBLE AT SPORTS.
SHHF
ACTS LIKE HE OWNS THE PLACE.
In the middle of all this, an angel descends from Heaven. What is it he wants?!
IT'S BEEN A WHILE...
FLUTTER
SINCE I WAS HUMAN.
Things take a sudden turn!
The fateful Volume 7 – Coming Soon!!

Devils and Realist vol. 6

story by **Madoka Takadono**
art by **Utako Yukihiro**

Cast of Characters

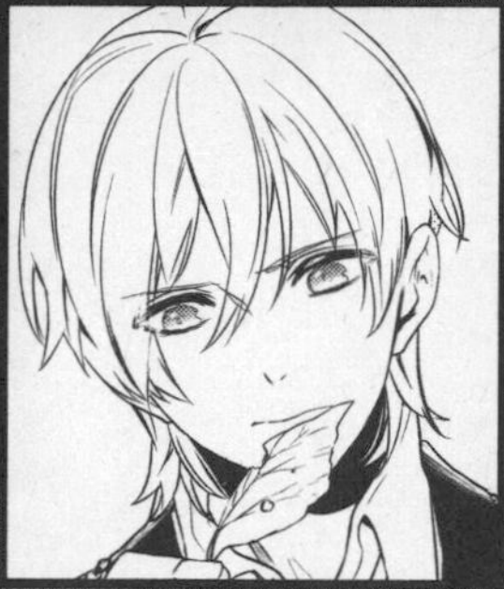

Kevin

William's capable yet gambling-addicted butler, who is also the pastor at the academy. In truth, he is the angel Uriel, who has been dispatched from Heaven.

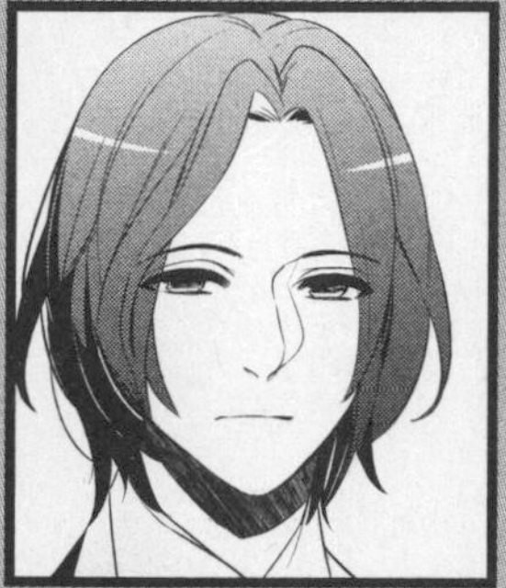

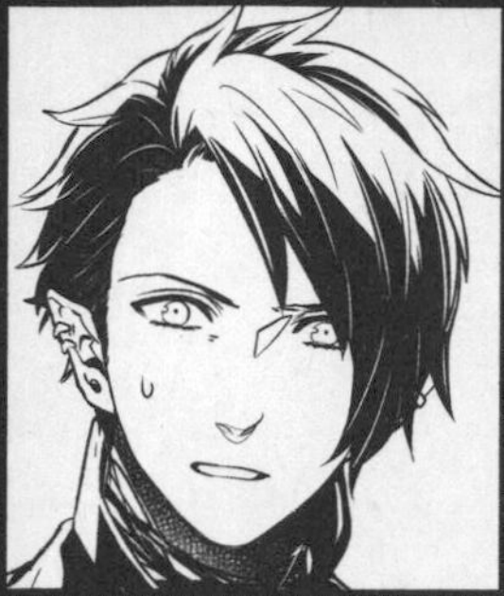

William

A brilliant realist from a famous noble family. As a descendant of King Solomon, he is the Elector with the authority to choose the representative king of Hell, though he is in denial of this fact.

Dantalion

Seventy-first Pillar of Hell, who commands its leading 36 armies. He is Grand Duke of the Underworld and a candidate to represent the king. At school, students rely on him during sporting events.

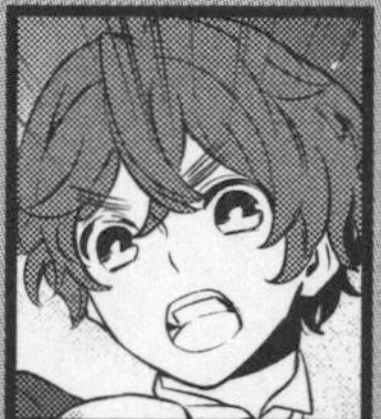

Isaac

William's classmate who is obsessed with supernatural phenomena.

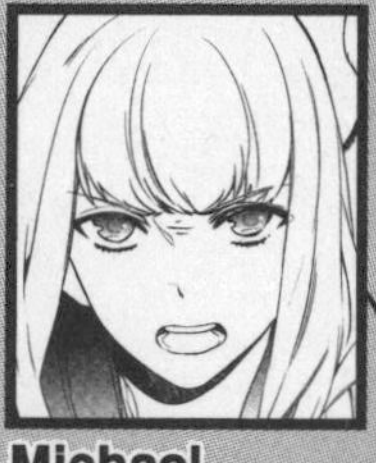

Michael

Vicious seraph who is planning to take William to Heaven. He visits Kevin to deliver a kick from time to time.

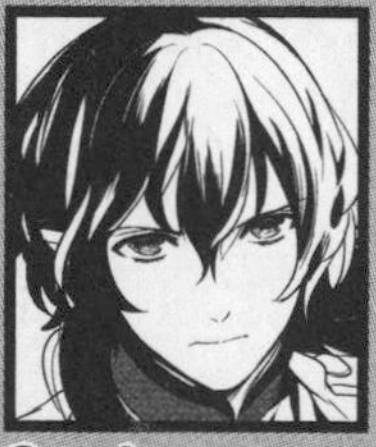

Camio

A candidate for representative king, Camio is Solomon's 53rd pillar and a Great President of Hell. He is an excellent student at school and serves as class representative.

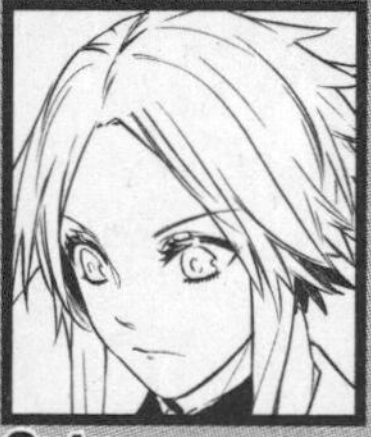

Sytry

Twelfth Pillar of Hell, who leads 60 armies. Sytry is Prince of Hell and a candidate to represent the king. He is treated like a princess at school because of his beautiful appearance.

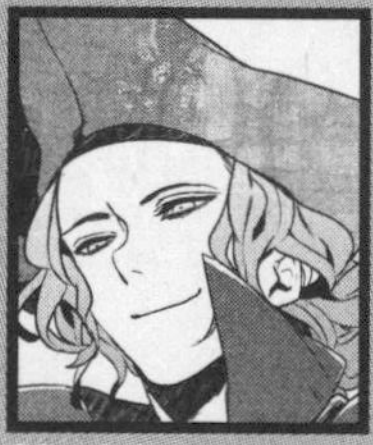

Mathers

A man who questions the duality of good and evil. Upon leaving the Church Army, he now calls himself Count Glenstrae.

The Story So Far

Demons Dantalion and Sytry appear suddenly before impoverished noble William Twining to tell him that he is the Elector--the person who will determine the representative king of Hell! The two of them masquerade as students at Stradford School, and William's life becomes more and more entangled in Hell's affairs. When the election of the representative king commences, the personality of Solomon manifests within William! However, Lucifer awakens, the election is postponed, and Solomon disappears. Meanwhile, in the human world, massacre rages in Paris while the angels plot to incite a religious ecstasy in William that would make him their pawn.

Pillar 32

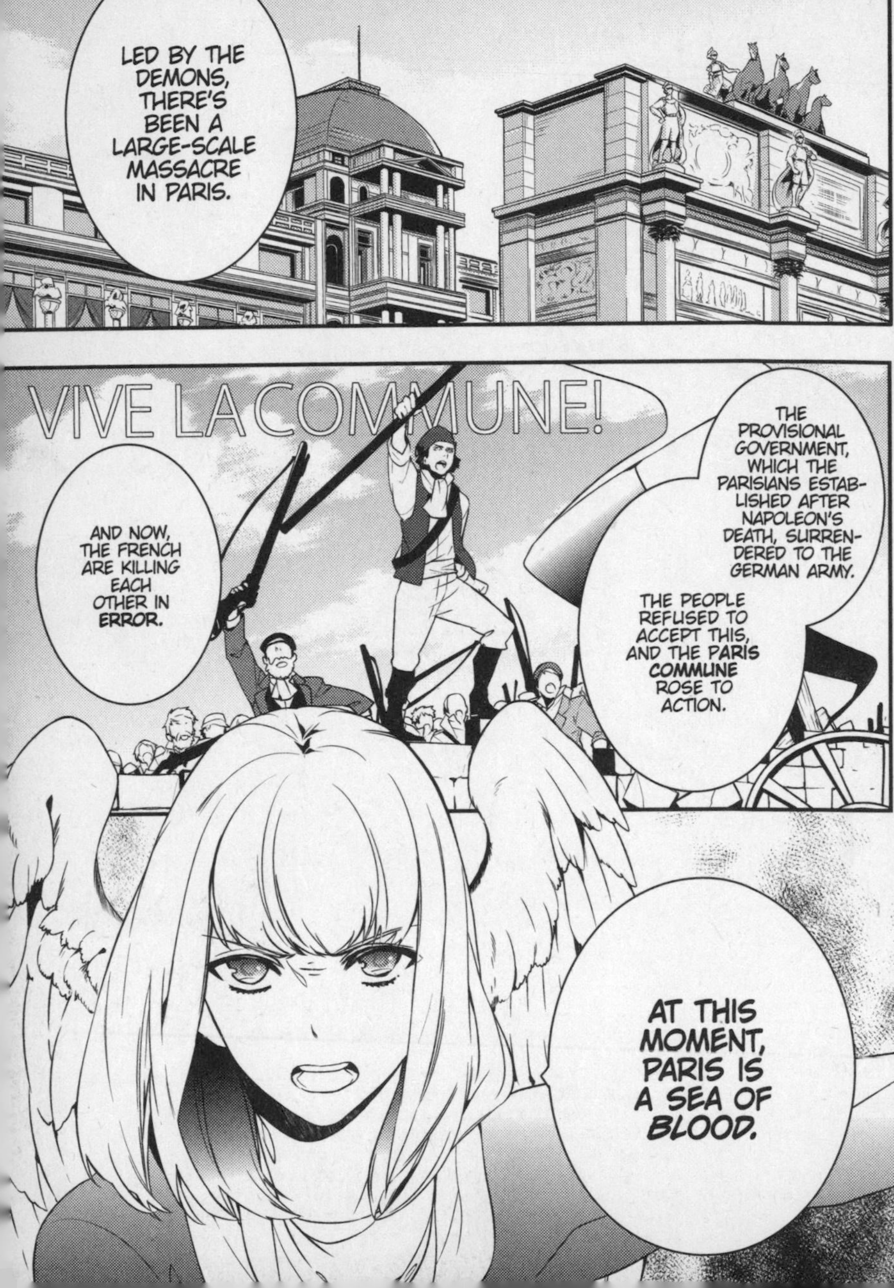
LED BY THE DEMONS, THERE'S BEEN A LARGE-SCALE MASSACRE IN PARIS.
THE PROVISIONAL GOVERNMENT, WHICH THE PARISIANS ESTAB-LISHED AFTER NAPOLEON'S DEATH, SURREN-DERED TO THE GERMAN ARMY.
THE PEOPLE REFUSED TO ACCEPT THIS, AND THE PARIS COMMUNE ROSE TO ACTION.
VIVE LA COMMUNE!
AND NOW, THE FRENCH ARE KILLING EACH OTHER IN ERROR.
AT THIS MOMENT, PARIS IS A SEA OF BLOOD.

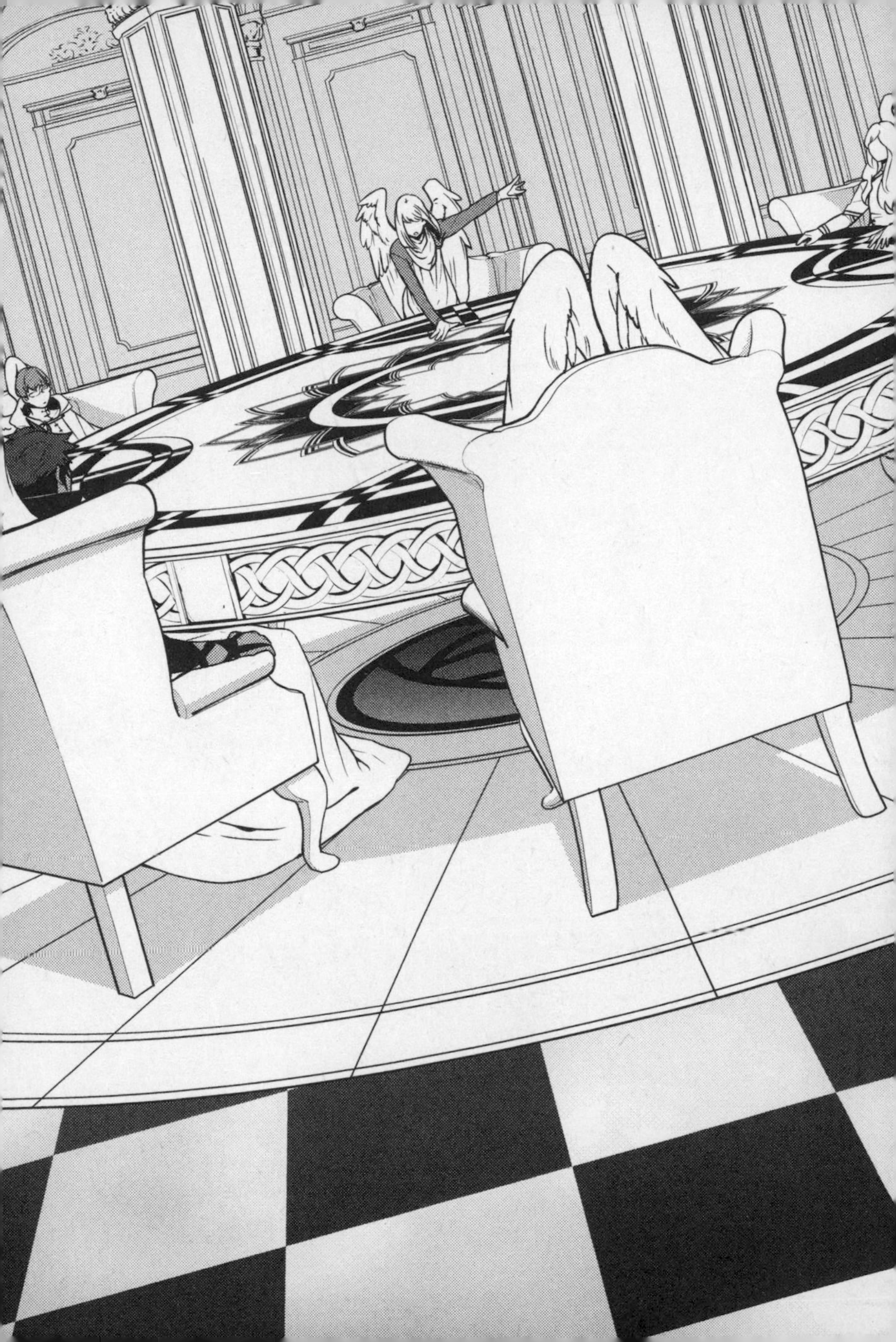

Pillar 32

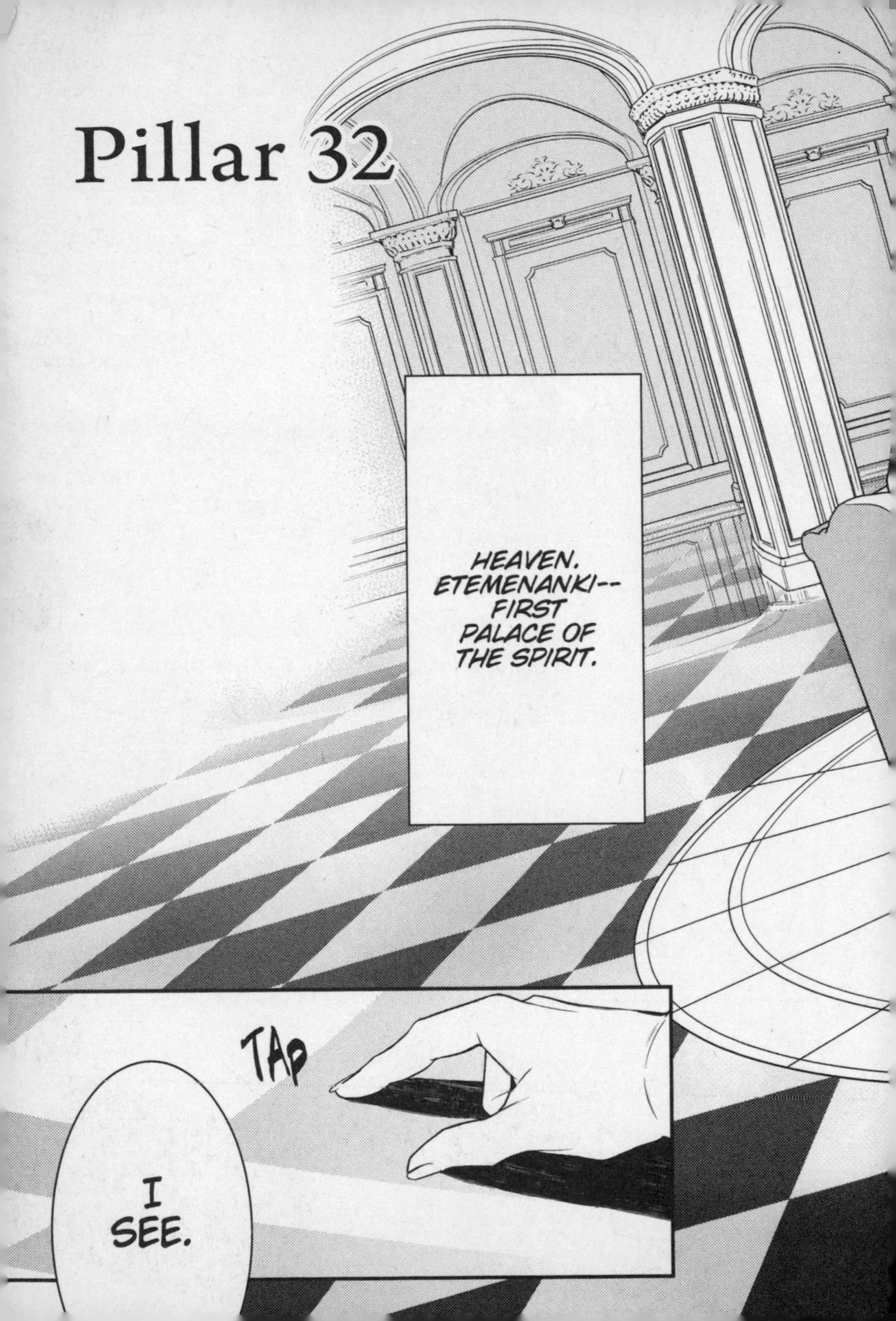
HEAVEN. ETEMENANKI-- FIRST PALACE OF THE SPIRIT.
TAp
I SEE.

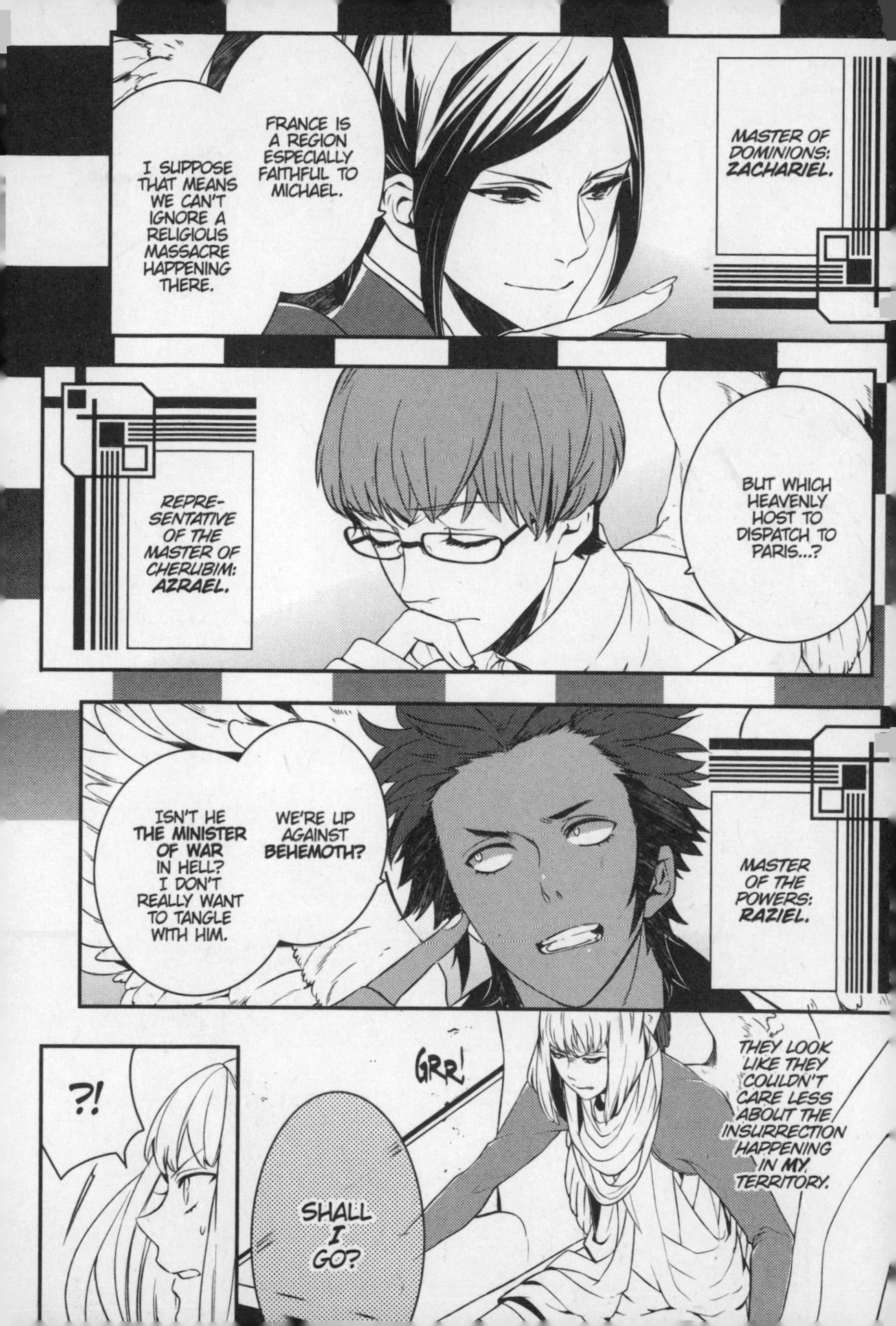
MASTER OF DOMINIONS: ZACHARIEL.
FRANCE IS A REGION ESPECIALLY FAITHFUL TO MICHAEL.
I SUPPOSE THAT MEANS WE CAN'T IGNORE A RELIGIOUS MASSACRE HAPPENING THERE.
BUT WHICH HEAVENLY HOST TO DISPATCH TO PARIS...?
REPRE-SENTATIVE OF THE MASTER OF CHERUBIM: AZRAEL.
MASTER OF THE POWERS: RAZIEL.
WE'RE UP AGAINST BEHEMOTH?
ISN'T HE THE MINISTER OF WAR IN HELL? I DON'T REALLY WANT TO TANGLE WITH HIM.
THEY LOOK LIKE THEY COULDN'T CARE LESS ABOUT THE INSURRECTION HAPPENING IN MY TERRITORY.
GRR!
SHALL I GO?
?!

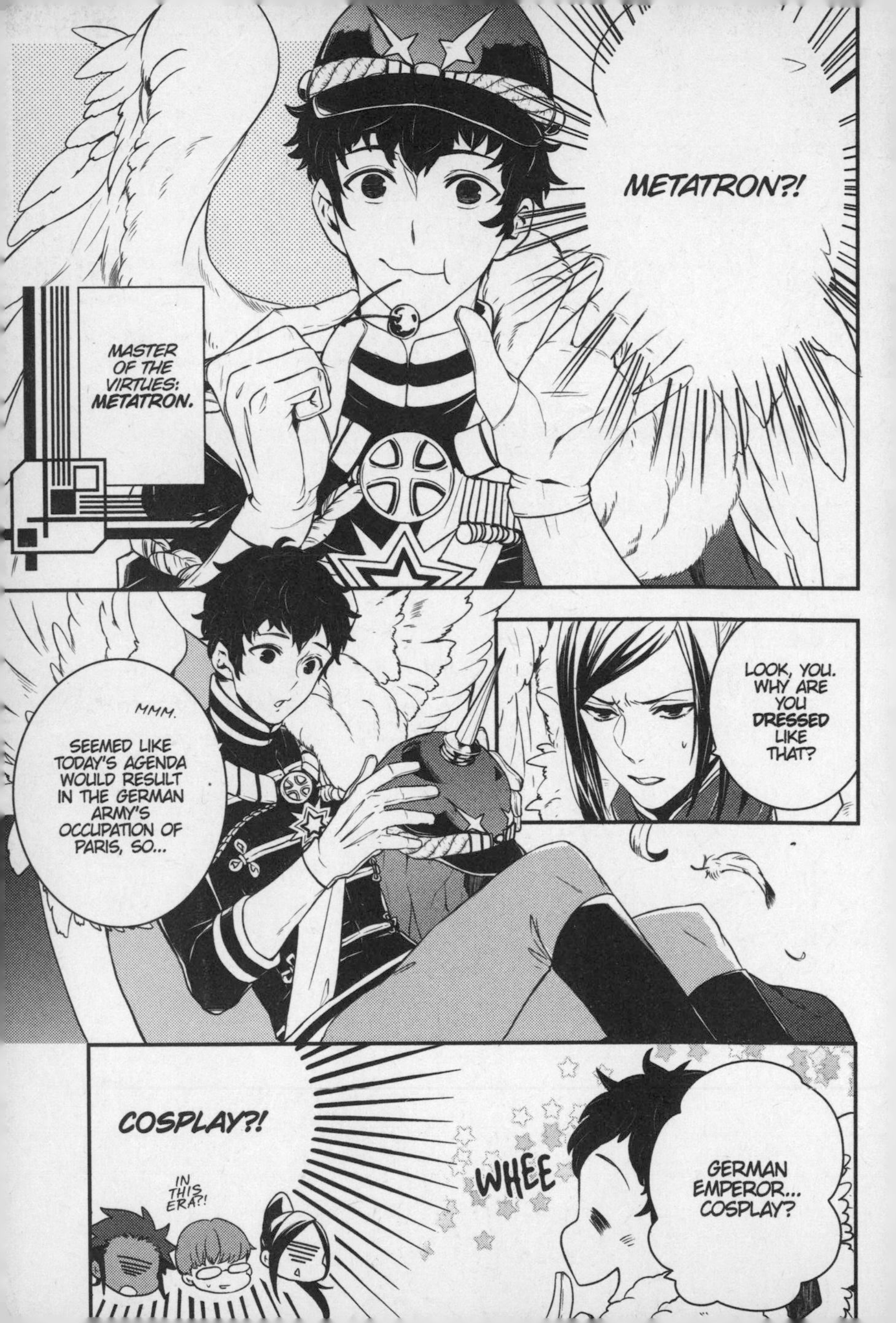
METATRON?!
MASTER OF THE VIRTUES: METATRON.
LOOK, YOU. WHY ARE YOU DRESSED LIKE THAT?
MMM.
SEEMED LIKE TODAY'S AGENDA WOULD RESULT IN THE GERMAN ARMY'S OCCUPATION OF PARIS, SO...
GERMAN EMPEROR... COSPLAY?
WHEE
COSPLAY?!
IN THIS ERA?!

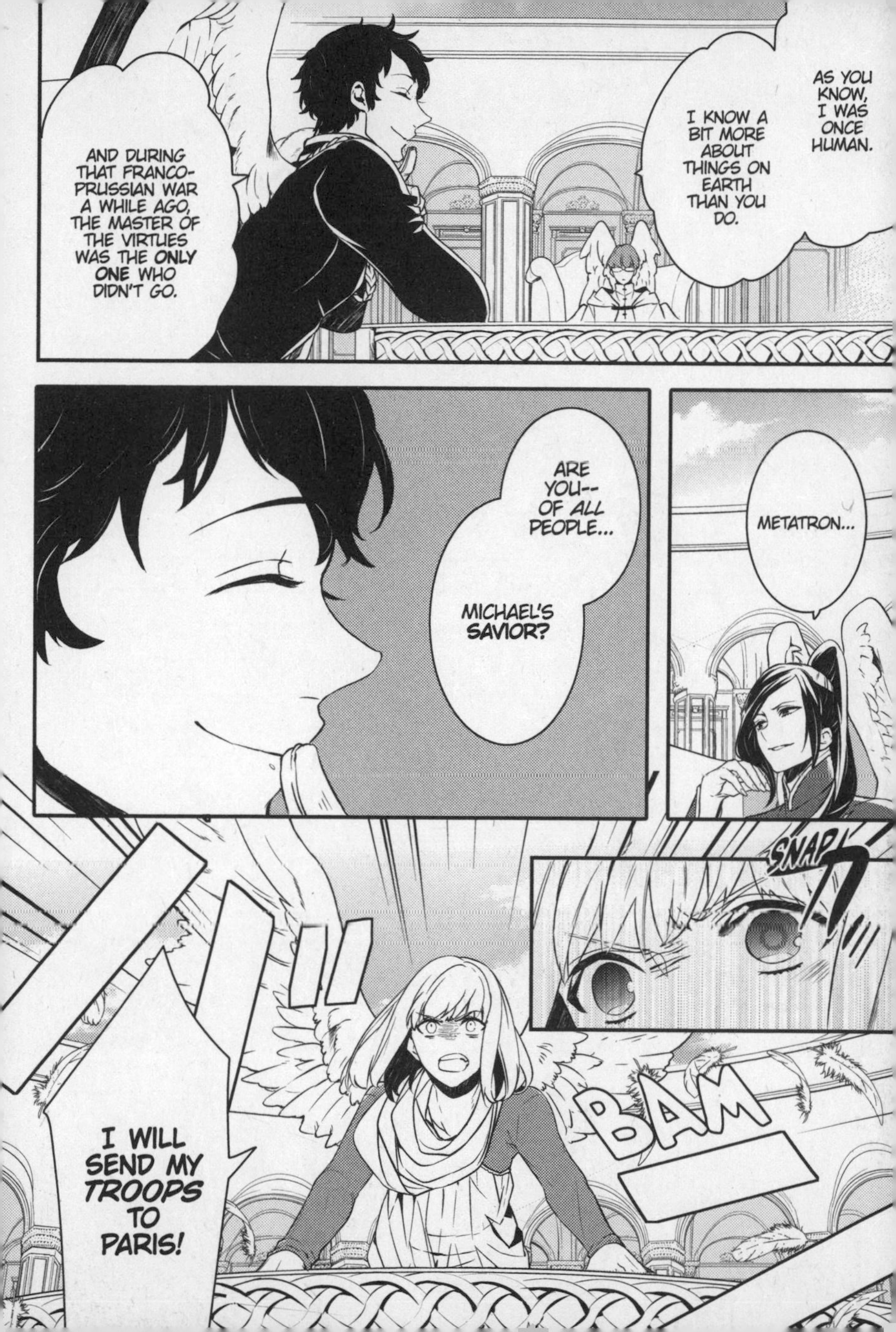
AS YOU KNOW, I WAS ONCE HUMAN.
I KNOW A BIT MORE ABOUT THINGS ON EARTH THAN YOU DO.
AND DURING THAT FRANCO-PRUSSIAN WAR A WHILE AGO, THE MASTER OF THE VIRTUES WAS THE ONLY ONE WHO DIDN'T GO.
METATRON...
ARE YOU-- OF ALL PEOPLE...
MICHAEL'S SAVIOR?
SNAP!
!!
BAM
I WILL SEND MY TROOPS TO PARIS!

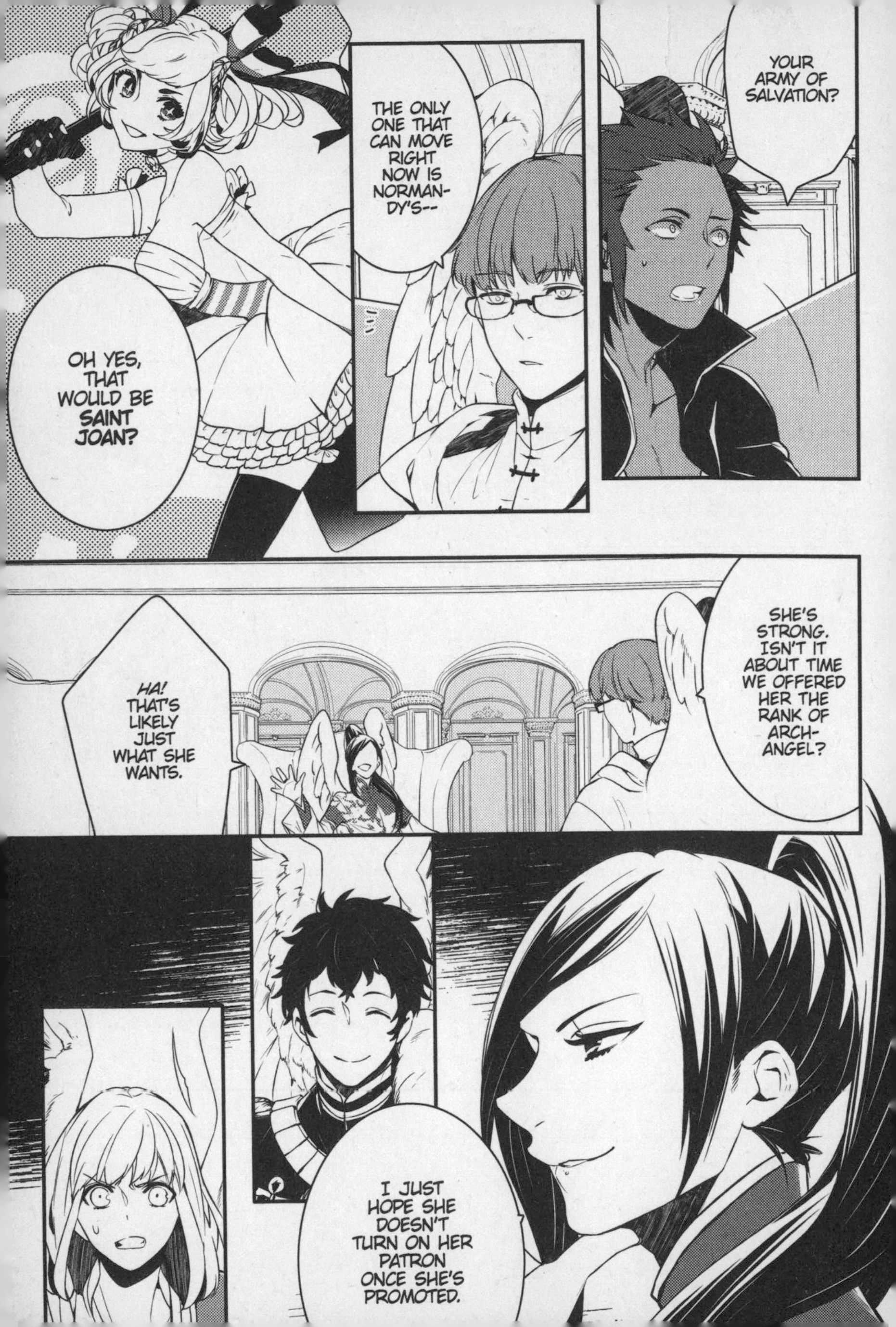
YOUR ARMY OF SALVATION?
THE ONLY ONE THAT CAN MOVE RIGHT NOW IS NORMAN-DY'S--
OH YES, THAT WOULD BE SAINT JOAN?
SHE'S STRONG. ISN'T IT ABOUT TIME WE OFFERED HER THE RANK OF ARCH-ANGEL?
HA! THAT'S LIKELY JUST WHAT SHE WANTS.
I JUST HOPE SHE DOESN'T TURN ON HER PATRON ONCE SHE'S PROMOTED.

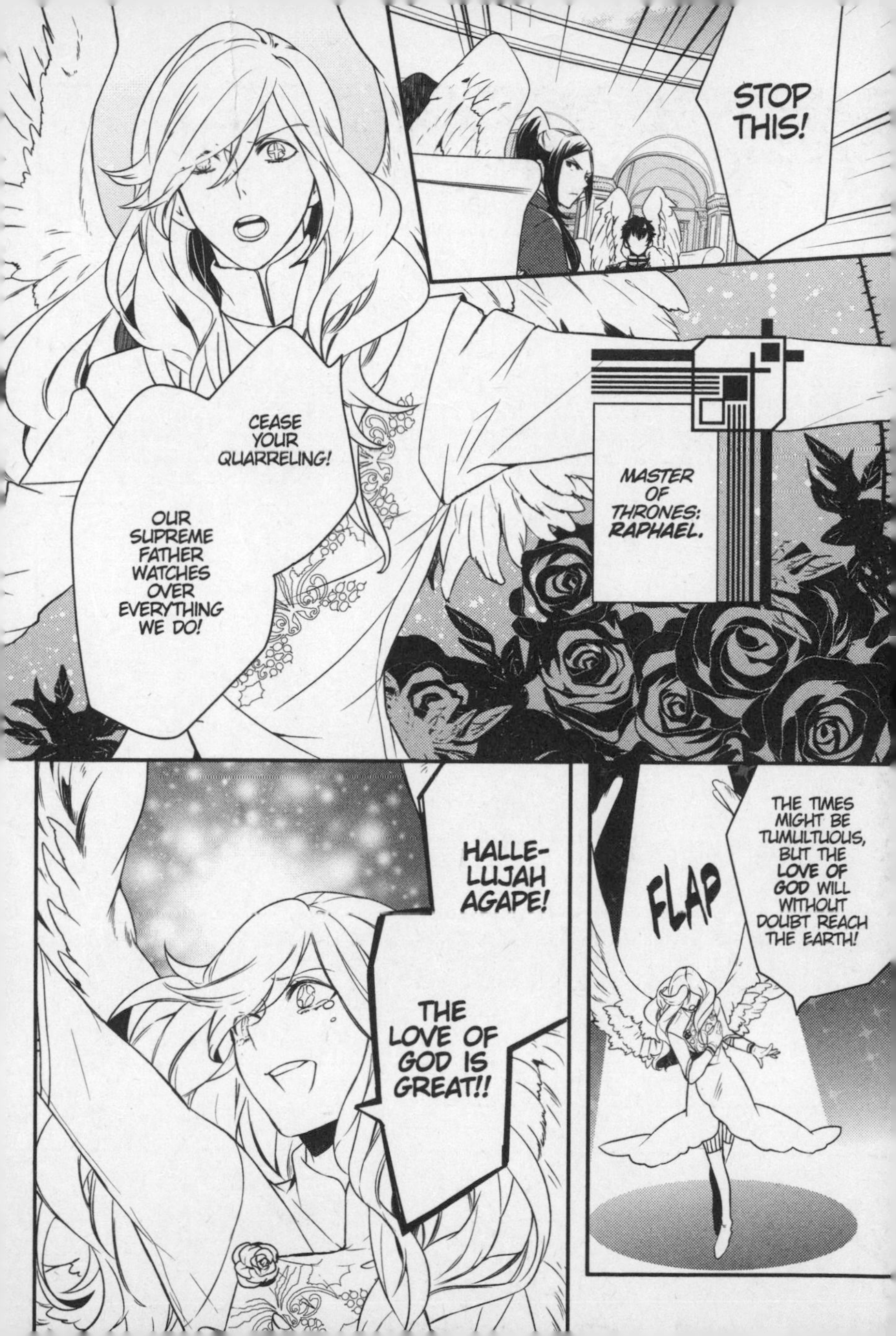
STOP THIS!
MASTER OF THRONES: RAPHAEL.
CEASE YOUR QUARRELING!
OUR SUPREME FATHER WATCHES OVER EVERYTHING WE DO!
THE TIMES MIGHT BE TUMULTUOUS, BUT THE LOVE OF GOD WILL WITHOUT DOUBT REACH THE EARTH!
FLAP
HALLE-LUJAH AGAPE!
THE LOVE OF GOD IS GREAT!!

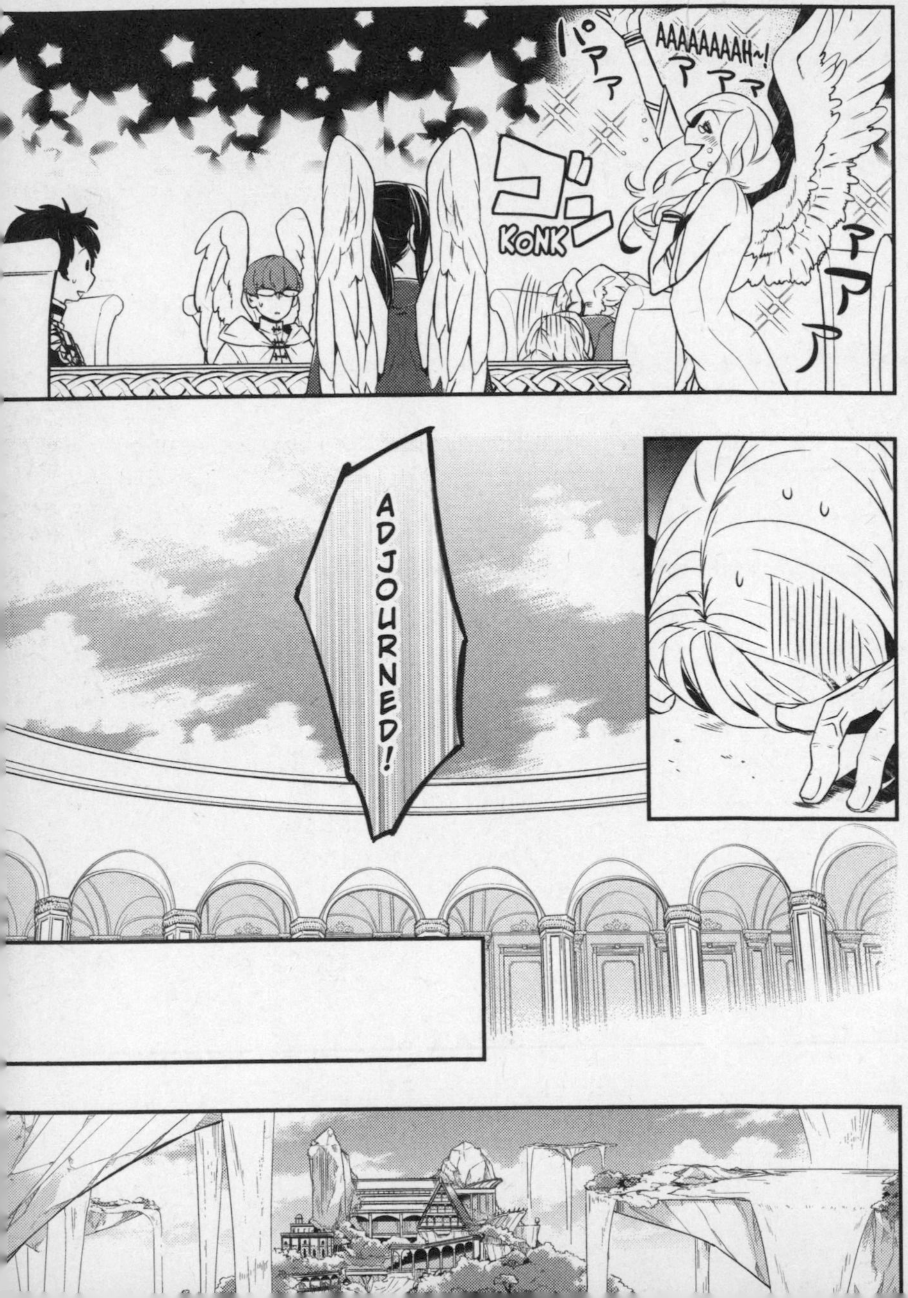
AAAAAAAAAH~!
KONK
ADJOURNED!

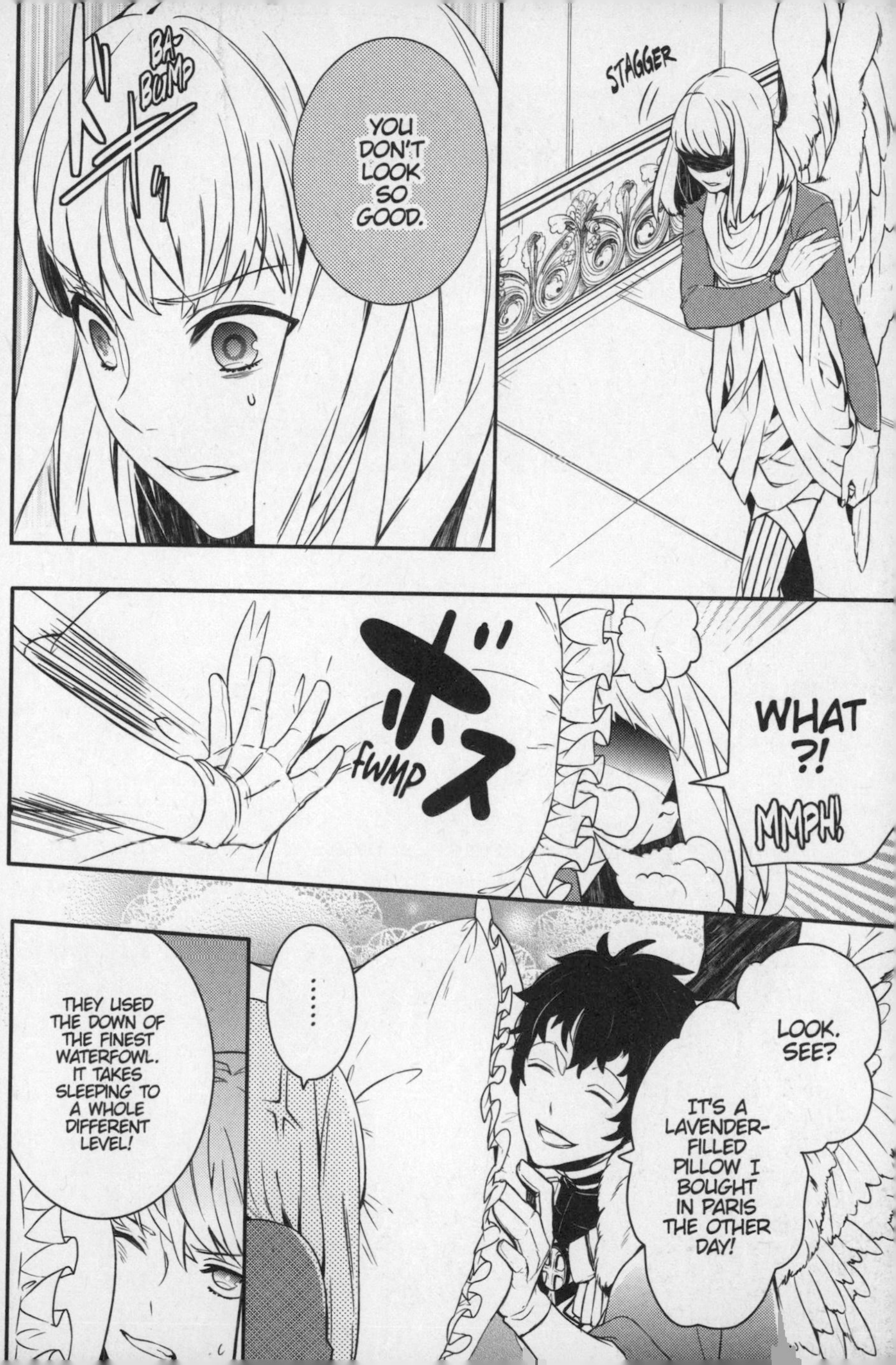
STAGGER
BA-BUMP
YOU DON'T LOOK SO GOOD.
WHAT?!
MMPH!
FWMP
LOOK. SEE?
IT'S A LAVENDER-FILLED PILLOW I BOUGHT IN PARIS THE OTHER DAY!
......
THEY USED THE DOWN OF THE FINEST WATERFOWL. IT TAKES SLEEPING TO A WHOLE DIFFERENT LEVEL!

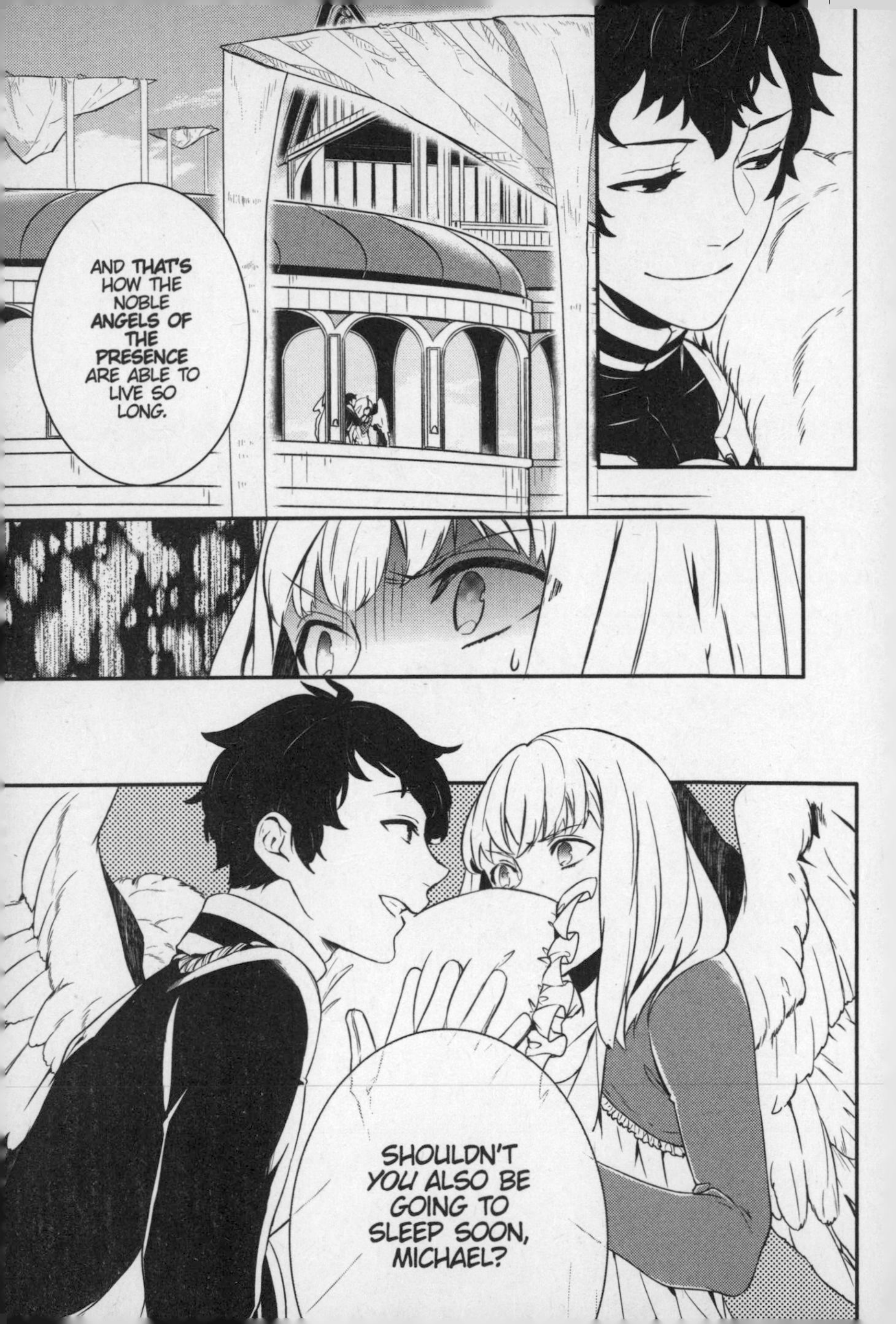
AND THAT'S HOW THE NOBLE ANGELS OF THE PRESENCE ARE ABLE TO LIVE SO LONG.
SHOULDN'T YOU ALSO BE GOING TO SLEEP SOON, MICHAEL?

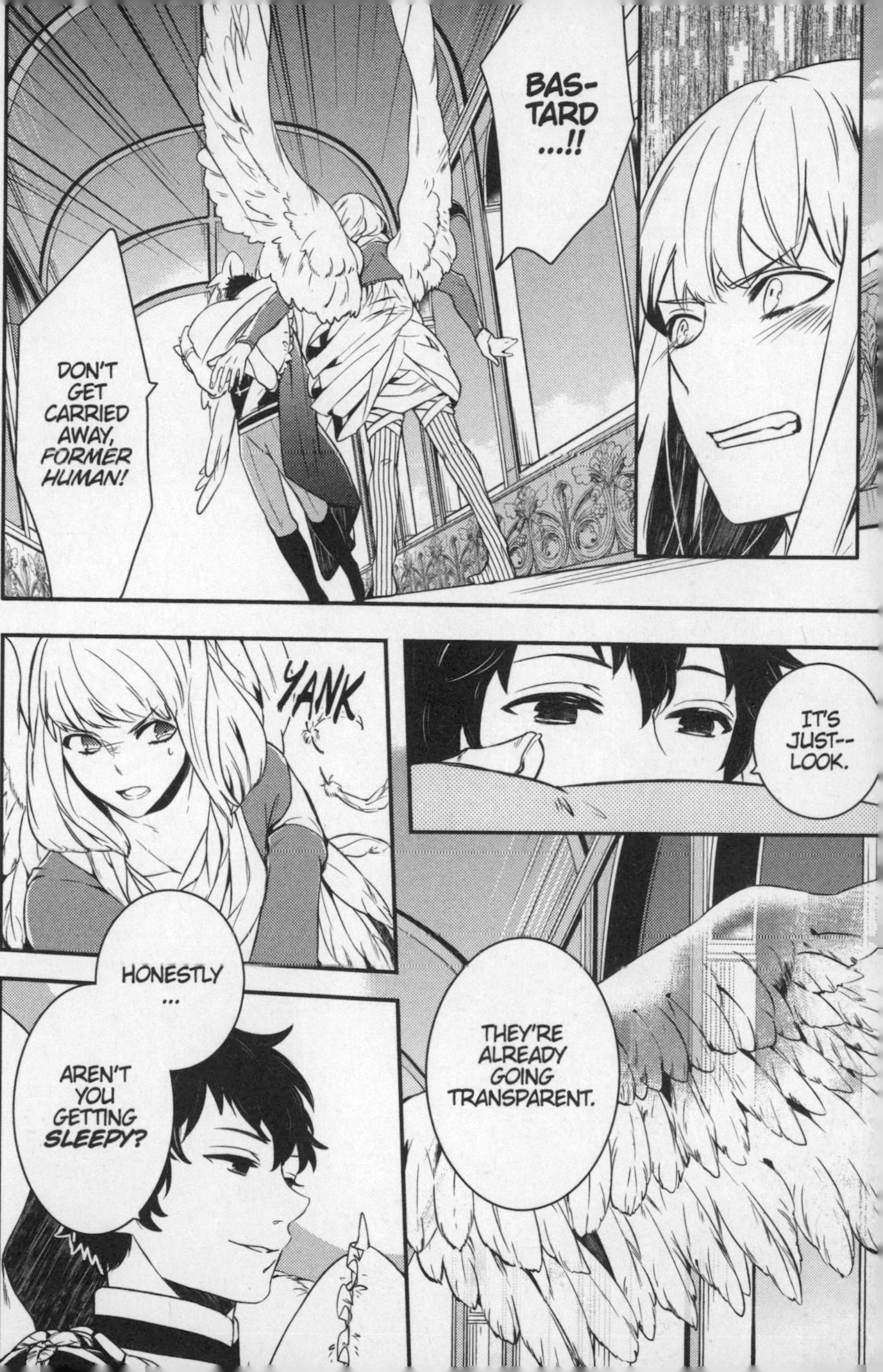
BAS-TARD ...!!
DON'T GET CARRIED AWAY, FORMER *HUMAN!*
IT'S JUST-- LOOK.
YANK
THEY'RE ALREADY GOING TRANSPARENT.
HONESTLY ...
AREN'T YOU GETTING ***SLEEPY?***

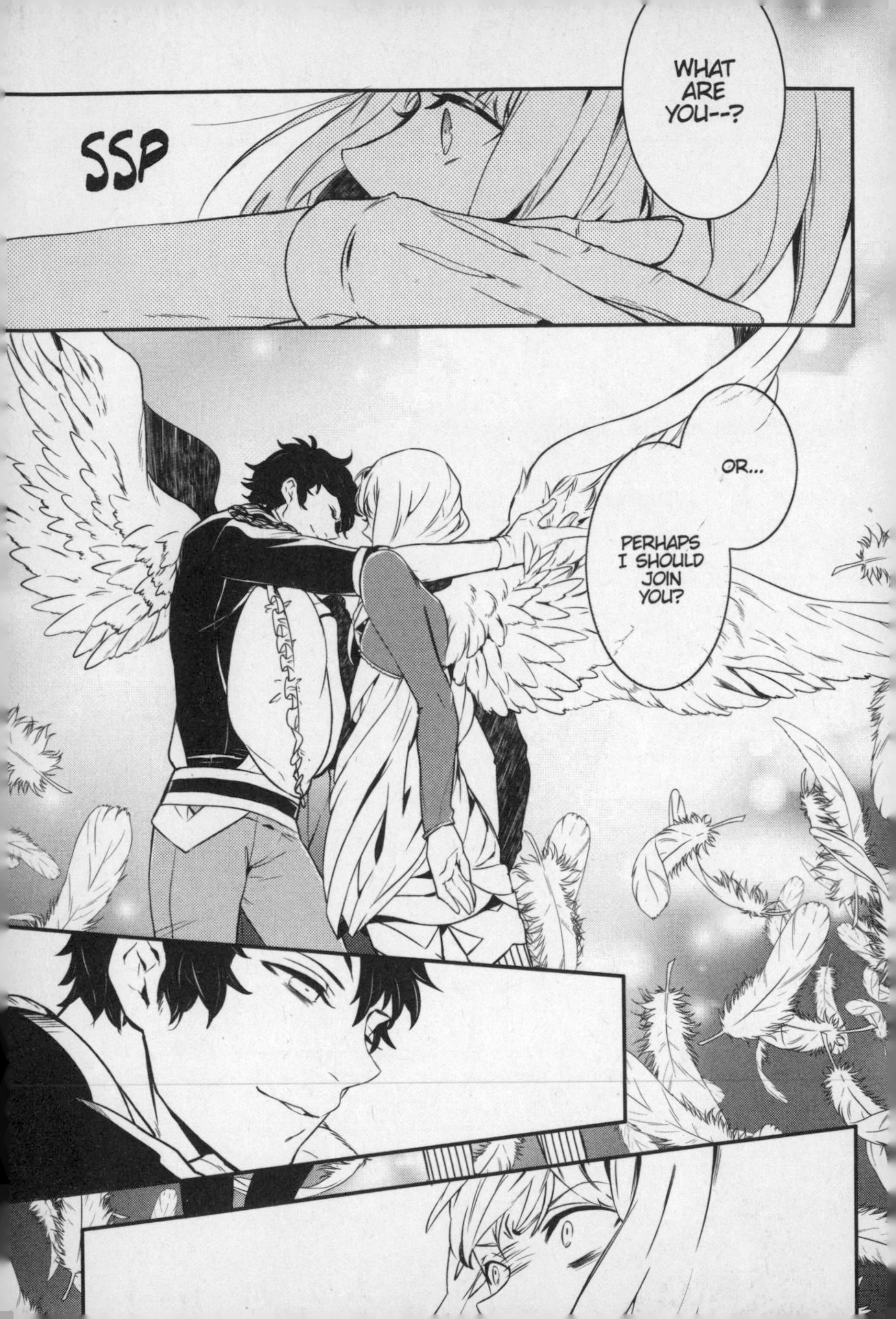
WHAT ARE YOU--?
SSP
OR...
PERHAPS I SHOULD JOIN YOU?

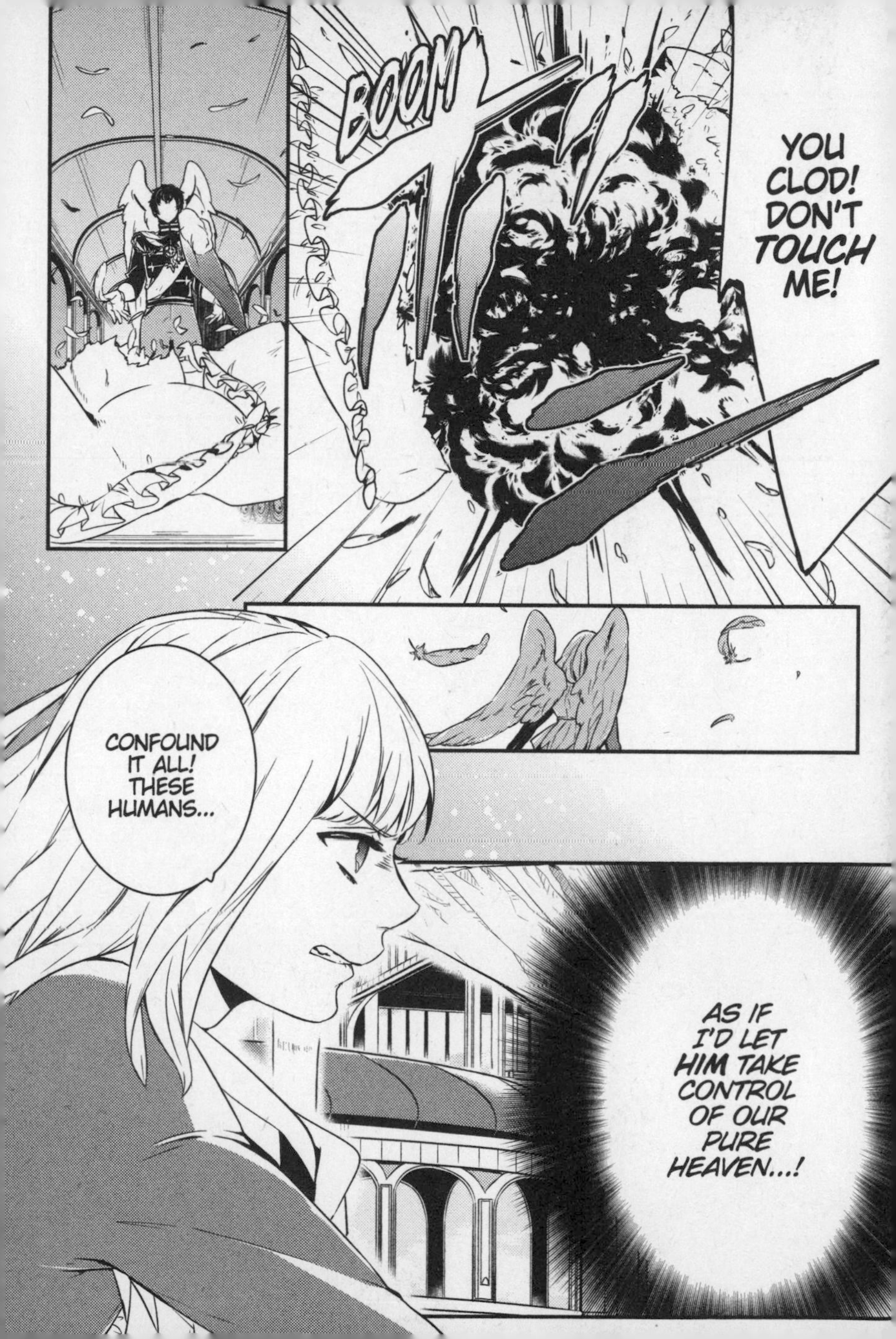
YOU CLOD! DON'T TOUCH ME!
BOOM
CONFOUND IT ALL! THESE HUMANS...
AS IF I'D LET HIM TAKE CONTROL OF OUR PURE HEAVEN...!

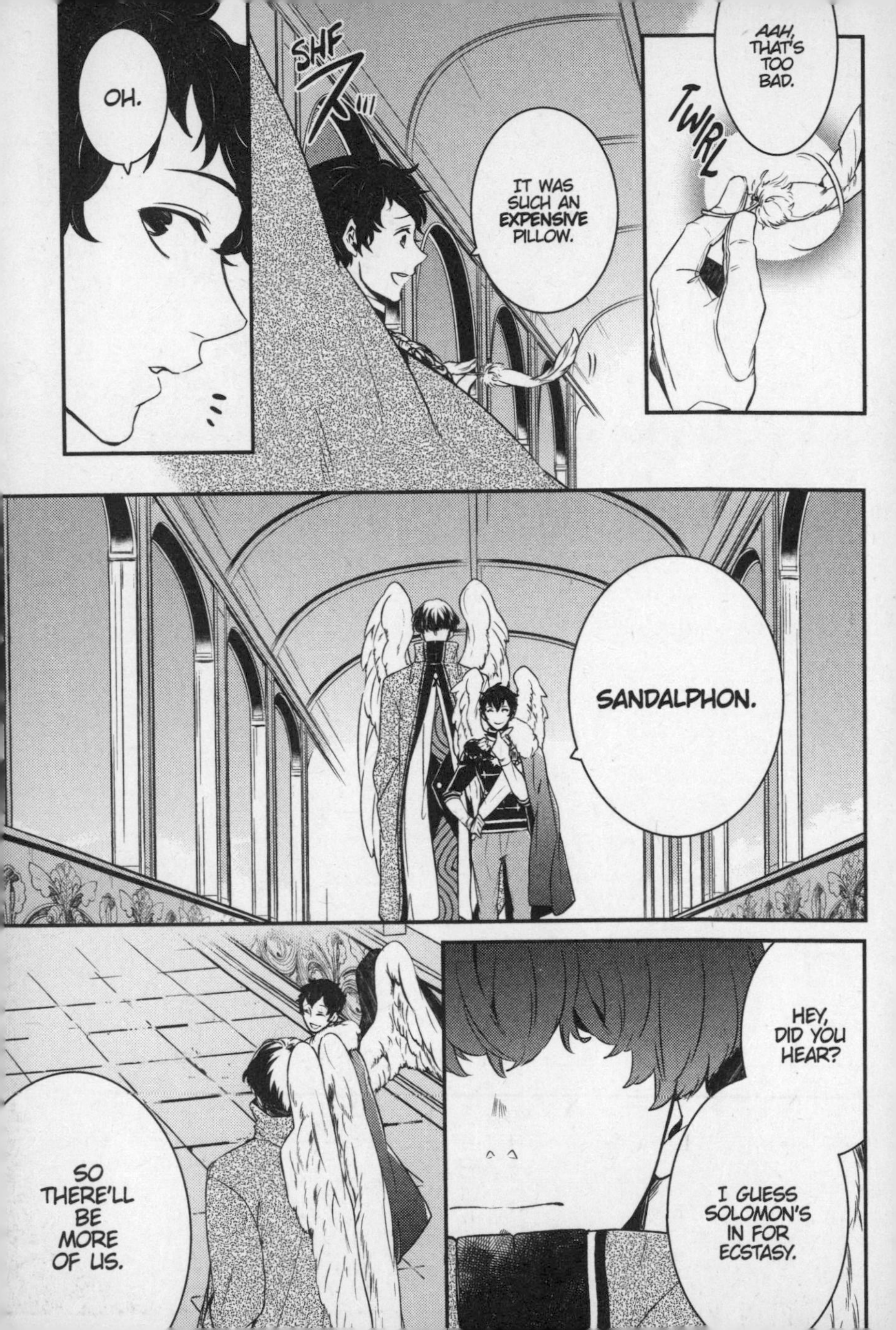
AAH, THAT'S TOO BAD.
TWIRL
IT WAS SUCH AN EXPENSIVE PILLOW.
SHF
OH.
SANDALPHON.
HEY, DID YOU HEAR?
I GUESS SOLOMON'S IN FOR ECSTASY.
SO THERE'LL BE MORE OF US.

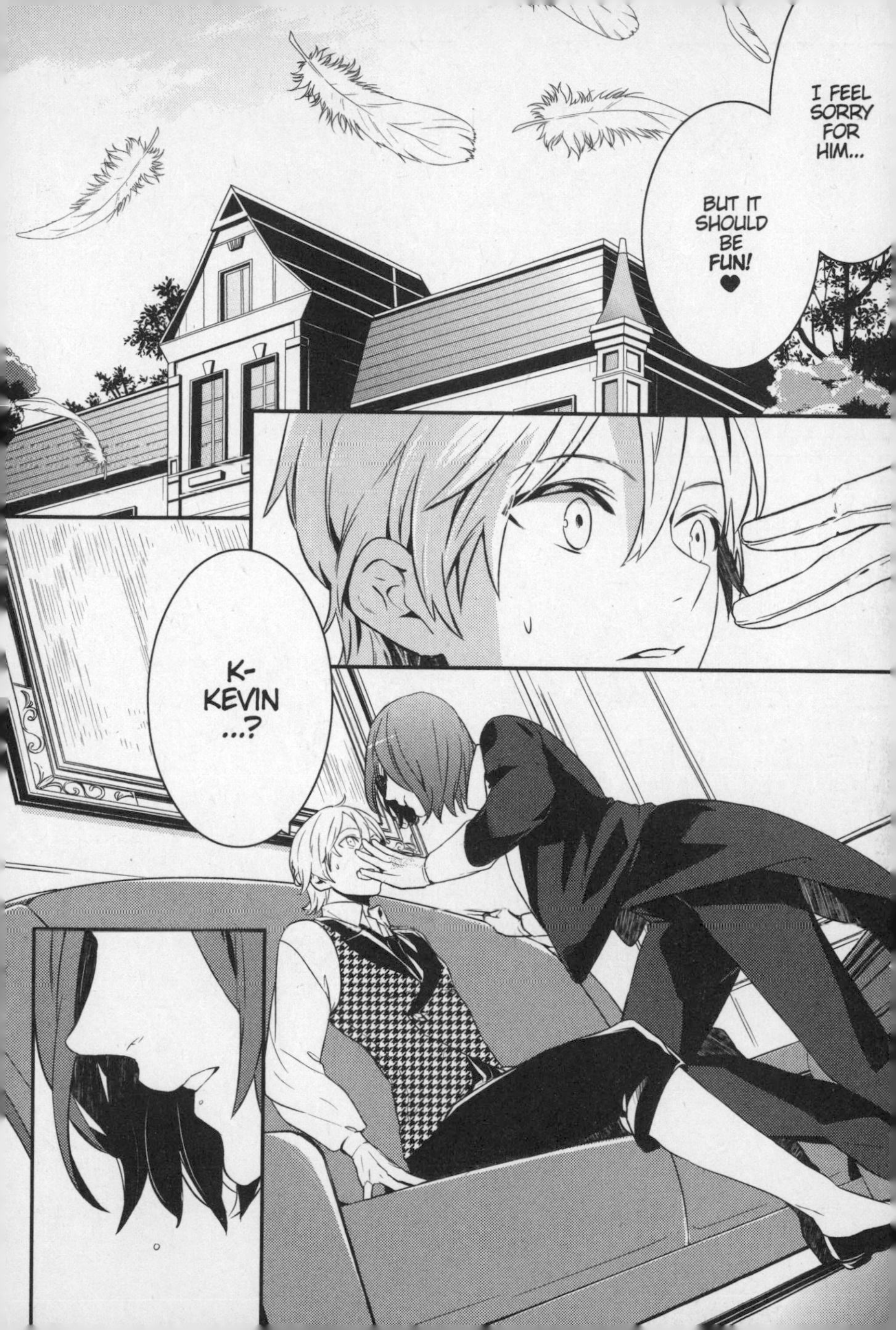
I FEEL SORRY FOR HIM...
BUT IT SHOULD BE FUN! ♥
K-KEVIN ...?

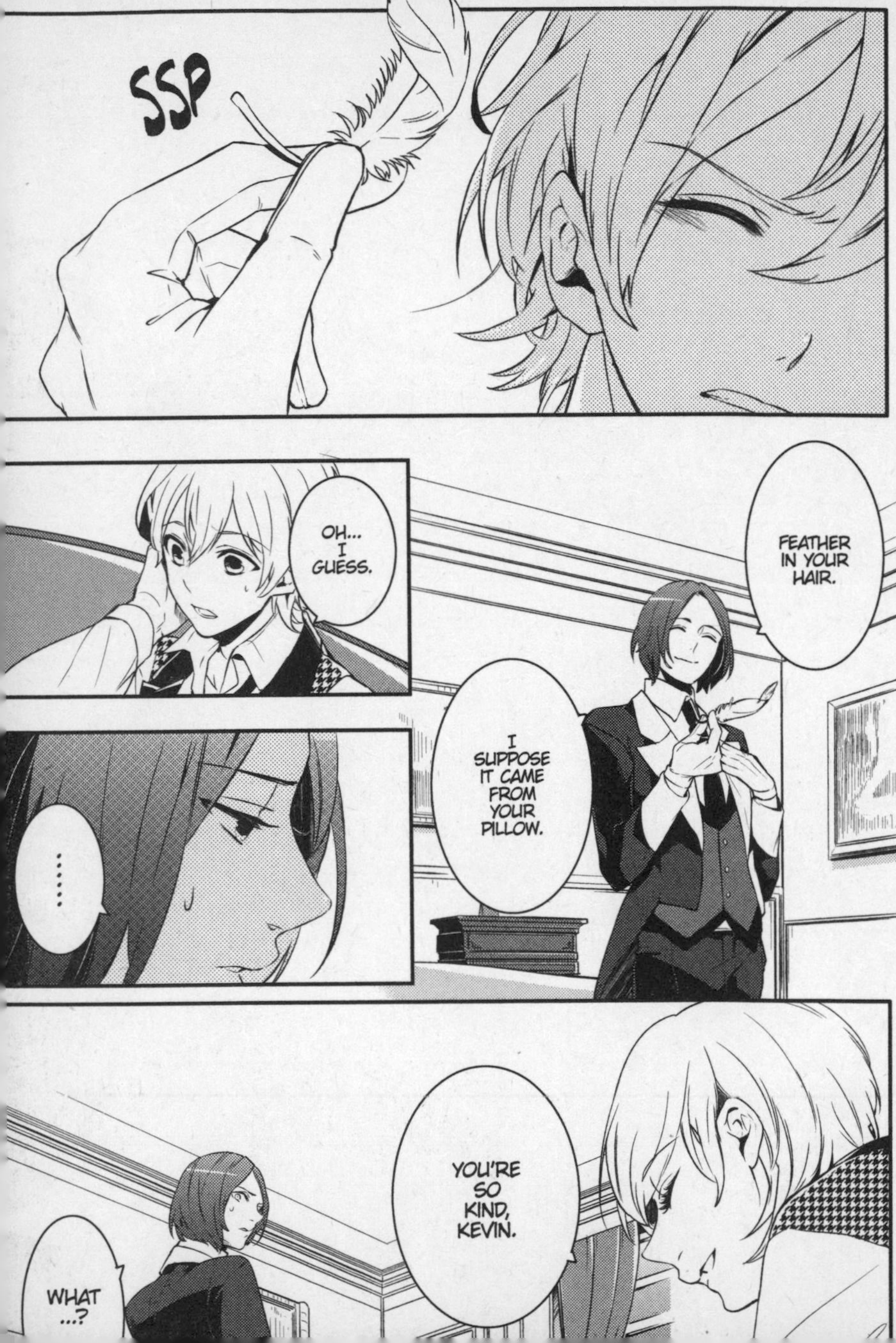
SSP
FEATHER IN YOUR HAIR.
I SUPPOSE IT CAME FROM YOUR PILLOW.
OH... I GUESS.
......
YOU'RE SO KIND, KEVIN.
WHAT ...?

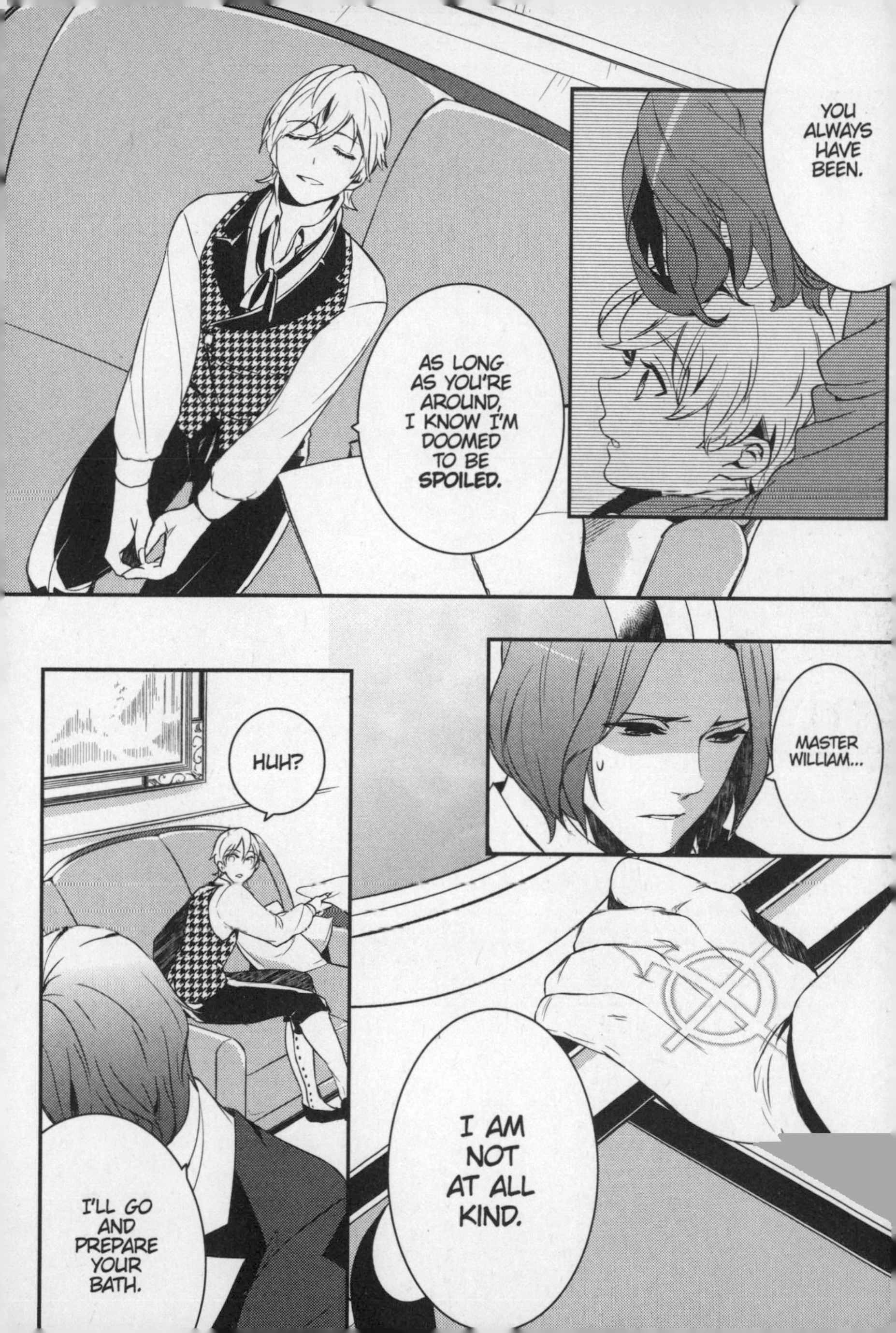
YOU ALWAYS HAVE BEEN.
AS LONG AS YOU'RE AROUND, I KNOW I'M DOOMED TO BE SPOILED.
MASTER WILLIAM...
I AM NOT AT ALL KIND.
HUH?
I'LL GO AND PREPARE YOUR BATH.

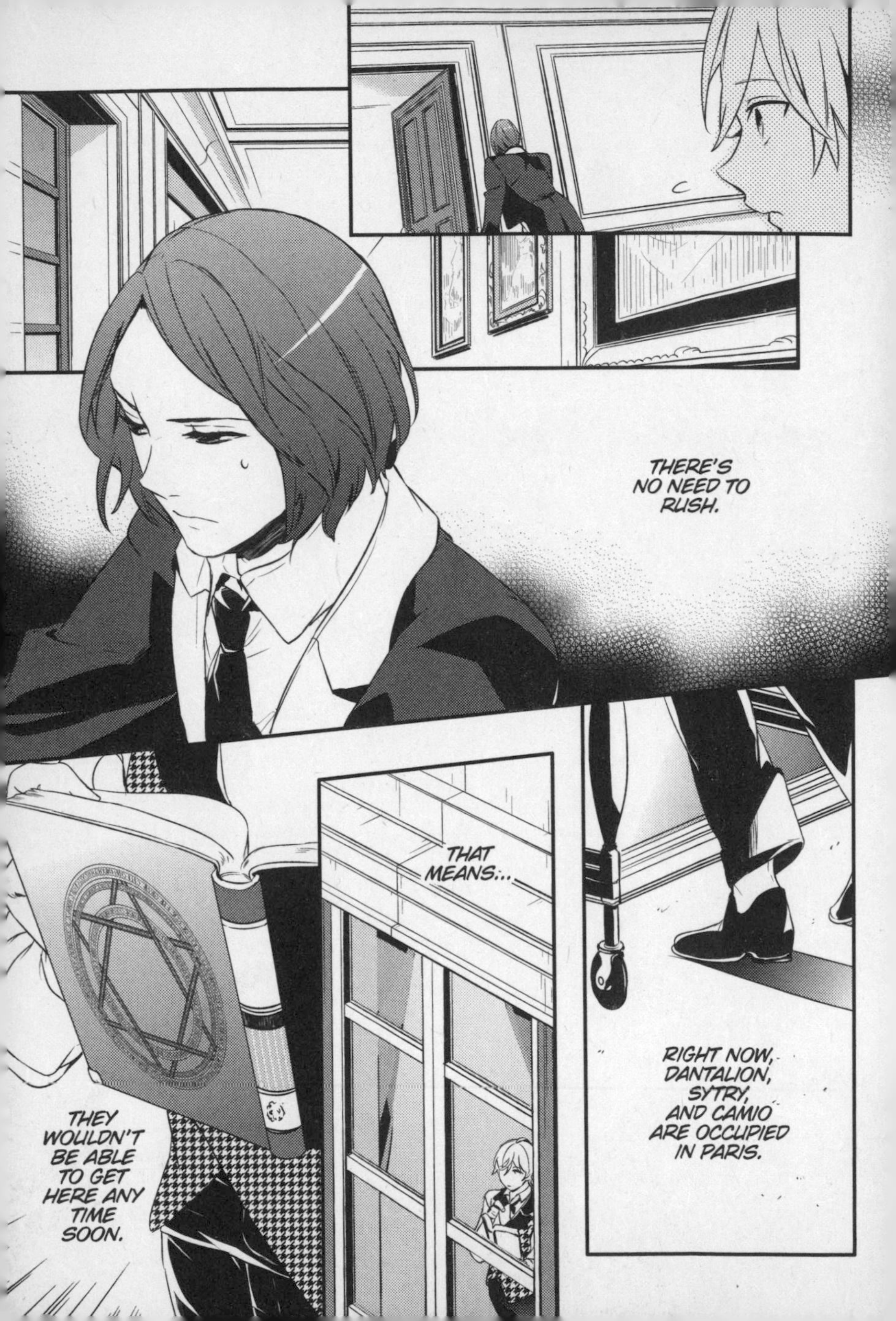
THERE'S NO NEED TO RUSH.
RIGHT NOW, DANTALION, SYTRY, AND CAMIO ARE OCCUPIED IN PARIS.
THAT MEANS...
THEY WOULDN'T BE ABLE TO GET HERE ANY TIME SOON.

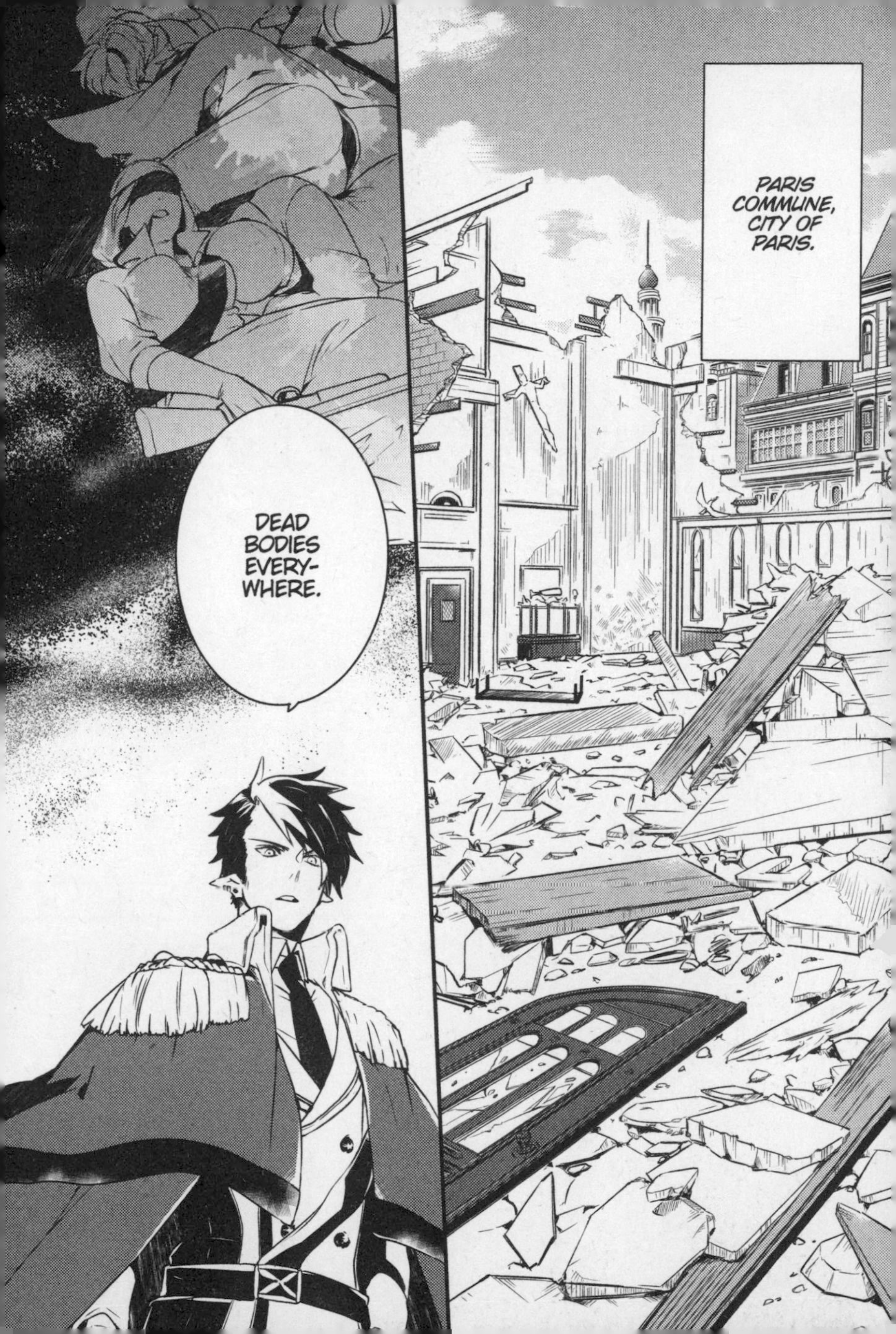
PARIS COMMUNE, CITY OF PARIS.
DEAD BODIES EVERY-WHERE.

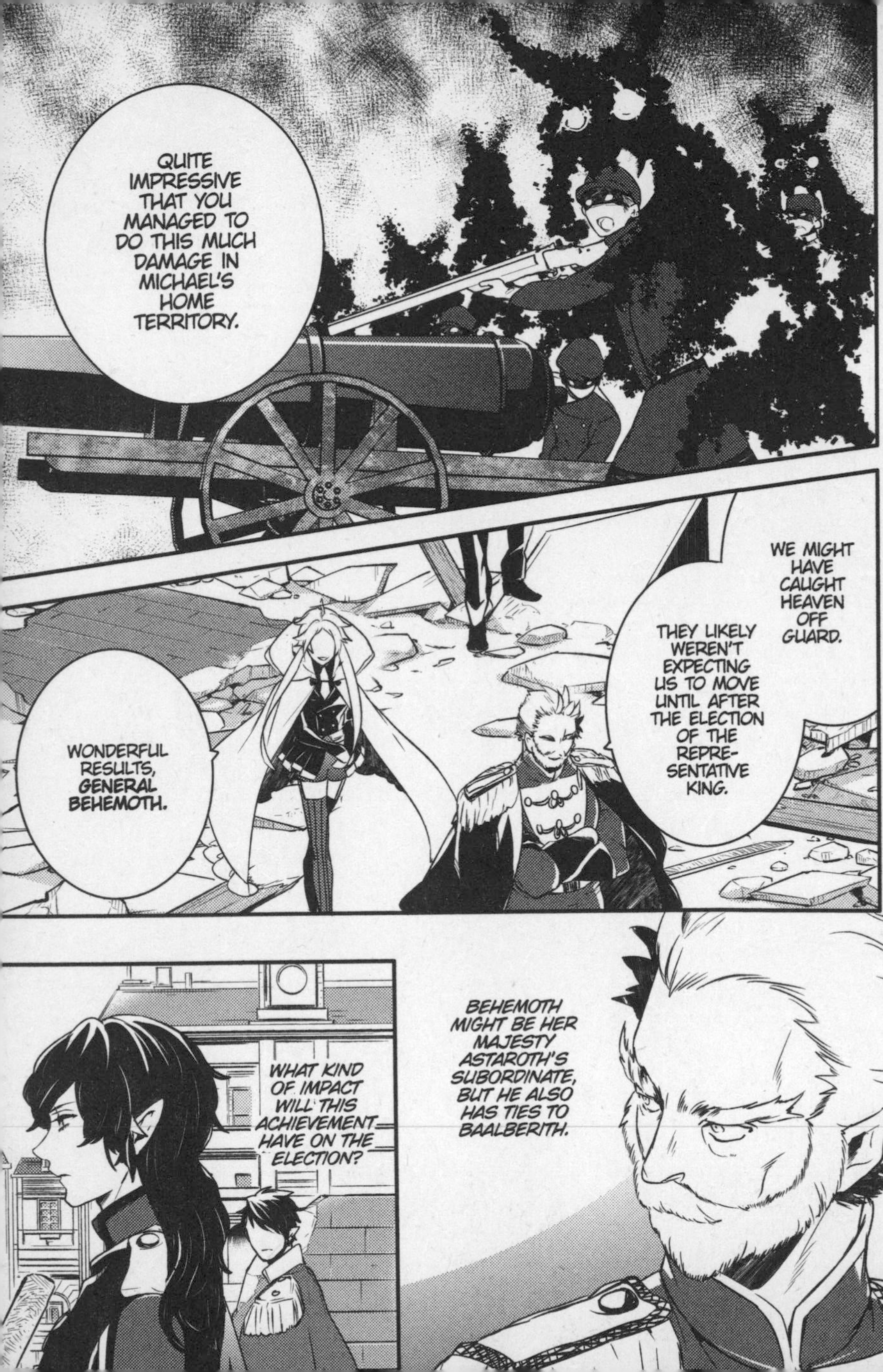
QUITE IMPRESSIVE THAT YOU MANAGED TO DO THIS MUCH DAMAGE IN MICHAEL'S HOME TERRITORY.
WE MIGHT HAVE CAUGHT HEAVEN OFF GUARD.
THEY LIKELY WEREN'T EXPECTING US TO MOVE UNTIL AFTER THE ELECTION OF THE REPRE-SENTATIVE KING.
WONDERFUL RESULTS, GENERAL BEHEMOTH.
BEHEMOTH MIGHT BE HER MAJESTY ASTAROTH'S SUBORDINATE, BUT HE ALSO HAS TIES TO BAALBERITH.
WHAT KIND OF IMPACT WILL THIS ACHIEVEMENT HAVE ON THE ELECTION?

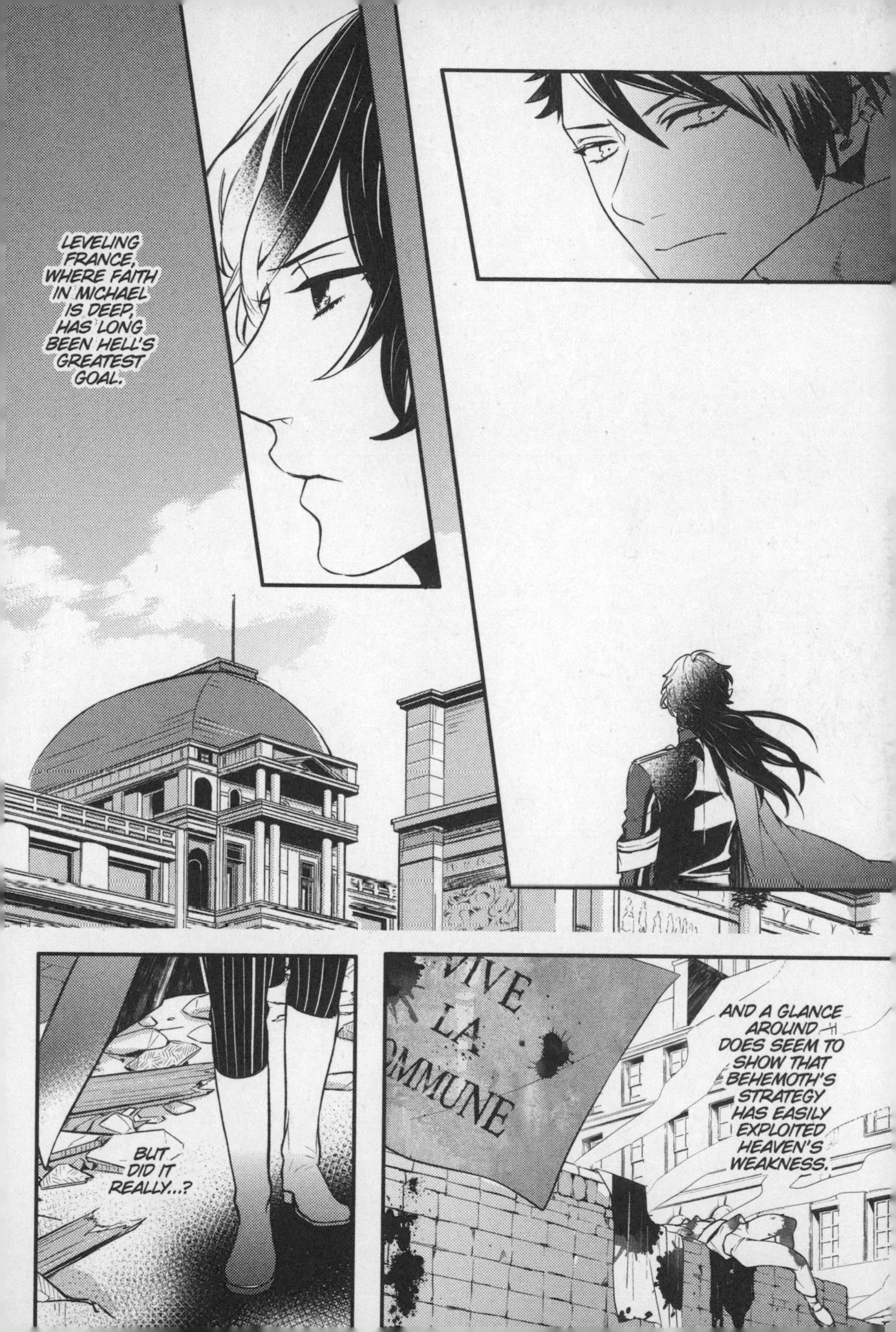
LEVELING FRANCE, WHERE FAITH IN MICHAEL IS DEEP, HAS LONG BEEN HELL'S GREATEST GOAL.
VIVE LA COMMUNE
AND A GLANCE AROUND DOES SEEM TO SHOW THAT BEHEMOTH'S STRATEGY HAS EASILY EXPLOITED HEAVEN'S WEAKNESS.
BUT DID IT REALLY...?

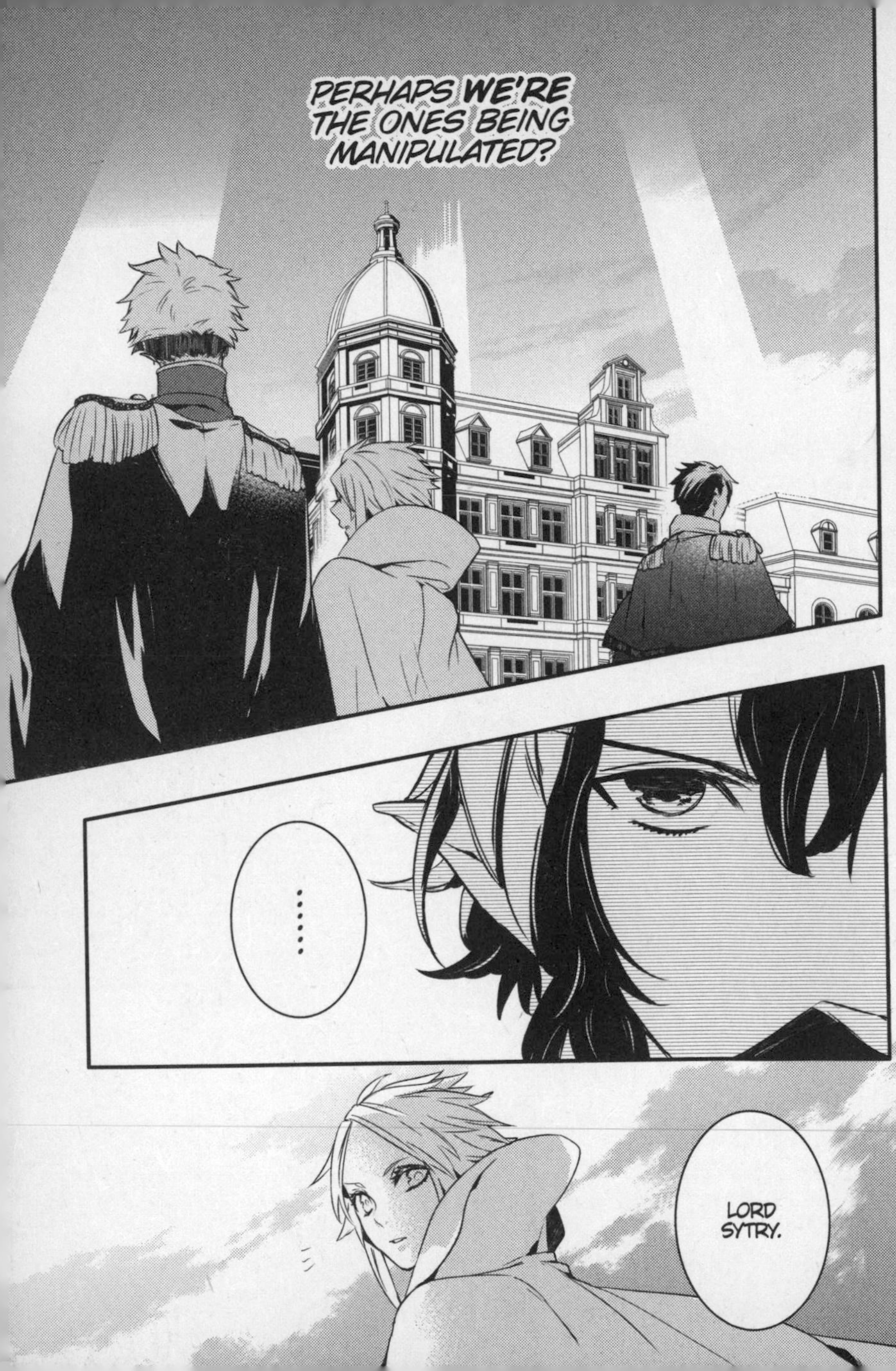
PERHAPS WE'RE THE ONES BEING MANIPULATED?
......
LORD SYTRY.

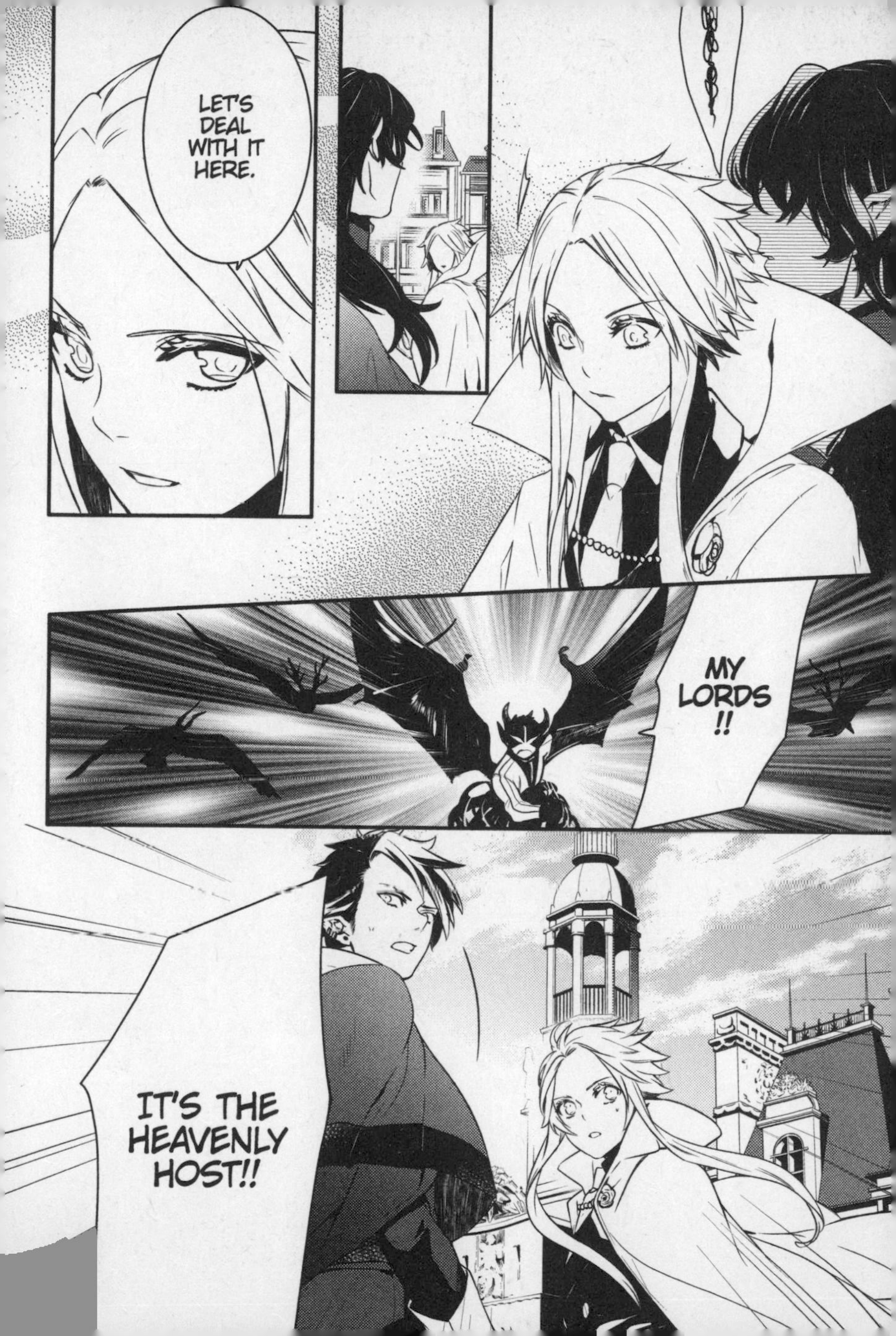
LET'S DEAL WITH IT HERE.
MY LORDS!!
IT'S THE HEAVENLY HOST!!

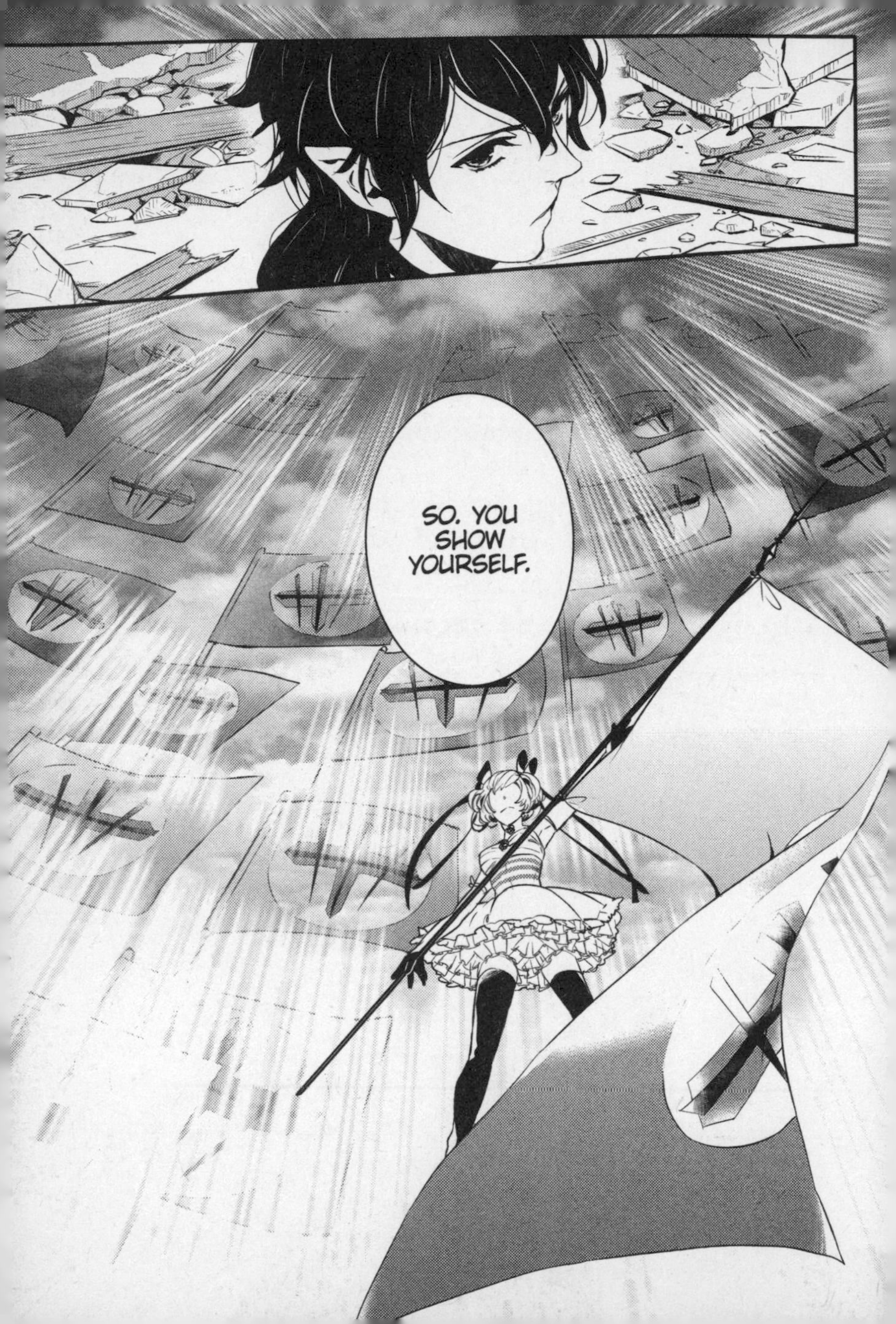
SO. YOU SHOW YOURSELF.

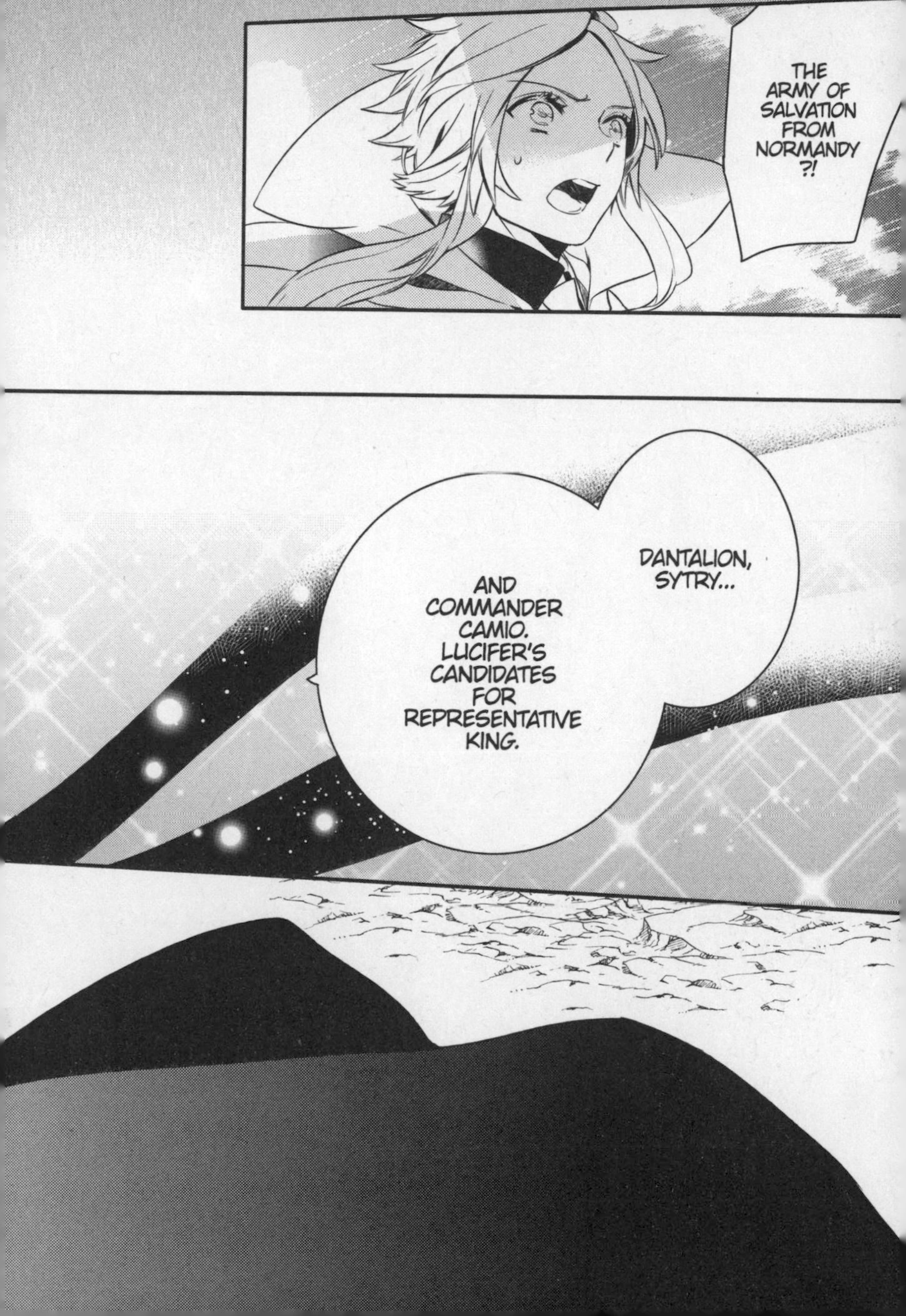
THE ARMY OF SALVATION FROM NORMANDY ?!
DANTALION, SYTRY...
AND COMMANDER CAMIO. LUCIFER'S CANDIDATES FOR REPRESENTATIVE KING.

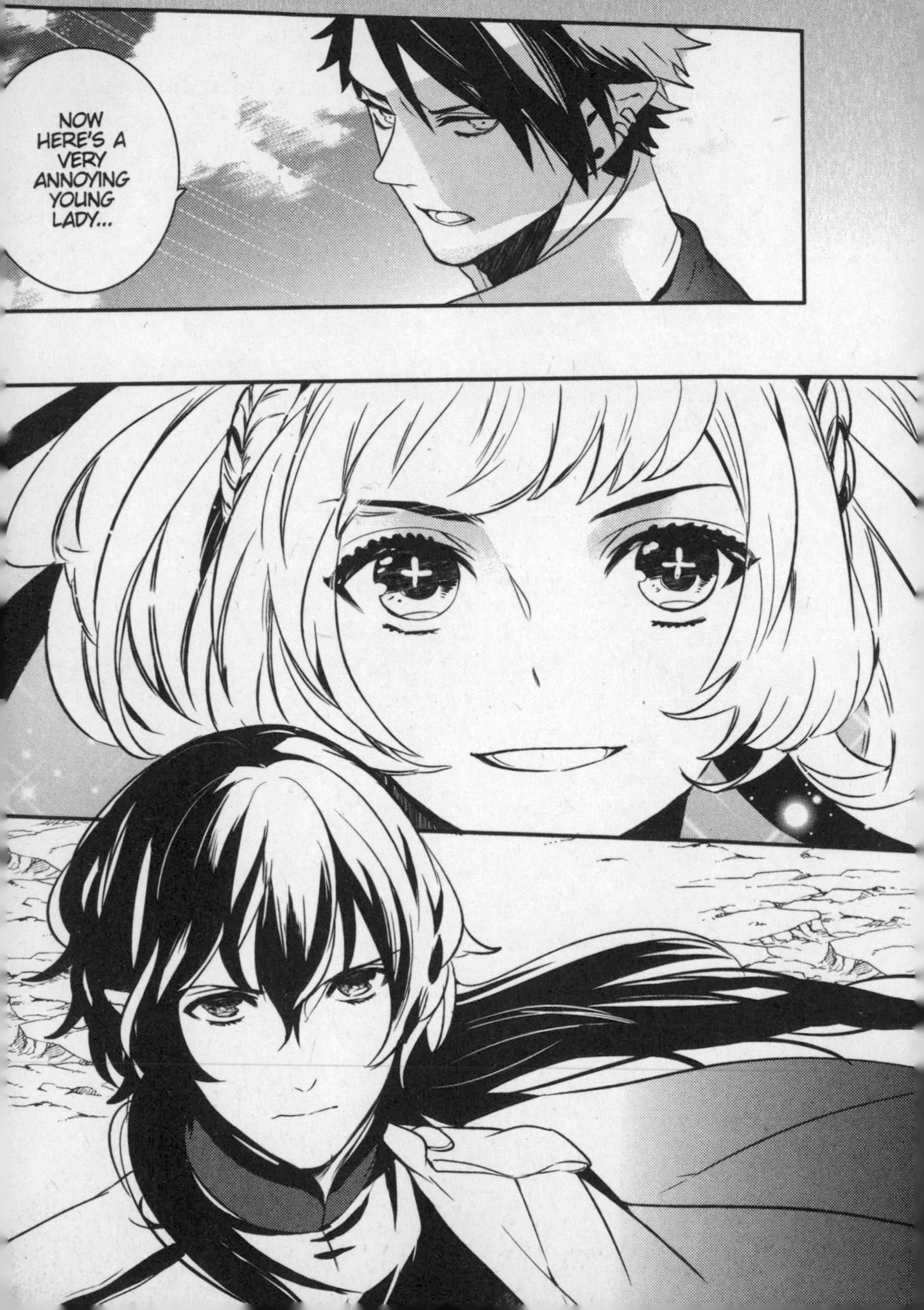
NOW HERE'S A VERY ANNOYING YOUNG LADY...

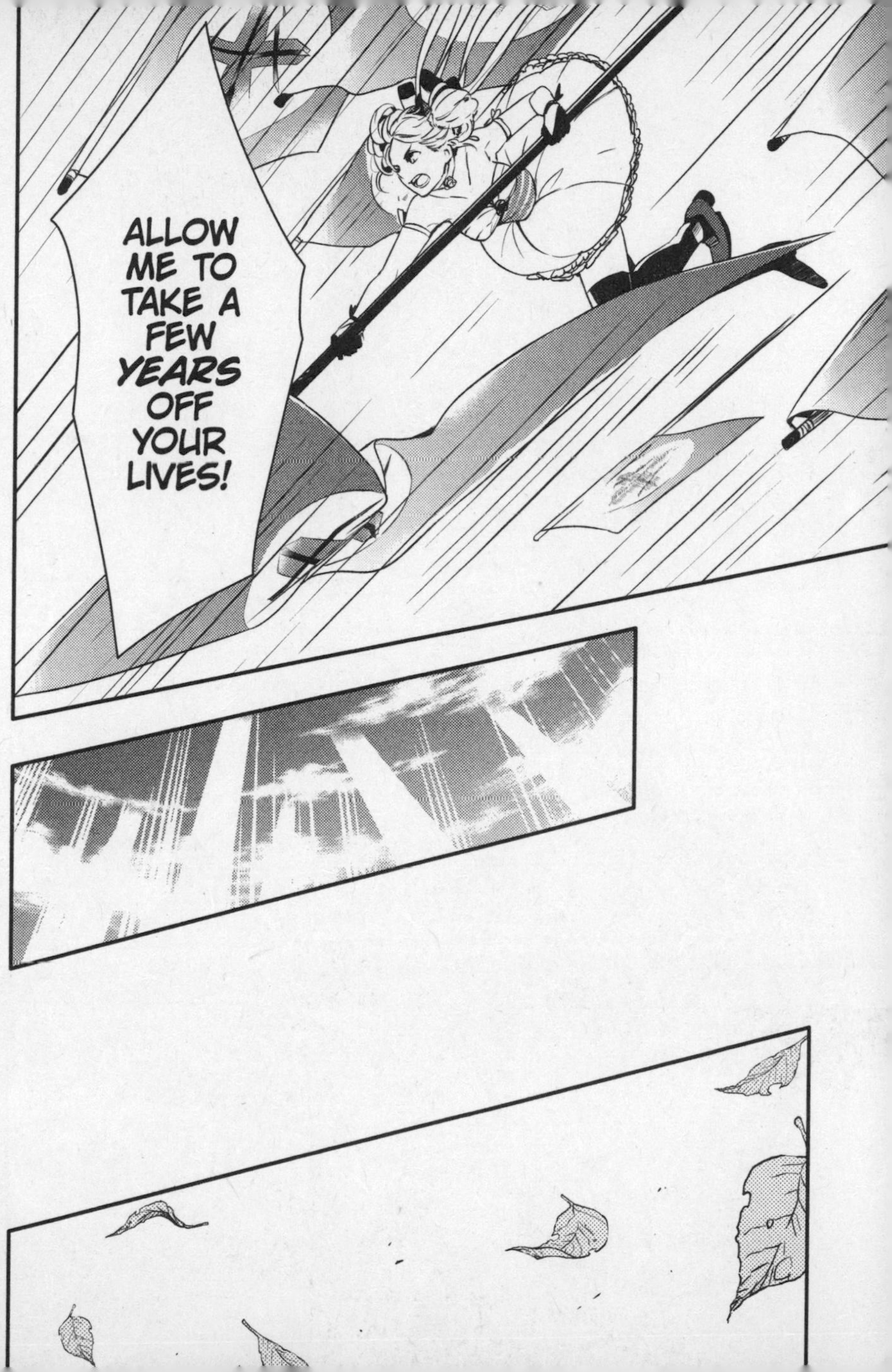
ALLOW ME TO TAKE A FEW YEARS OFF YOUR LIVES!

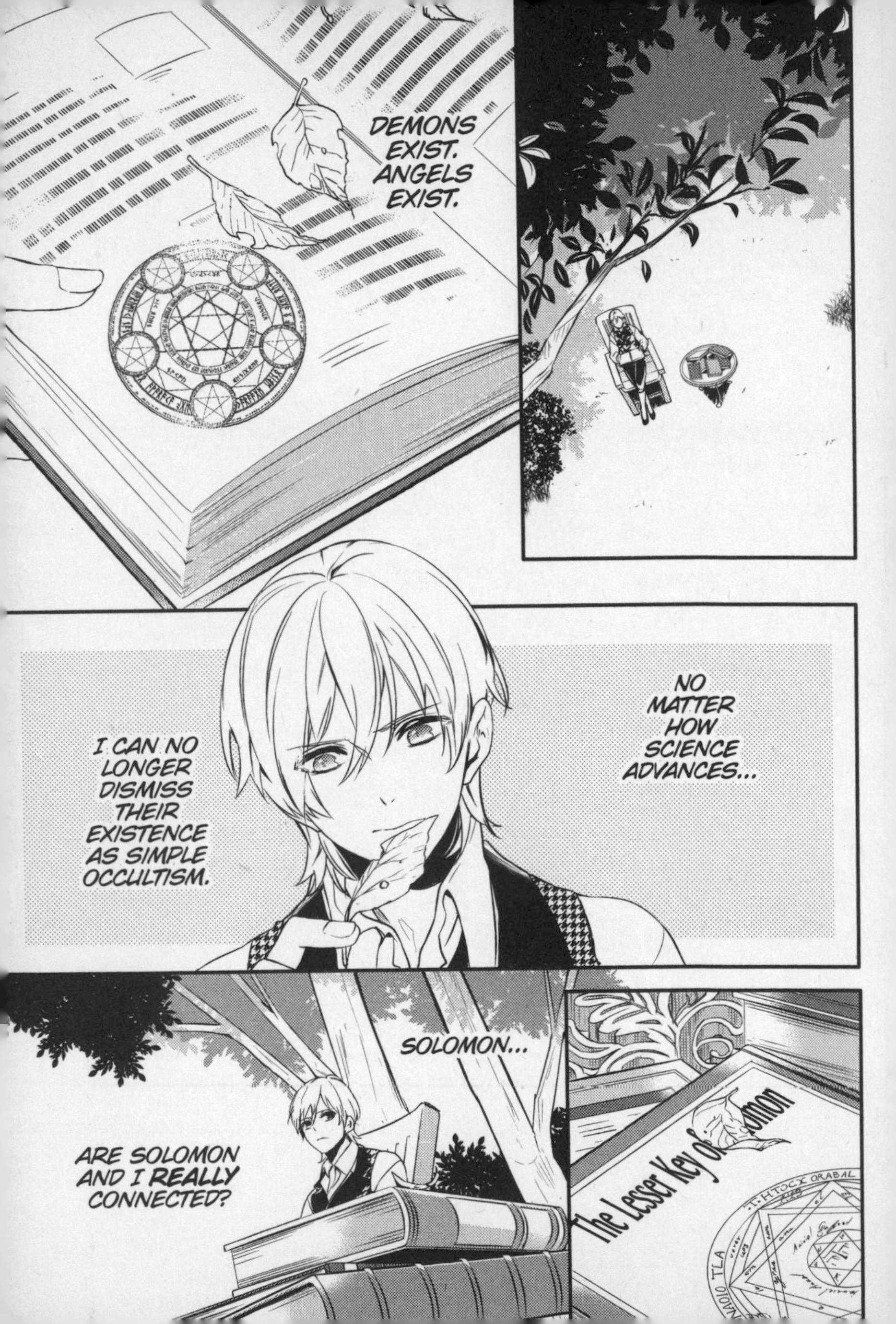
DEMONS EXIST. ANGELS EXIST.
NO MATTER HOW SCIENCE ADVANCES...
I CAN NO LONGER DISMISS THEIR EXISTENCE AS SIMPLE OCCULTISM.
The Lesser Key of
SOLOMON...
ARE SOLOMON AND I **REALLY** CONNECTED?

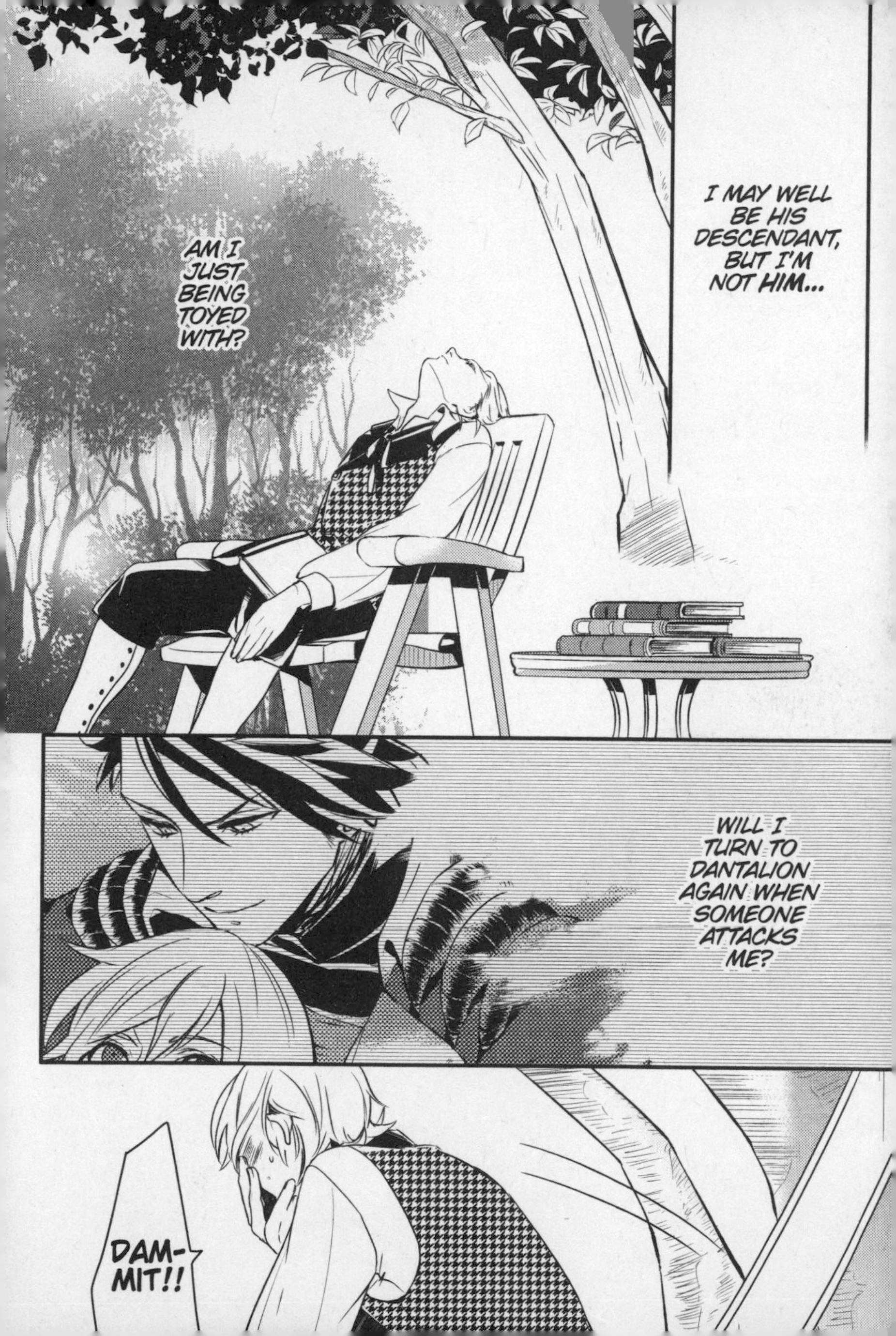
I MAY WELL BE HIS DESCENDANT, BUT I'M NOT HIM...
AM I JUST BEING TOYED WITH?
WILL I TURN TO DANTALION AGAIN WHEN SOMEONE ATTACKS ME?
DAM-MIT!!

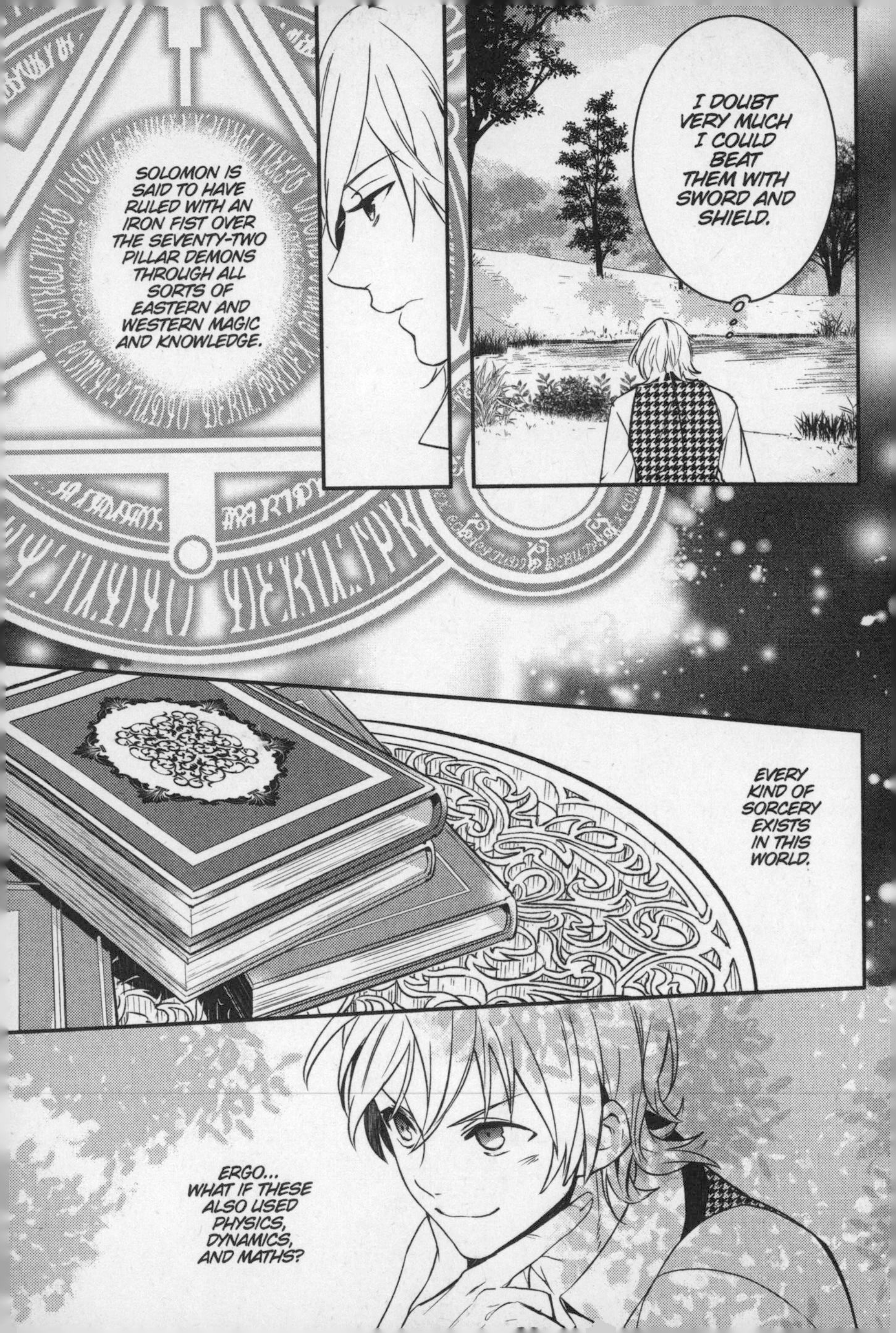
I DOUBT VERY MUCH I COULD BEAT THEM WITH SWORD AND SHIELD.
SOLOMON IS SAID TO HAVE RULED WITH AN IRON FIST OVER THE SEVENTY-TWO PILLAR DEMONS THROUGH ALL SORTS OF EASTERN AND WESTERN MAGIC AND KNOWLEDGE.
EVERY KIND OF SORCERY EXISTS IN THIS WORLD.
ERGO... WHAT IF THESE ALSO USED PHYSICS, DYNAMICS, AND MATHS?

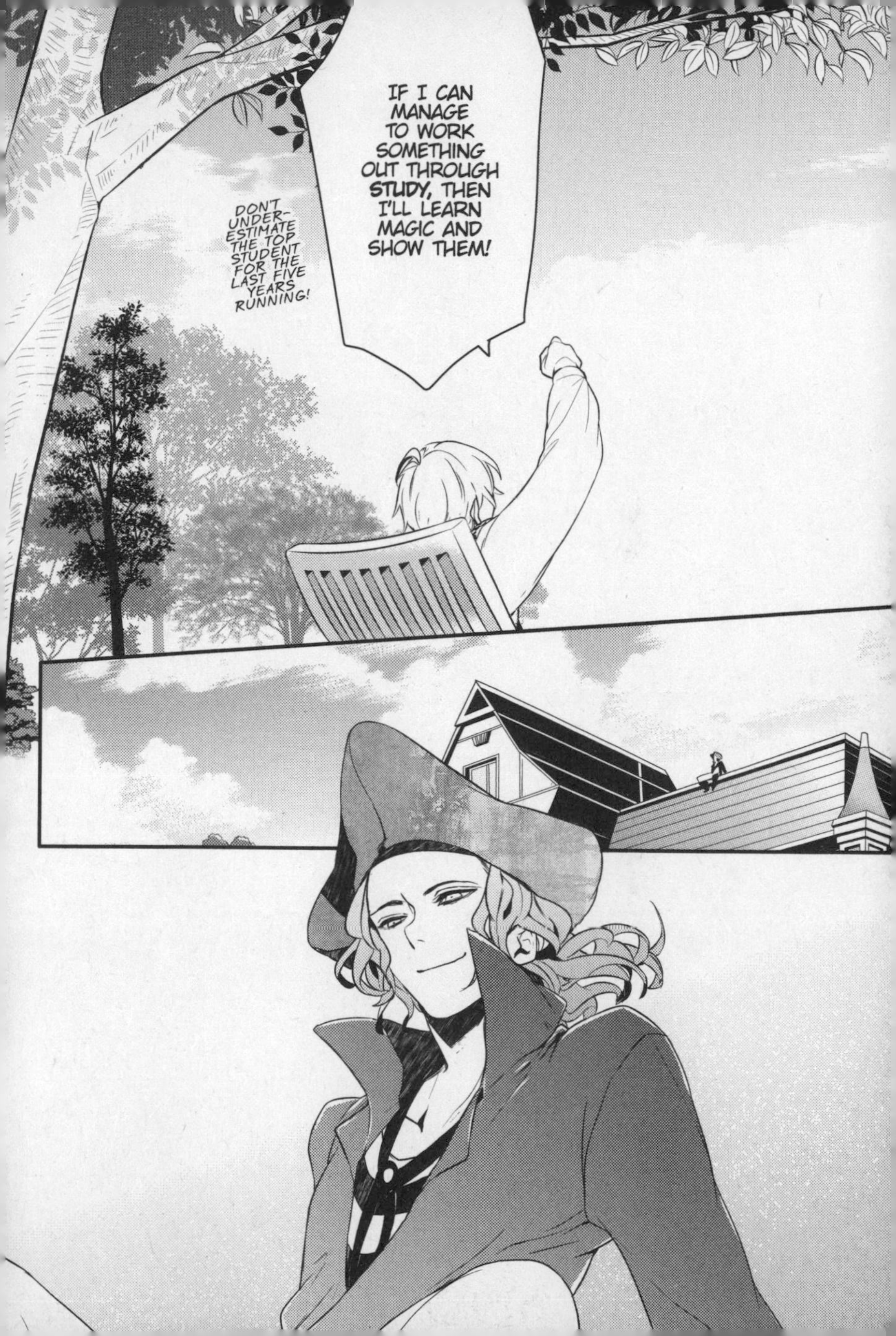
IF I CAN MANAGE TO WORK SOMETHING OUT THROUGH STUDY, THEN I'LL LEARN MAGIC AND SHOW THEM!
DON'T UNDER-ESTIMATE THE TOP STUDENT FOR THE LAST FIVE YEARS RUNNING!

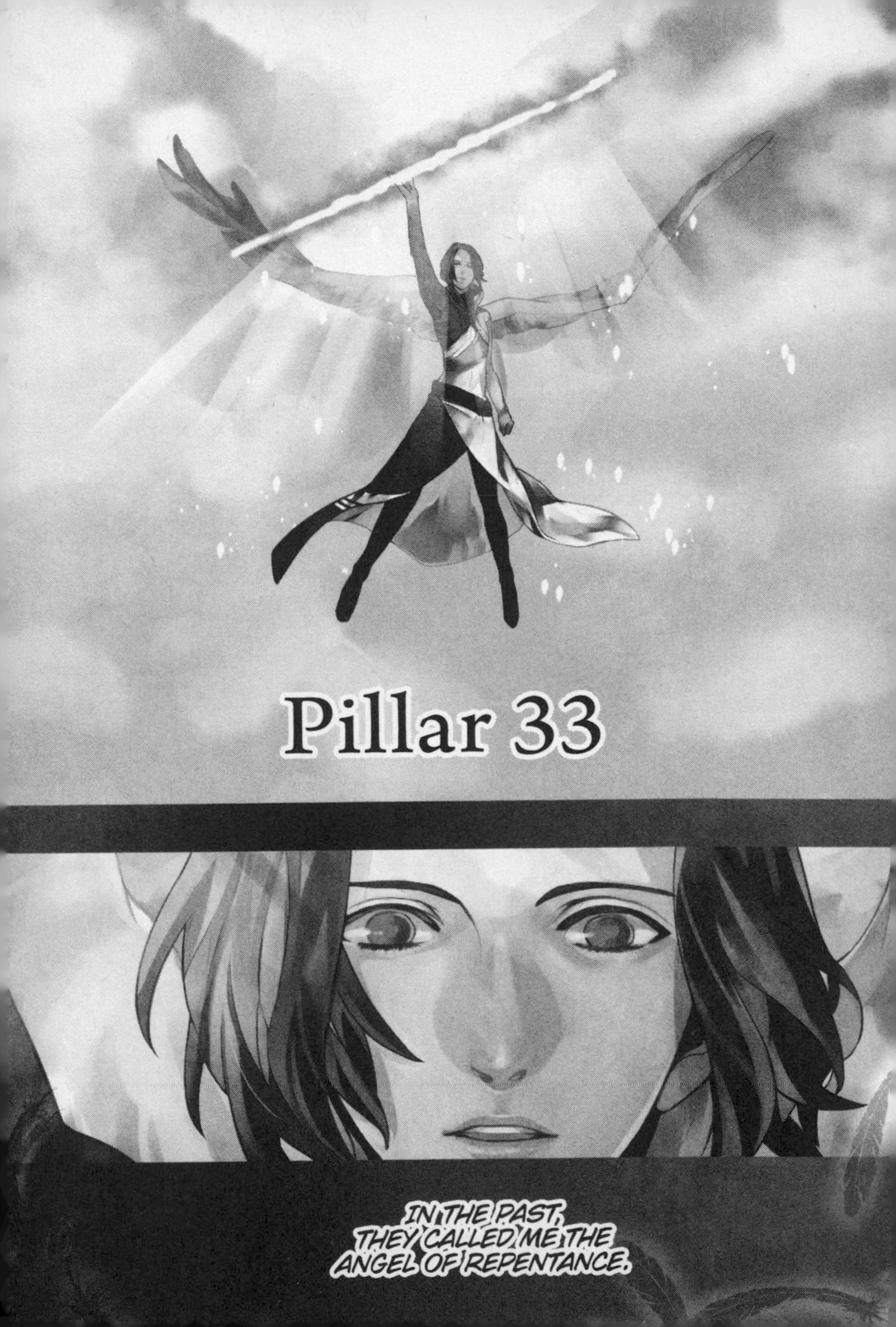
Pillar 33
IN THE PAST, THEY CALLED ME THE ANGEL OF REPENTANCE.

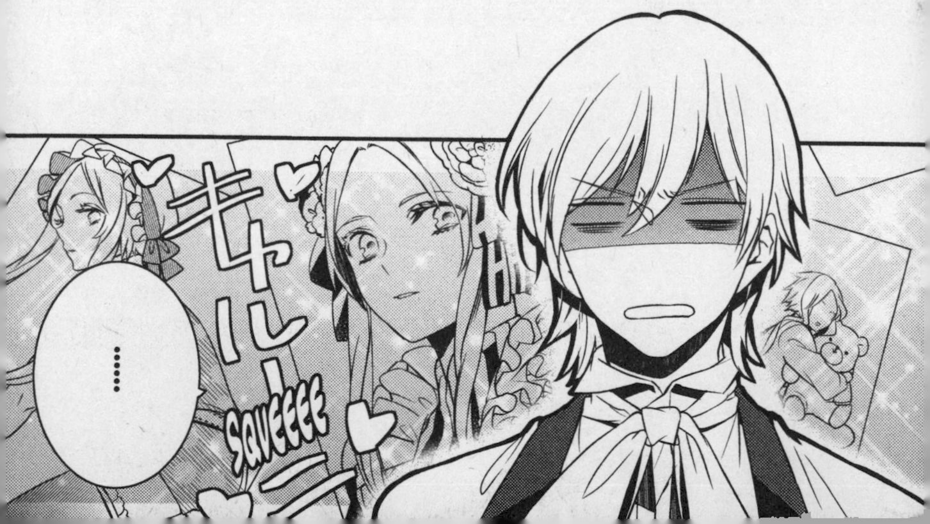
キャー
SQUEEEE
......

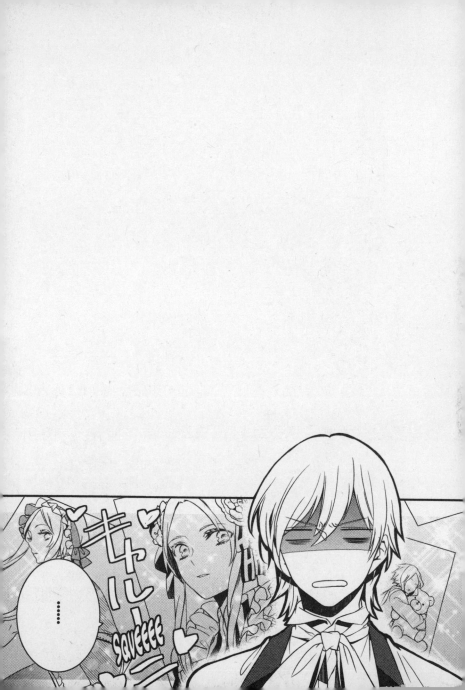

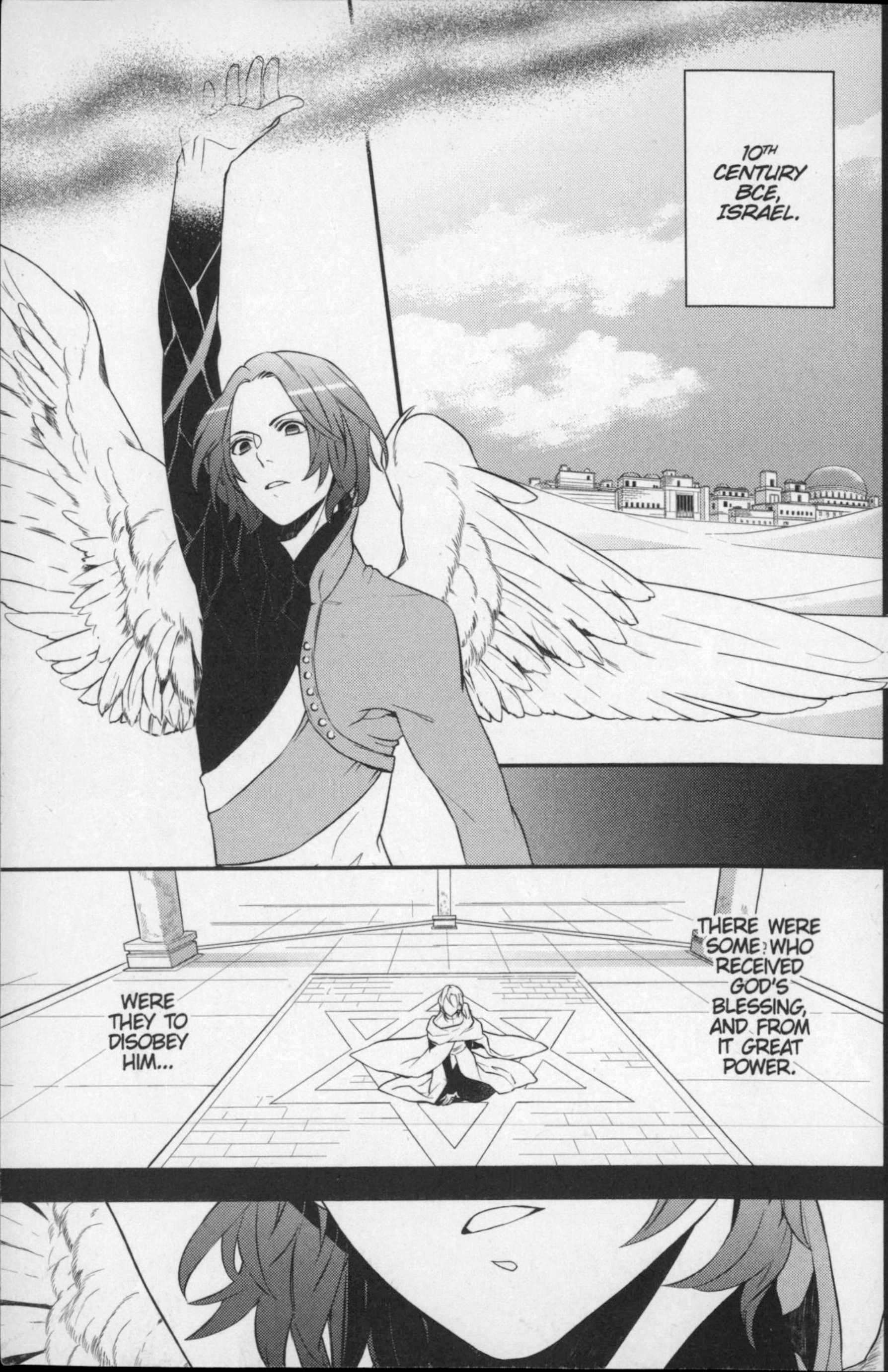
10TH CENTURY BCE, ISRAEL.
THERE WERE SOME WHO RECEIVED GOD'S BLESSING, AND FROM IT GREAT POWER.
WERE THEY TO DISOBEY HIM...

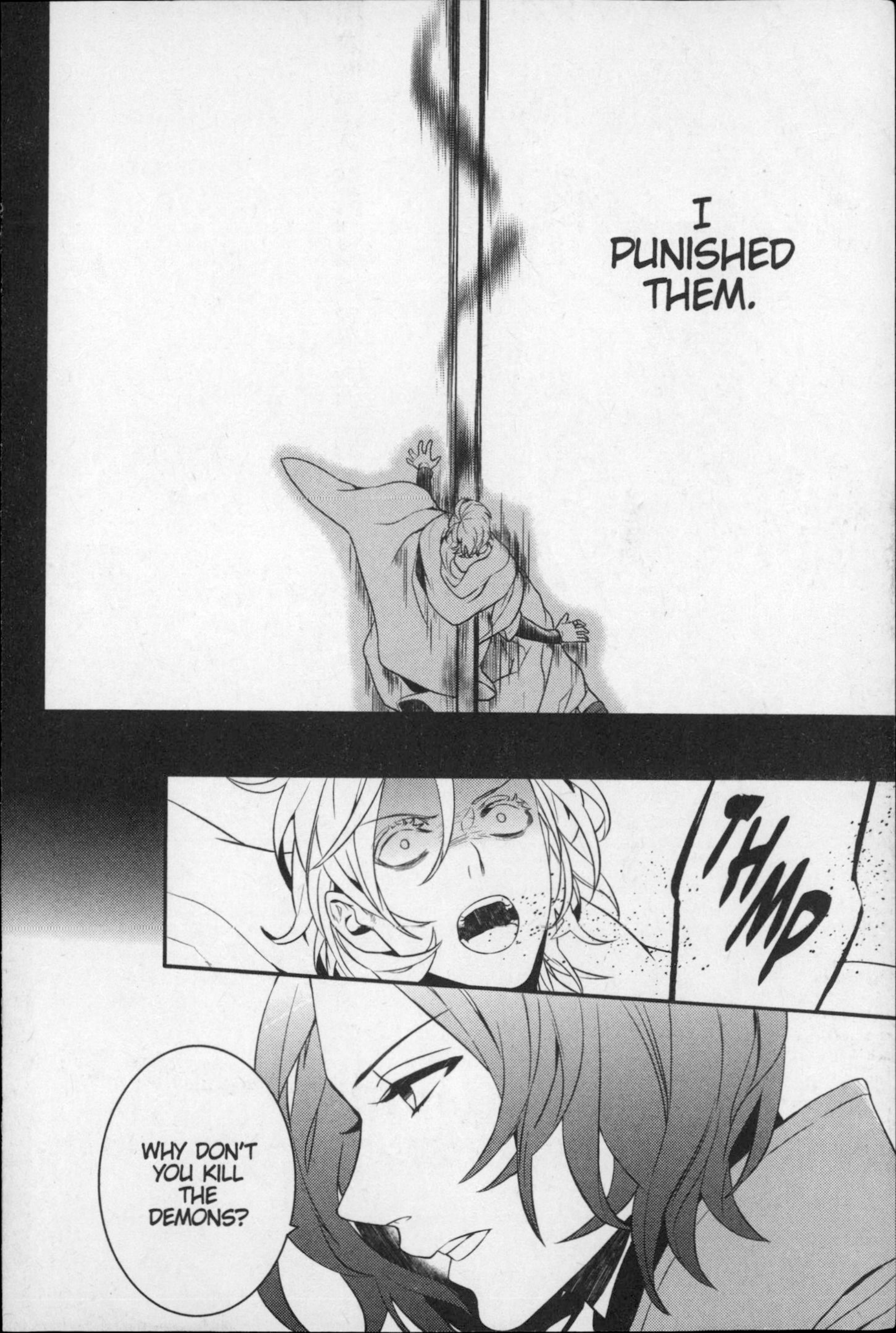
I PUNISHED THEM.
THMP
WHY DON'T YOU KILL THE DEMONS?

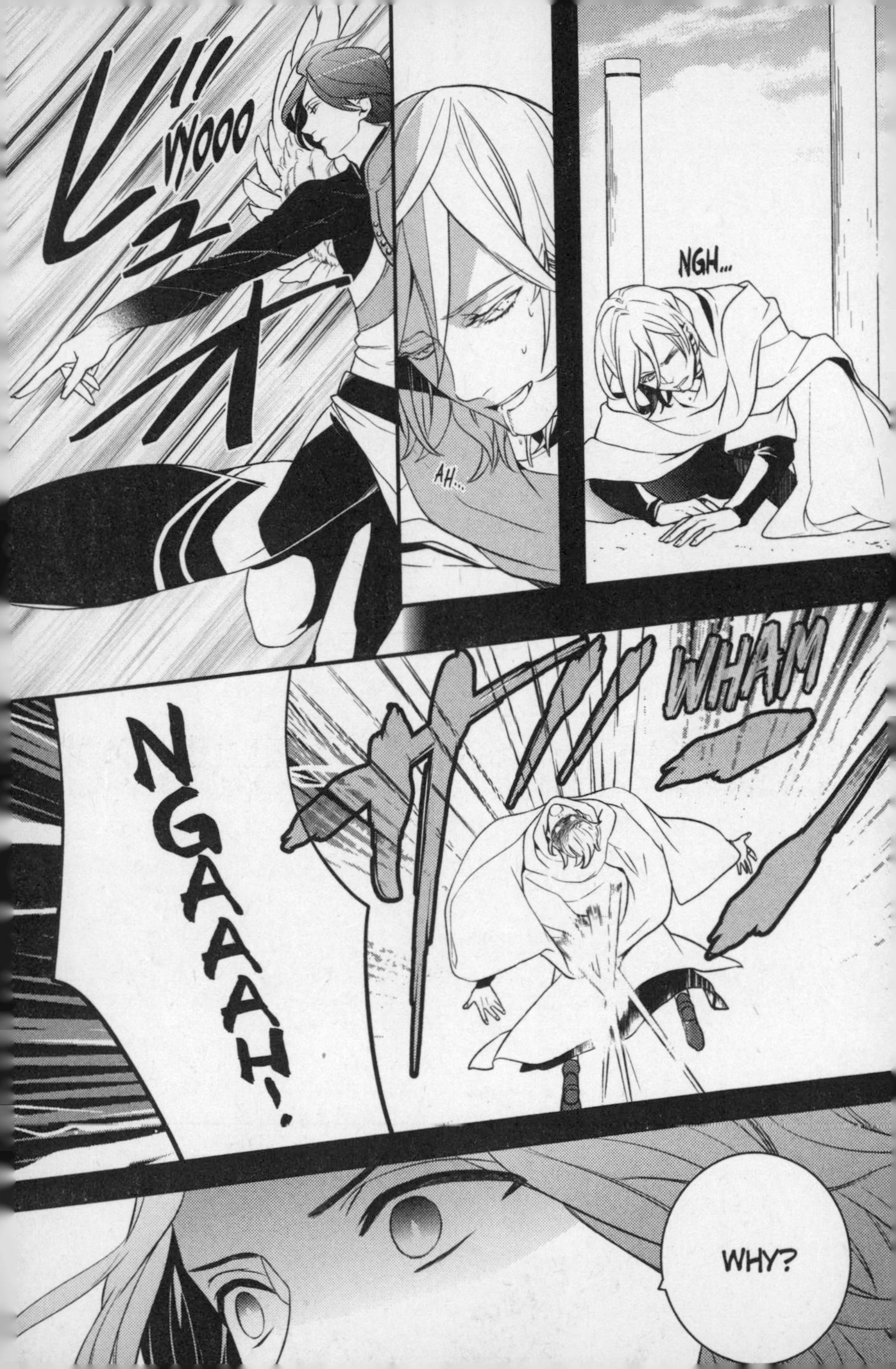
NGH...
AH...
VYOOO
WHAM
NGAAAH!
WHY?

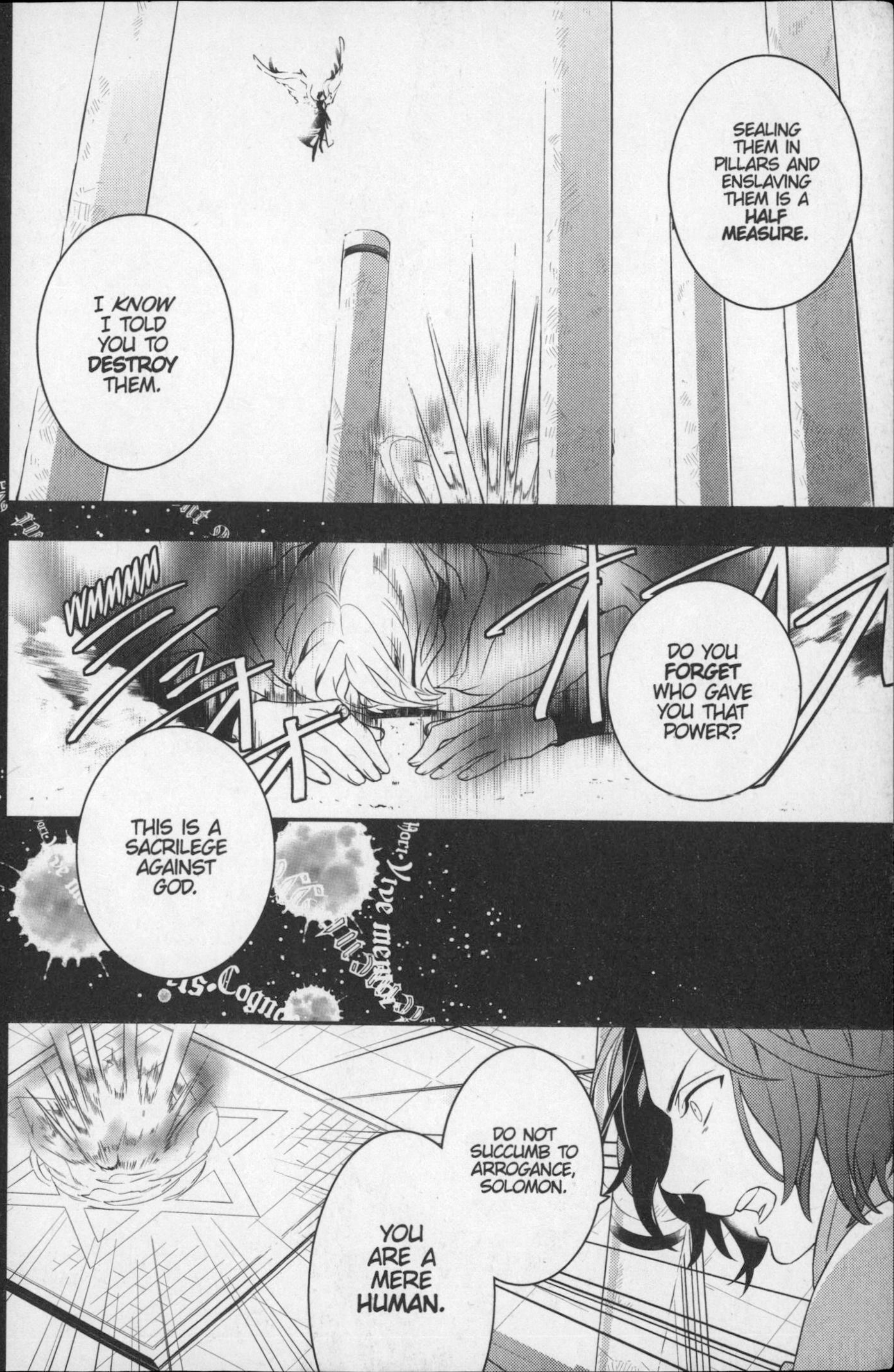
SEALING THEM IN PILLARS AND ENSLAVING THEM IS A **HALF MEASURE.**
I *KNOW* I TOLD YOU TO **DESTROY** THEM.
WMMMM
DO YOU **FORGET** WHO GAVE YOU THAT POWER?
THIS IS A SACRILEGE AGAINST GOD.
DO NOT SUCCUMB TO ARROGANCE, SOLOMON.
YOU ARE A MERE HUMAN.

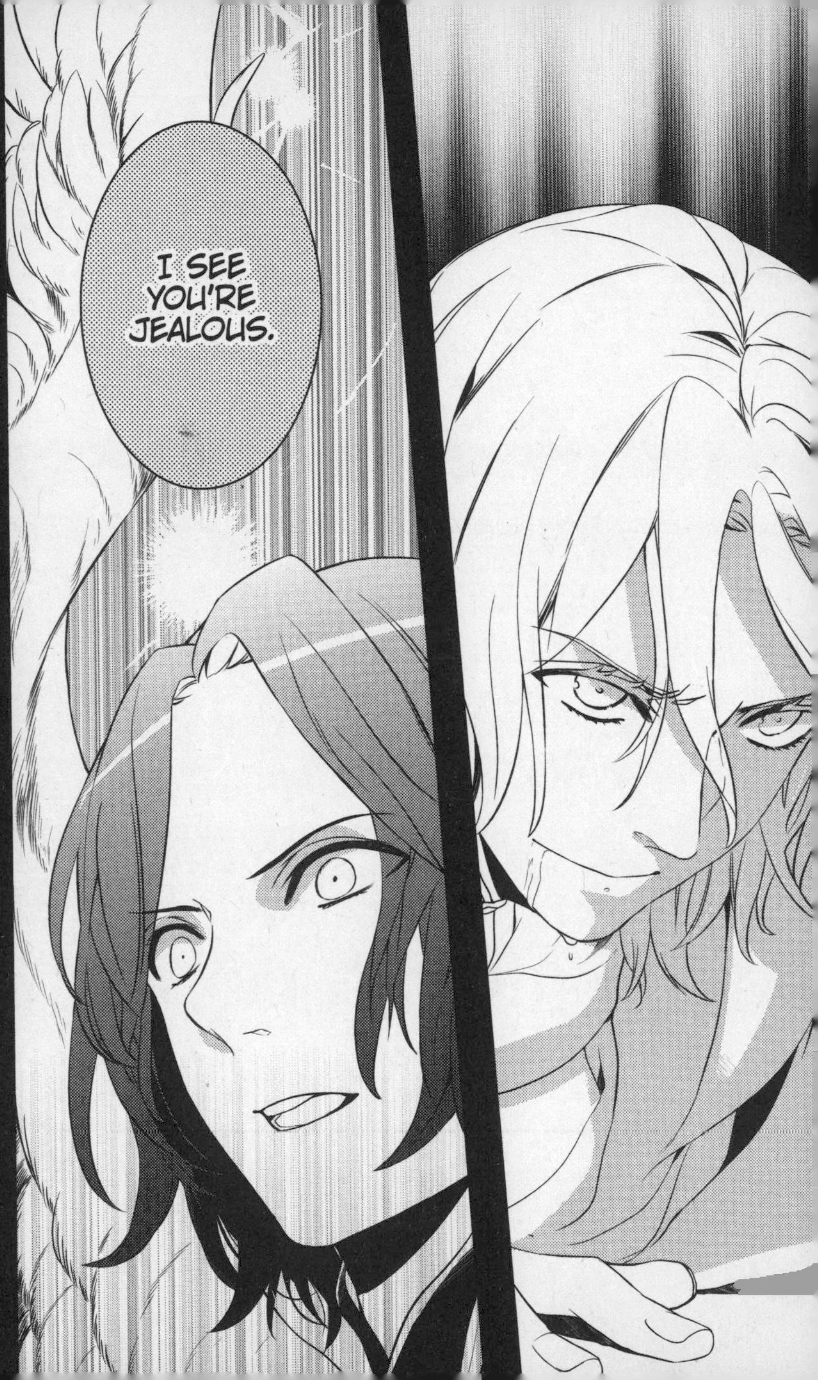
I SEE YOU'RE JEALOUS.

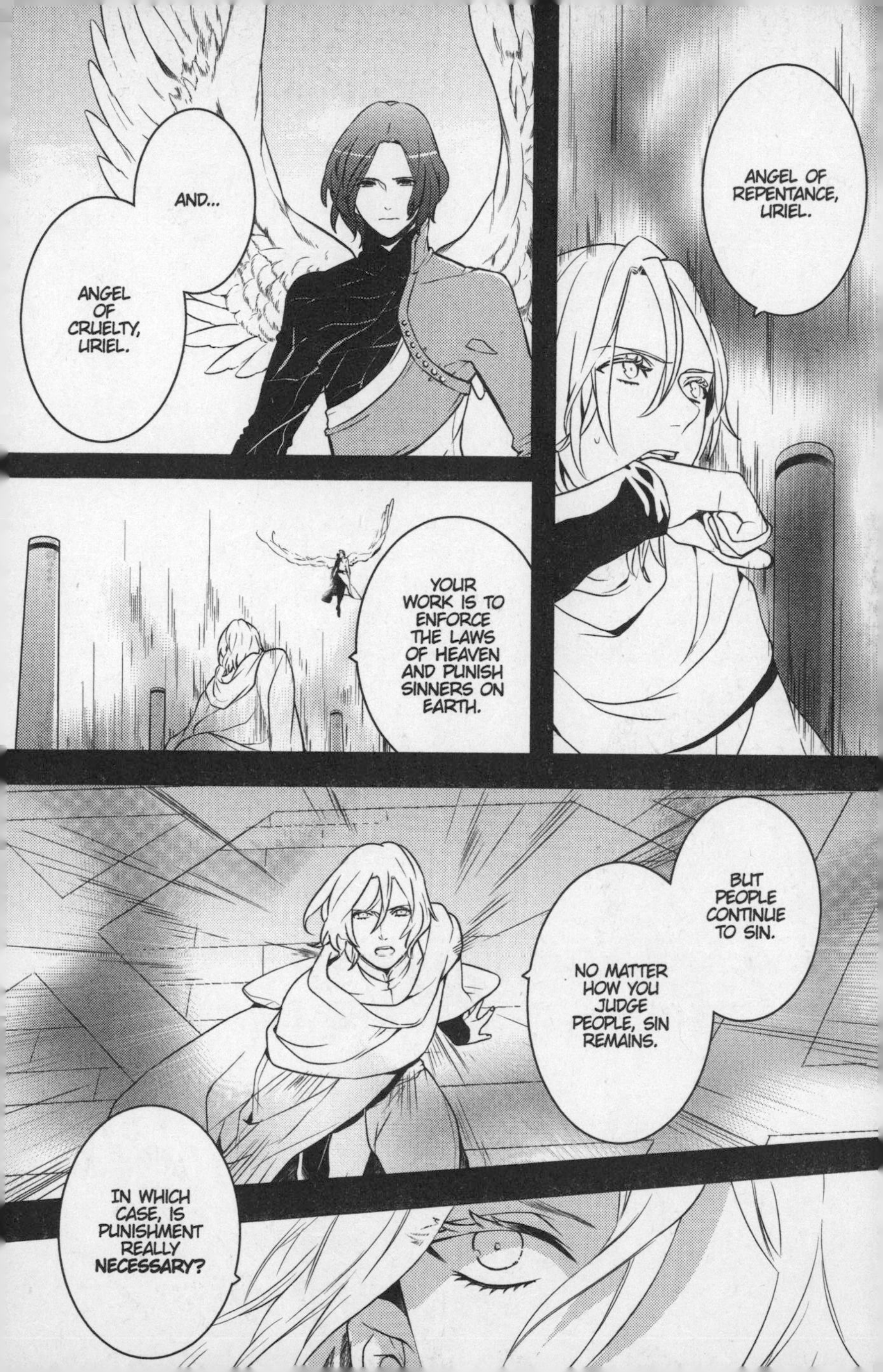
ANGEL OF REPENTANCE, URIEL.
AND...
ANGEL OF CRUELTY, URIEL.
YOUR WORK IS TO ENFORCE THE LAWS OF HEAVEN AND PUNISH SINNERS ON EARTH.
BUT PEOPLE CONTINUE TO SIN.
NO MATTER HOW YOU JUDGE PEOPLE, SIN REMAINS.
IN WHICH CASE, IS PUNISHMENT REALLY NECESSARY?

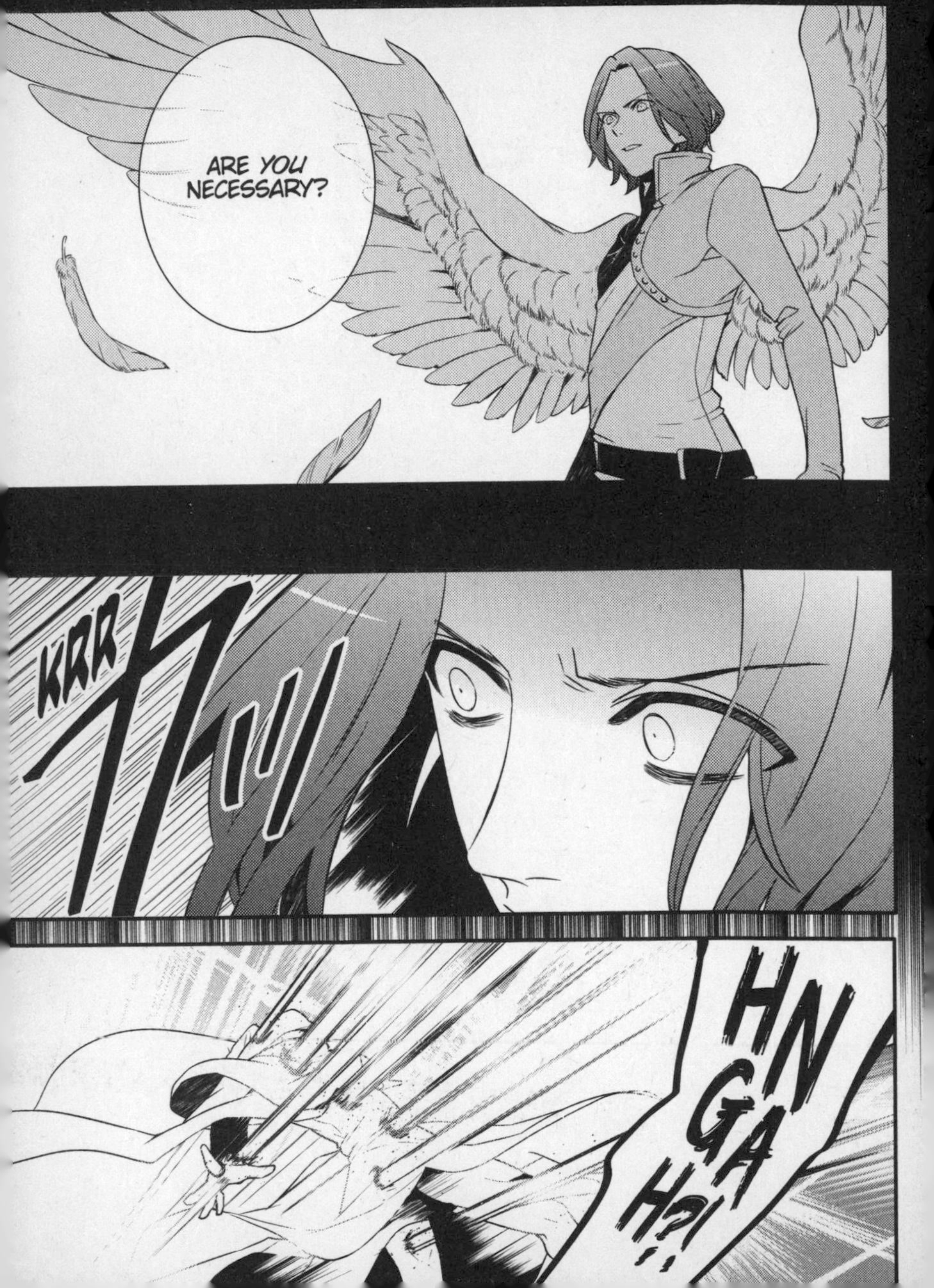
ARE YOU NECESSARY?
KRR
HNGAH?!

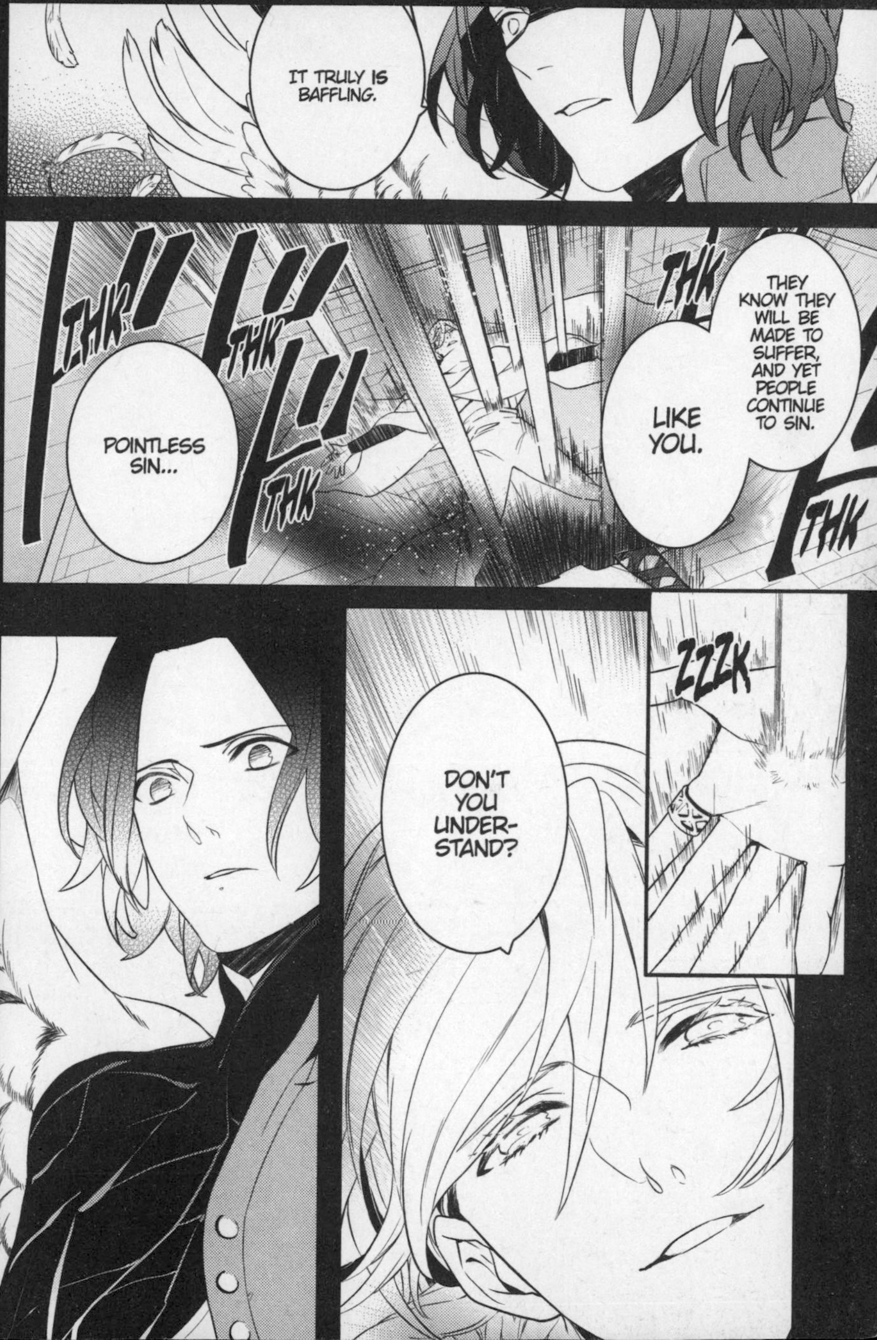
IT TRULY IS BAFFLING.
THK
THEY KNOW THEY WILL BE MADE TO SUFFER, AND YET PEOPLE CONTINUE TO SIN.
LIKE YOU.
THK
THK
THK
POINTLESS SIN...
THK
ZZZK
DON'T YOU UNDER-STAND?

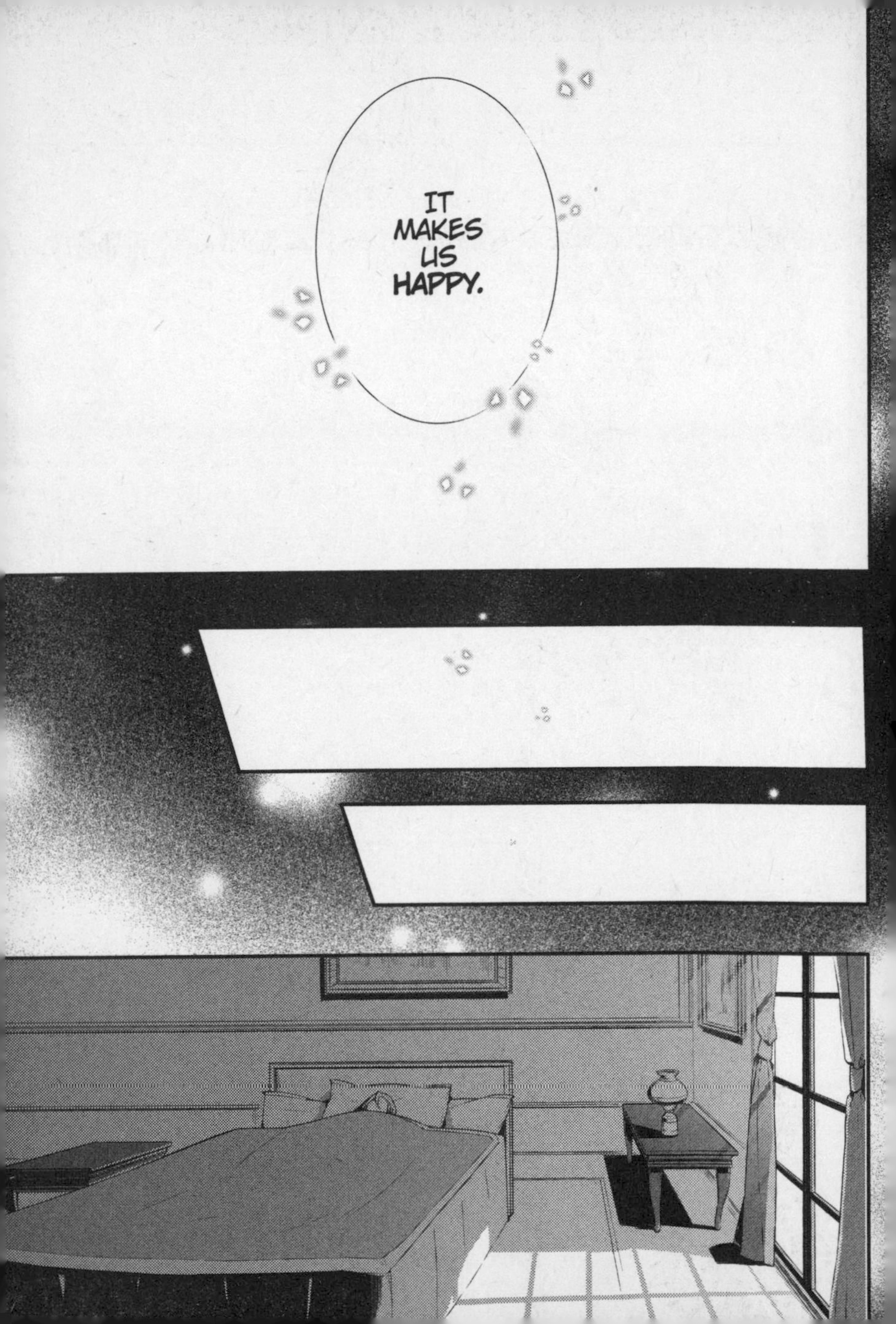
IT MAKES US HAPPY.

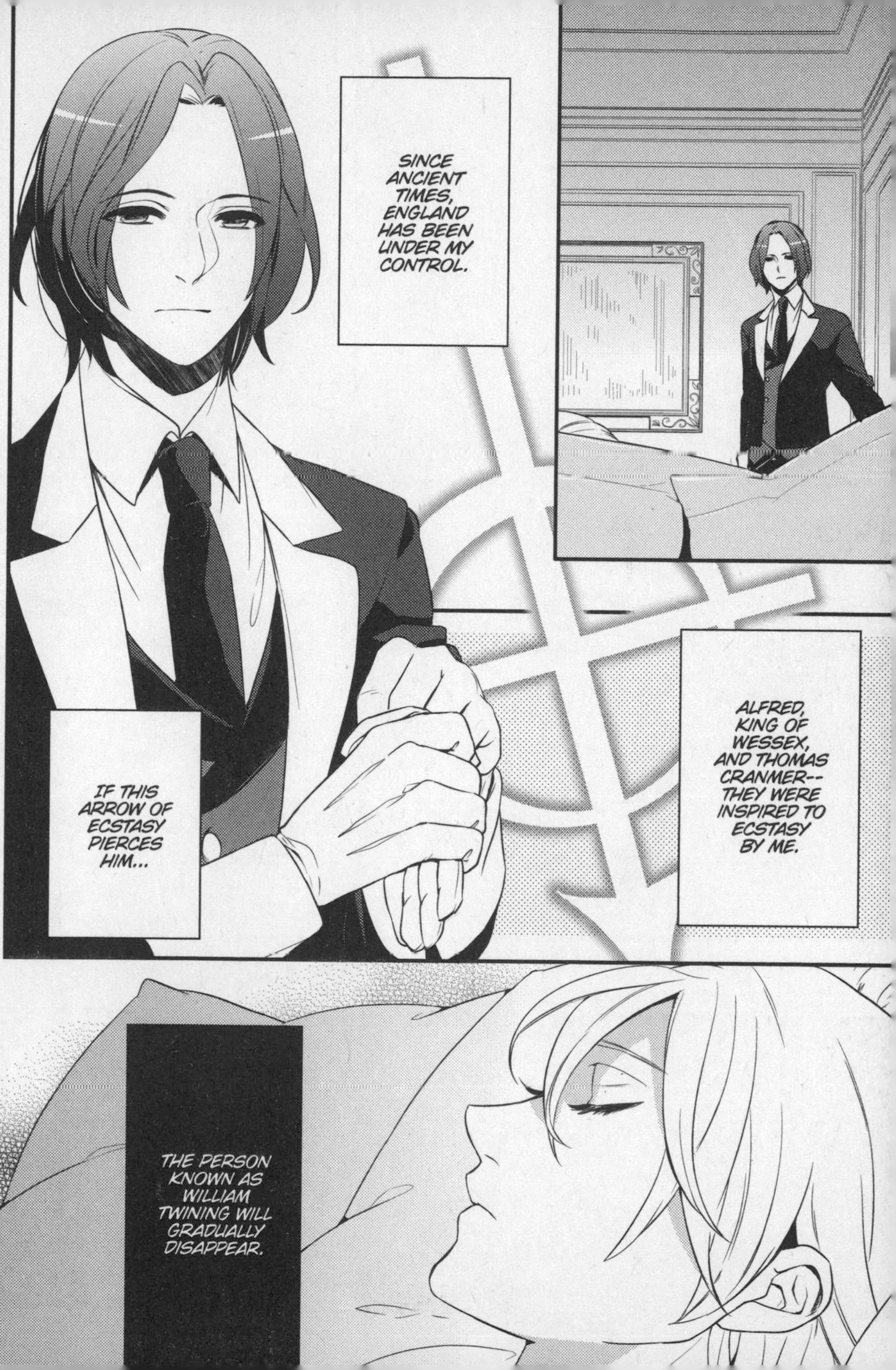
SINCE ANCIENT TIMES, ENGLAND HAS BEEN UNDER MY CONTROL.
ALFRED, KING OF WESSEX, AND THOMAS CRANMER-- THEY WERE INSPIRED TO ECSTASY BY ME.
IF THIS ARROW OF ECSTASY PIERCES HIM...
THE PERSON KNOWN AS WILLIAM TWINING WILL GRADUALLY DISAPPEAR.

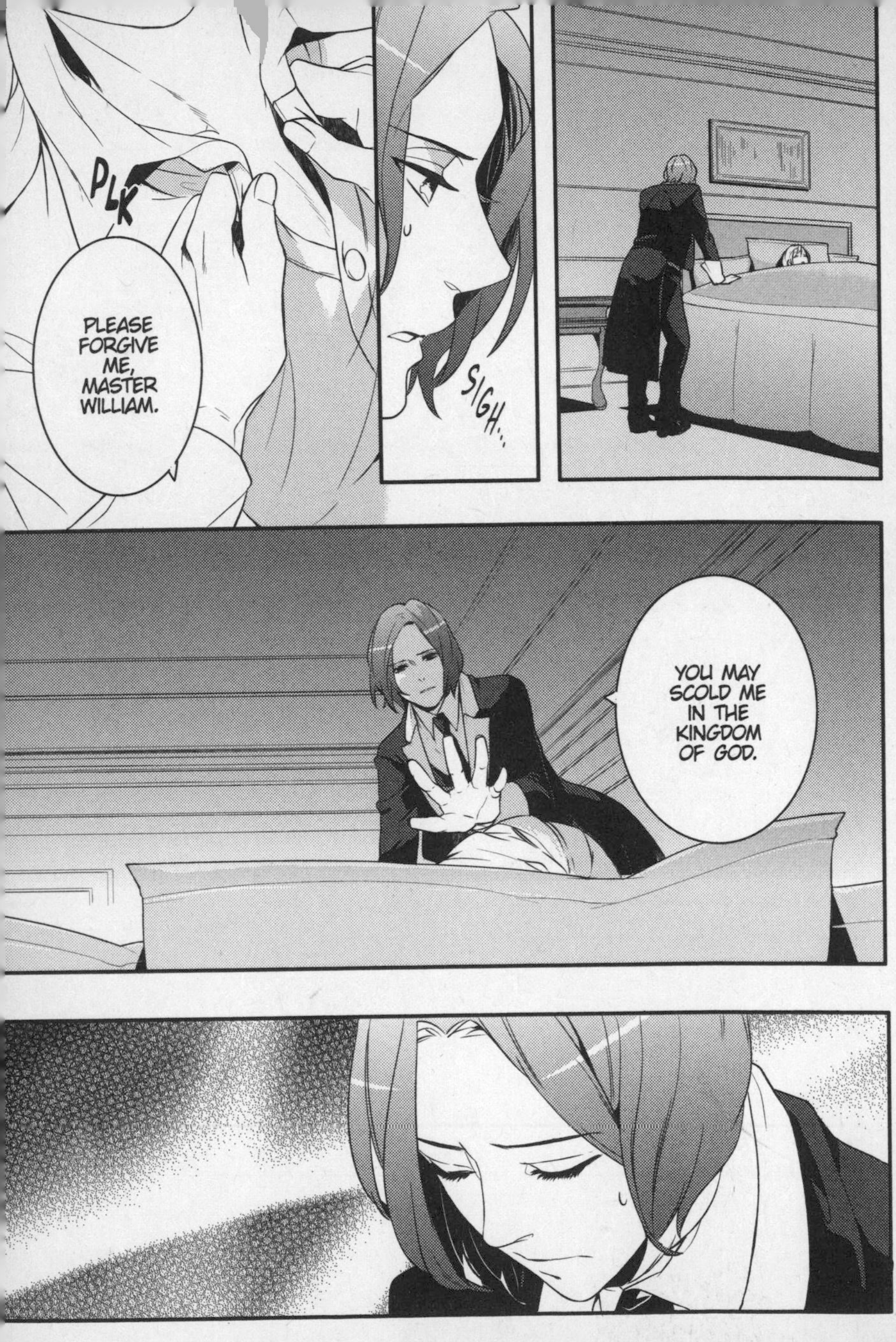
SIGH...
PLK
PLEASE FORGIVE ME, MASTER WILLIAM.
YOU MAY SCOLD ME IN THE KINGDOM OF GOD.

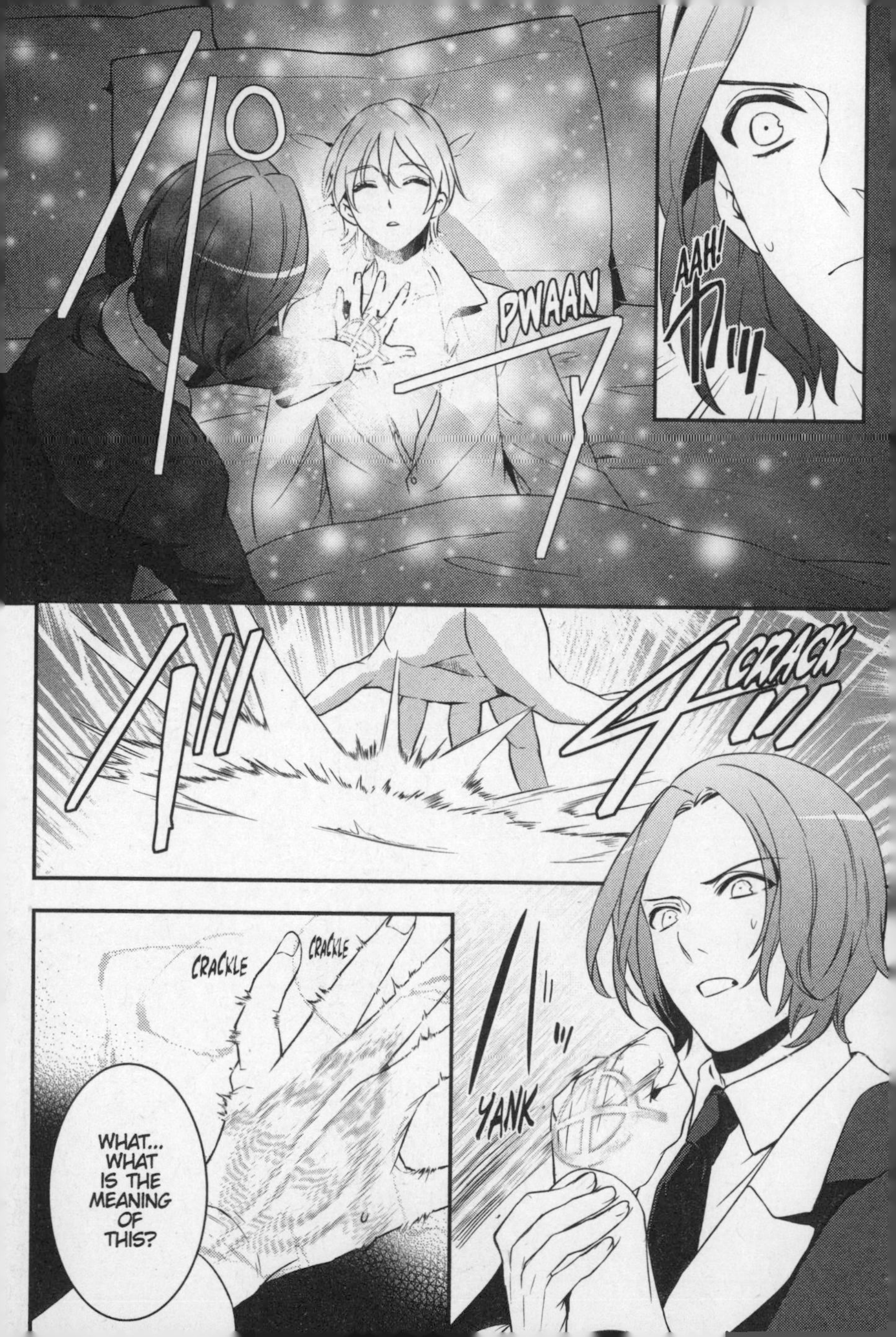
AAH!
PWAAN
CRACK
YANK
CRACKLE
CRACKLE
WHAT... WHAT IS THE MEANING OF THIS?

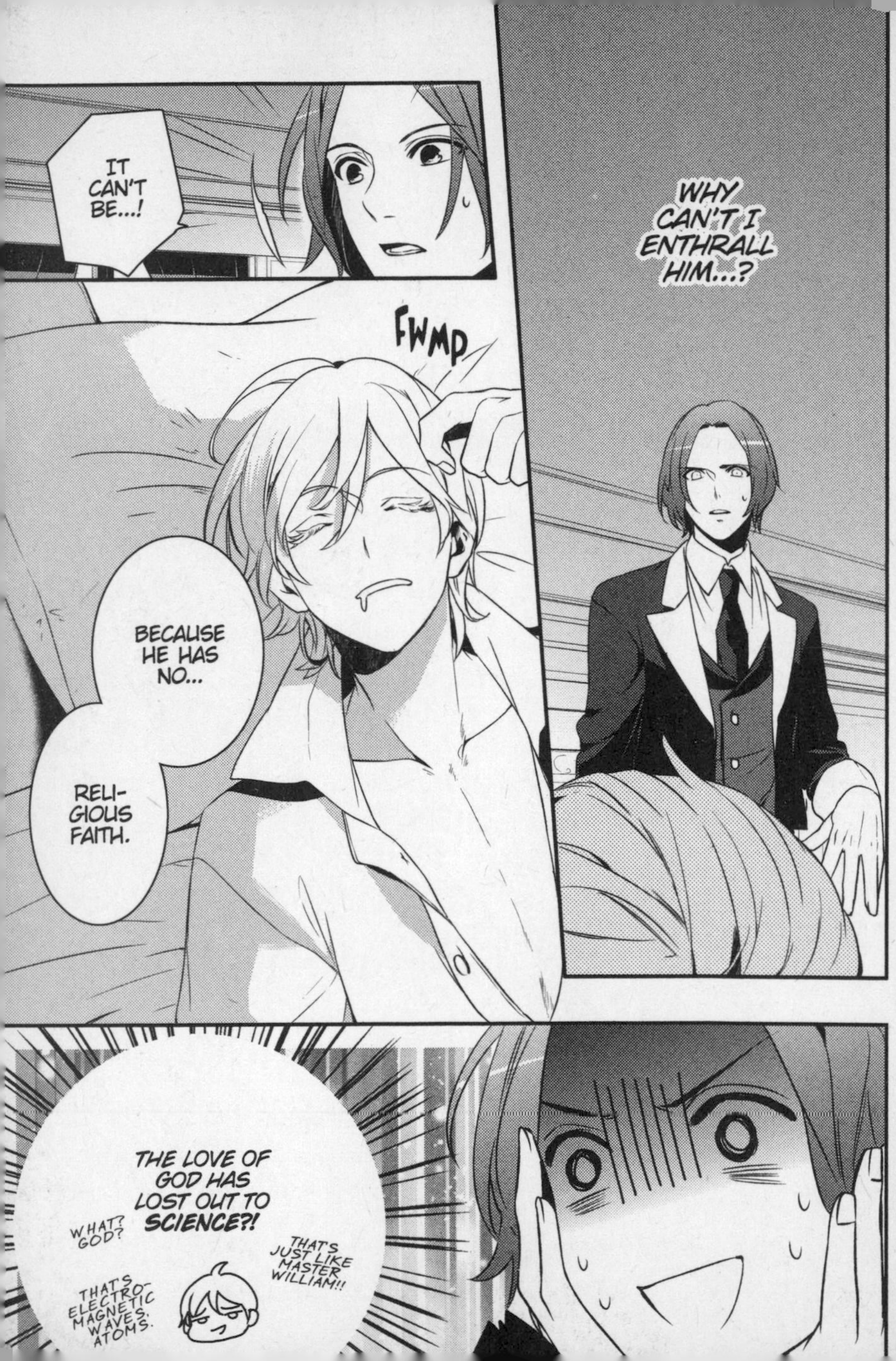
WHY CAN'T I ENTHRALL HIM...?
IT CAN'T BE...!
FWMP
BECAUSE HE HAS NO...
RELI-GIOUS FAITH.
THE LOVE OF GOD HAS LOST OUT TO **SCIENCE**?!
THAT'S JUST LIKE MASTER WILLIAM!!
WHAT? GOD?
THAT'S ELECTRO-MAGNETIC WAVES, ATOMS.

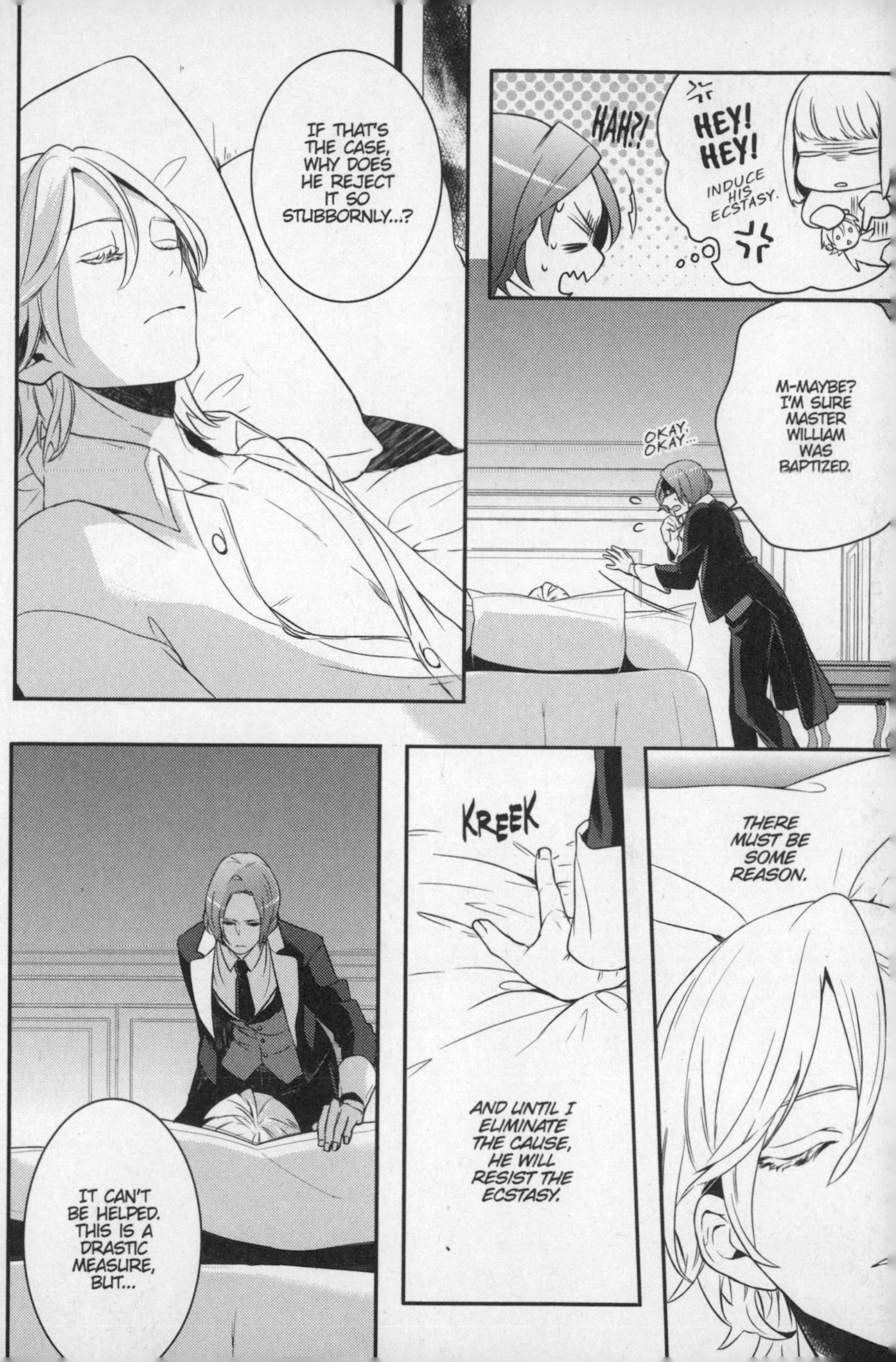
HEY! HEY!
INDUCE HIS ECSTASY.
HAH?!
M-MAYBE? I'M SURE MASTER WILLIAM WAS BAPTIZED.
OKAY, OKAY...
IF THAT'S THE CASE, WHY DOES HE REJECT IT SO STUBBORNLY...?
THERE MUST BE SOME REASON.
KREEK
AND UNTIL I ELIMINATE THE CAUSE, HE WILL RESIST THE ECSTASY.
IT CAN'T BE HELPED. THIS IS A DRASTIC MEASURE, BUT...

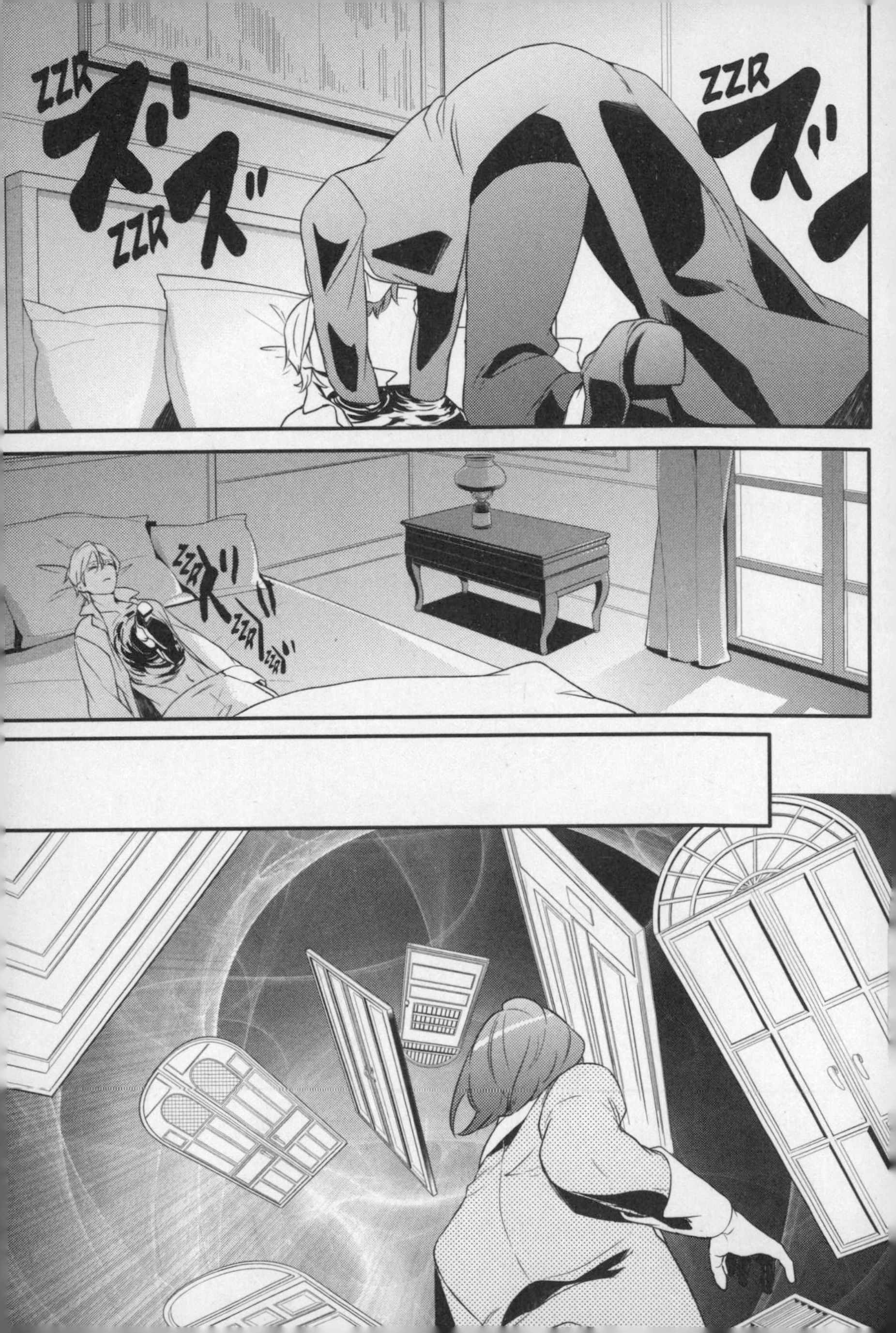
ZZR
ズ
ZZR
ズ
ZZR
ズ
ZZR
ズリ
ZZR
ZZR

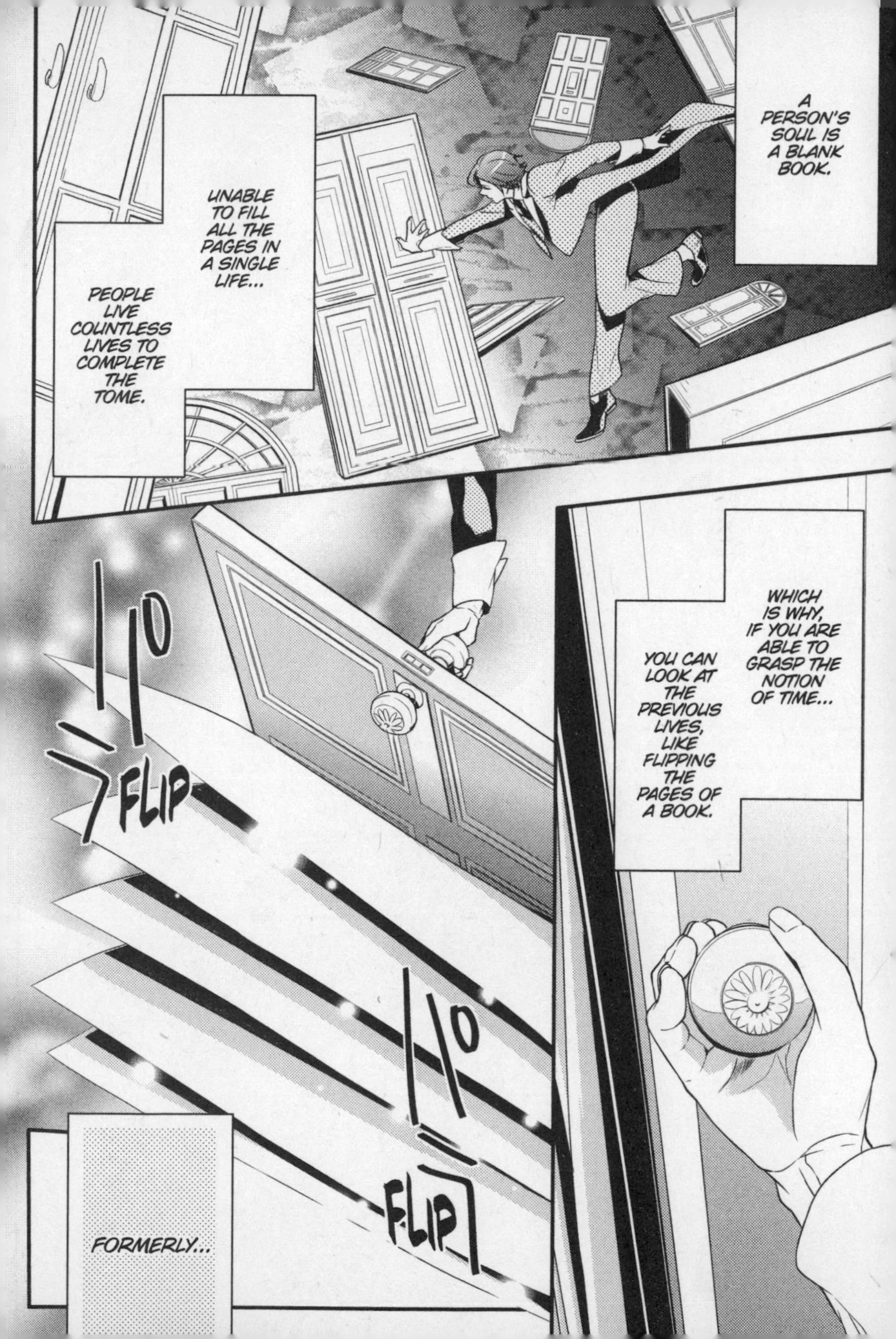
A PERSON'S SOUL IS A BLANK BOOK.
UNABLE TO FILL ALL THE PAGES IN A SINGLE LIFE...
PEOPLE LIVE COUNTLESS LIVES TO COMPLETE THE TOME.
WHICH IS WHY, IF YOU ARE ABLE TO GRASP THE NOTION OF TIME...
YOU CAN LOOK AT THE PREVIOUS LIVES, LIKE FLIPPING THE PAGES OF A BOOK.
FLIP
FLIP
FORMERLY...

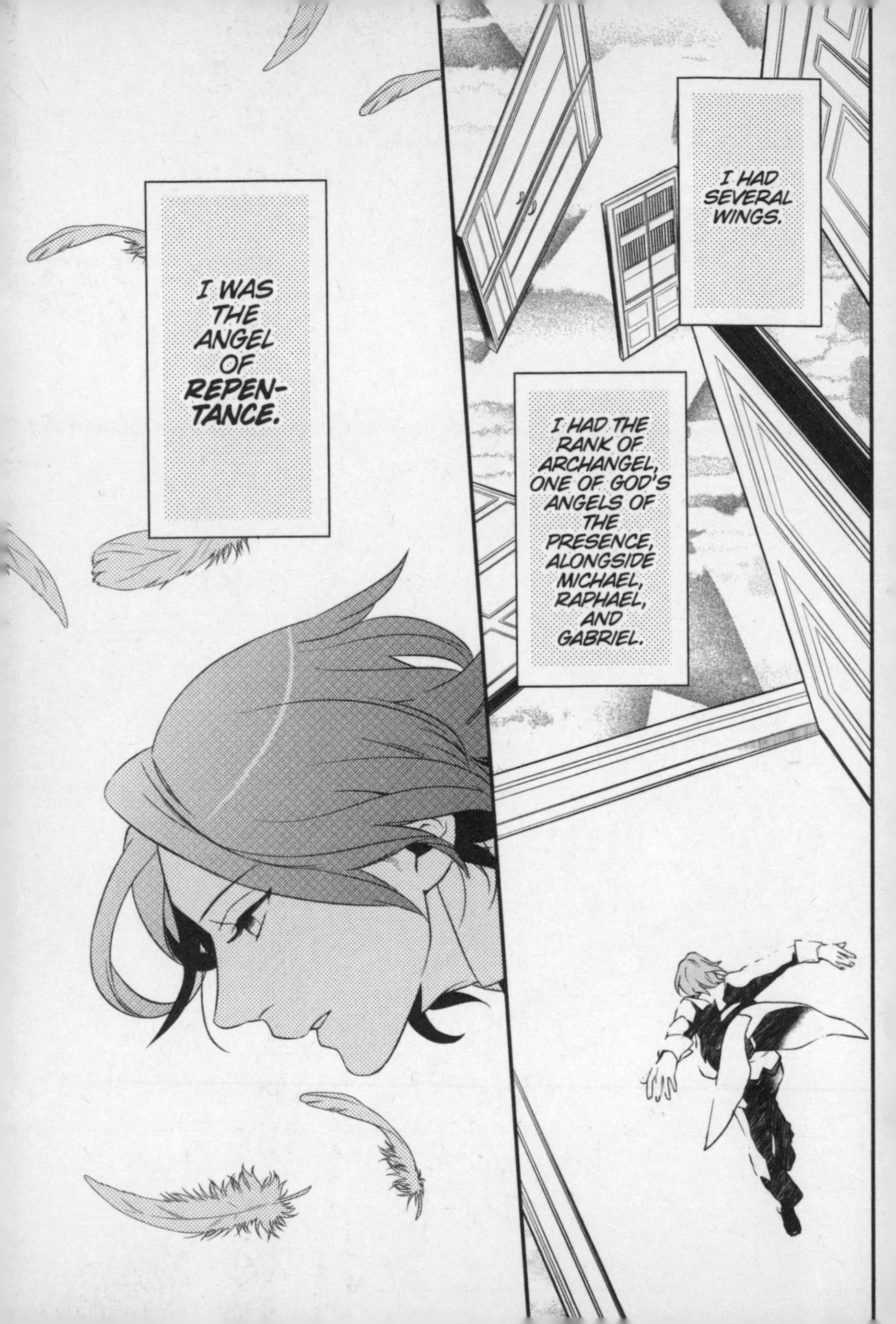
I HAD SEVERAL WINGS.
I HAD THE RANK OF ARCHANGEL, ONE OF GOD'S ANGELS OF THE PRESENCE, ALONGSIDE MICHAEL, RAPHAEL, AND GABRIEL.
I WAS THE ANGEL OF REPENTANCE.

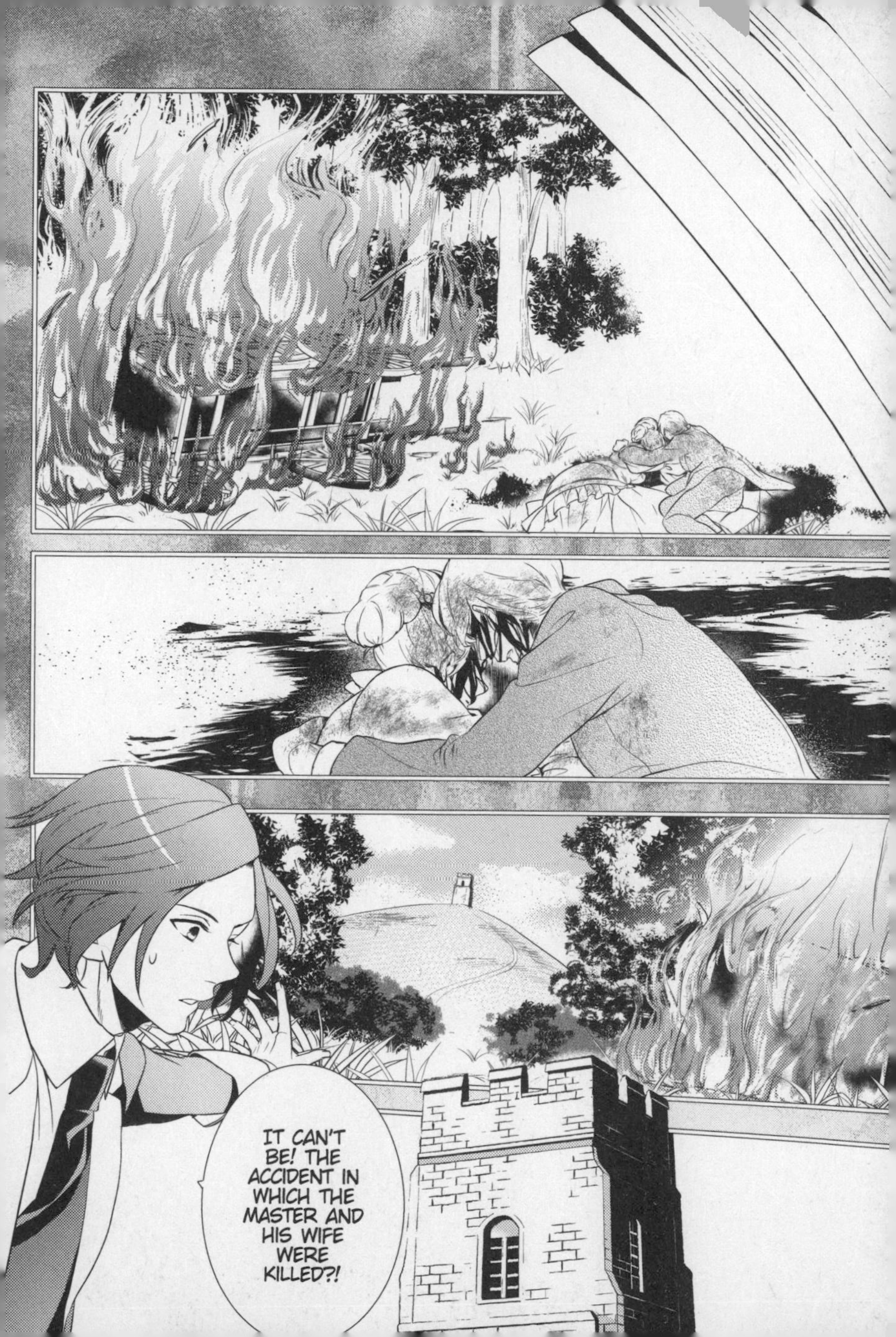
IT CAN'T BE! THE ACCIDENT IN WHICH THE MASTER AND HIS WIFE WERE KILLED?!

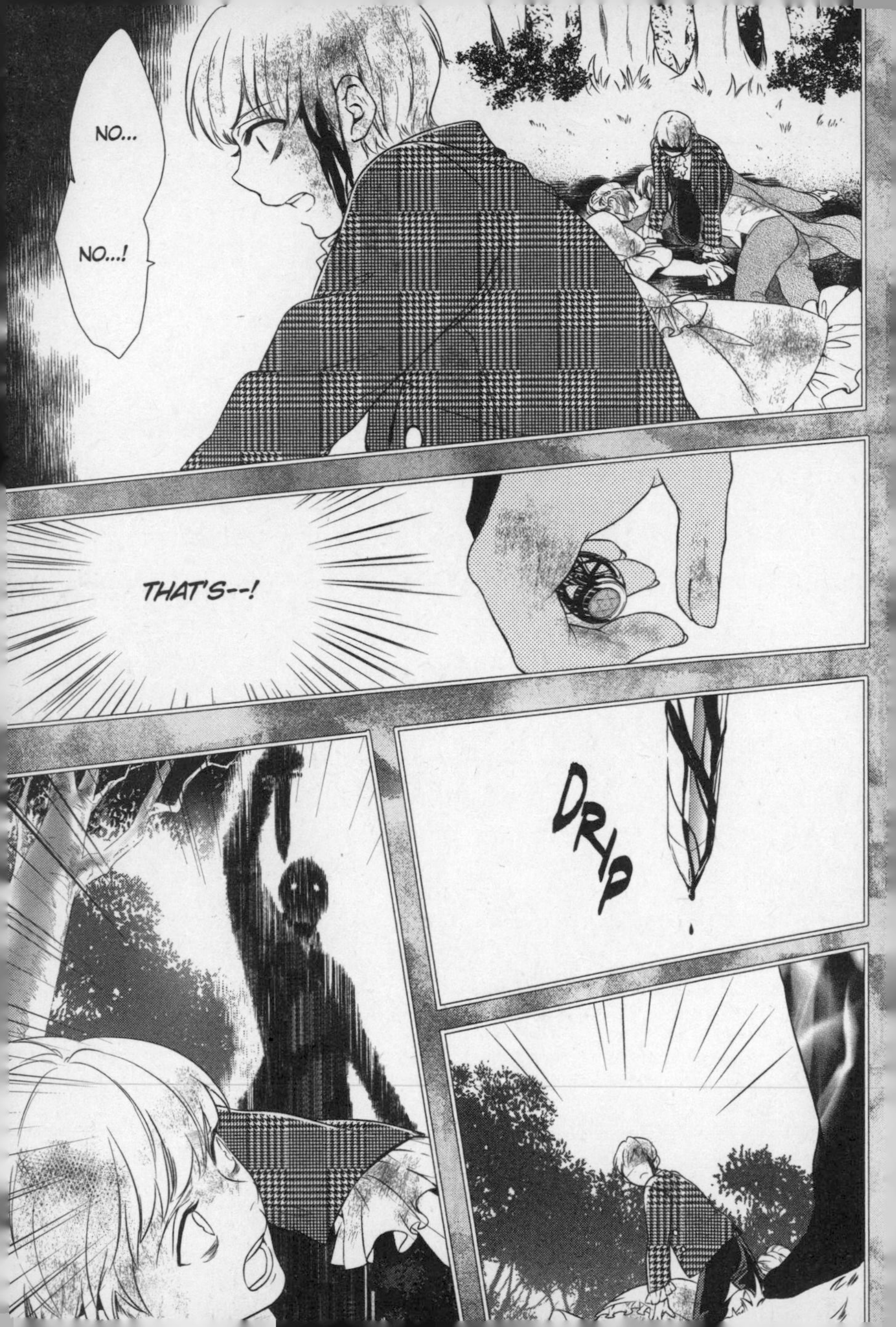
NO...
NO...!
THAT'S--!
DRIP

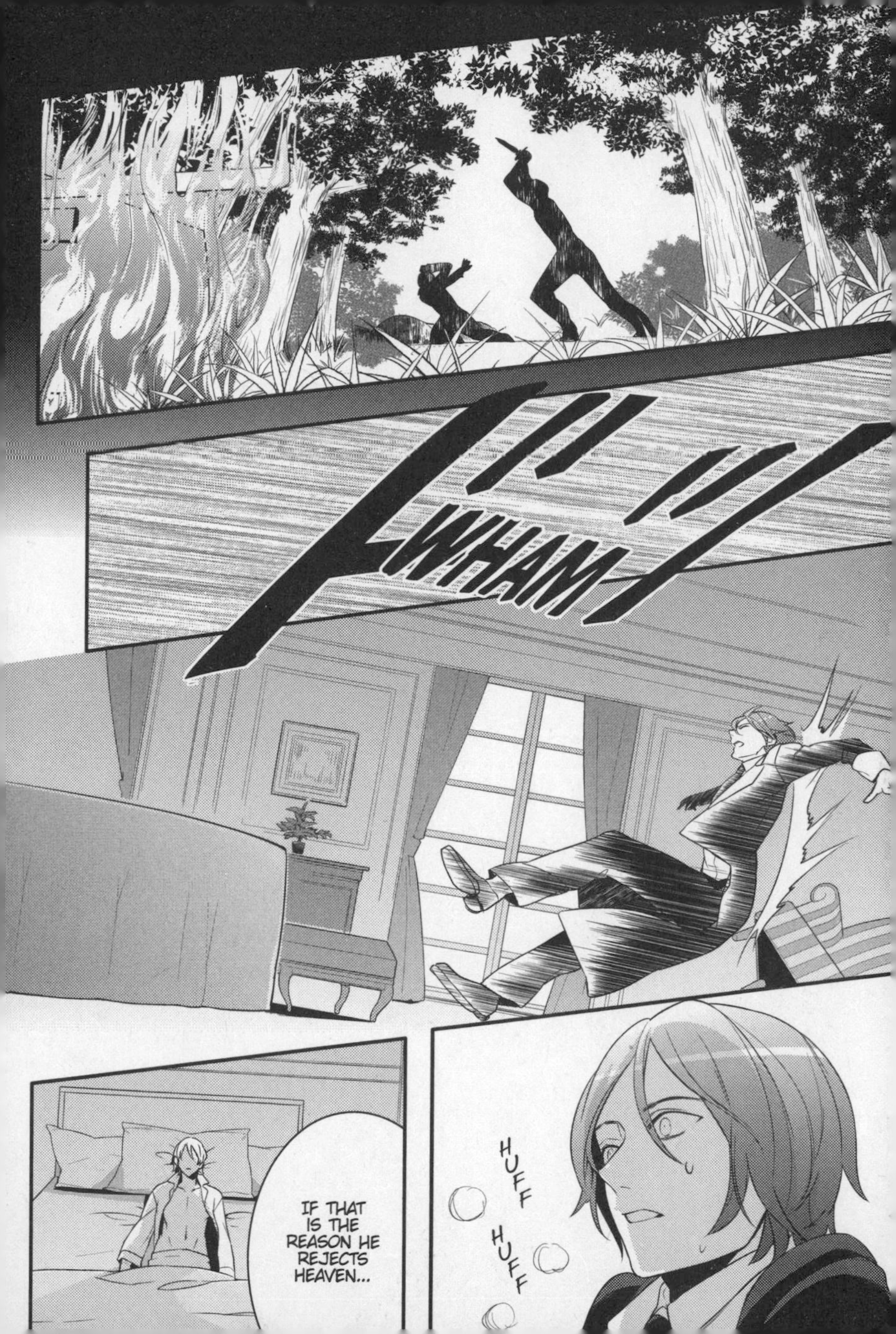
WHAM
HUFF
HUFF
IF THAT IS THE REASON HE REJECTS HEAVEN...

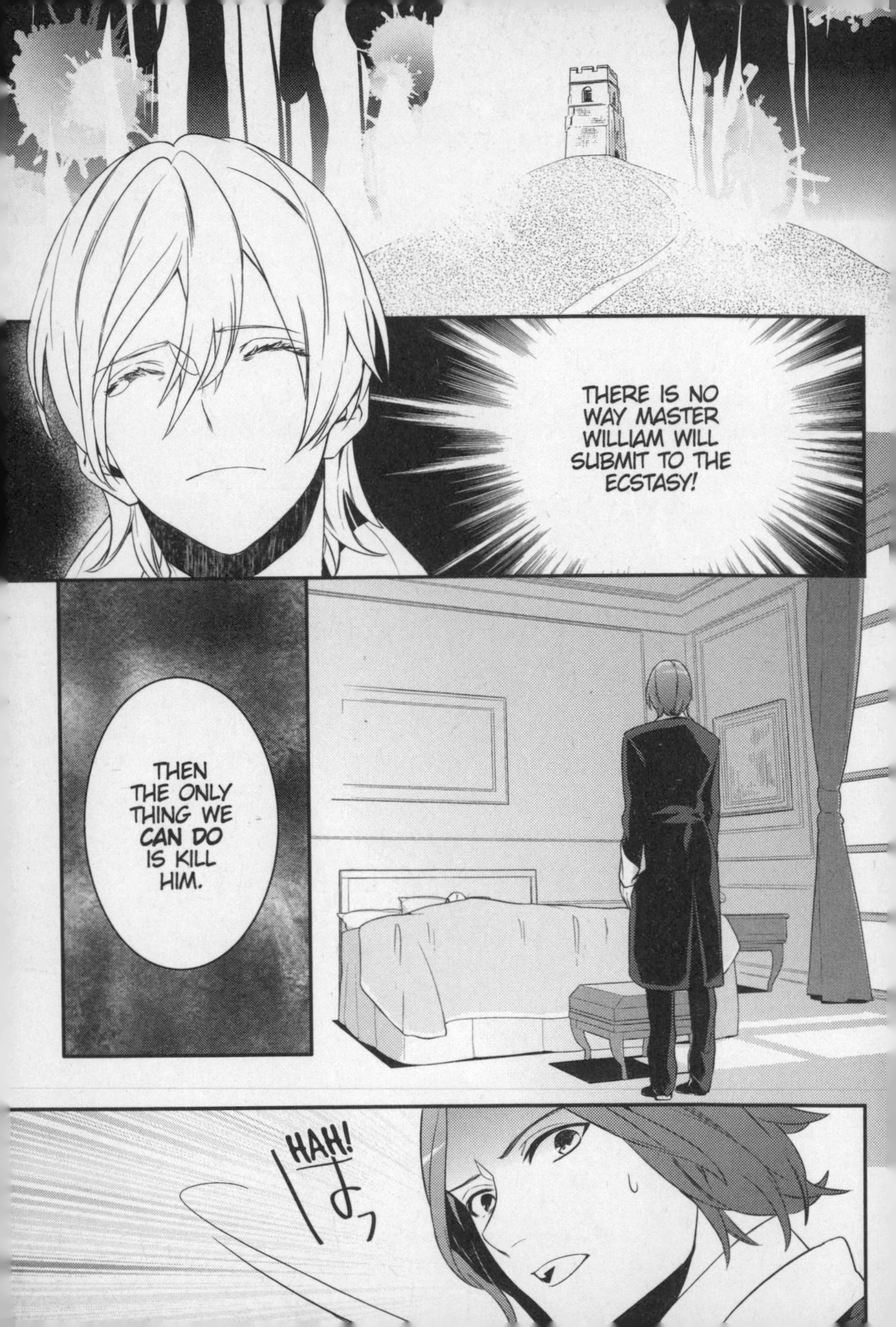
THERE IS NO WAY MASTER WILLIAM WILL SUBMIT TO THE ECSTASY!
THEN THE ONLY THING WE CAN DO IS KILL HIM.
HAH!
はっ

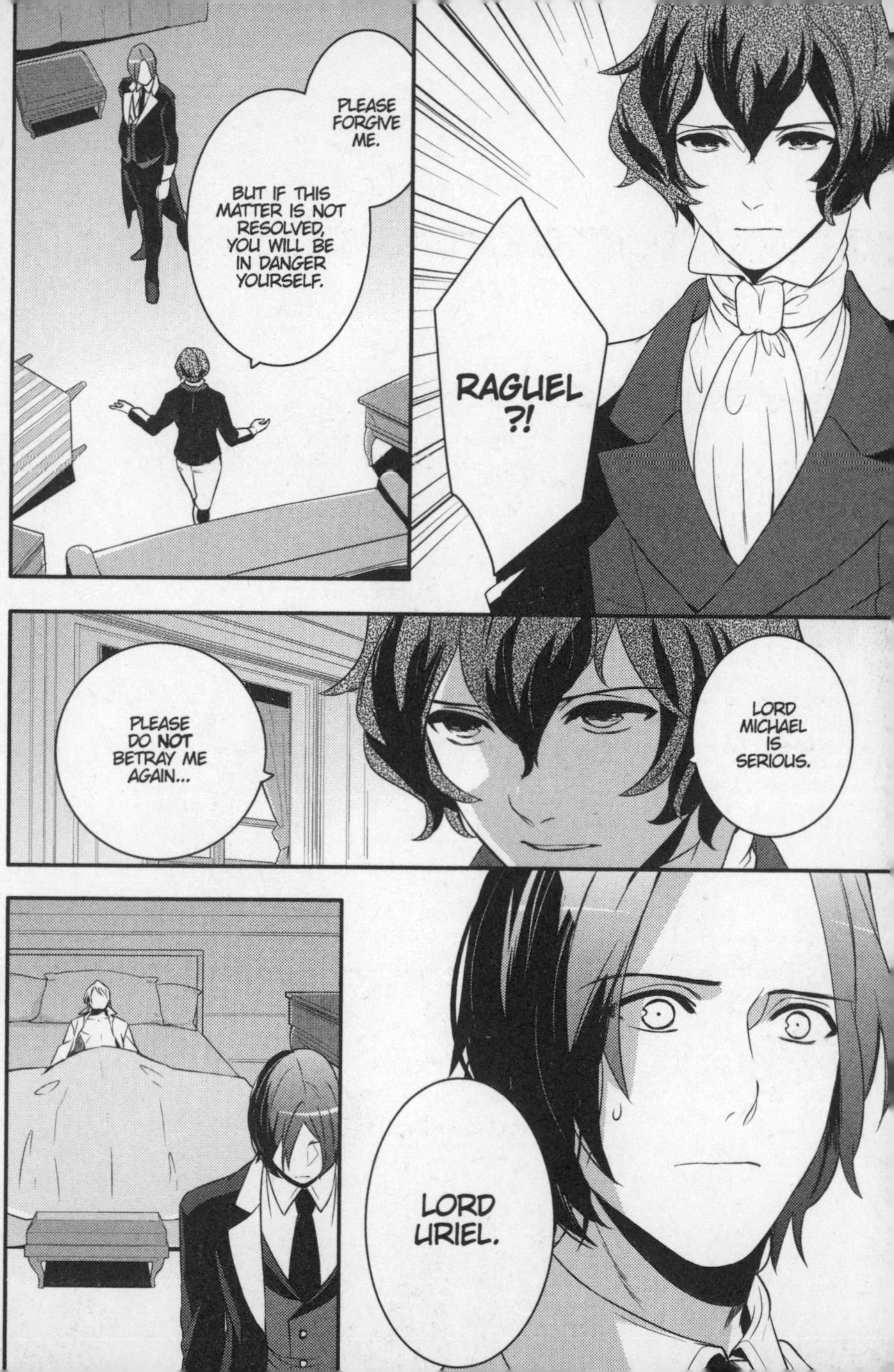
RAGUEL ?!
PLEASE FORGIVE ME.
BUT IF THIS MATTER IS NOT RESOLVED, YOU WILL BE IN DANGER YOURSELF.
LORD MICHAEL IS SERIOUS.
PLEASE DO NOT BETRAY ME AGAIN...
LORD URIEL.

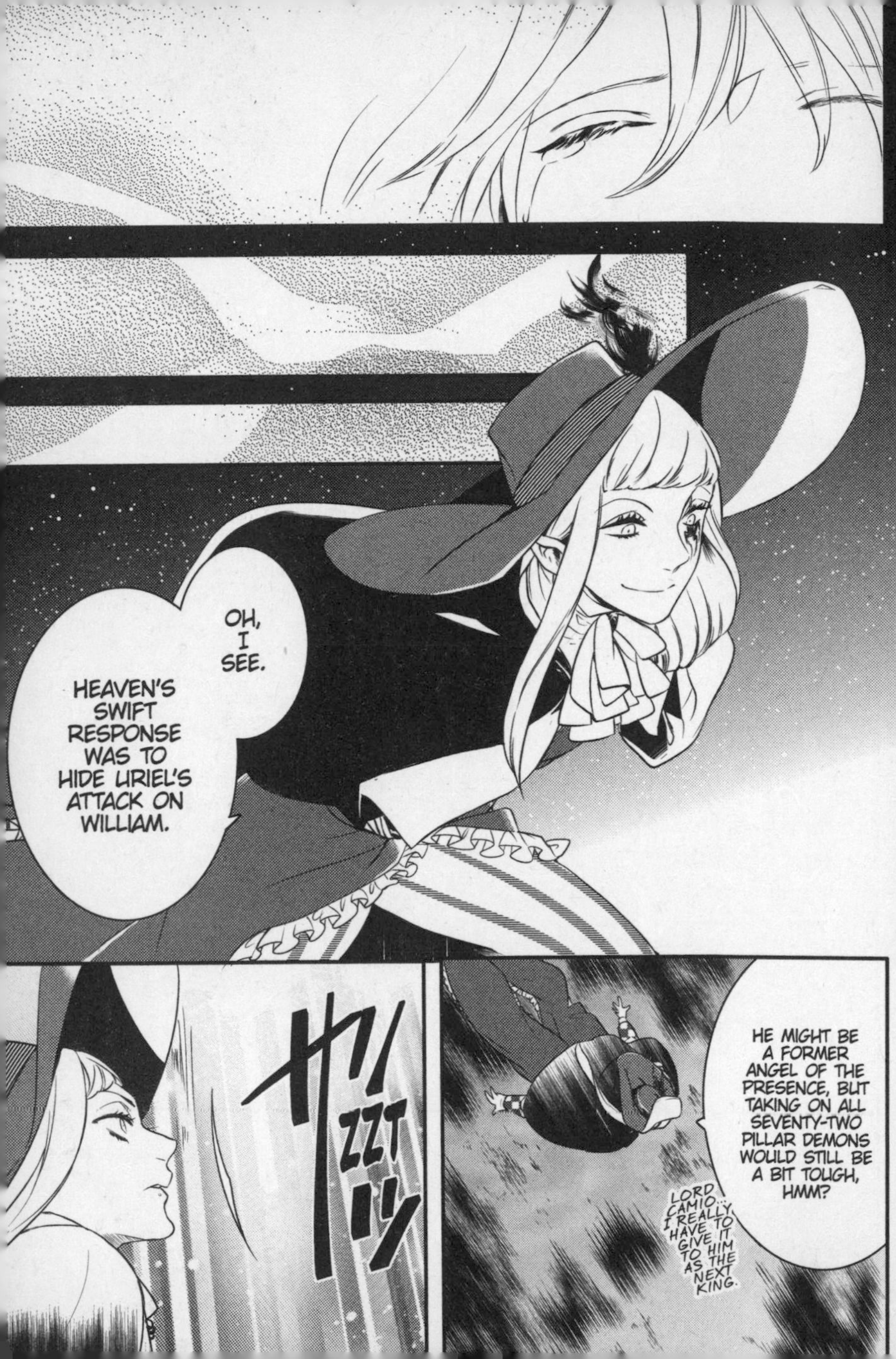
OH, I SEE.
HEAVEN'S SWIFT RESPONSE WAS TO HIDE URIEL'S ATTACK ON WILLIAM.
HE MIGHT BE A FORMER ANGEL OF THE PRESENCE, BUT TAKING ON ALL SEVENTY-TWO PILLAR DEMONS WOULD STILL BE A BIT TOUGH, HMM?
LORD CAMIO... I REALLY HAVE TO GIVE IT TO HIM AS THE NEXT KING.
ZZT

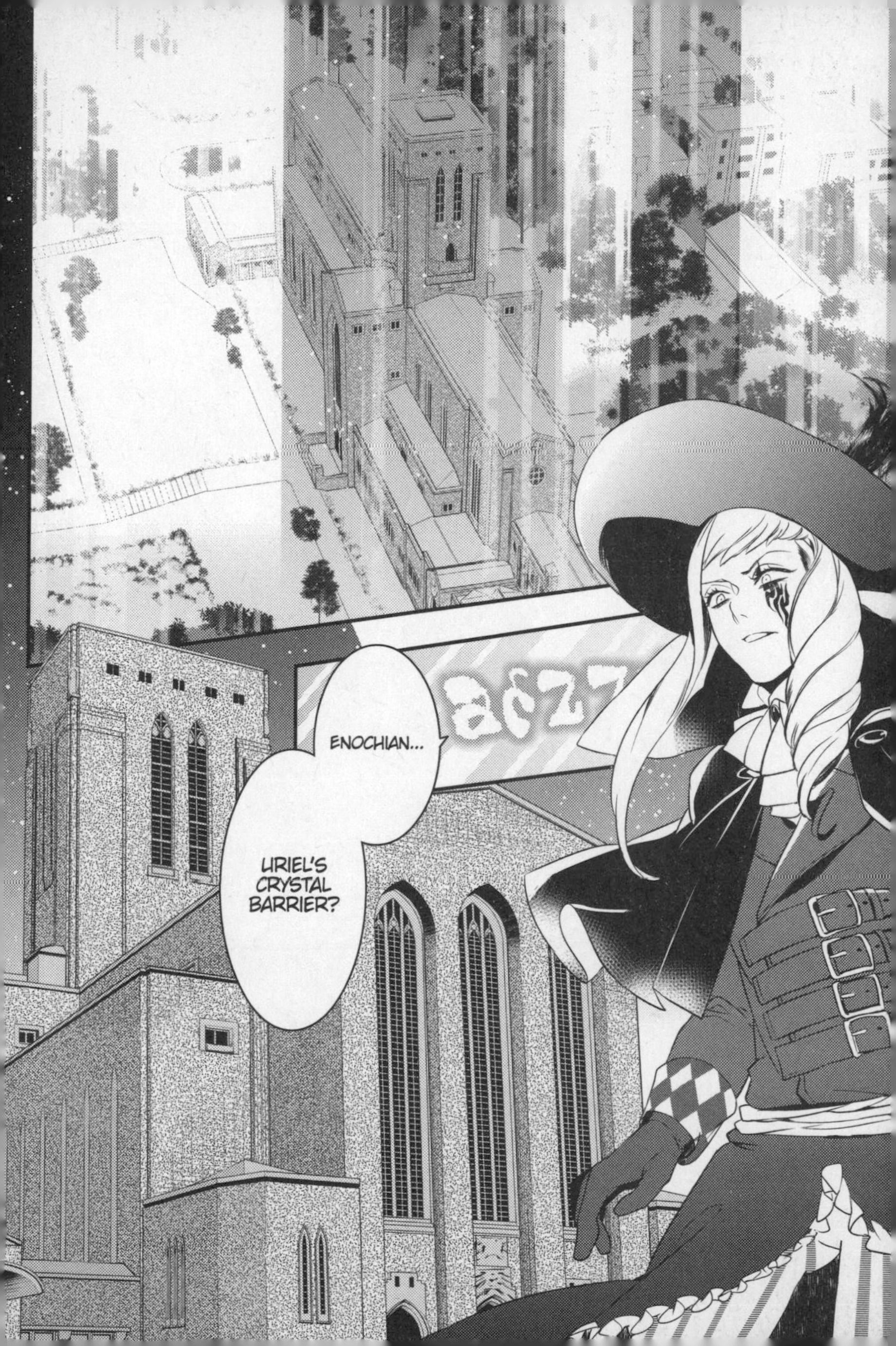
ENOCHIAN...
URIEL'S CRYSTAL BARRIER?

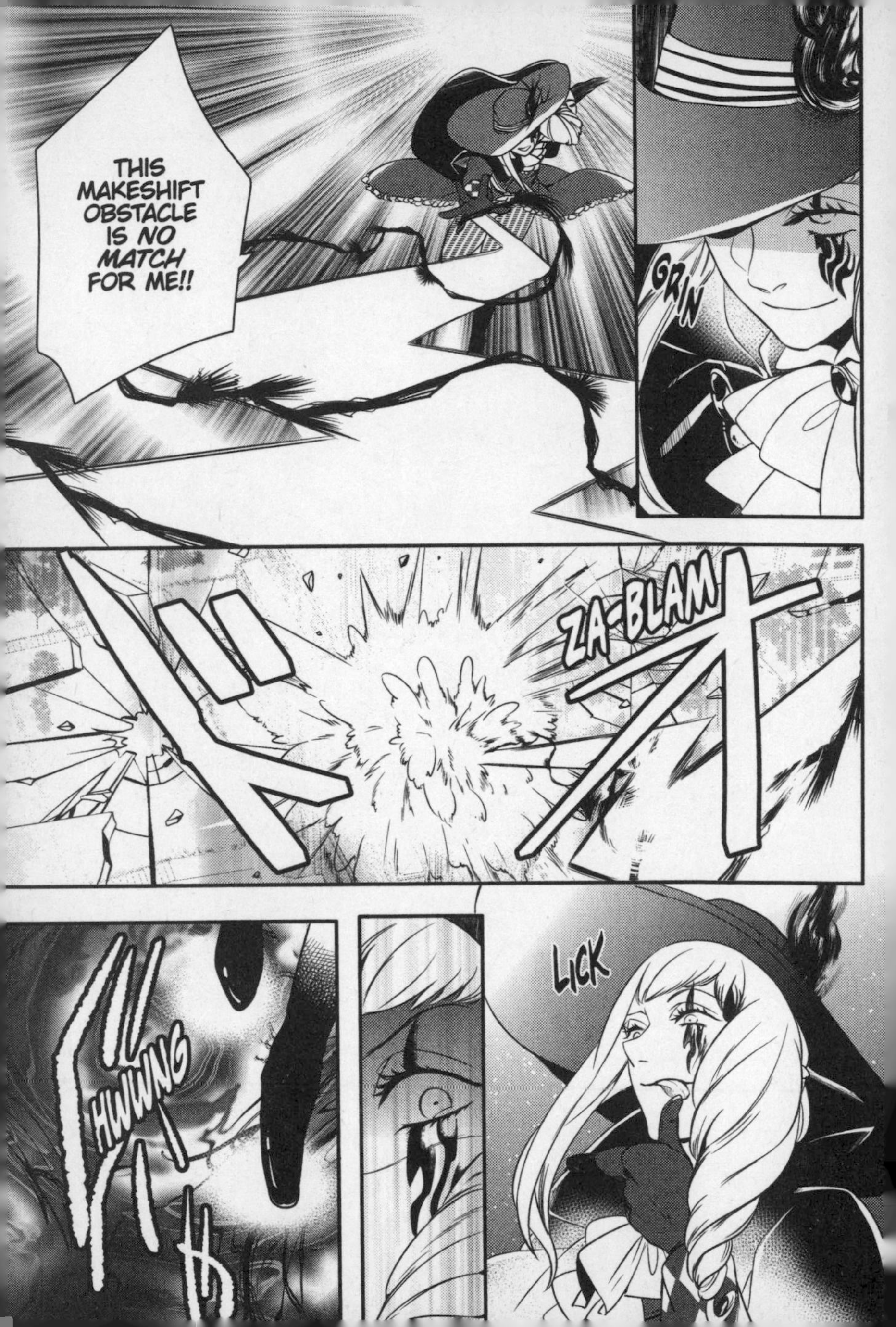
GRIN
THIS MAKESHIFT OBSTACLE IS NO MATCH FOR ME!!
ZA-BLAM
LICK
HWWNG

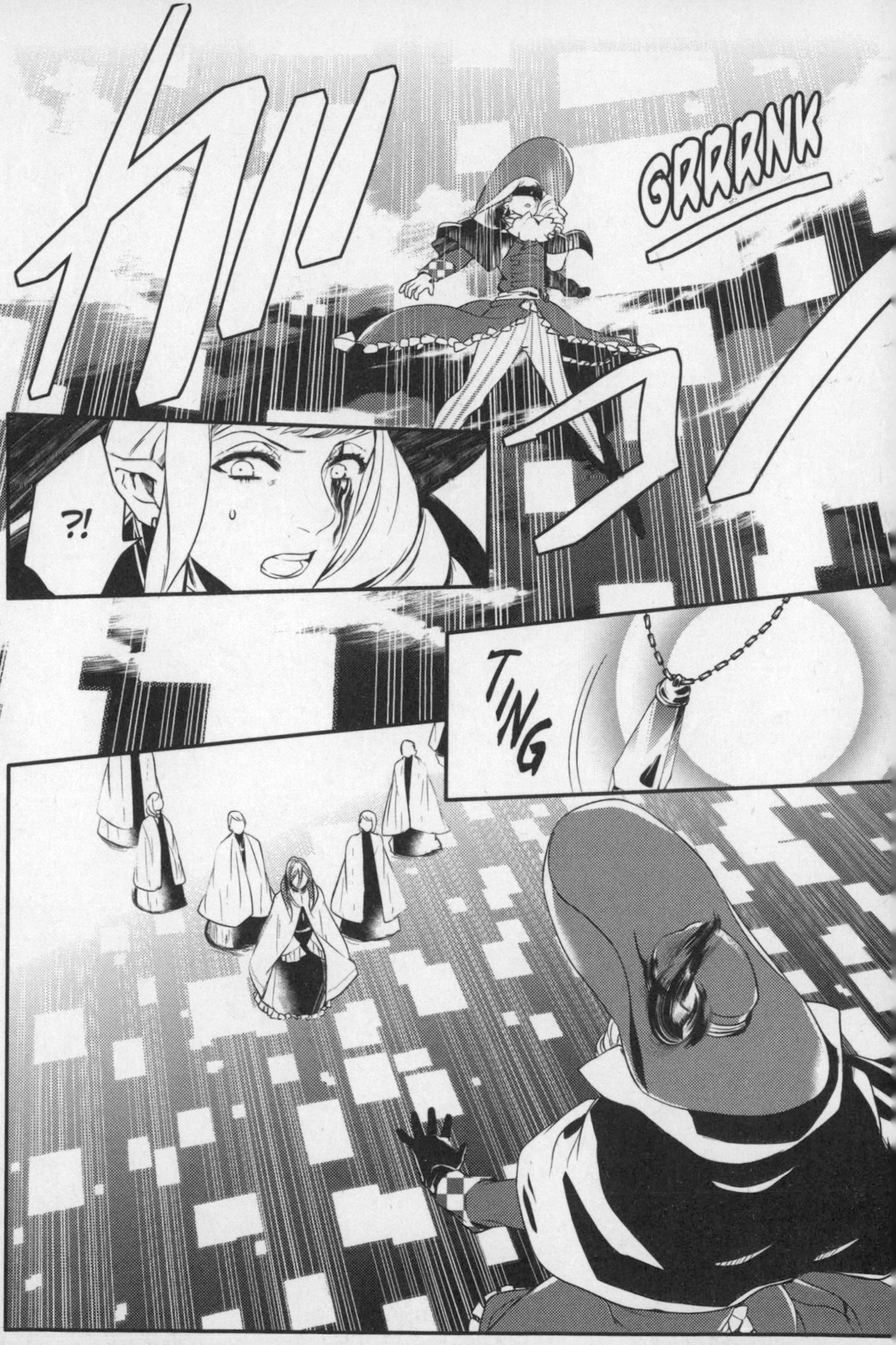
GRRRNK
?!
TING

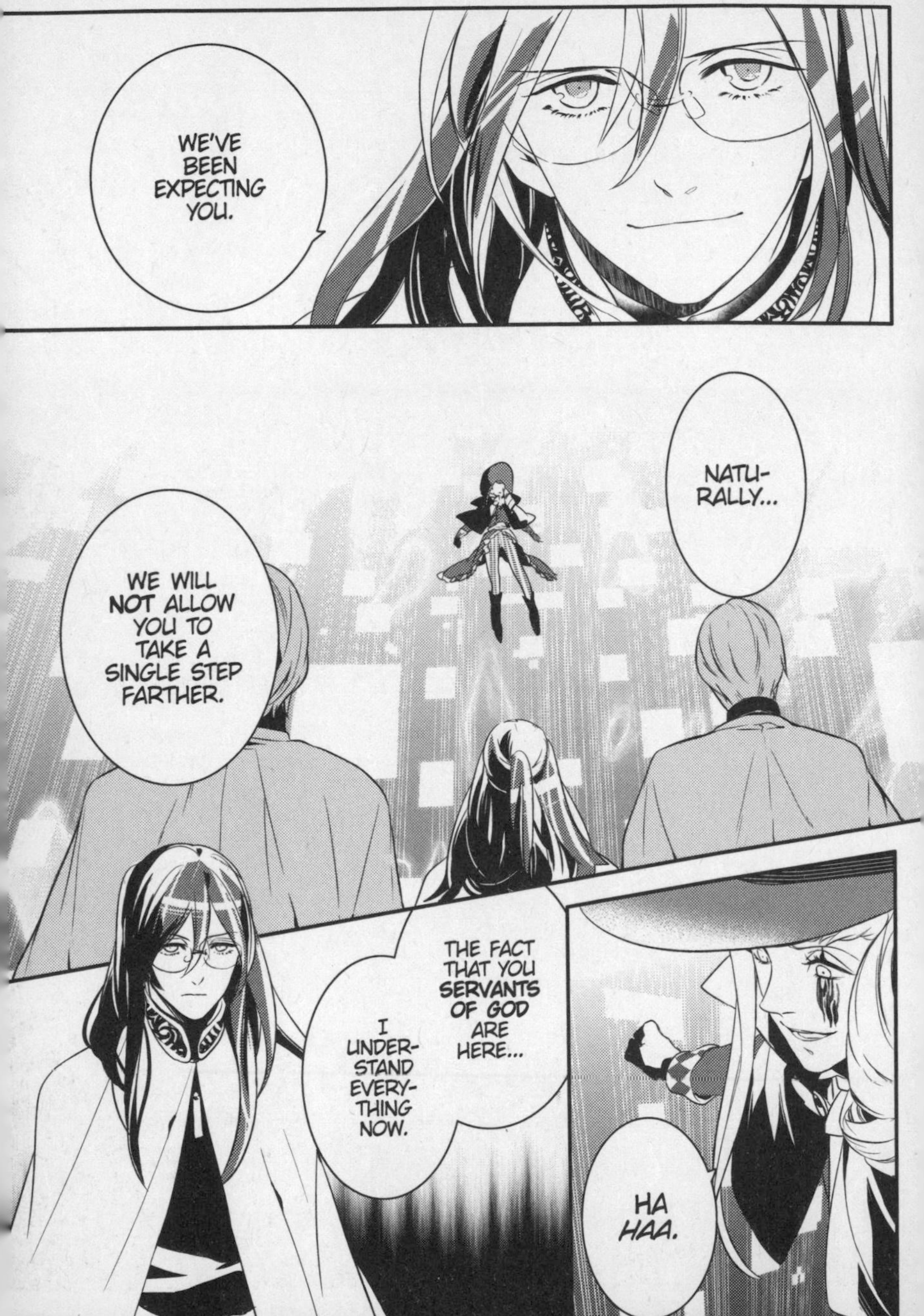
WE'VE BEEN EXPECTING YOU.
NATU-RALLY...
WE WILL NOT ALLOW YOU TO TAKE A SINGLE STEP FARTHER.
HA HAA.
THE FACT THAT YOU SERVANTS OF GOD ARE HERE...
I UNDER-STAND EVERY-THING NOW.

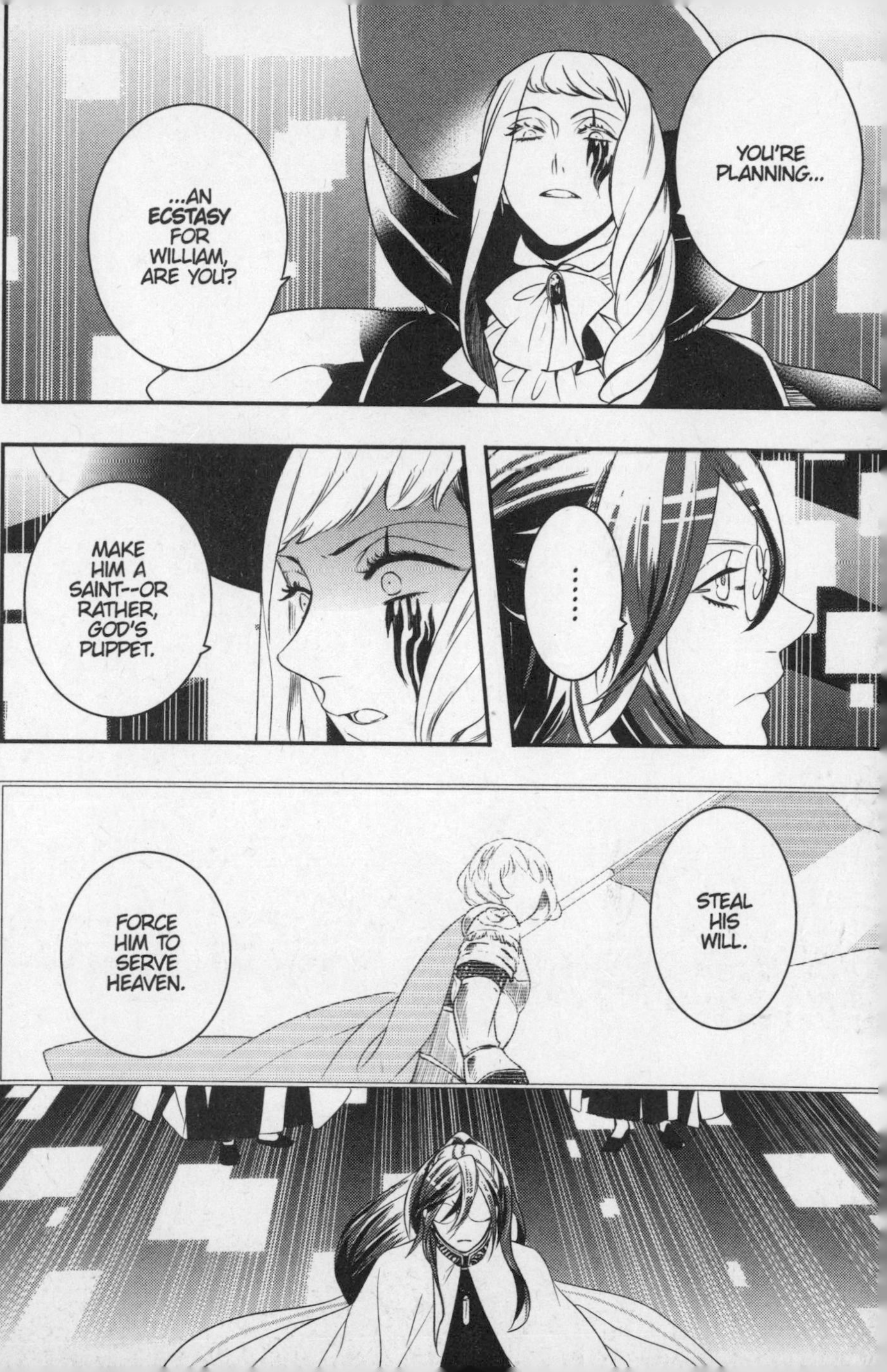
YOU'RE PLANNING...
...AN ECSTASY FOR WILLIAM, ARE YOU?
......
MAKE HIM A SAINT--OR RATHER, GOD'S PUPPET.
STEAL HIS WILL.
FORCE HIM TO SERVE HEAVEN.

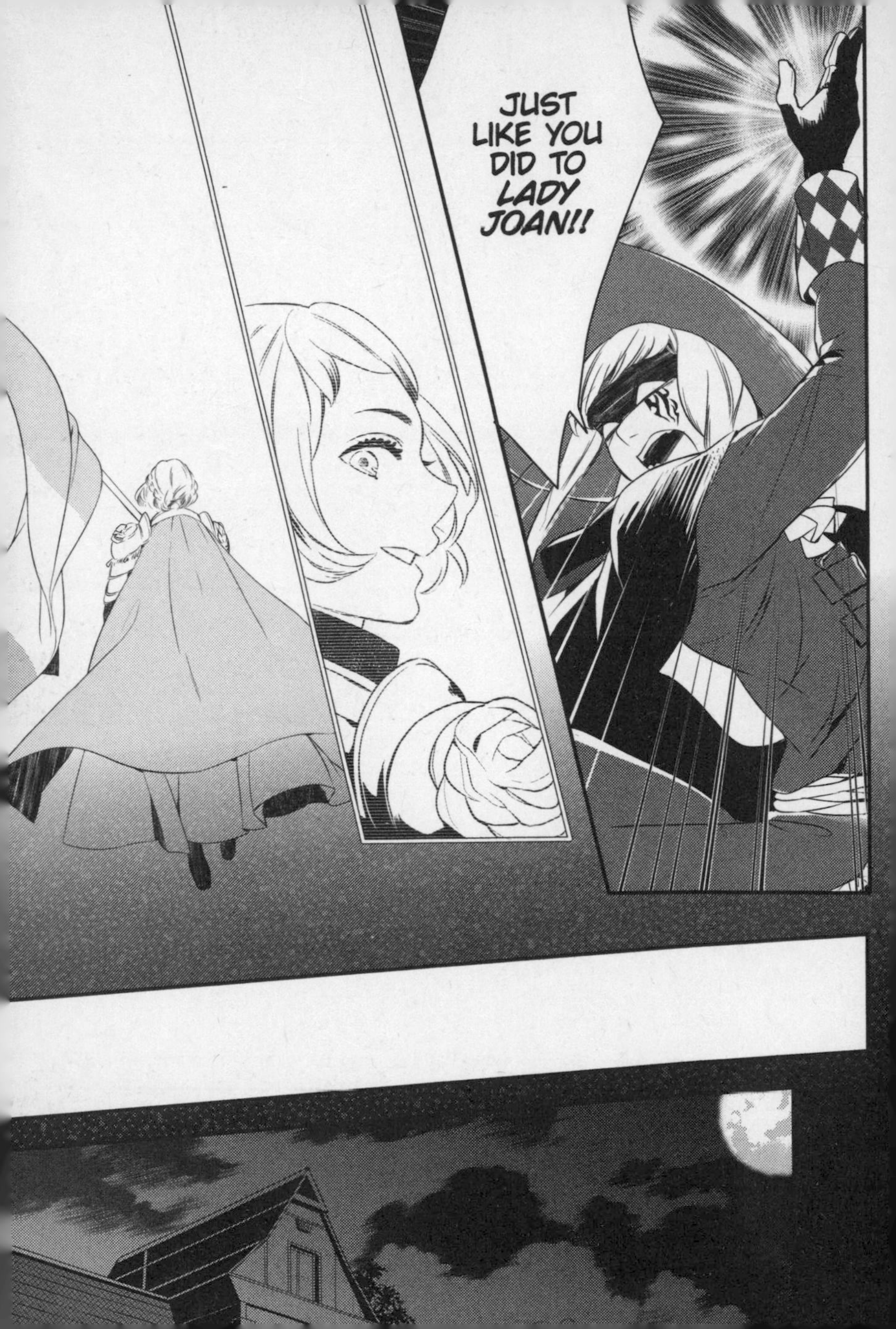
JUST LIKE YOU DID TO LADY JOAN!!

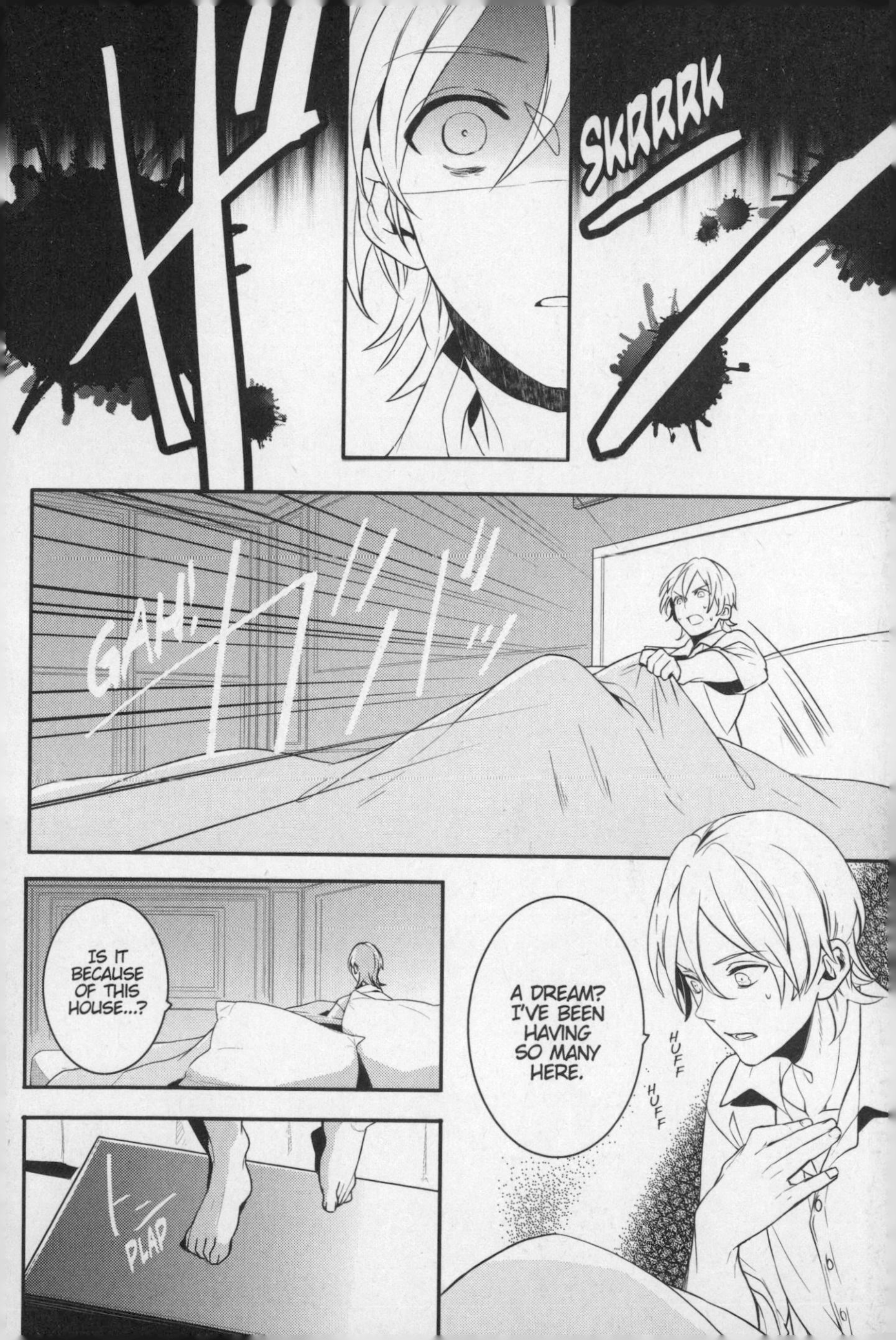
SKRRRK
GAH!
A DREAM? I'VE BEEN HAVING SO MANY HERE.
HUFF
HUFF
IS IT BECAUSE OF THIS HOUSE...?
PLAP

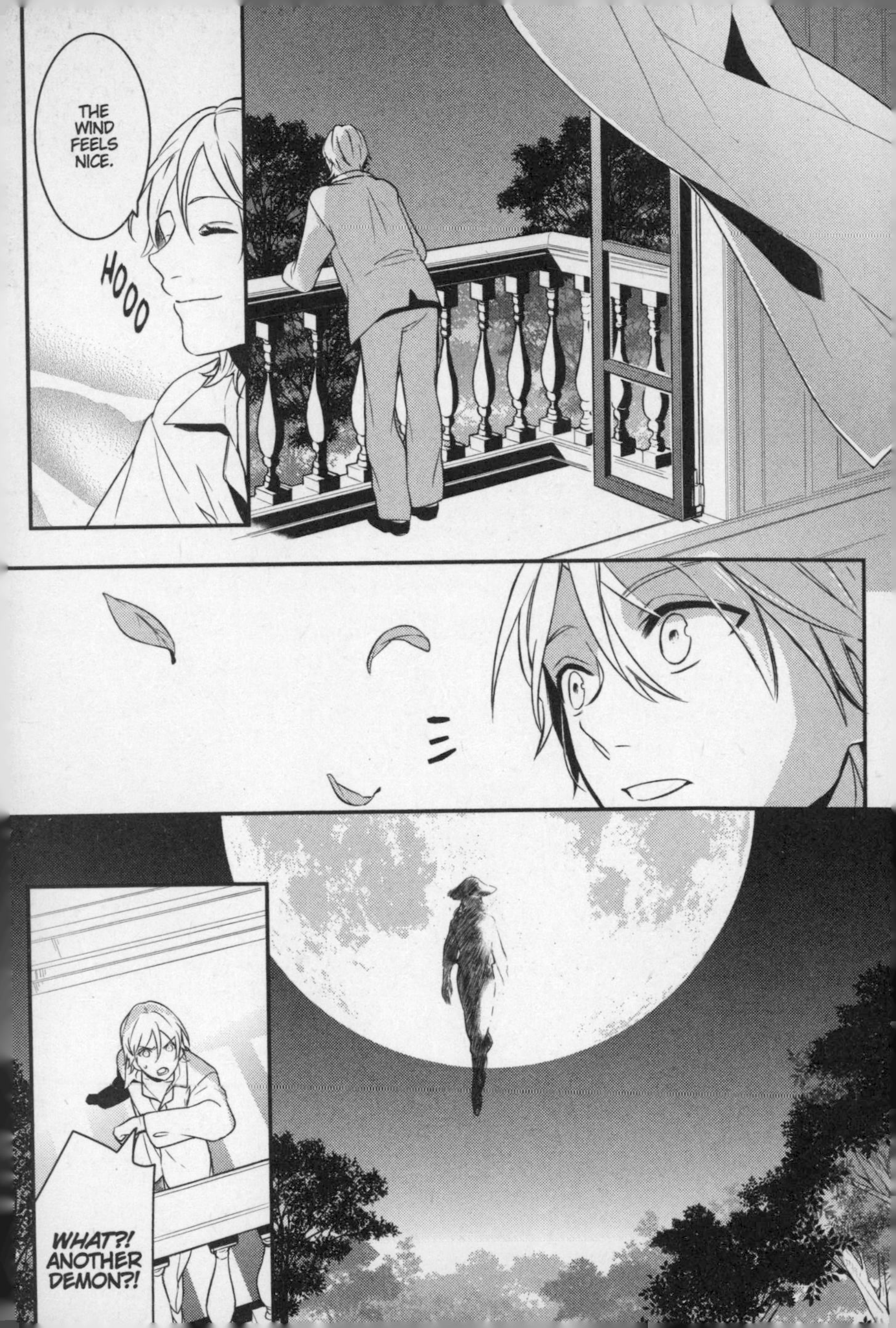
THE WIND FEELS NICE.
HOOO
WHAT?! ANOTHER DEMON?!

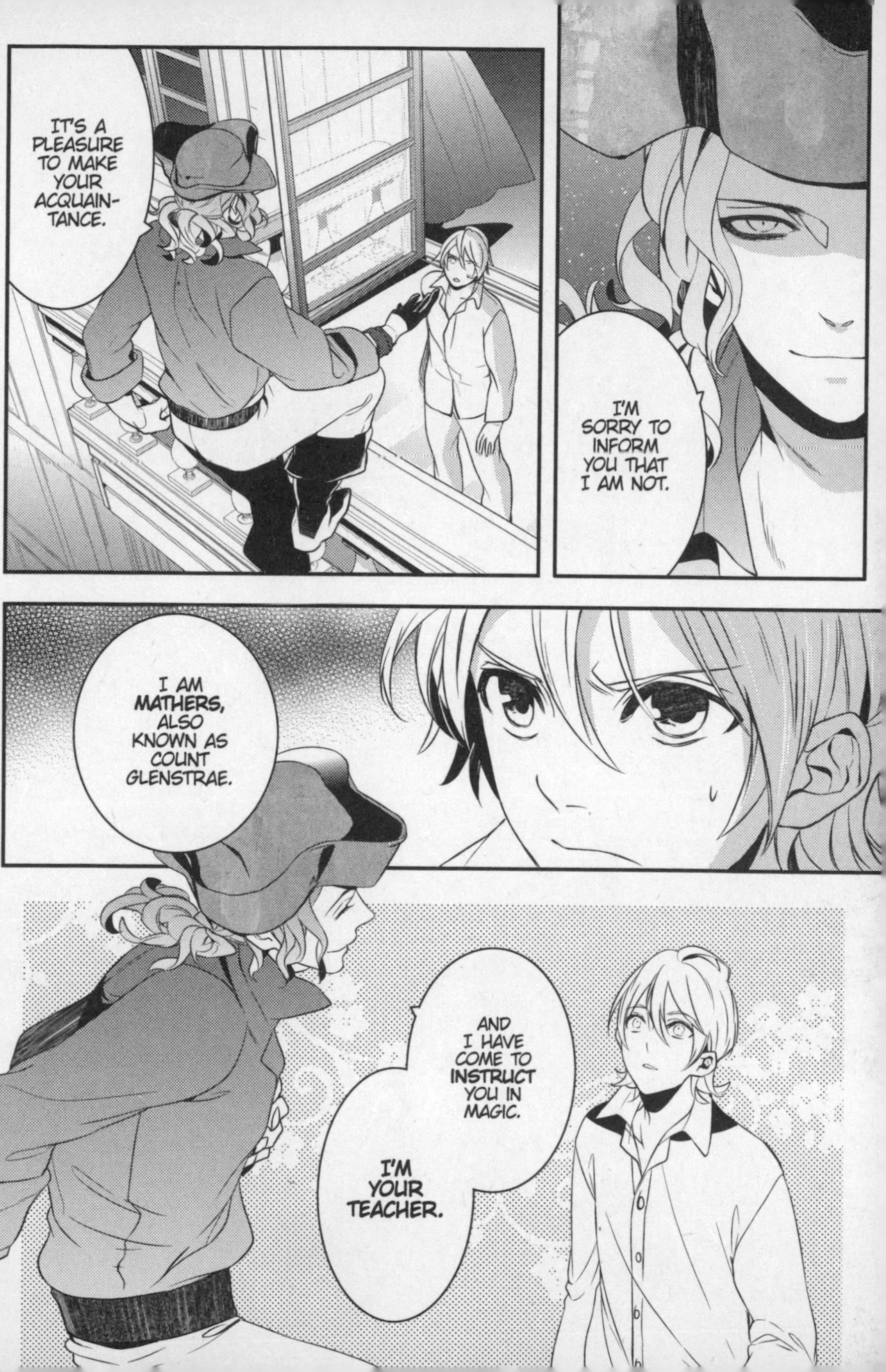
I'M SORRY TO INFORM YOU THAT I AM NOT.
IT'S A PLEASURE TO MAKE YOUR ACQUAIN-TANCE.
I AM MATHERS, ALSO KNOWN AS COUNT GLENSTRAE.
AND I HAVE COME TO INSTRUCT YOU IN MAGIC.
I'M YOUR TEACHER.

Pillar 34

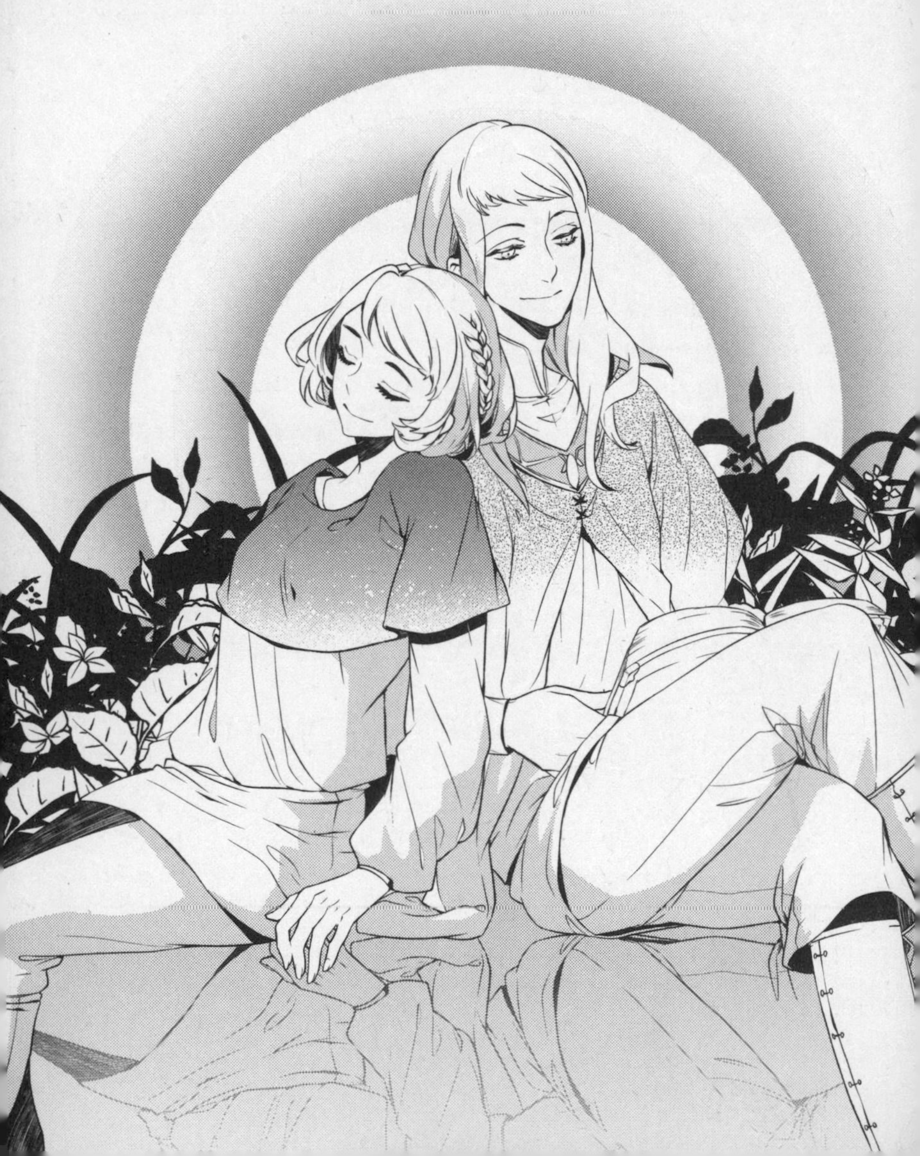

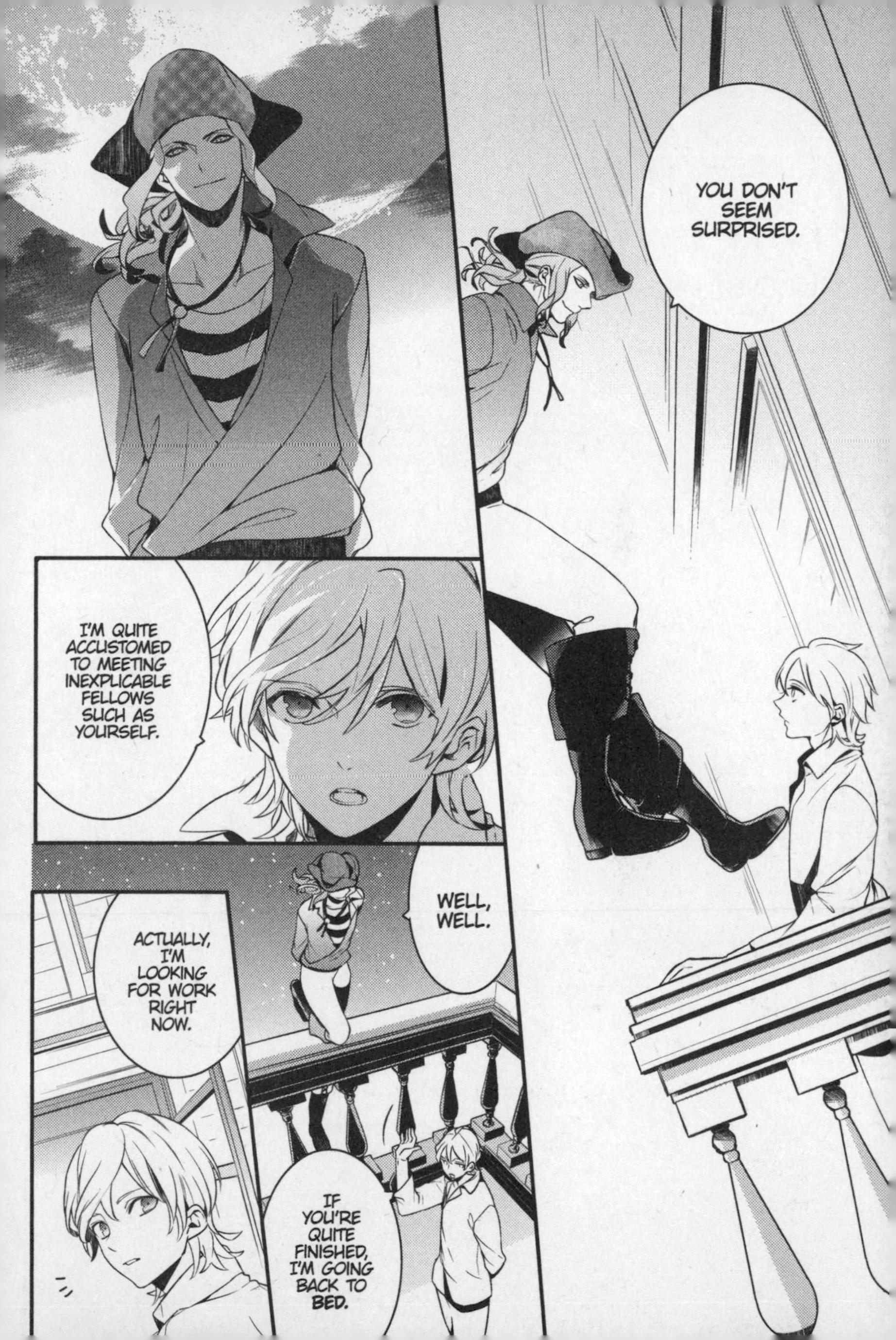
YOU DON'T SEEM SURPRISED.
I'M QUITE ACCUSTOMED TO MEETING INEXPLICABLE FELLOWS SUCH AS YOURSELF.
WELL, WELL.
IF YOU'RE QUITE FINISHED, I'M GOING BACK TO BED.
ACTUALLY, I'M LOOKING FOR WORK RIGHT NOW.

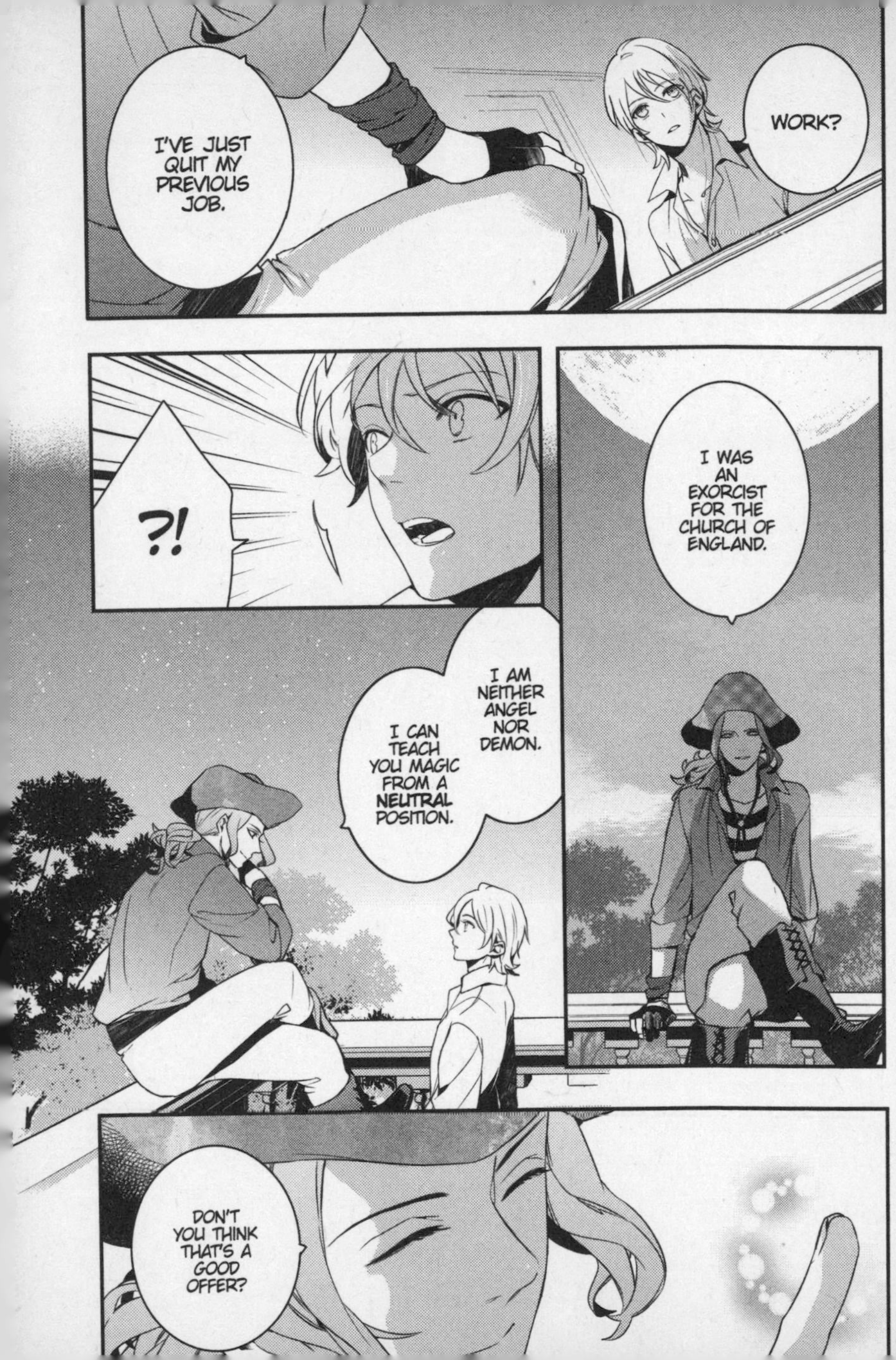
WORK?
I'VE JUST QUIT MY PREVIOUS JOB.
I WAS AN EXORCIST FOR THE CHURCH OF ENGLAND.
?!
I AM NEITHER ANGEL NOR DEMON.
I CAN TEACH YOU MAGIC FROM A **NEUTRAL** POSITION.
DON'T YOU THINK THAT'S A GOOD OFFER?

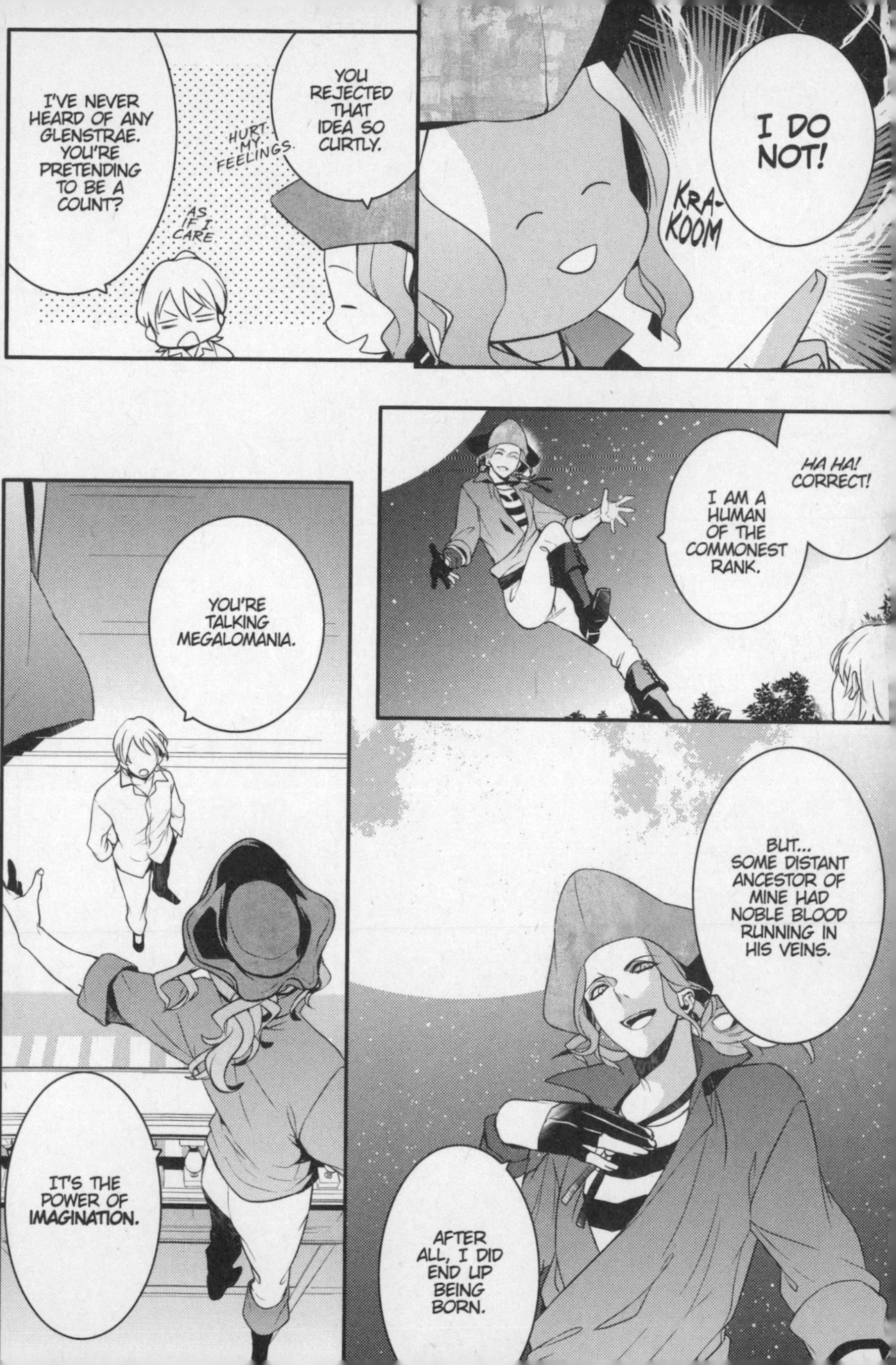
I DO NOT!
KRA-KOOM
YOU REJECTED THAT IDEA SO CURTLY.
HURT MY FEELINGS.
I'VE NEVER HEARD OF ANY GLENSTRAE. YOU'RE PRETENDING TO BE A COUNT?
AS IF I CARE
HA HA! CORRECT!
I AM A HUMAN OF THE COMMONEST RANK.
BUT... SOME DISTANT ANCESTOR OF MINE HAD NOBLE BLOOD RUNNING IN HIS VEINS.
AFTER ALL, I DID END UP BEING BORN.
YOU'RE TALKING MEGALOMANIA.
IT'S THE POWER OF IMAGINATION.

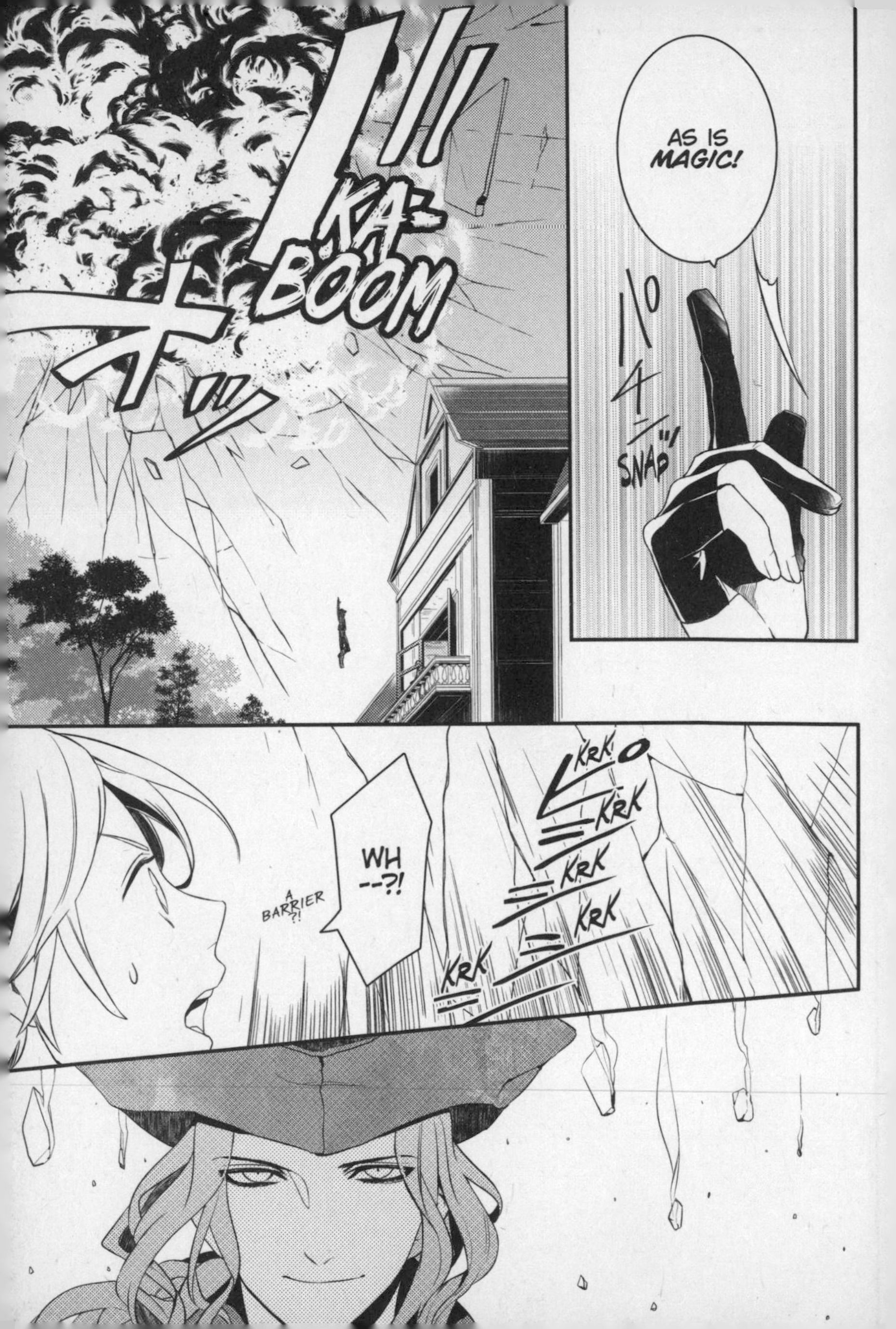
AS IS MAGIC!
SNAP
KA-BOOM
WH--?!
A BARRIER?!
KRK KRK KRK KRK KRK

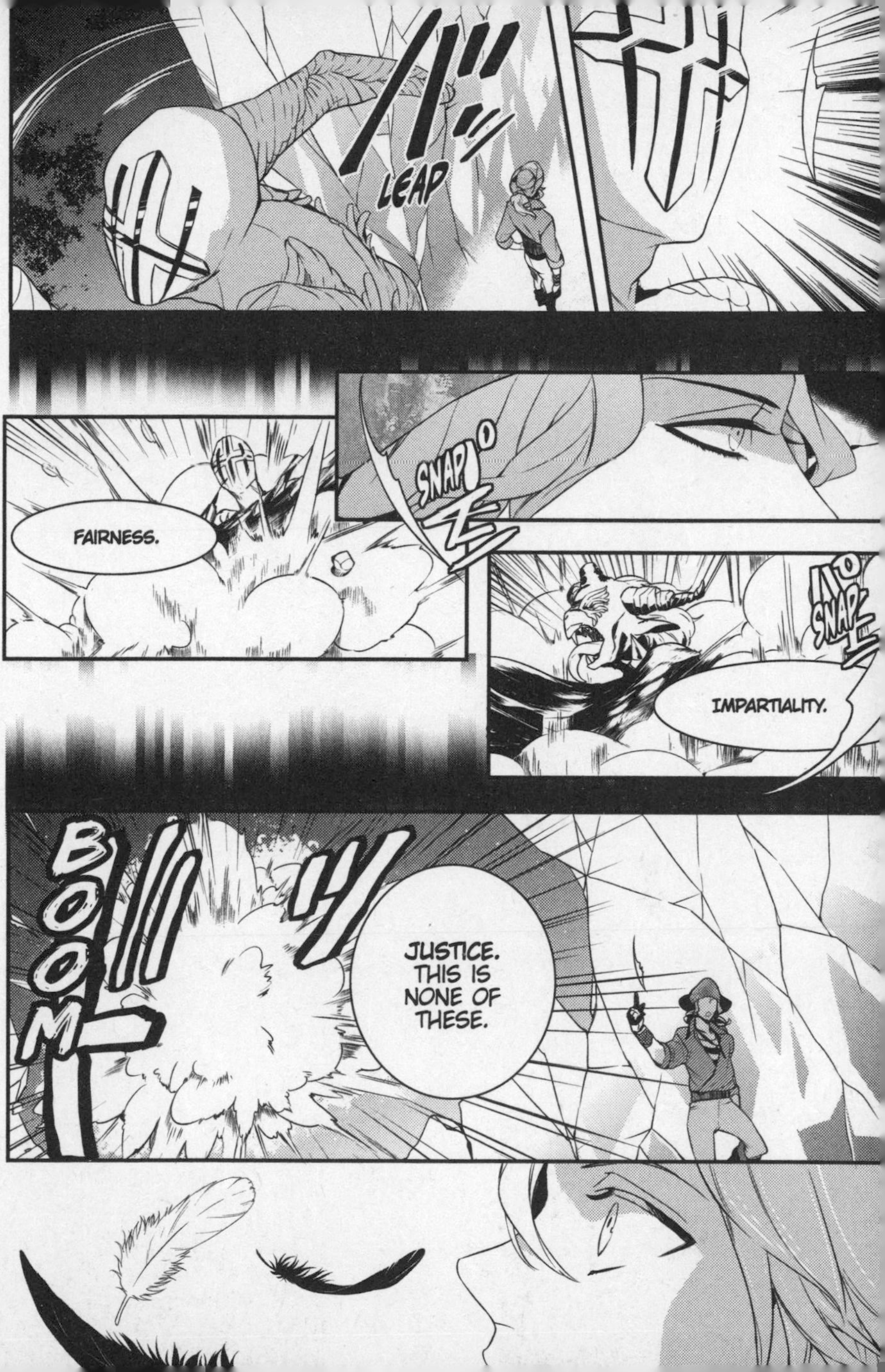
LEAP
SNAP
FAIRNESS.
SNAP
IMPARTIALITY.
BOOM
JUSTICE. THIS IS NONE OF THESE.

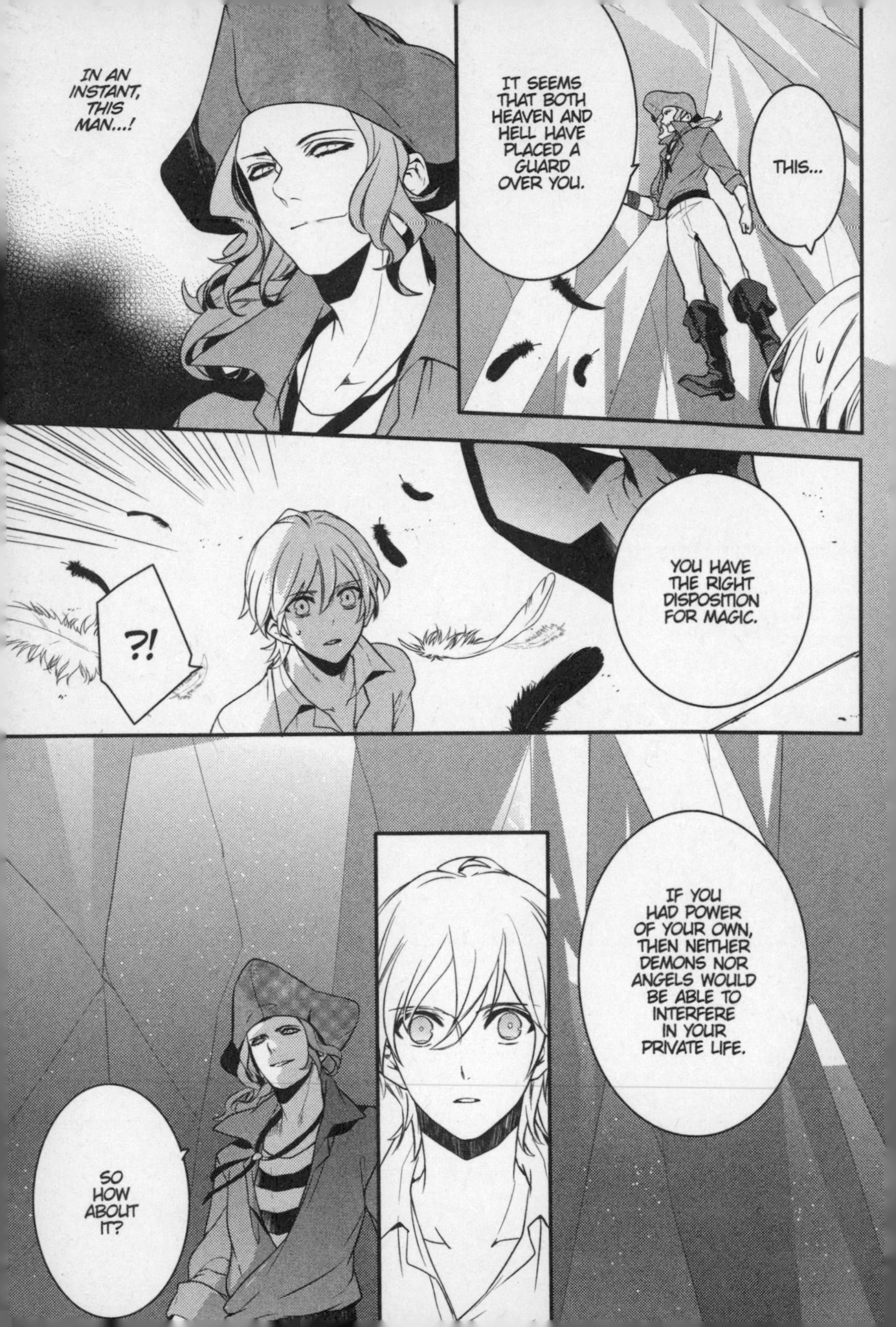
THIS...
IT SEEMS THAT BOTH HEAVEN AND HELL HAVE PLACED A GUARD OVER YOU.
IN AN INSTANT, THIS MAN...!
YOU HAVE THE RIGHT DISPOSITION FOR MAGIC.
?!
IF YOU HAD POWER OF YOUR OWN, THEN NEITHER DEMONS NOR ANGELS WOULD BE ABLE TO INTERFERE IN YOUR PRIVATE LIFE.
SO HOW ABOUT IT?

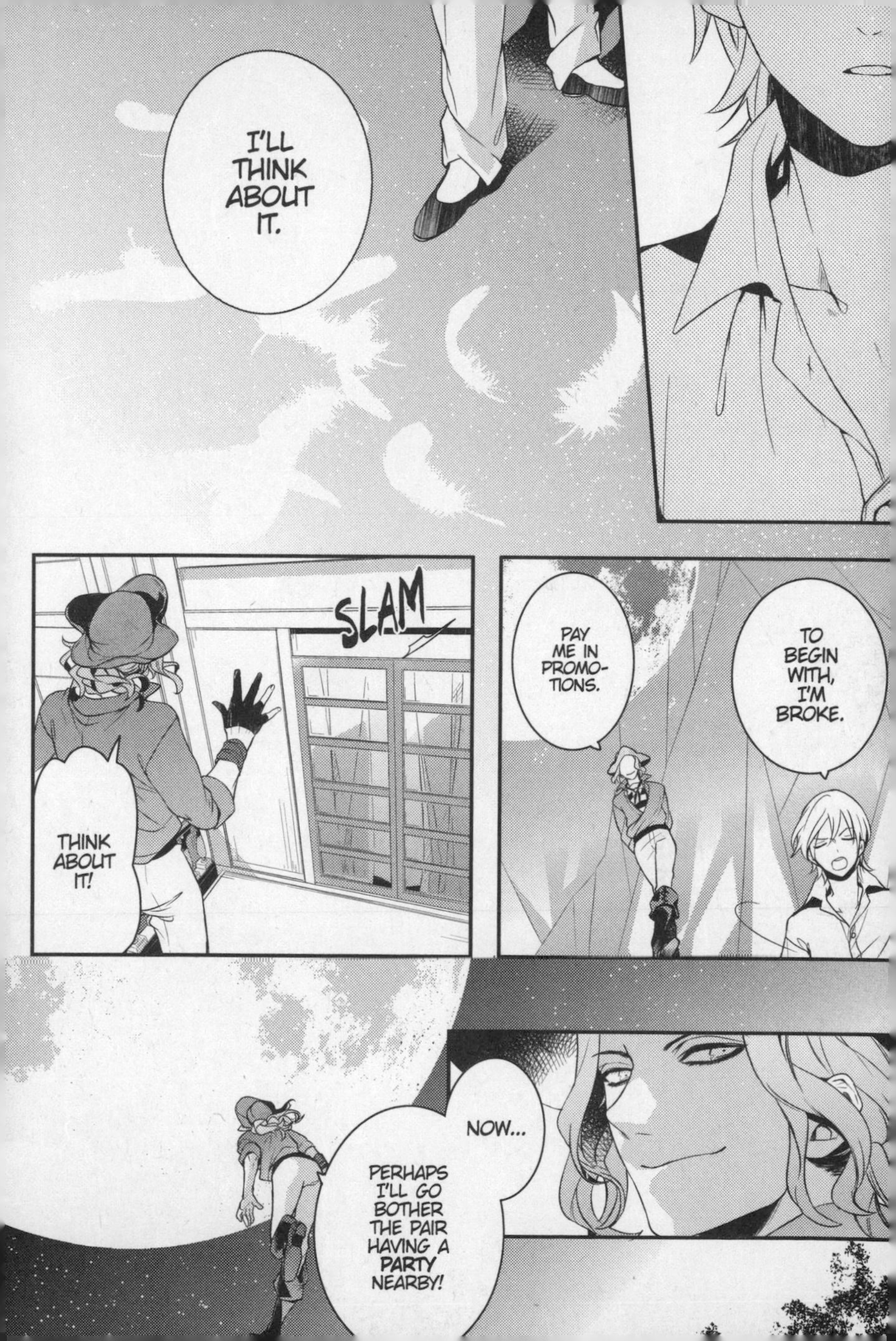
I'LL THINK ABOUT IT.
TO BEGIN WITH, I'M BROKE.
PAY ME IN PROMOTIONS.
SLAM
THINK ABOUT IT!
NOW...
PERHAPS I'LL GO BOTHER THE PAIR HAVING A PARTY NEARBY!

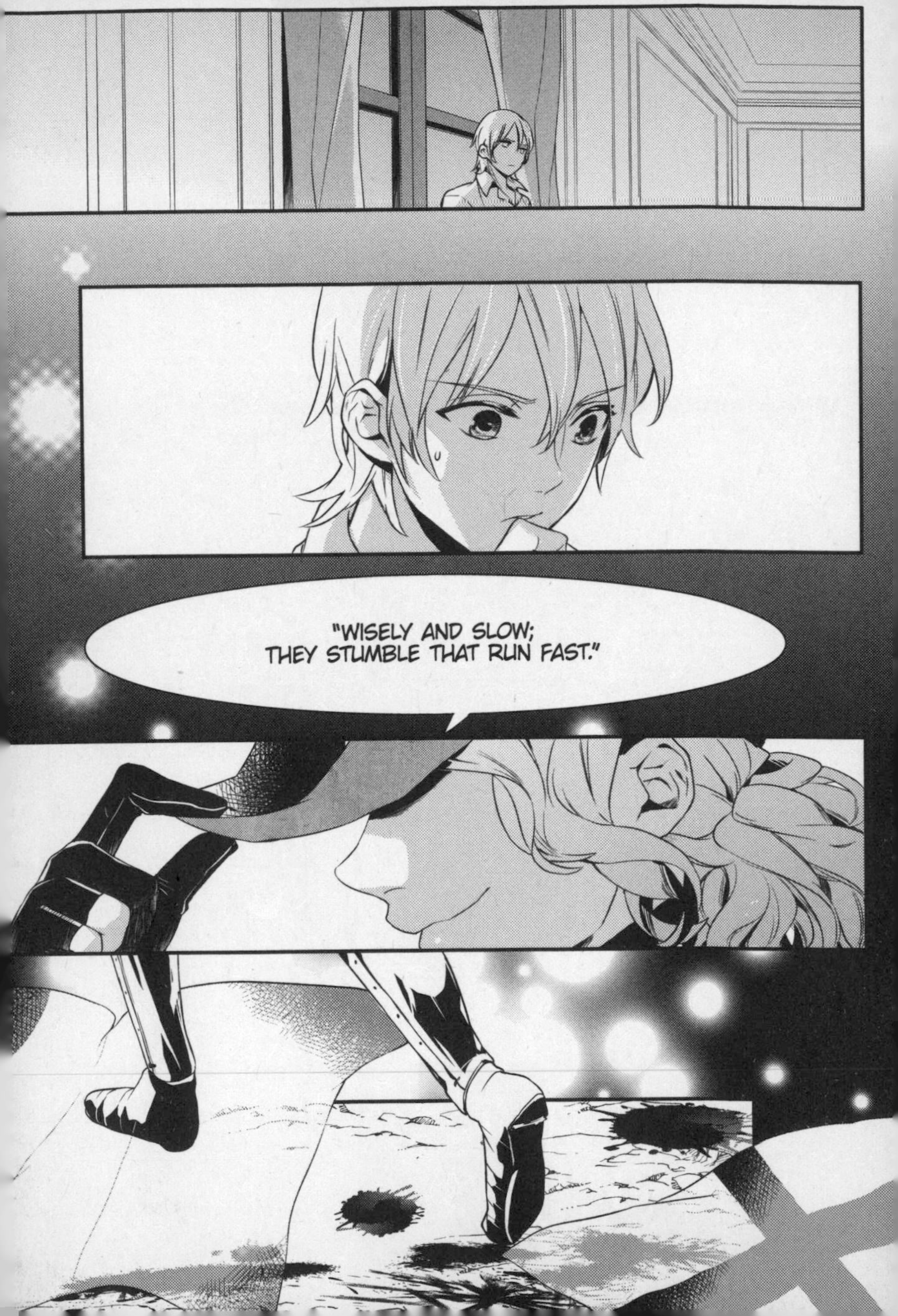
"WISELY AND SLOW;
THEY STUMBLE THAT RUN FAST."

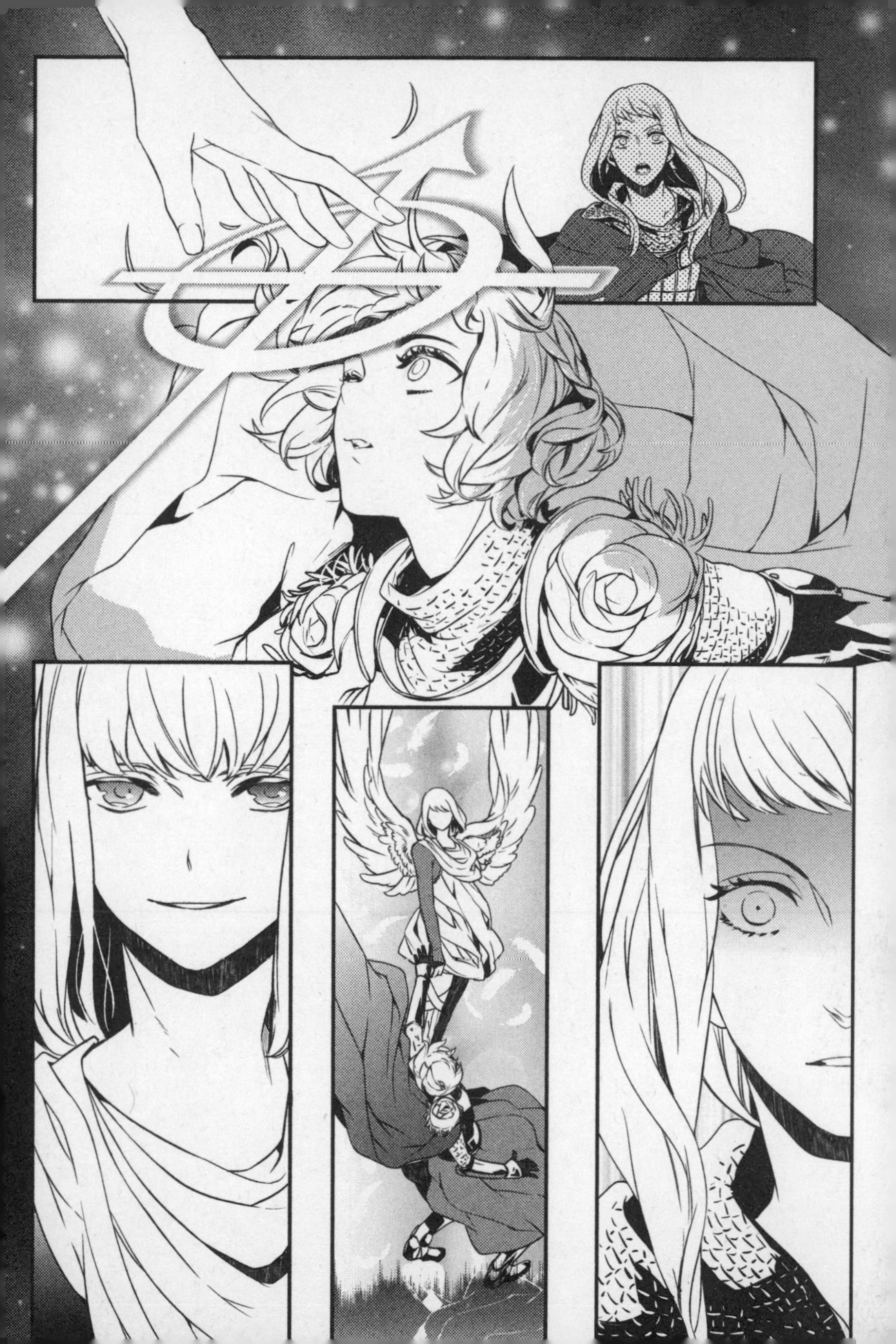

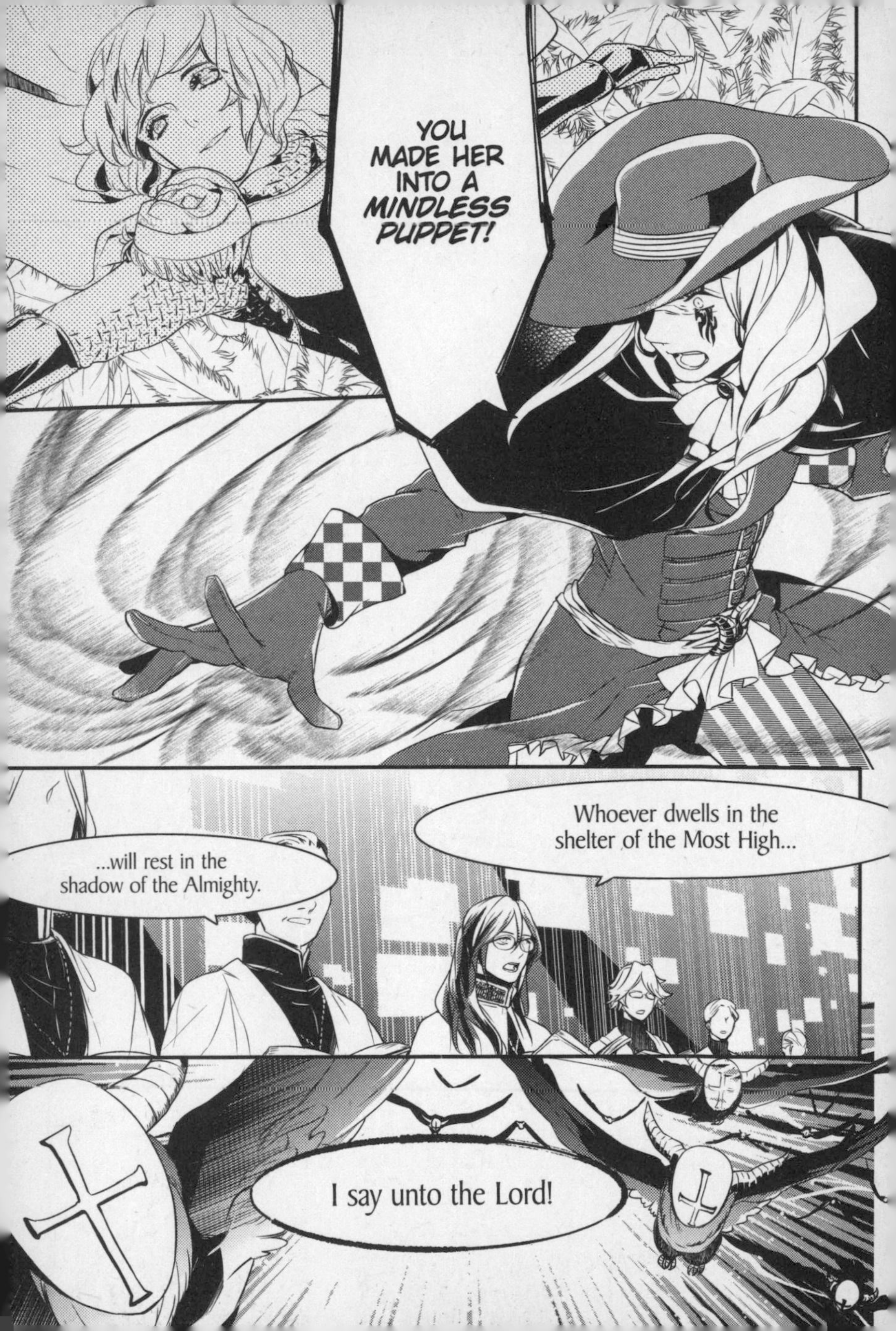
YOU MADE HER INTO A MINDLESS PUPPET!
Whoever dwells in the shelter of the Most High...
...will rest in the shadow of the Almighty.
I say unto the Lord!

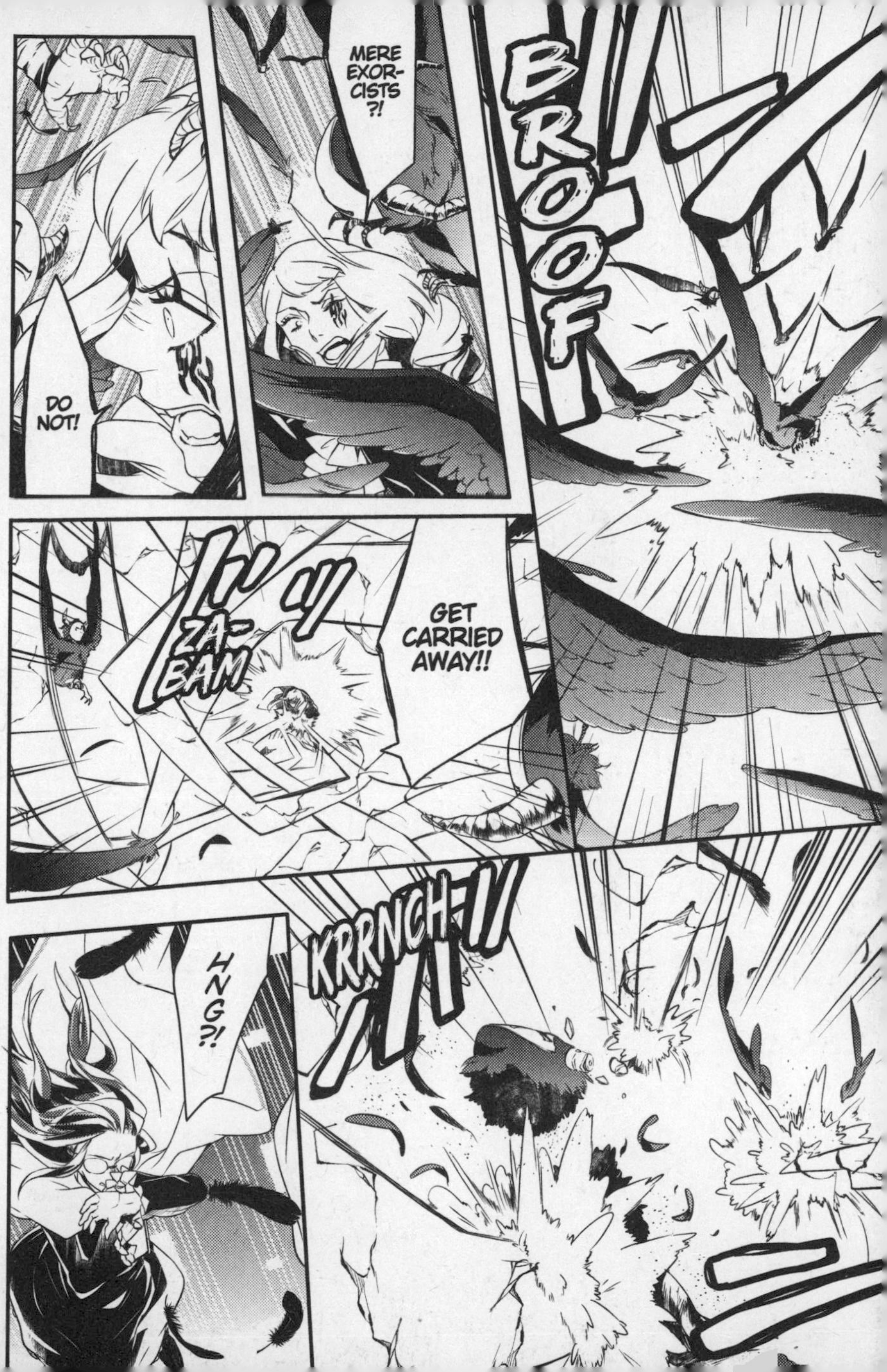
BROOOF
MERE EXORCISTS?!
DO NOT!
GET CARRIED AWAY!!
ZA-BAM
KRRNCH
HNG?!

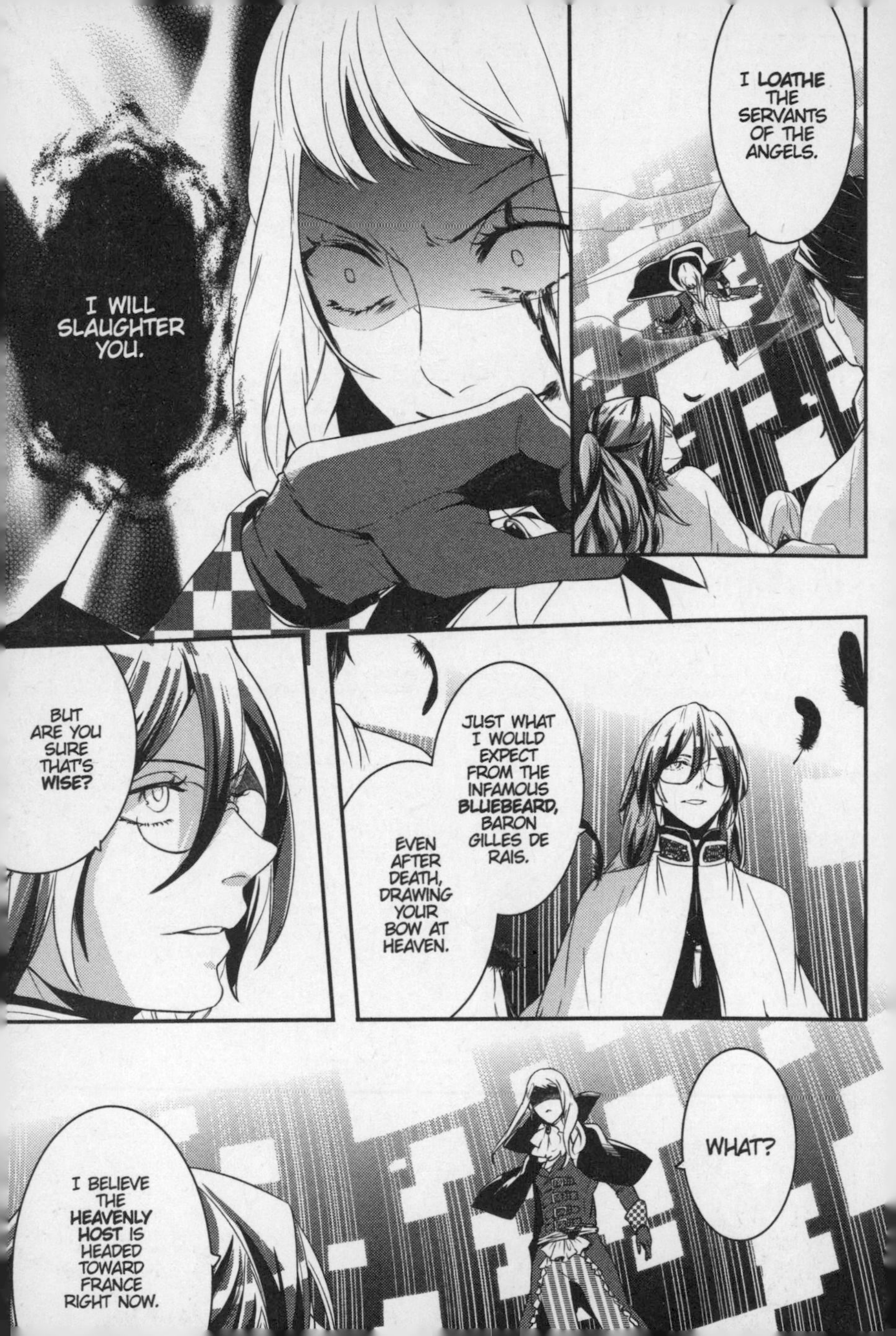
I LOATHE THE SERVANTS OF THE ANGELS.
I WILL SLAUGHTER YOU.
JUST WHAT I WOULD EXPECT FROM THE INFAMOUS BLUEBEARD, BARON GILLES DE RAIS.
EVEN AFTER DEATH, DRAWING YOUR BOW AT HEAVEN.
BUT ARE YOU SURE THAT'S WISE?
WHAT?
I BELIEVE THE HEAVENLY HOST IS HEADED TOWARD FRANCE RIGHT NOW.

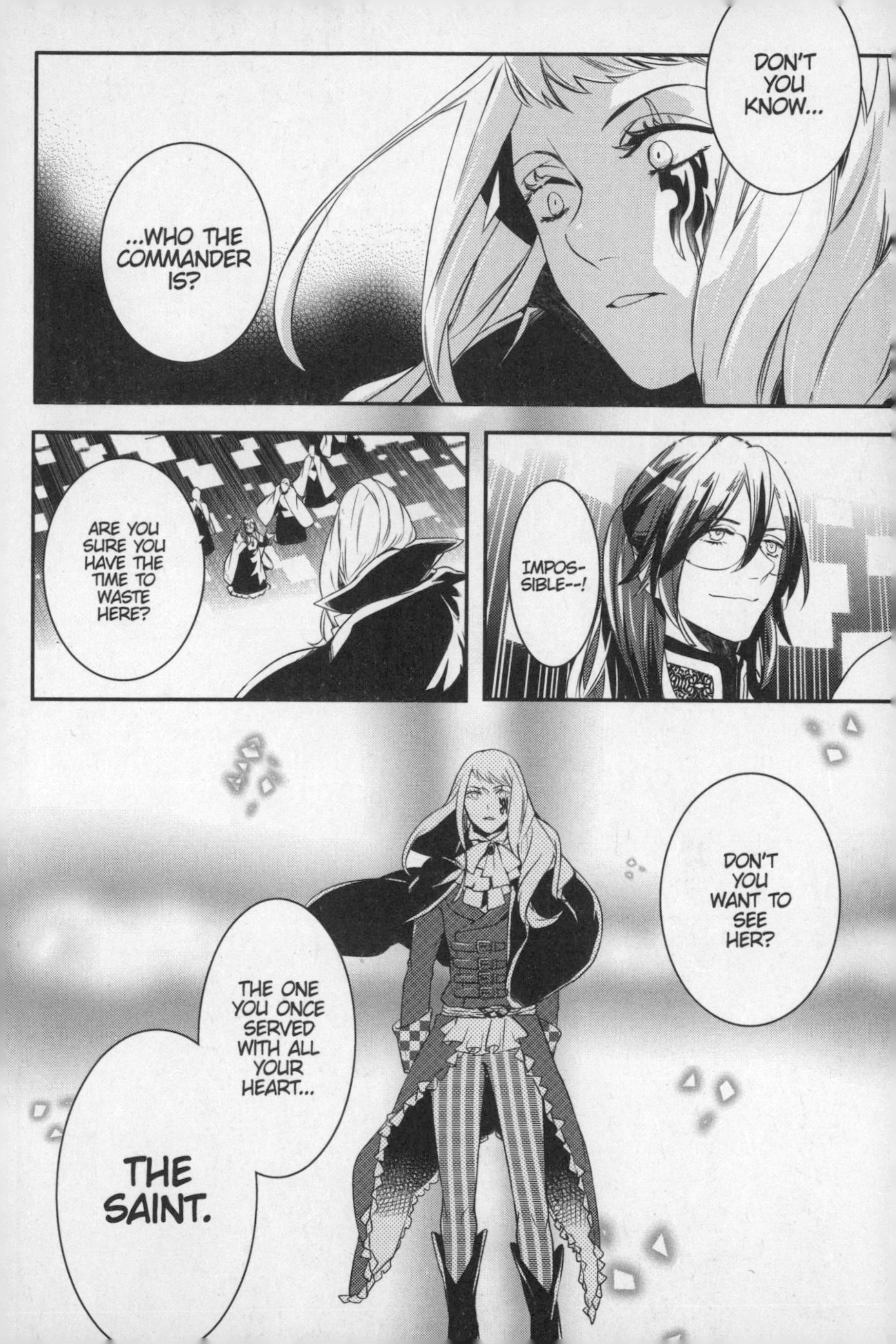
DON'T YOU KNOW...
...WHO THE COMMANDER IS?
IMPOS-SIBLE--!
ARE YOU SURE YOU HAVE THE TIME TO WASTE HERE?
DON'T YOU WANT TO SEE HER?
THE ONE YOU ONCE SERVED WITH ALL YOUR HEART...
THE SAINT.

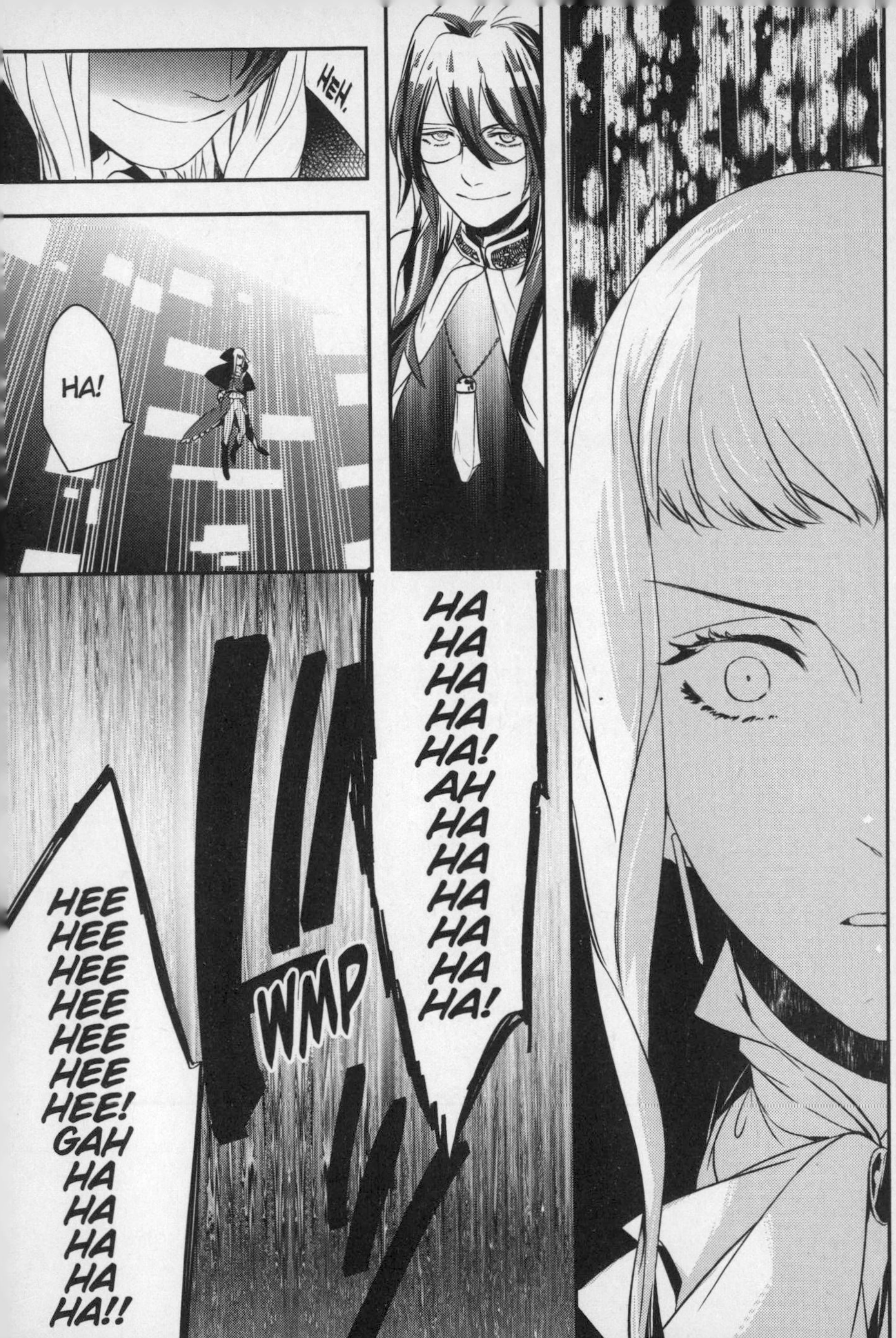
HEH.
HA!
HA HA HA HA HA! AH HA HA HA HA HA HA HA!
WMP
HEE HEE HEE HEE HEE HEE HEE! GAH HA HA HA HA HA!!

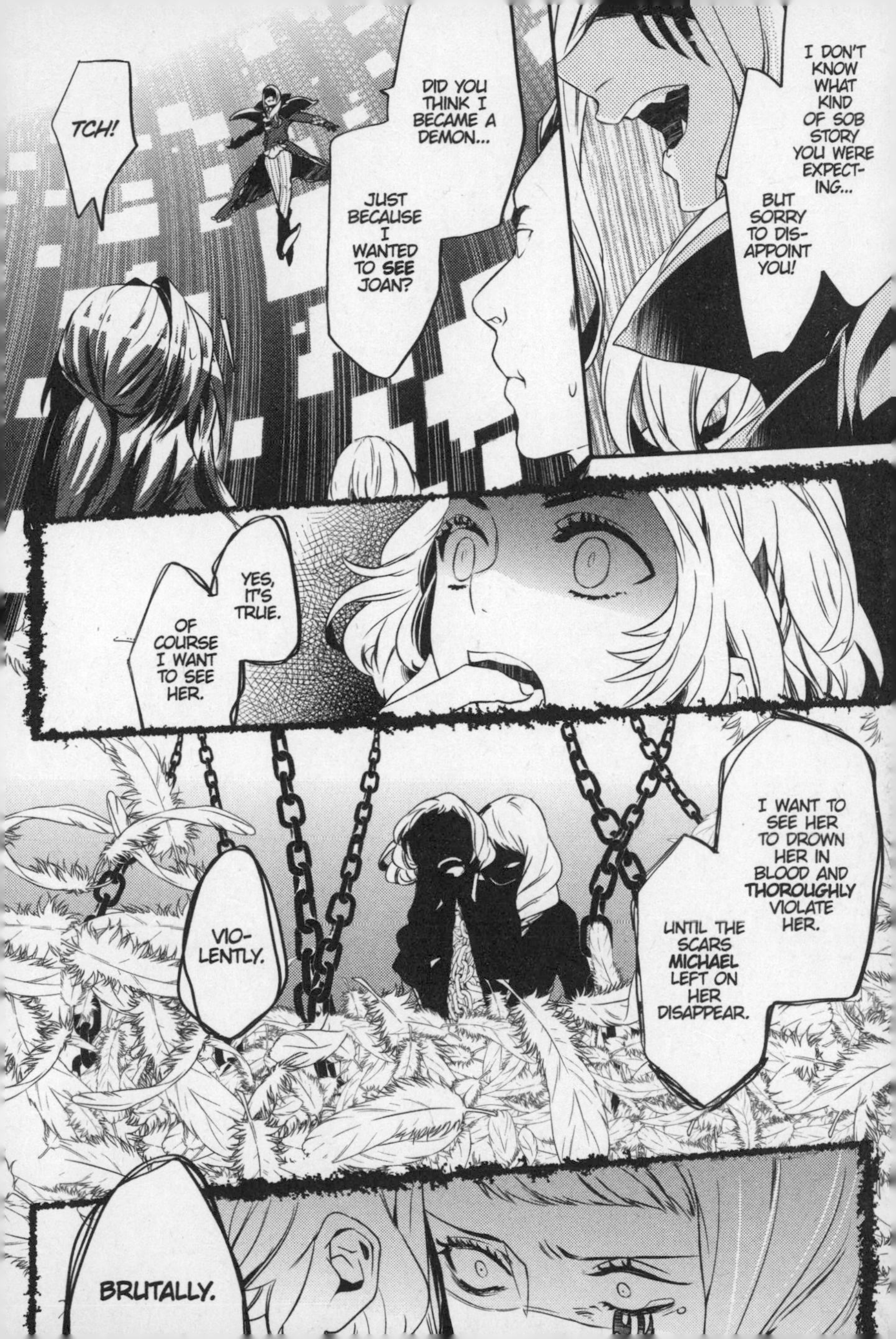
I DON'T KNOW WHAT KIND OF SOB STORY YOU WERE EXPECTING...
BUT SORRY TO DISAPPOINT YOU!
DID YOU THINK I BECAME A DEMON...
JUST BECAUSE I WANTED TO SEE JOAN?
TCH!
YES, IT'S TRUE.
OF COURSE I WANT TO SEE HER.
I WANT TO SEE HER TO DROWN HER IN BLOOD AND THOROUGHLY VIOLATE HER.
UNTIL THE SCARS MICHAEL LEFT ON HER DISAPPEAR.
VIOLENTLY.
BRUTALLY.

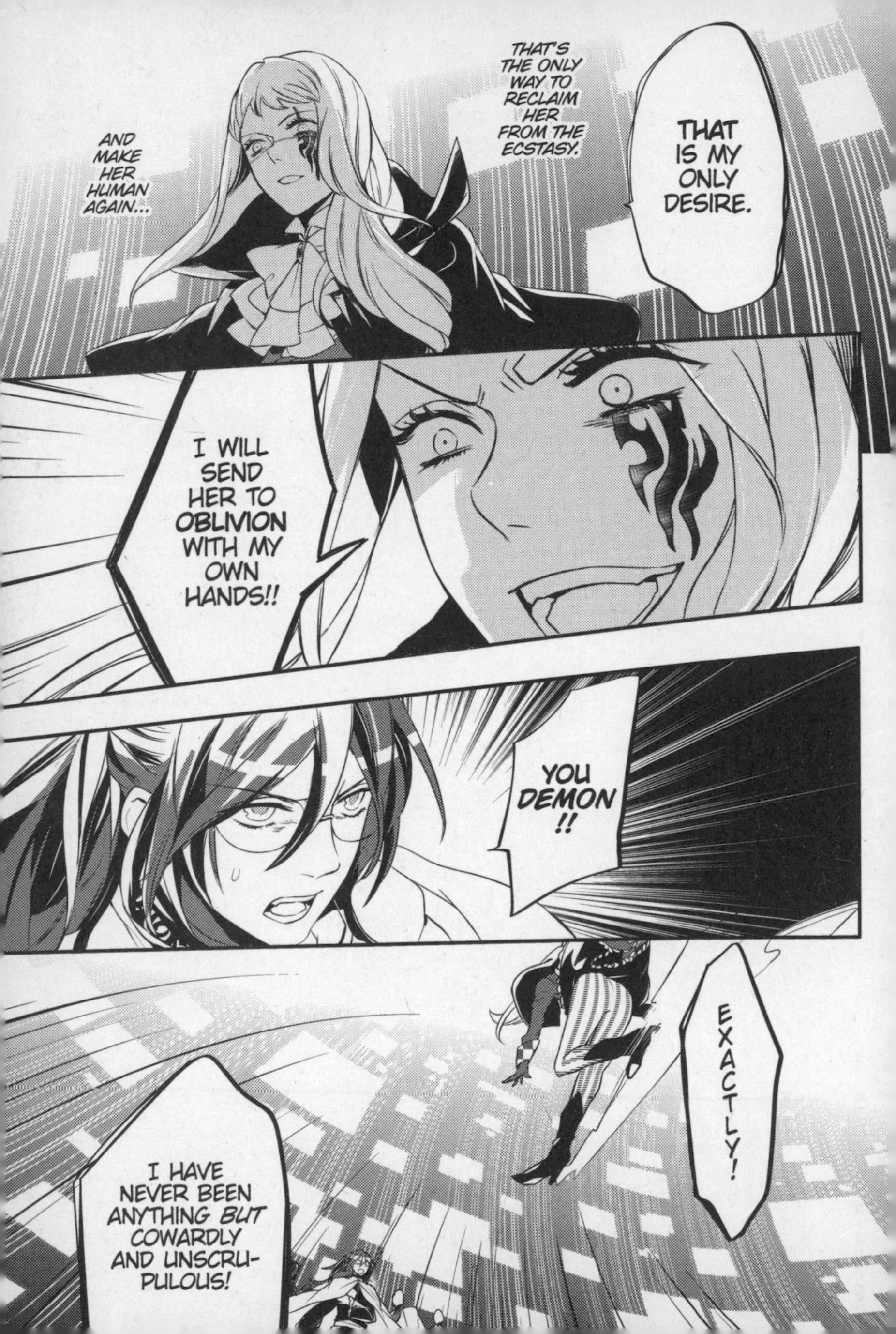
THAT IS MY ONLY DESIRE.
THAT'S THE ONLY WAY TO RECLAIM HER FROM THE ECSTASY.
AND MAKE HER HUMAN AGAIN...
I WILL SEND HER TO OBLIVION WITH MY OWN HANDS!!
YOU DEMON!!
EXACTLY!
I HAVE NEVER BEEN ANYTHING *BUT* COWARDLY AND UNSCRU-PULOUS!

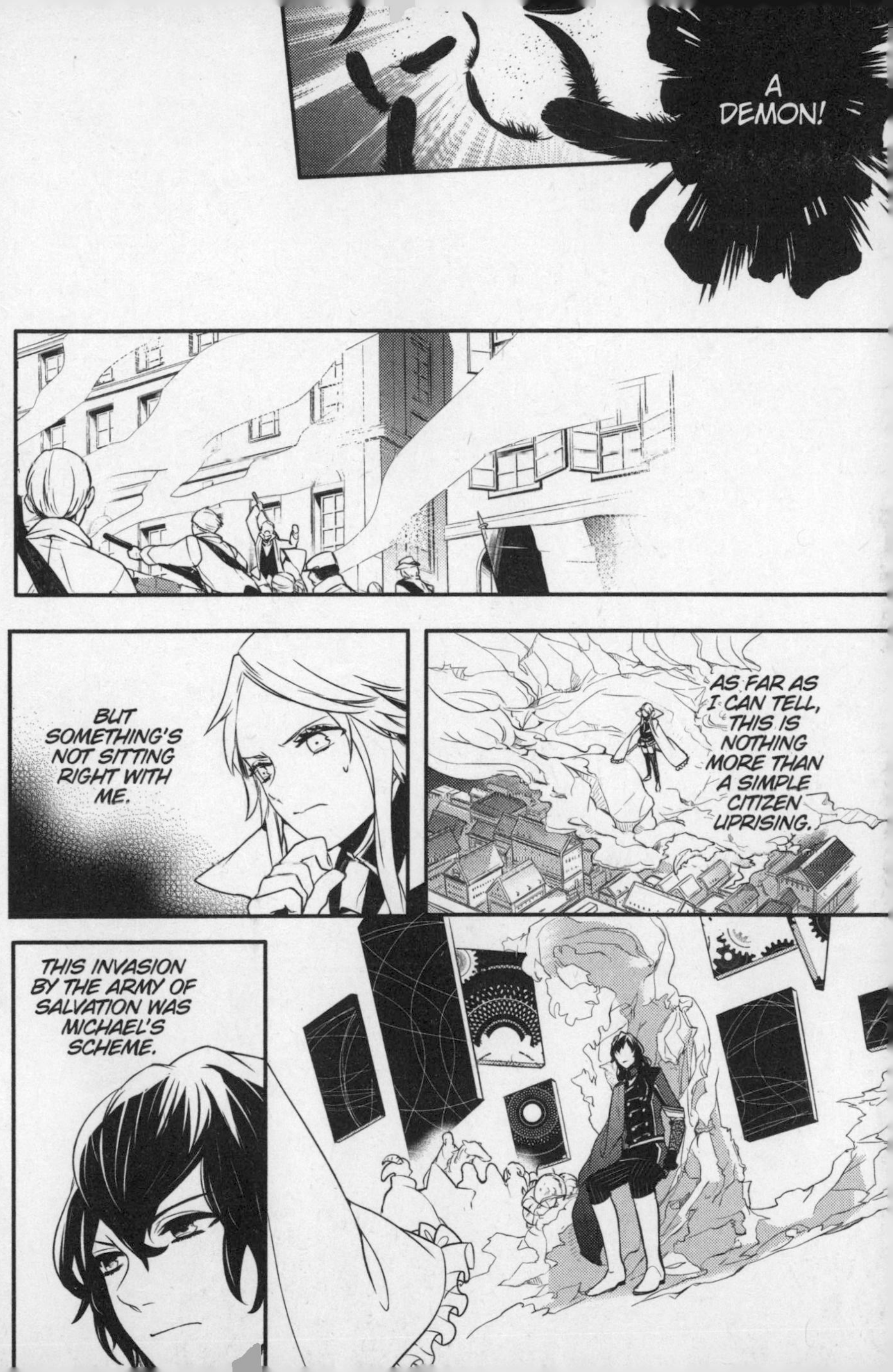
A DEMON!
AS FAR AS I CAN TELL, THIS IS NOTHING MORE THAN A SIMPLE CITIZEN UPRISING.
BUT SOMETHING'S NOT SITTING RIGHT WITH ME.
THIS INVASION BY THE ARMY OF SALVATION WAS MICHAEL'S SCHEME.

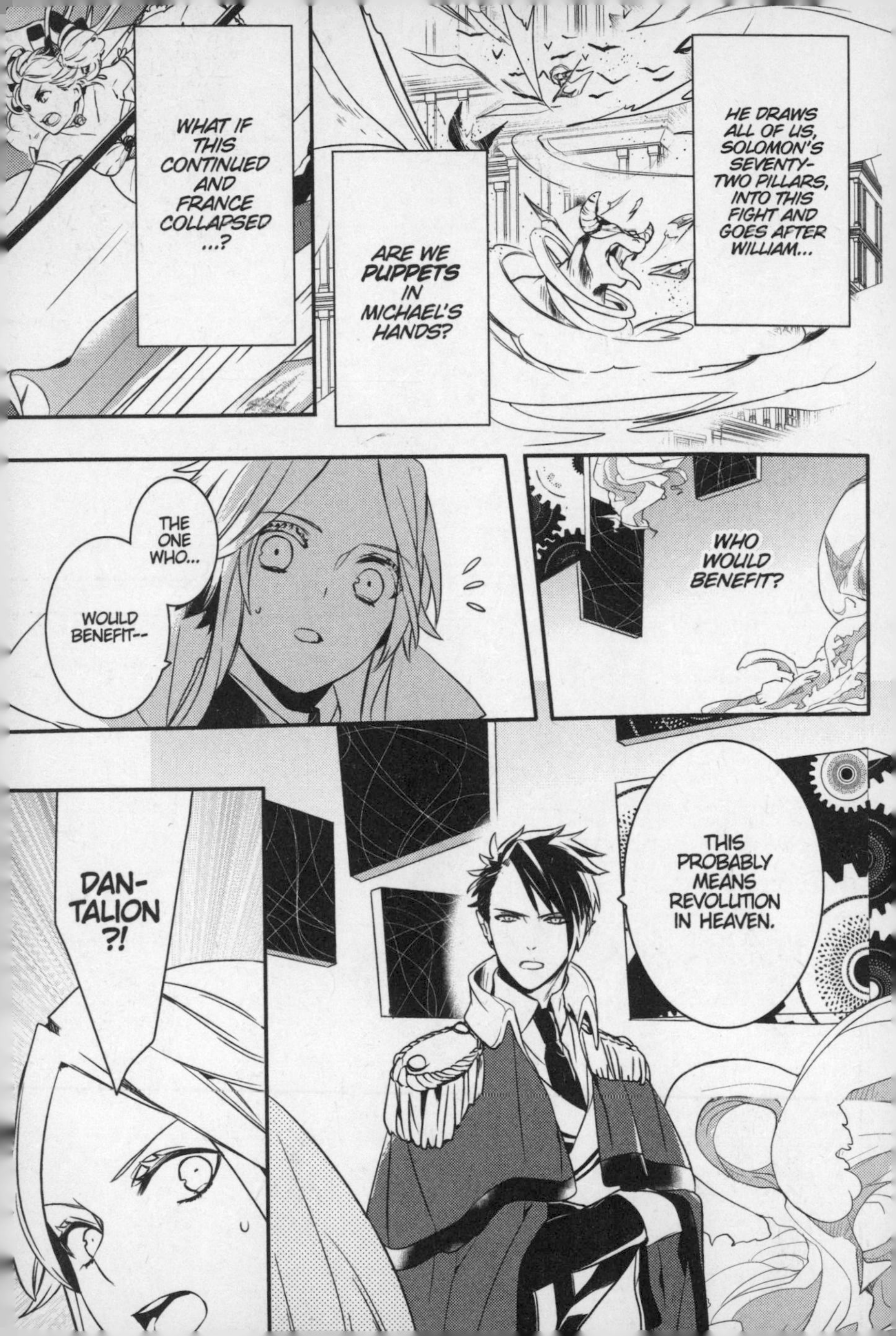
HE DRAWS ALL OF US, SOLOMON'S SEVENTY-TWO PILLARS, INTO THIS FIGHT AND GOES AFTER WILLIAM...
ARE WE PUPPETS IN MICHAEL'S HANDS?
WHAT IF THIS CONTINUED AND FRANCE COLLAPSED ...?
WHO WOULD BENEFIT?
THE ONE WHO...
WOULD BENEFIT--
THIS PROBABLY MEANS REVOLUTION IN HEAVEN.
DAN-TALION ?!

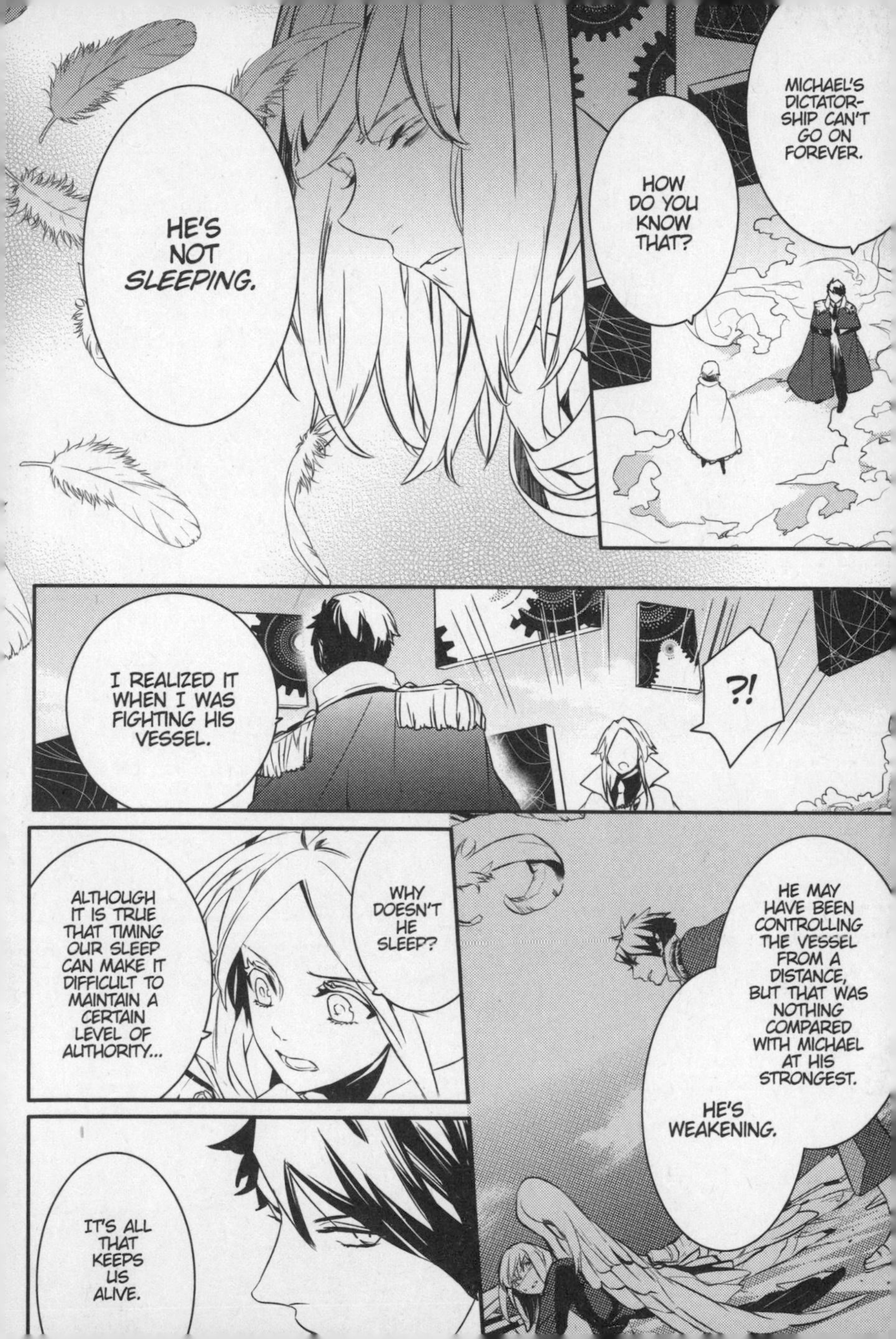
MICHAEL'S DICTATOR-SHIP CAN'T GO ON FOREVER.
HOW DO YOU KNOW THAT?
HE'S NOT SLEEPING.
?!
I REALIZED IT WHEN I WAS FIGHTING HIS VESSEL.
HE MAY HAVE BEEN CONTROLLING THE VESSEL FROM A DISTANCE, BUT THAT WAS NOTHING COMPARED WITH MICHAEL AT HIS STRONGEST.
HE'S WEAKENING.
WHY DOESN'T HE SLEEP?
ALTHOUGH IT IS TRUE THAT TIMING OUR SLEEP CAN MAKE IT DIFFICULT TO MAINTAIN A CERTAIN LEVEL OF AUTHORITY...
IT'S ALL THAT KEEPS US ALIVE.

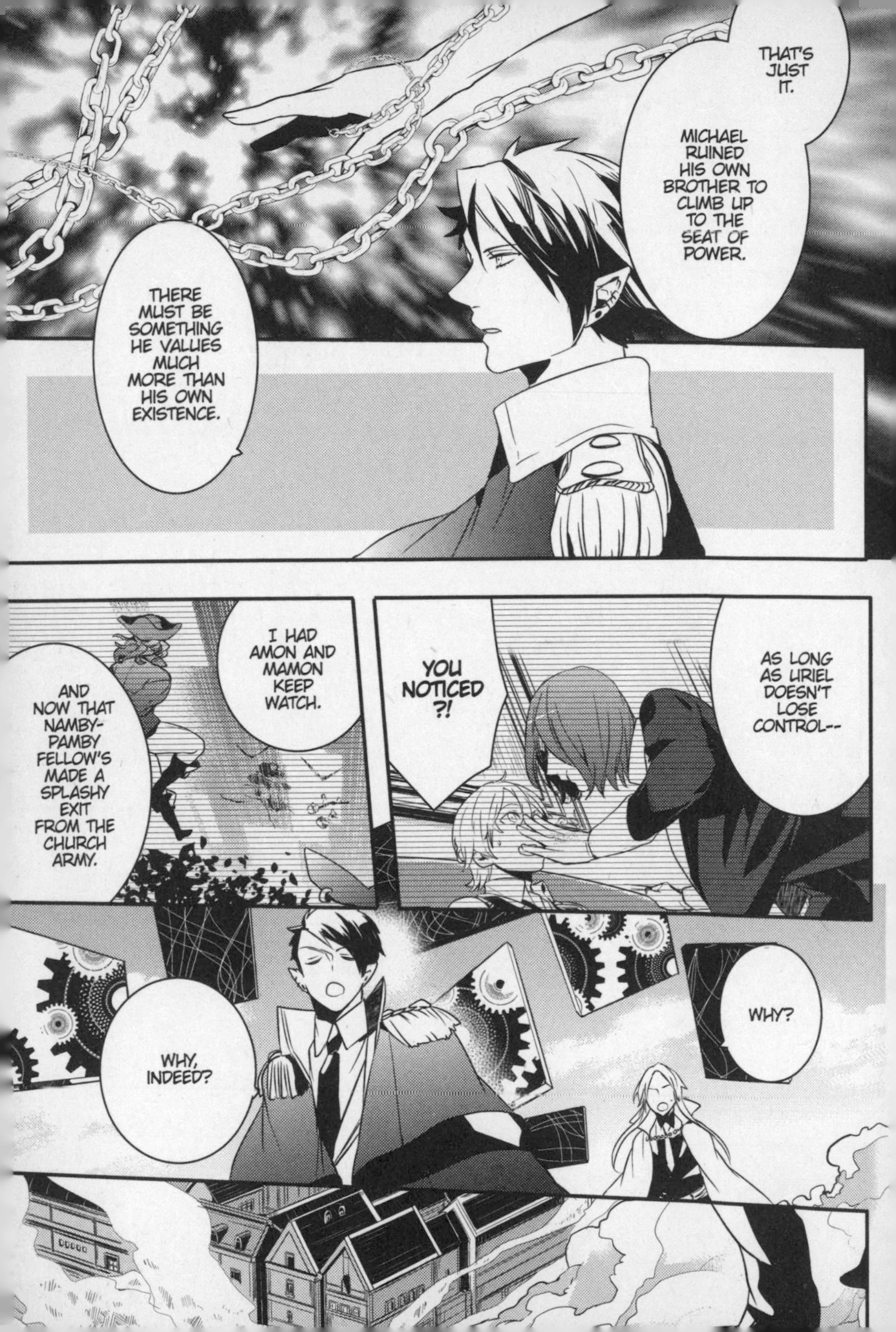
THAT'S JUST IT.
MICHAEL RUINED HIS OWN BROTHER TO CLIMB UP TO THE SEAT OF POWER.
THERE MUST BE SOMETHING HE VALUES MUCH MORE THAN HIS OWN EXISTENCE.
AS LONG AS URIEL DOESN'T LOSE CONTROL--
YOU NOTICED ?!
I HAD AMON AND MAMON KEEP WATCH.
AND NOW THAT NAMBY-PAMBY FELLOW'S MADE A SPLASHY EXIT FROM THE CHURCH ARMY.
WHY?
WHY, INDEED?

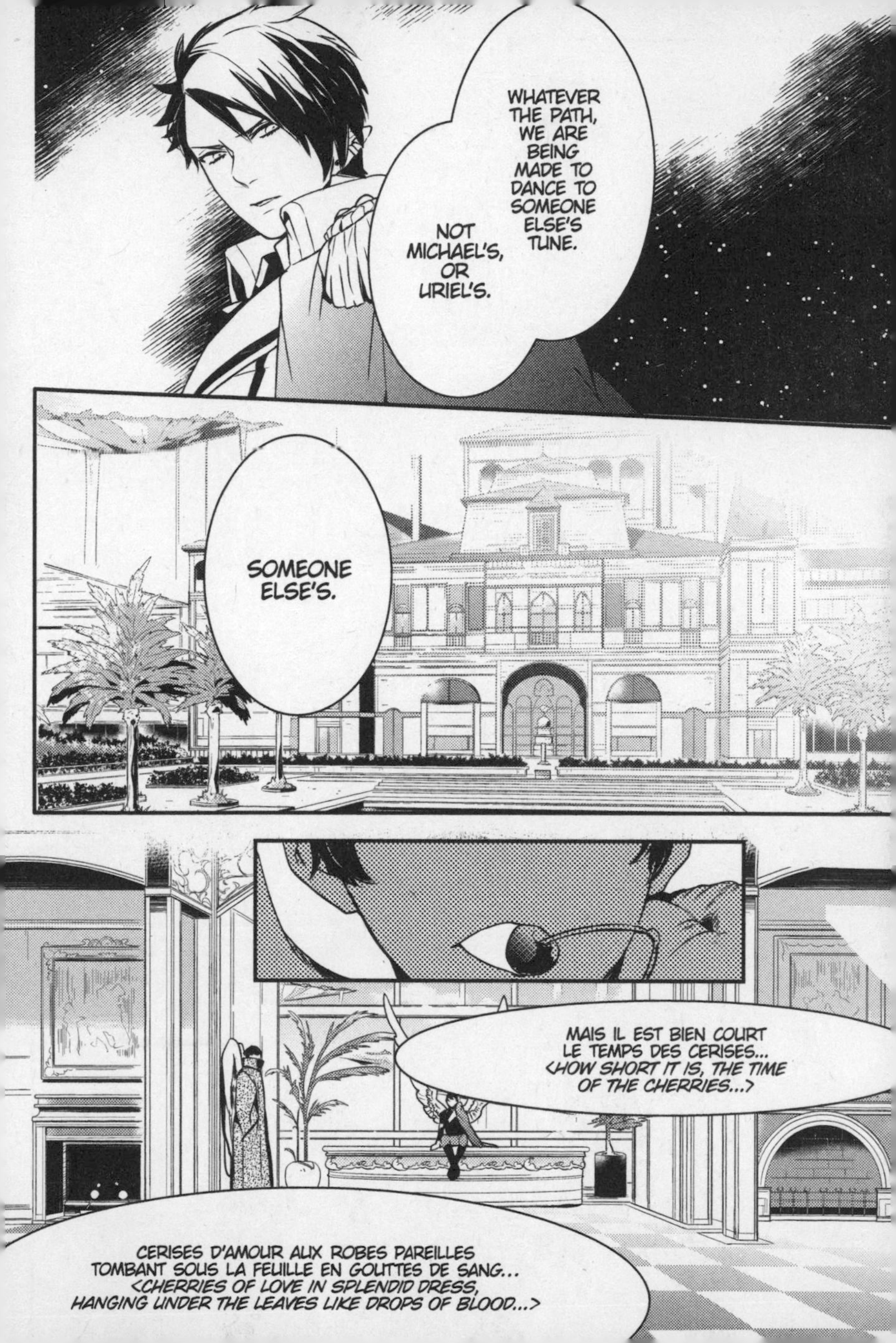
WHATEVER THE PATH, WE ARE BEING MADE TO DANCE TO SOMEONE ELSE'S TUNE.
NOT MICHAEL'S, OR URIEL'S.
SOMEONE ELSE'S.
MAIS IL EST BIEN COURT LE TEMPS DES CERISES... <HOW SHORT IT IS, THE TIME OF THE CHERRIES...>
CERISES D'AMOUR AUX ROBES PAREILLES TOMBANT SOUS LA FEUILLE EN GOUTTES DE SANG... <CHERRIES OF LOVE IN SPLENDID DRESS, HANGING UNDER THE LEAVES LIKE DROPS OF BLOOD...>

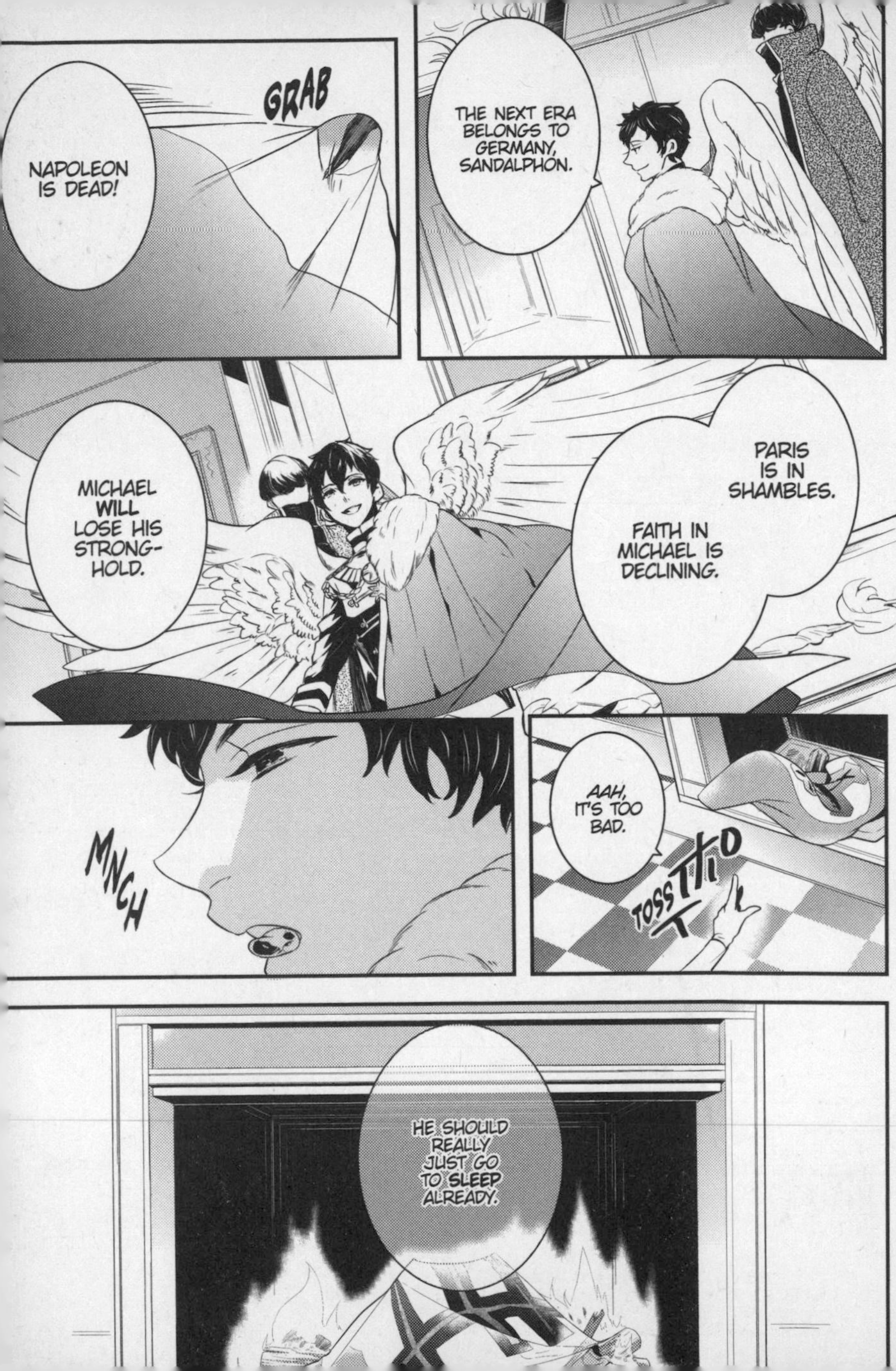
THE NEXT ERA BELONGS TO GERMANY, SANDALPHON.
GRAB
NAPOLEON IS DEAD!
PARIS IS IN SHAMBLES.
FAITH IN MICHAEL IS DECLINING.
MICHAEL WILL LOSE HIS STRONG-HOLD.
AAH, IT'S TOO BAD.
TOSS
MNCH
HE SHOULD REALLY JUST GO TO SLEEP ALREADY.

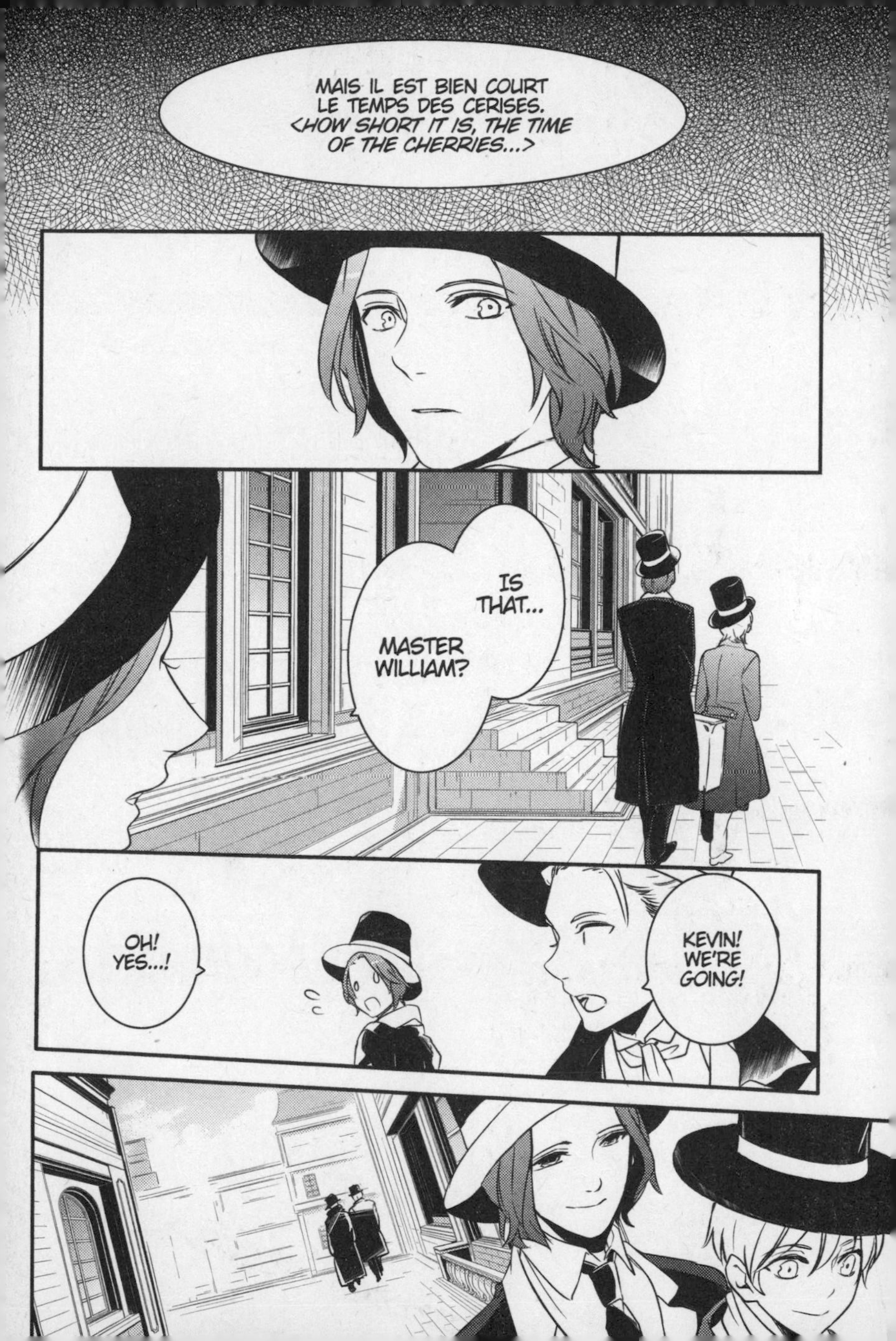
MAIS IL EST BIEN COURT LE TEMPS DES CERISES. <HOW SHORT IT IS, THE TIME OF THE CHERRIES...>
IS THAT...
MASTER WILLIAM?
KEVIN! WE'RE GOING!
OH! YES...!

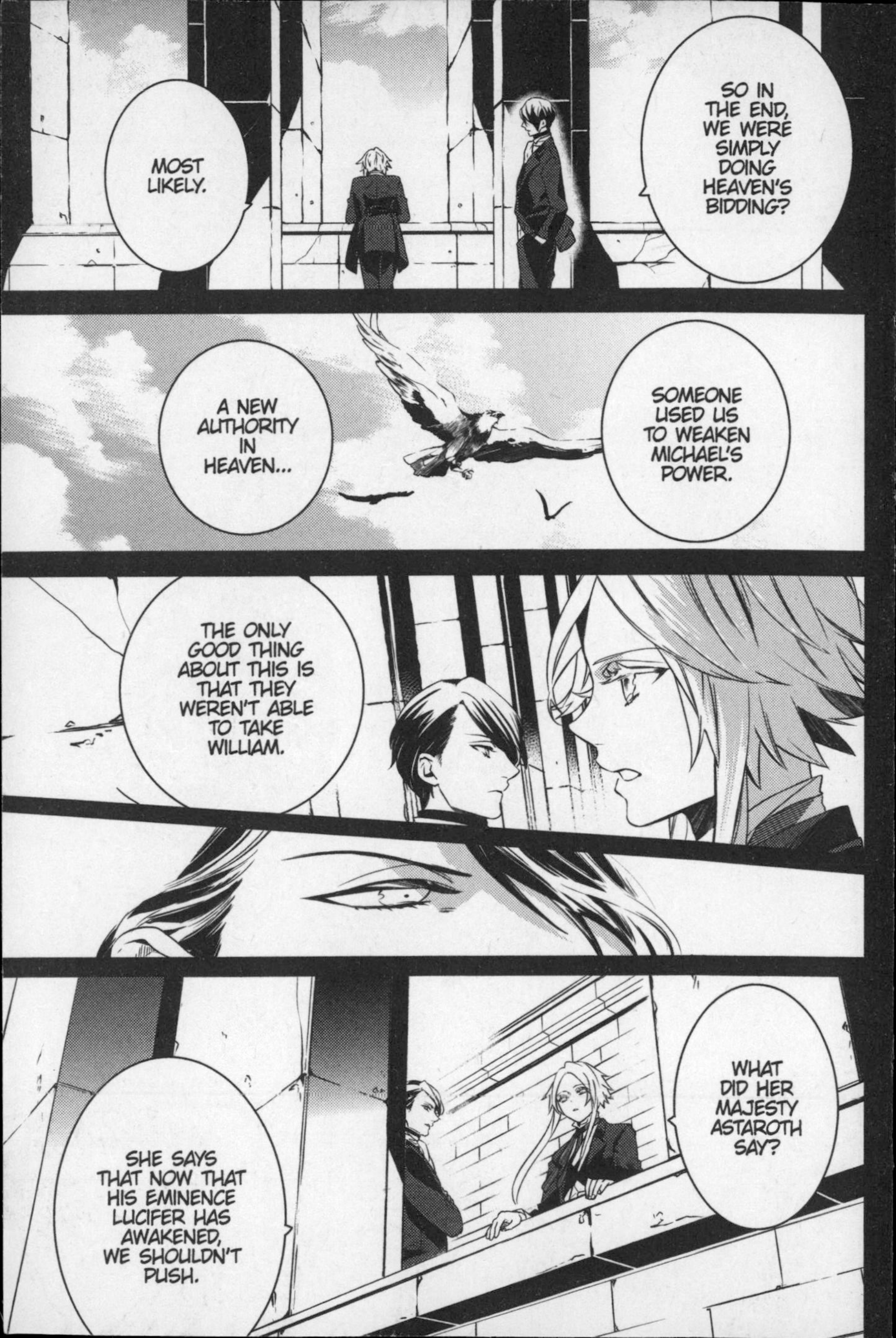
SO IN THE END, WE WERE SIMPLY DOING HEAVEN'S BIDDING?
MOST LIKELY.
SOMEONE USED US TO WEAKEN MICHAEL'S POWER.
A NEW AUTHORITY IN HEAVEN...
THE ONLY GOOD THING ABOUT THIS IS THAT THEY WEREN'T ABLE TO TAKE WILLIAM.
WHAT DID HER MAJESTY ASTAROTH SAY?
SHE SAYS THAT NOW THAT HIS EMINENCE LUCIFER HAS AWAKENED, WE SHOULDN'T PUSH.

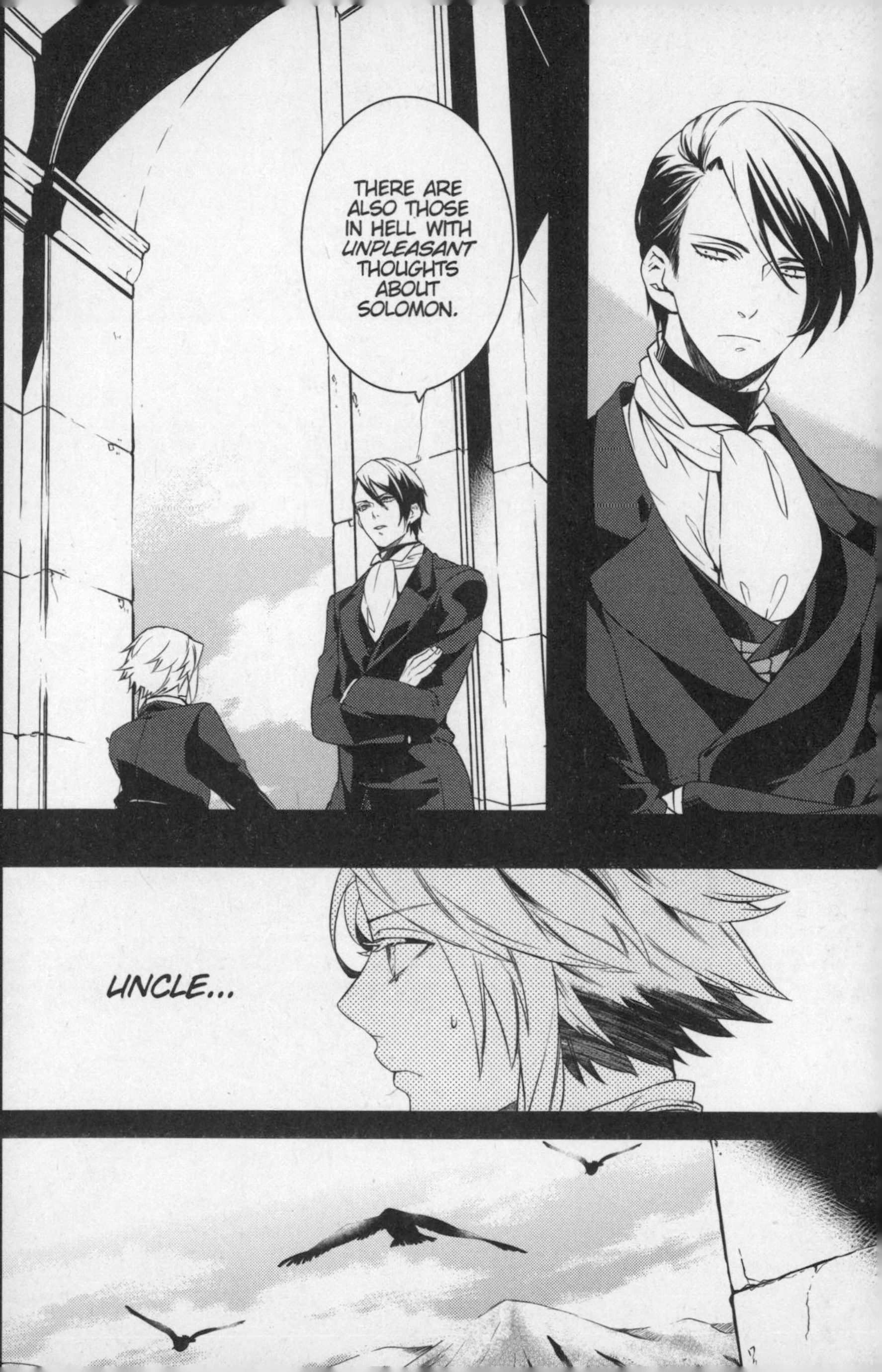
THERE ARE ALSO THOSE IN HELL WITH *UNPLEASANT* THOUGHTS ABOUT SOLOMON.
UNCLE...

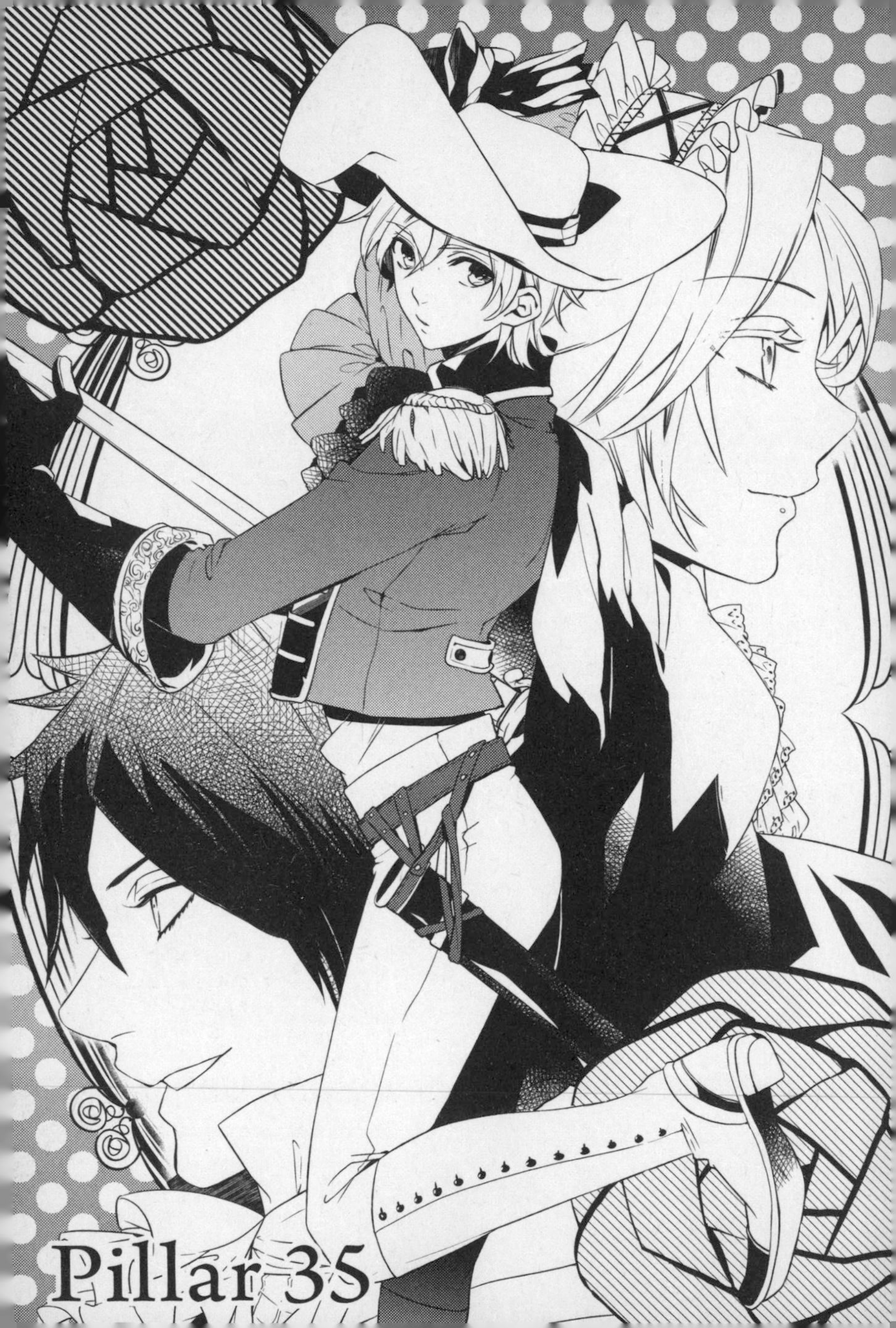
Pillar 35

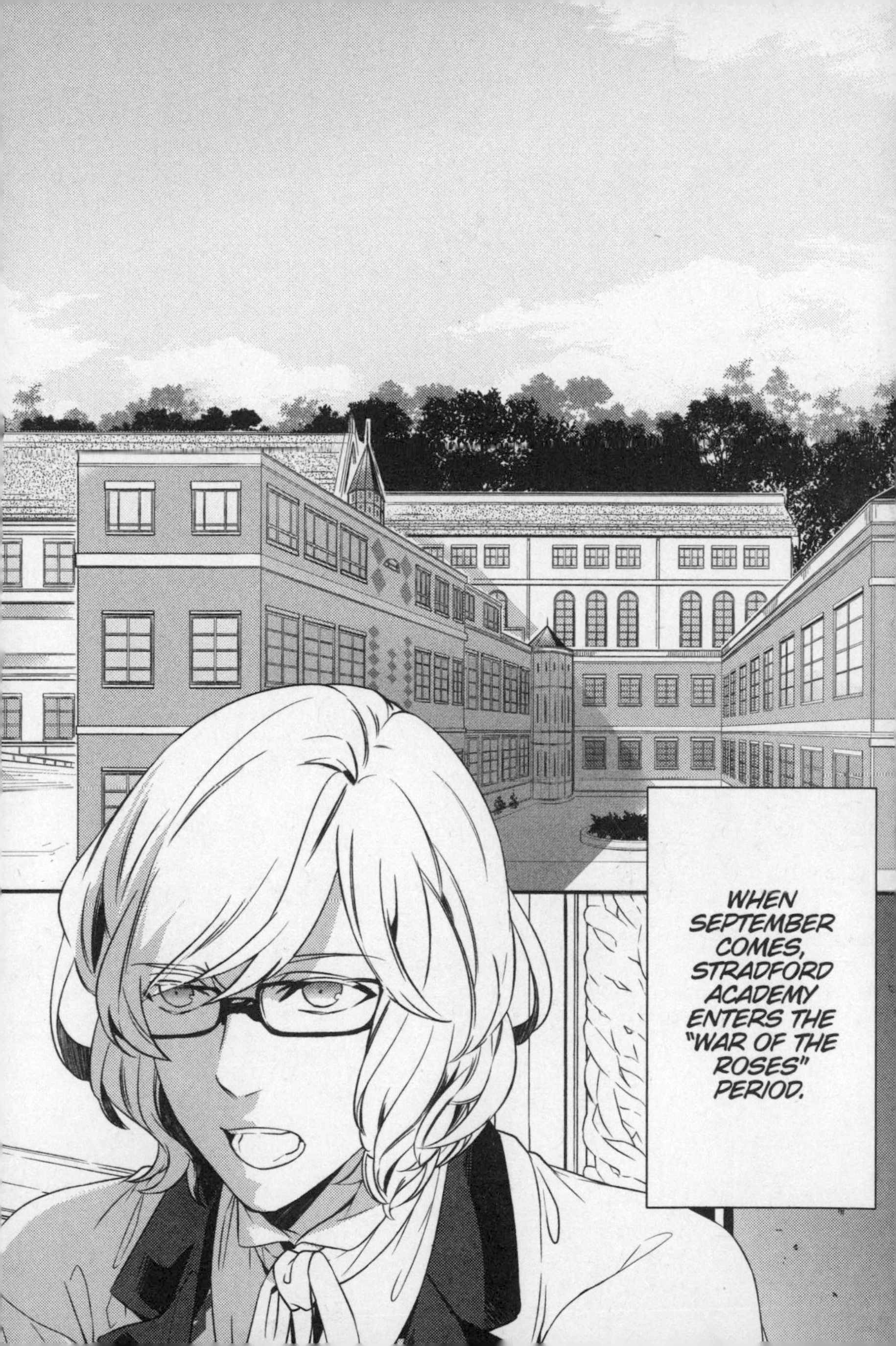
WHEN SEPTEMBER COMES, STRADFORD ACADEMY ENTERS THE "WAR OF THE ROSES" PERIOD.

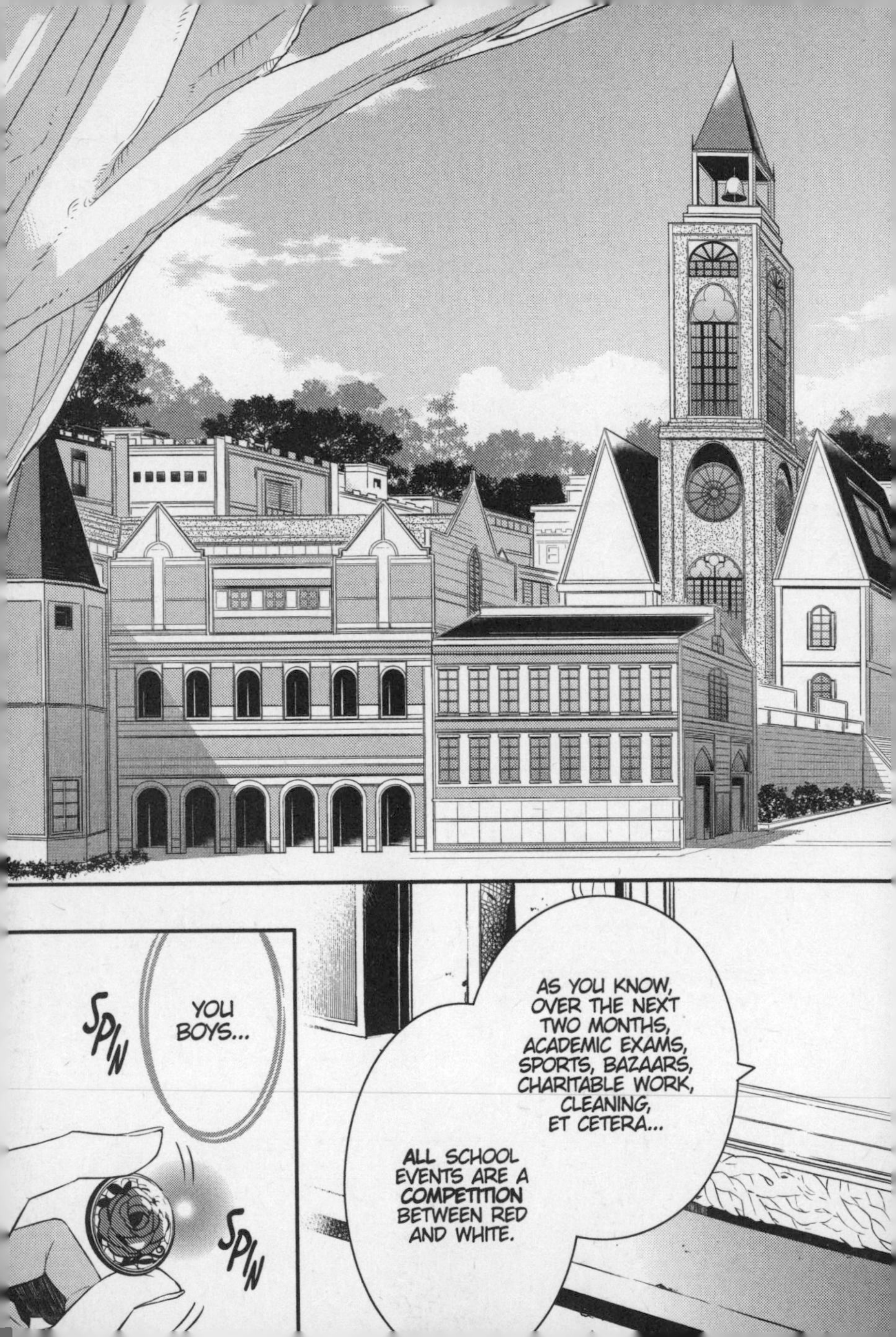
AS YOU KNOW, OVER THE NEXT TWO MONTHS, ACADEMIC EXAMS, SPORTS, BAZAARS, CHARITABLE WORK, CLEANING, ET CETERA...
ALL SCHOOL EVENTS ARE A **COMPETITION** BETWEEN RED AND WHITE.
YOU BOYS...
SPIN
SPIN

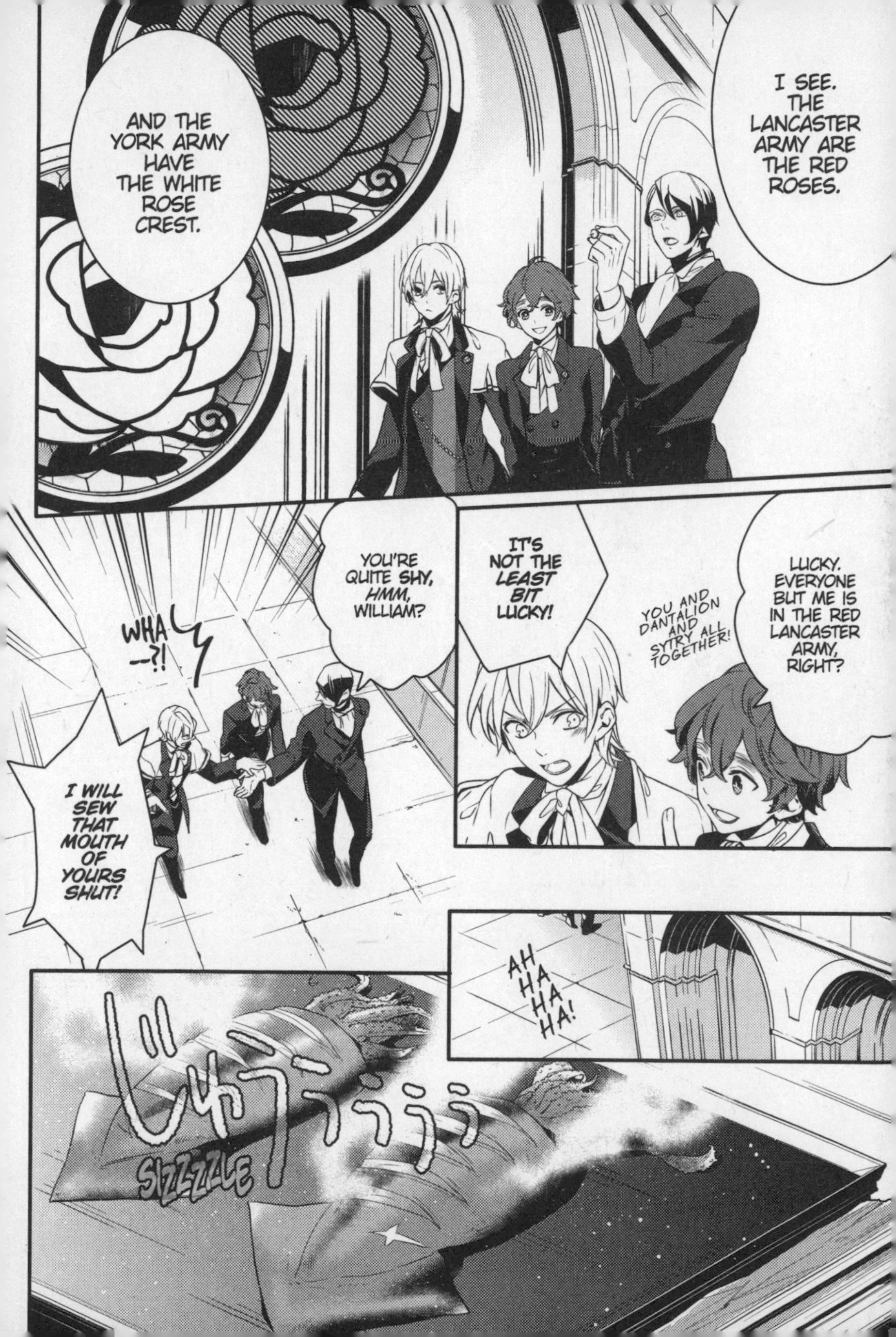

I SEE. THE LANCASTER ARMY ARE THE RED ROSES.
AND THE YORK ARMY HAVE THE WHITE ROSE CREST.
LUCKY. EVERYONE BUT ME IS IN THE RED LANCASTER ARMY, RIGHT?
YOU AND DANTALION AND SYTRY ALL TOGETHER!
IT'S NOT THE *LEAST* BIT LUCKY!
YOU'RE QUITE SHY, *HMM*, WILLIAM?
WHA--?!
I WILL SEW THAT MOUTH OF YOURS SHUT!
AH HA HA HA HA!
SIZZZZLE

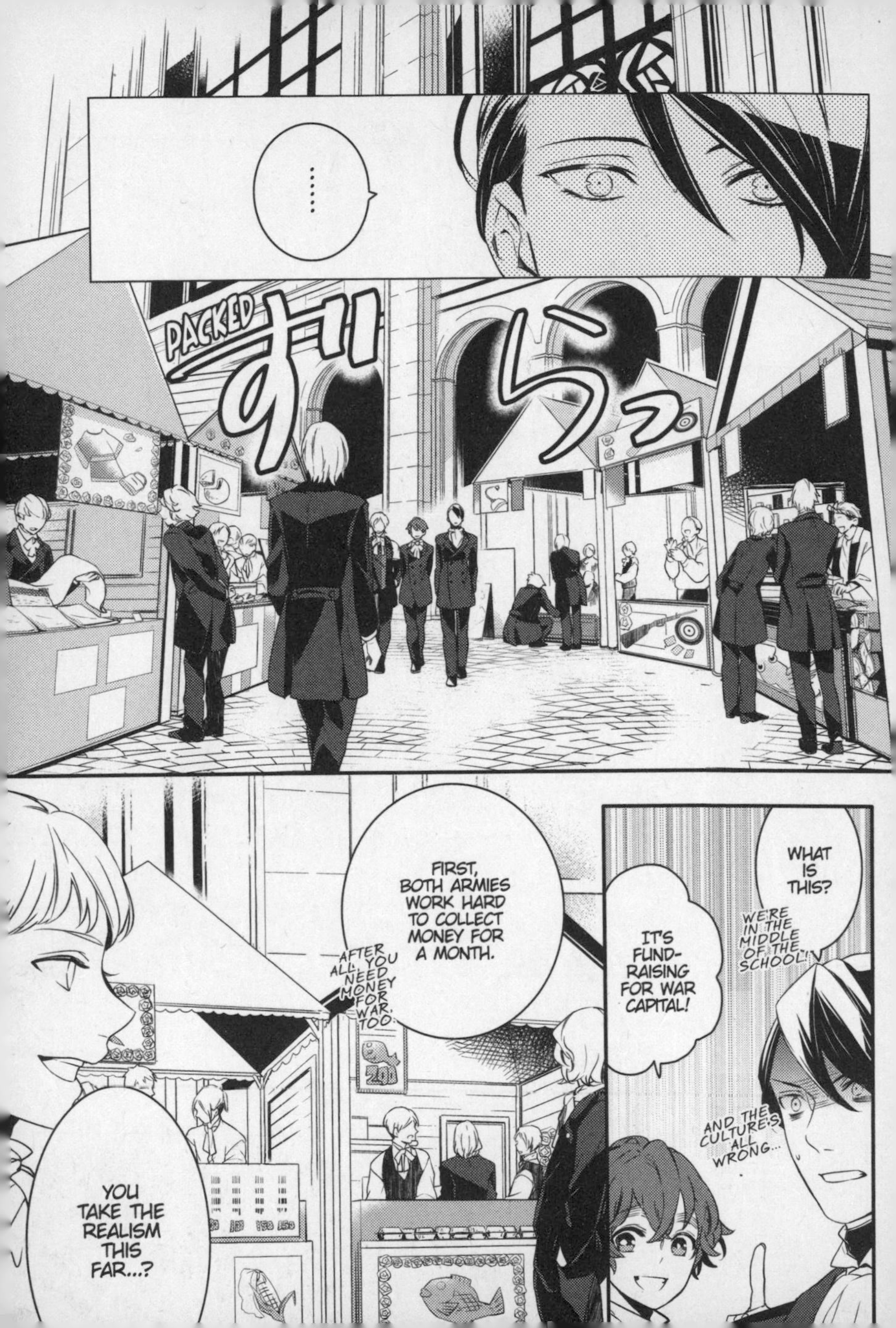
......
PACKED
WHAT IS THIS?
WE'RE IN THE MIDDLE OF THE SCHOOL!
AND THE CULTURE'S ALL WRONG...
IT'S FUND-RAISING FOR WAR CAPITAL!
FIRST, BOTH ARMIES WORK HARD TO COLLECT MONEY FOR A MONTH.
AFTER ALL YOU NEED MONEY FOR WAR, TOO.
YOU TAKE THE REALISM THIS FAR...?

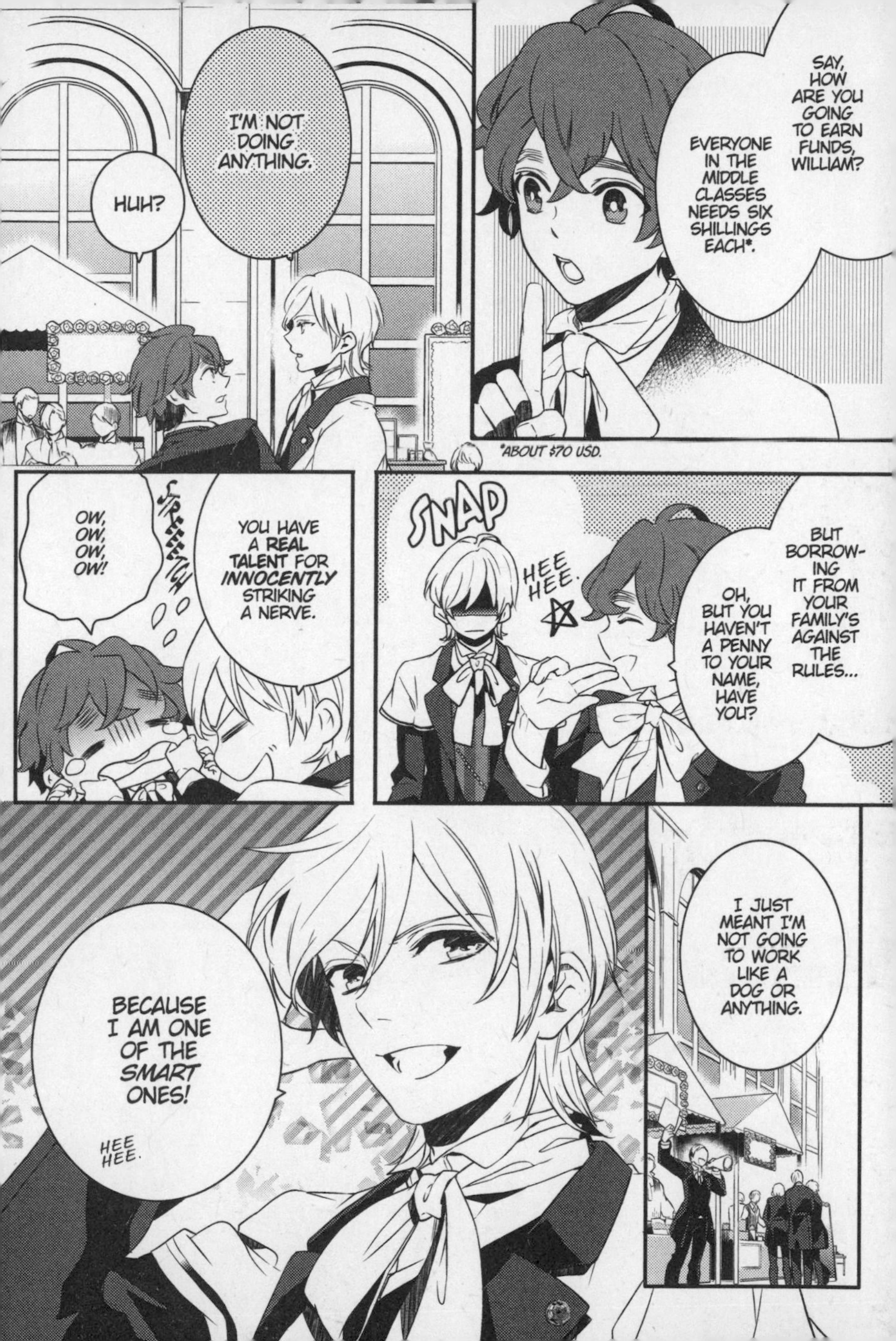
SAY, HOW ARE YOU GOING TO EARN FUNDS, WILLIAM?
EVERYONE IN THE MIDDLE CLASSES NEEDS SIX SHILLINGS EACH*.
I'M NOT DOING ANYTHING.
HUH?
*ABOUT $70 USD.
BUT BORROWING IT FROM YOUR FAMILY'S AGAINST THE RULES...
OH, BUT YOU HAVEN'T A PENNY TO YOUR NAME, HAVE YOU?
HEE HEE.
SNAP
YOU HAVE A REAL TALENT FOR INNOCENTLY STRIKING A NERVE.
STREEEETCH
OW, OW, OW, OW!
I JUST MEANT I'M NOT GOING TO WORK LIKE A DOG OR ANYTHING.
BECAUSE I AM ONE OF THE SMART ONES!
HEE HEE.

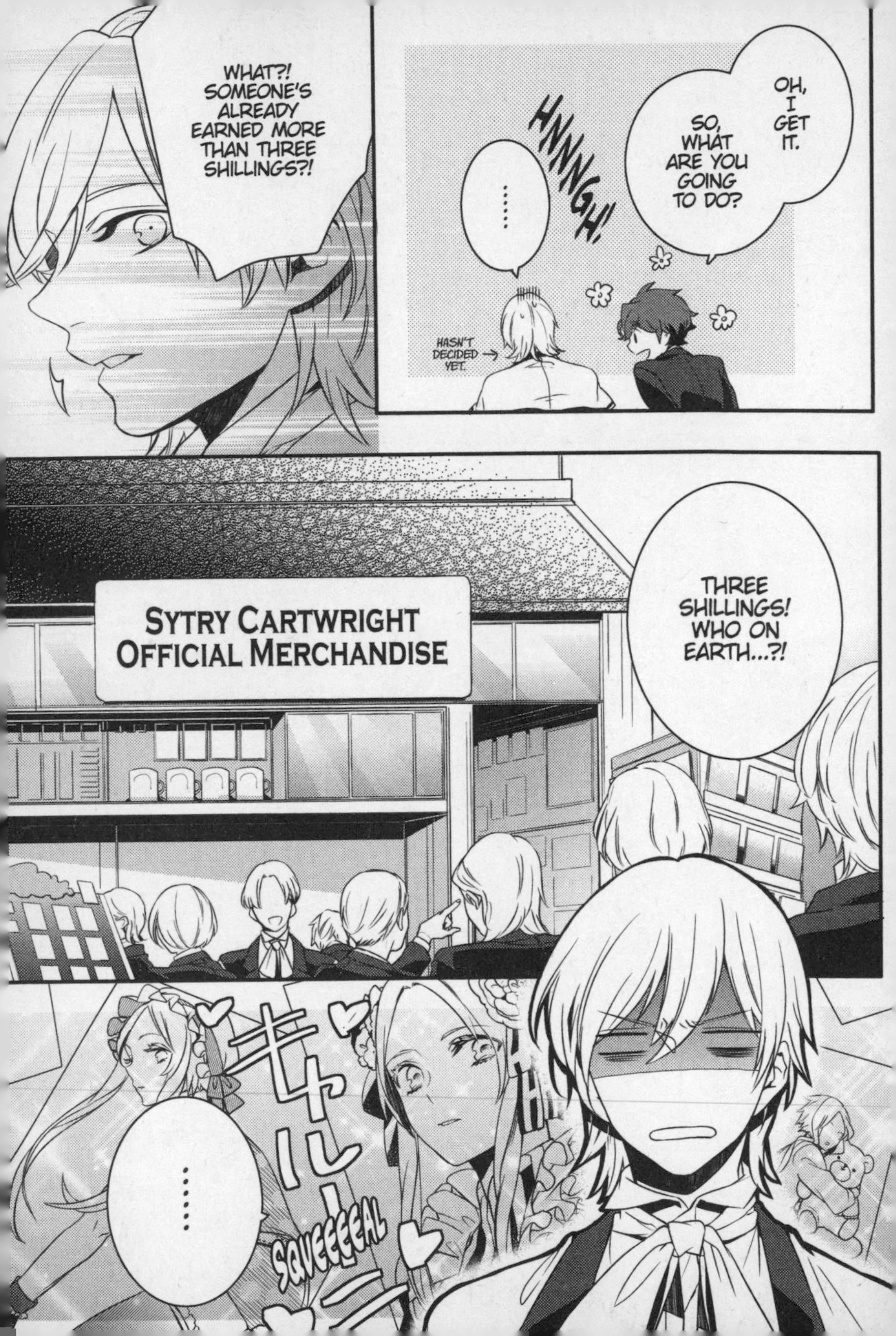

OH, I GET IT. SO, WHAT ARE YOU GOING TO DO?
HNNNGH!
......
HASN'T DECIDED YET.
WHAT?! SOMEONE'S ALREADY EARNED MORE THAN THREE SHILLINGS?!
SYTRY CARTWRIGHT OFFICIAL MERCHANDISE
THREE SHILLINGS! WHO ON EARTH...?!
......
SQUEEEEAL

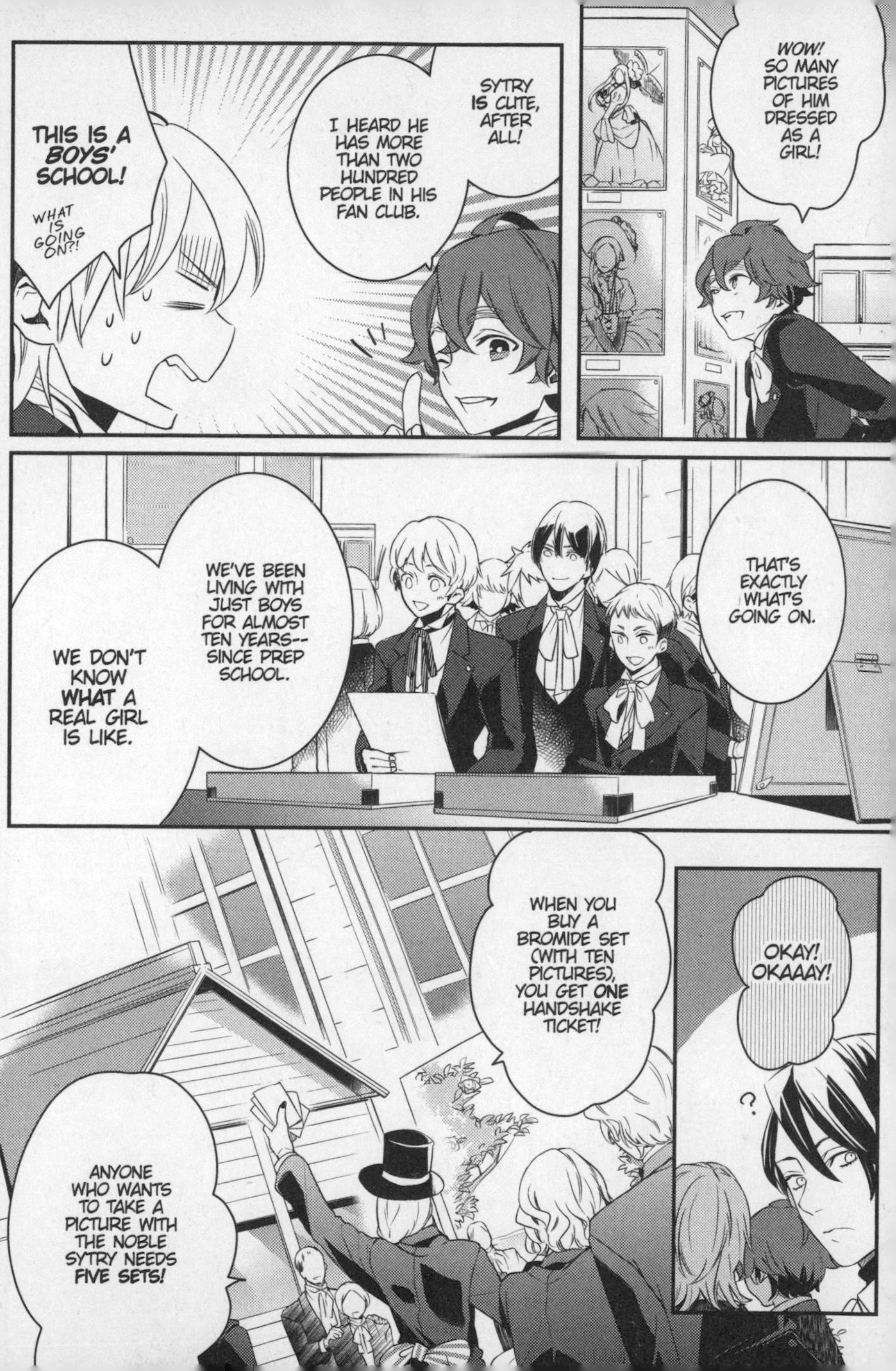
WOW! SO MANY PICTURES OF HIM DRESSED AS A GIRL!
SYTRY IS CUTE, AFTER ALL!
I HEARD HE HAS MORE THAN TWO HUNDRED PEOPLE IN HIS FAN CLUB.
THIS IS A *BOYS'* SCHOOL!
WHAT IS GOING ON?!
THAT'S EXACTLY WHAT'S GOING ON.
WE'VE BEEN LIVING WITH JUST BOYS FOR ALMOST TEN YEARS-- SINCE PREP SCHOOL.
WE DON'T KNOW WHAT A REAL GIRL IS LIKE.
OKAY! OKAAAY!
?
WHEN YOU BUY A BROMIDE SET (WITH TEN PICTURES), YOU GET ONE HANDSHAKE TICKET!
ANYONE WHO WANTS TO TAKE A PICTURE WITH THE NOBLE SYTRY NEEDS FIVE SETS!

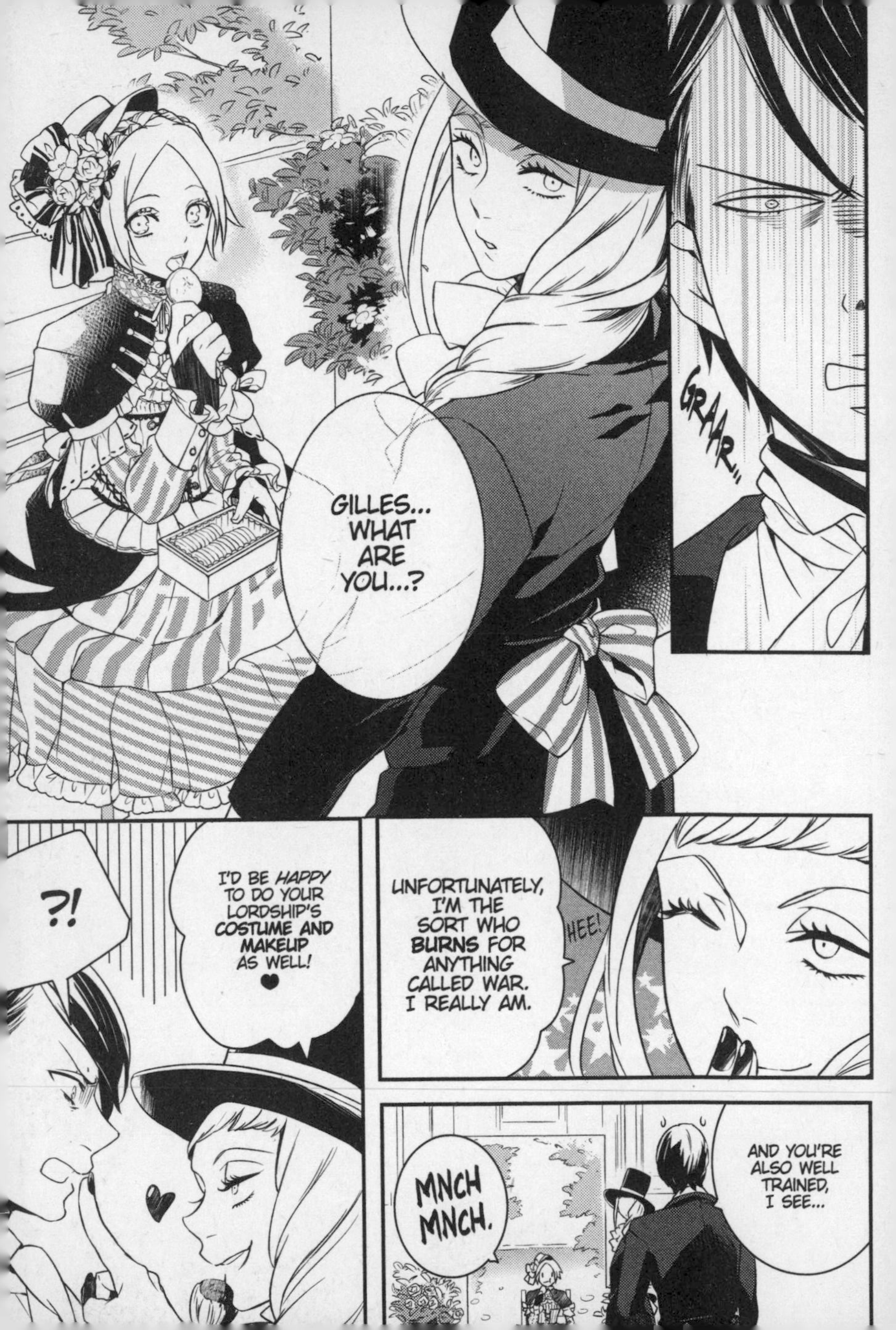
GRAAR..
GILLES... WHAT ARE YOU...?
UNFORTUNATELY, I'M THE SORT WHO BURNS FOR ANYTHING CALLED WAR. I REALLY AM.
HEE!
AND YOU'RE ALSO WELL TRAINED, I SEE...
MNCH MNCH.
I'D BE HAPPY TO DO YOUR LORDSHIP'S COSTUME AND MAKEUP AS WELL! ♥
?!

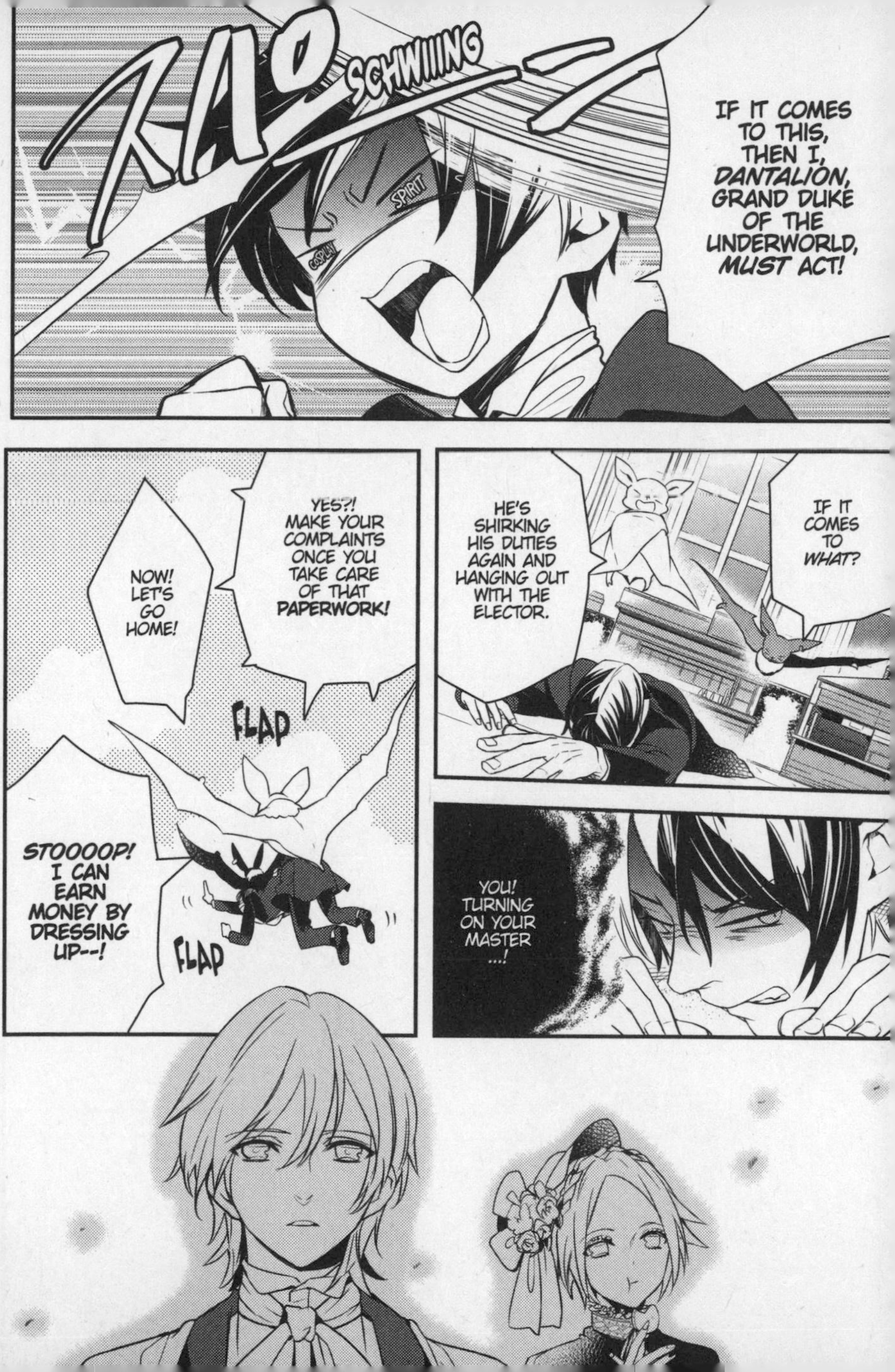
SCHWIIING
SPIRIT
COSPLAY
IF IT COMES TO THIS, THEN I, DANTALION, GRAND DUKE OF THE UNDERWORLD, MUST ACT!
IF IT COMES TO WHAT?
HE'S SHIRKING HIS DUTIES AGAIN AND HANGING OUT WITH THE ELECTOR.
YOU! TURNING ON YOUR MASTER ...!
YES?! MAKE YOUR COMPLAINTS ONCE YOU TAKE CARE OF THAT PAPERWORK!
NOW! LET'S GO HOME!
FLAP
STOOOOP! I CAN EARN MONEY BY DRESSING UP--!
FLAP

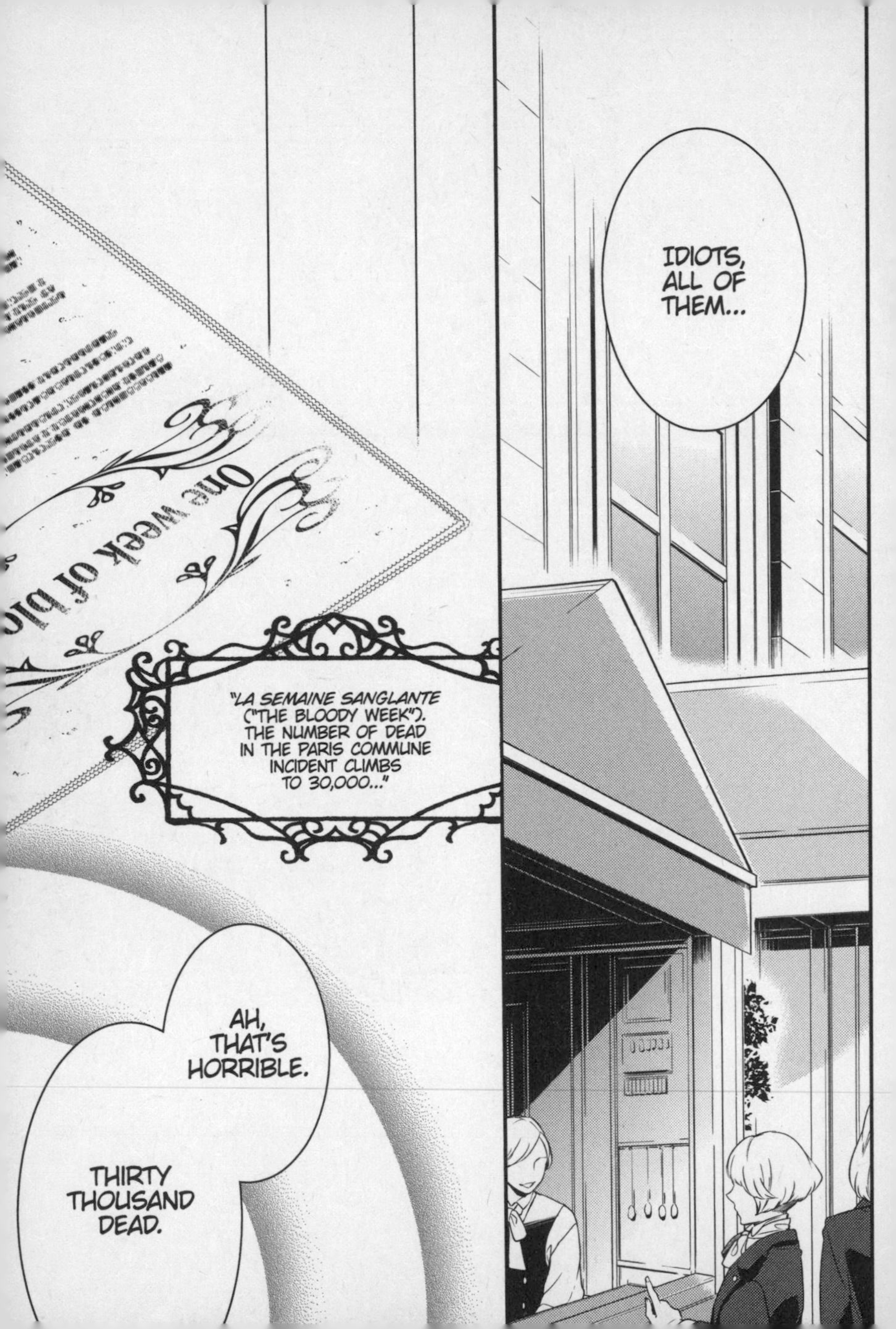
IDIOTS, ALL OF THEM...
"LA SEMAINE SANGLANTE ("THE BLOODY WEEK"). THE NUMBER OF DEAD IN THE PARIS COMMUNE INCIDENT CLIMBS TO 30,000..."
AH, THAT'S HORRIBLE.
THIRTY THOUSAND DEAD.

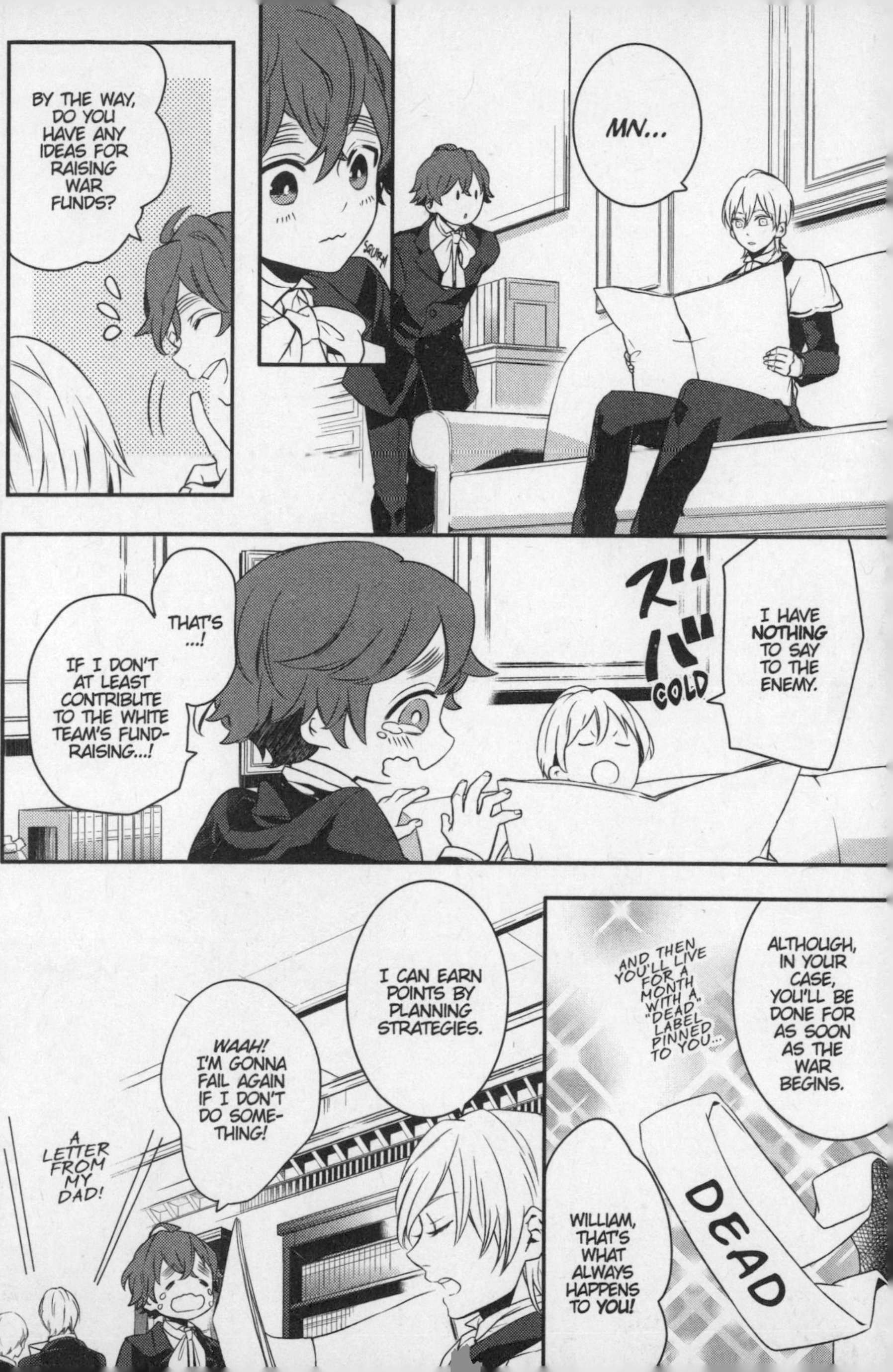
MN...
SQUIRM
BY THE WAY, DO YOU HAVE ANY IDEAS FOR RAISING WAR FUNDS?
ズバ
COLD
I HAVE NOTHING TO SAY TO THE ENEMY.
THAT'S ...!
IF I DON'T AT LEAST CONTRIBUTE TO THE WHITE TEAM'S FUND-RAISING...!
ALTHOUGH, IN YOUR CASE, YOU'LL BE DONE FOR AS SOON AS THE WAR BEGINS.
AND THEN YOU'LL LIVE FOR A MONTH WITH A "DEAD" LABEL PINNED TO YOU...
DEAD
WILLIAM, THAT'S WHAT ALWAYS HAPPENS TO YOU!
I CAN EARN POINTS BY PLANNING STRATEGIES.
WAAH! I'M GONNA FAIL AGAIN IF I DON'T DO SOME-THING!
A LETTER FROM MY DAD!

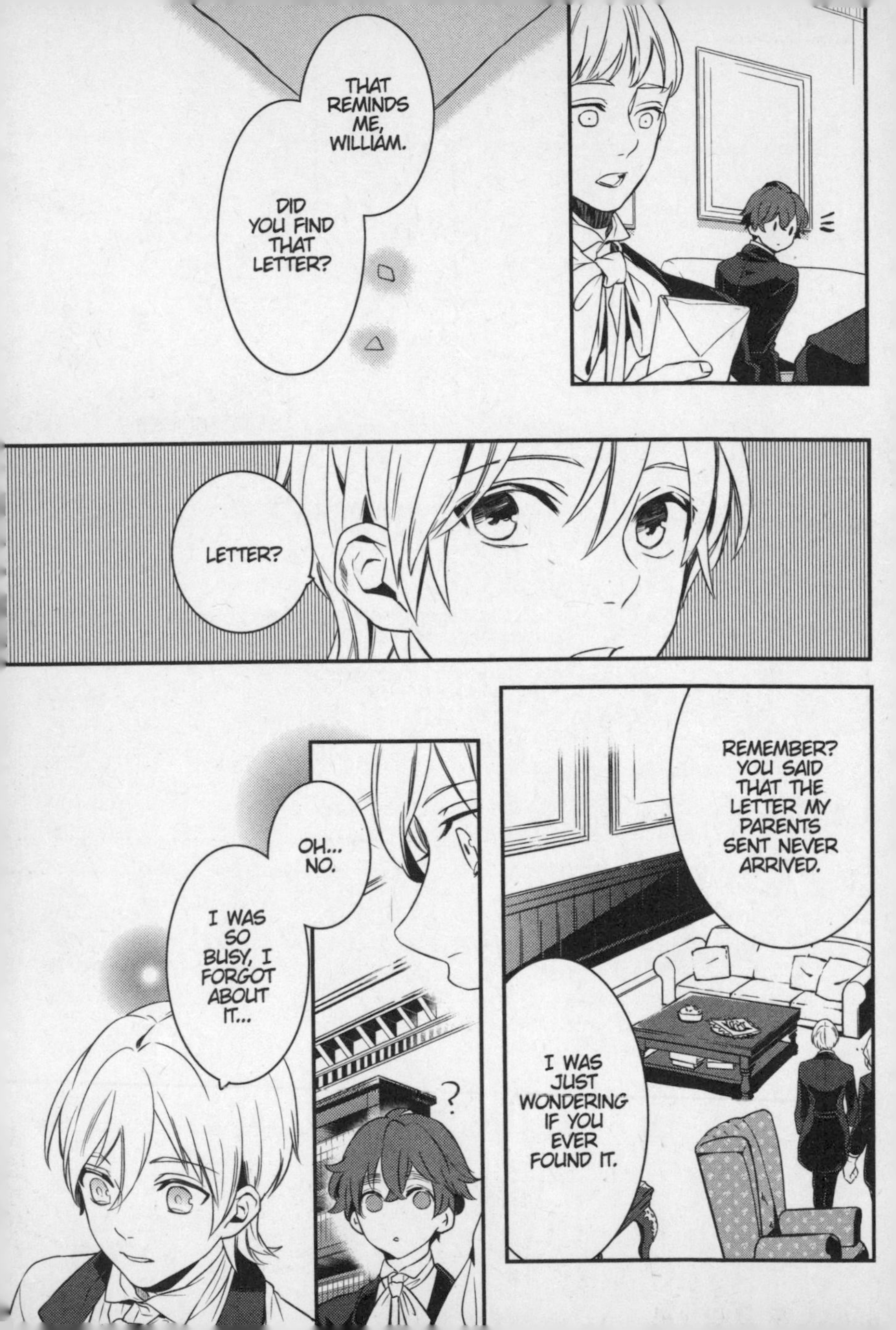
THAT REMINDS ME, WILLIAM.
DID YOU FIND THAT LETTER?
LETTER?
REMEMBER? YOU SAID THAT THE LETTER MY PARENTS SENT NEVER ARRIVED.
I WAS JUST WONDERING IF YOU EVER FOUND IT.
OH... NO.
I WAS SO BUSY, I FORGOT ABOUT IT...

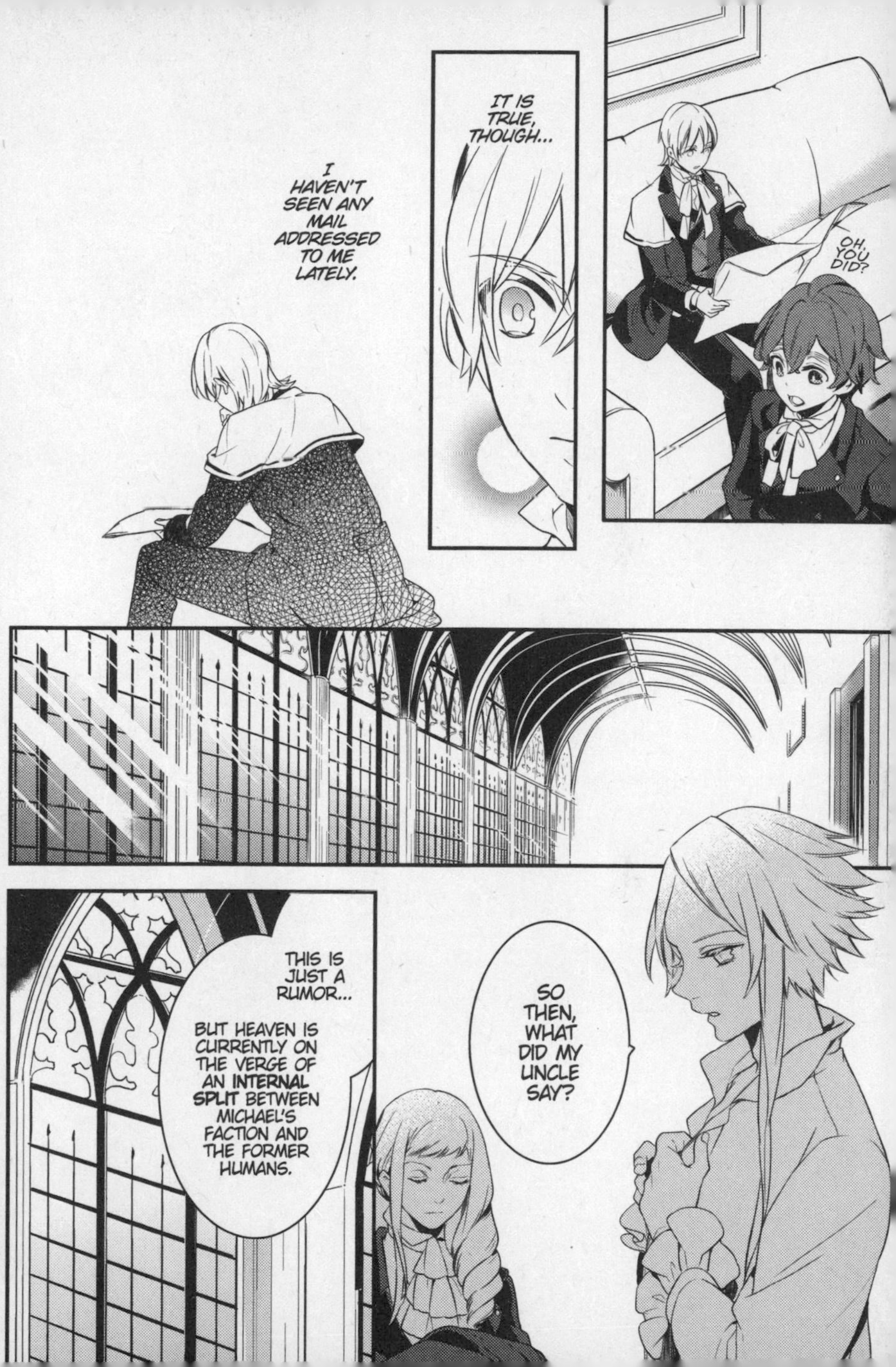
OH, YOU DID?
IT IS TRUE, THOUGH...
I HAVEN'T SEEN ANY MAIL ADDRESSED TO ME LATELY.
SO THEN, WHAT DID MY UNCLE SAY?
THIS IS JUST A RUMOR...
BUT HEAVEN IS CURRENTLY ON THE VERGE OF AN INTERNAL SPLIT BETWEEN MICHAEL'S FACTION AND THE FORMER HUMANS.

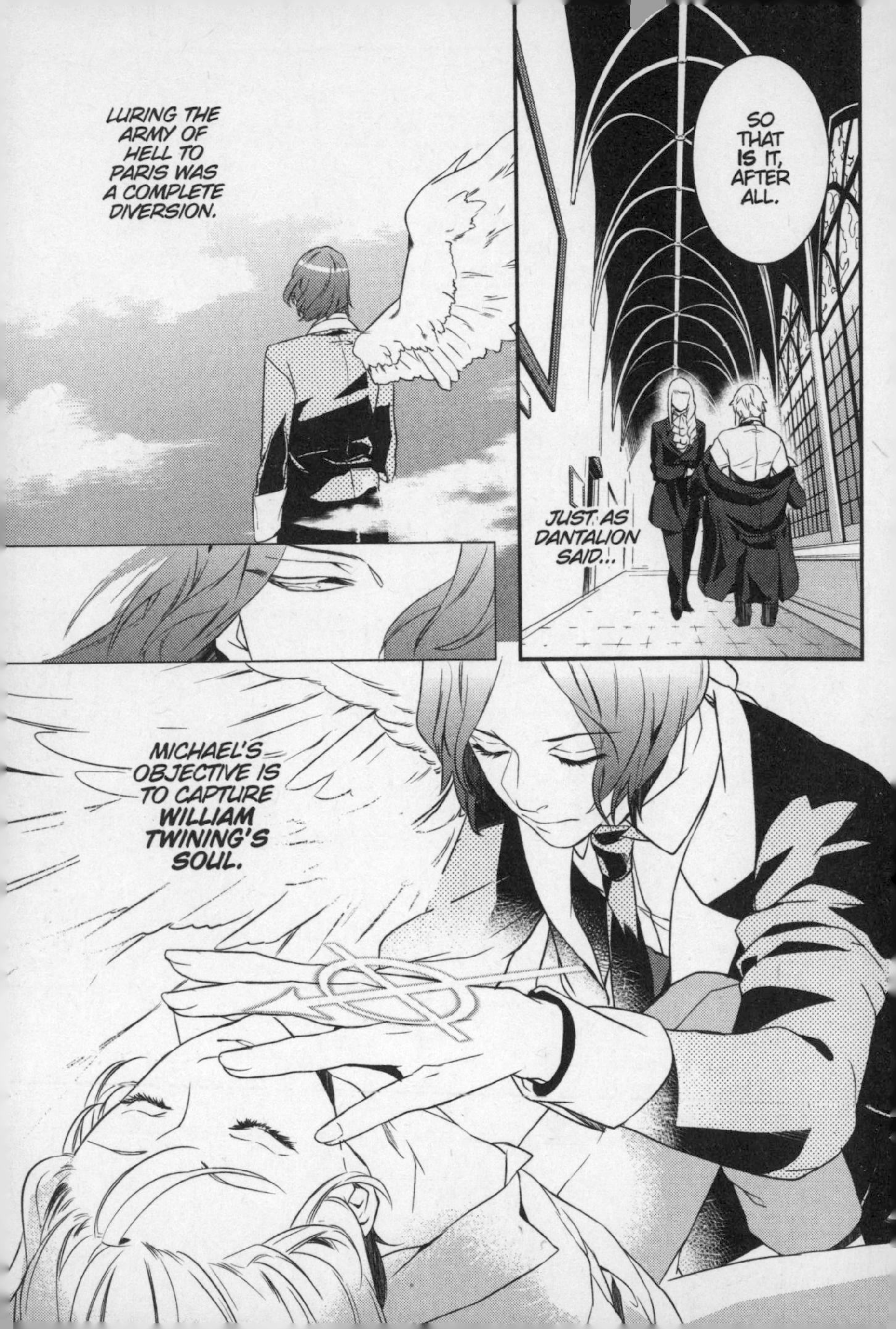
SO THAT IS IT, AFTER ALL.
JUST AS DANTALION SAID...
LURING THE ARMY OF HELL TO PARIS WAS A COMPLETE DIVERSION.
MICHAEL'S OBJECTIVE IS TO CAPTURE WILLIAM TWINING'S SOUL.

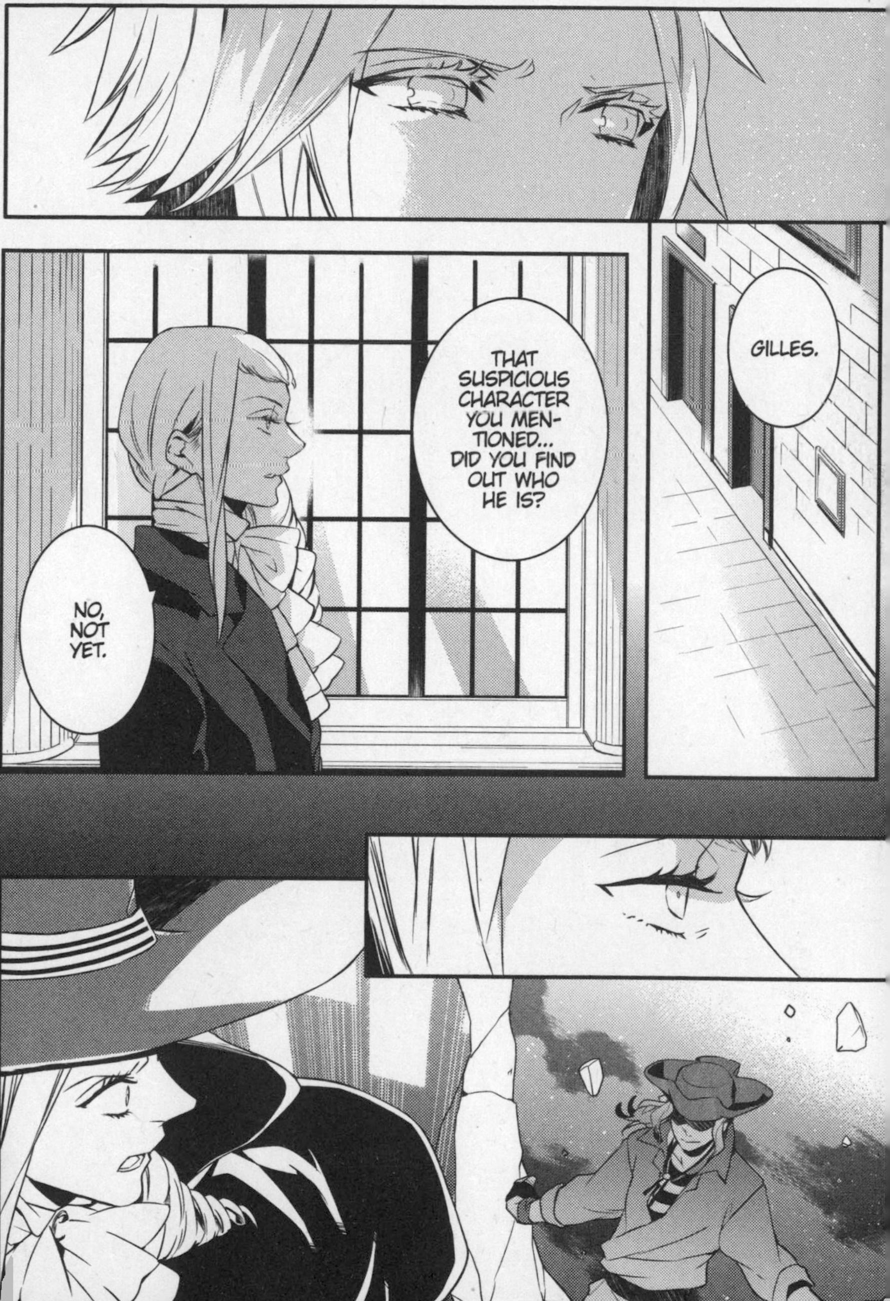
GILLES.
THAT SUSPICIOUS CHARACTER YOU MEN-TIONED... DID YOU FIND OUT WHO HE IS?
NO, NOT YET.

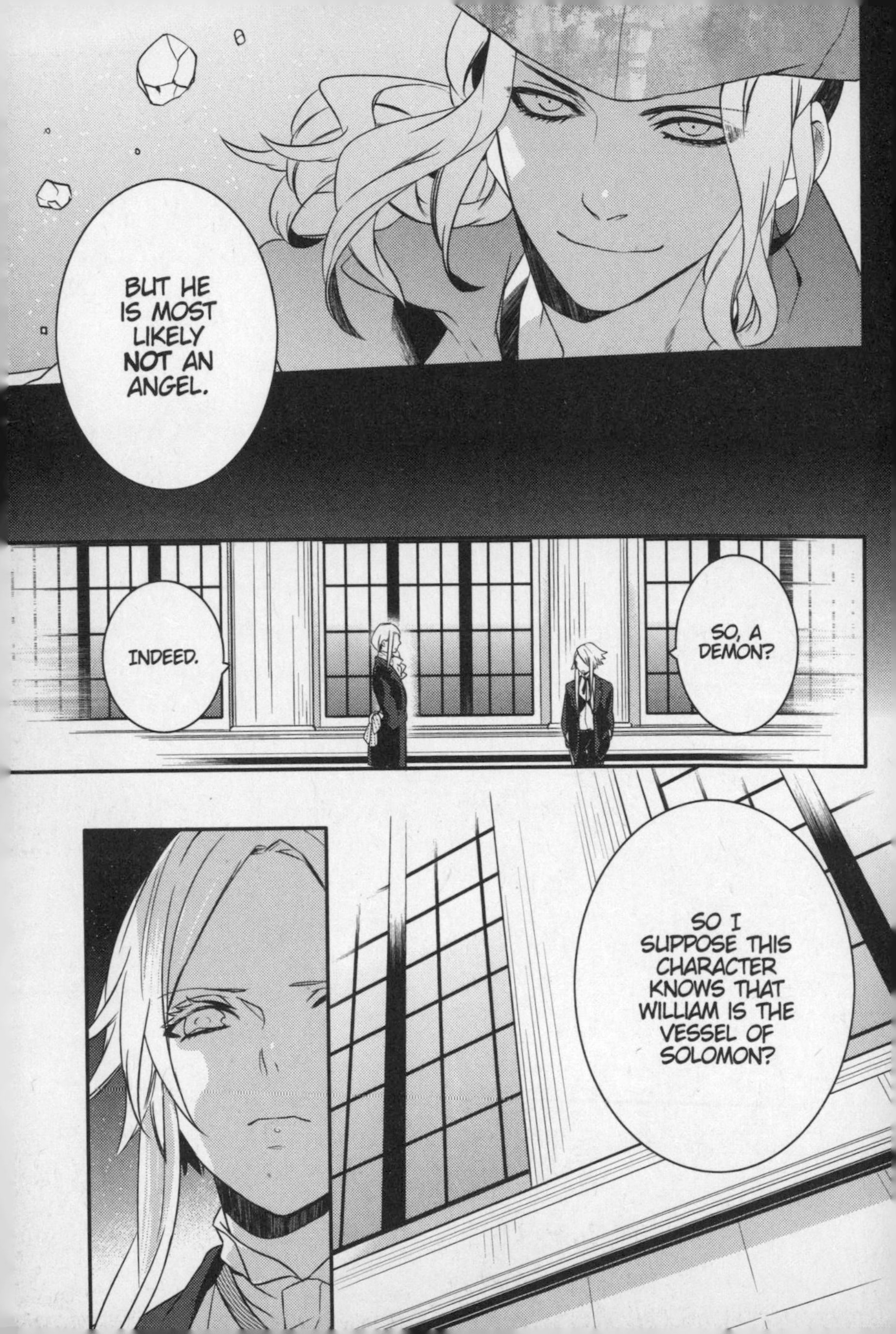
BUT HE IS MOST LIKELY NOT AN ANGEL.
SO, A DEMON?
INDEED.
SO I SUPPOSE THIS CHARACTER KNOWS THAT WILLIAM IS THE VESSEL OF SOLOMON?

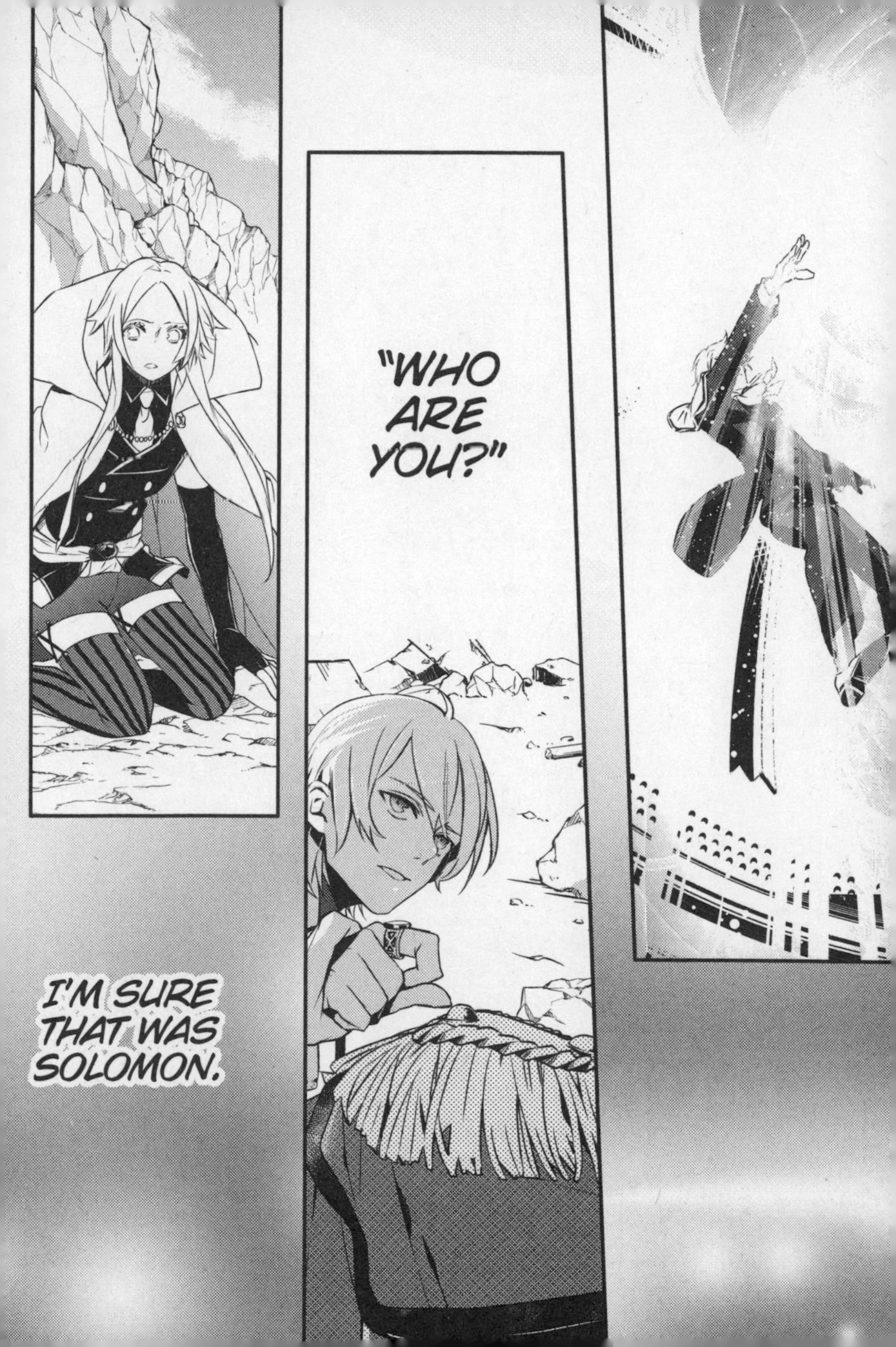
"WHO ARE YOU?"
I'M SURE THAT WAS SOLOMON.

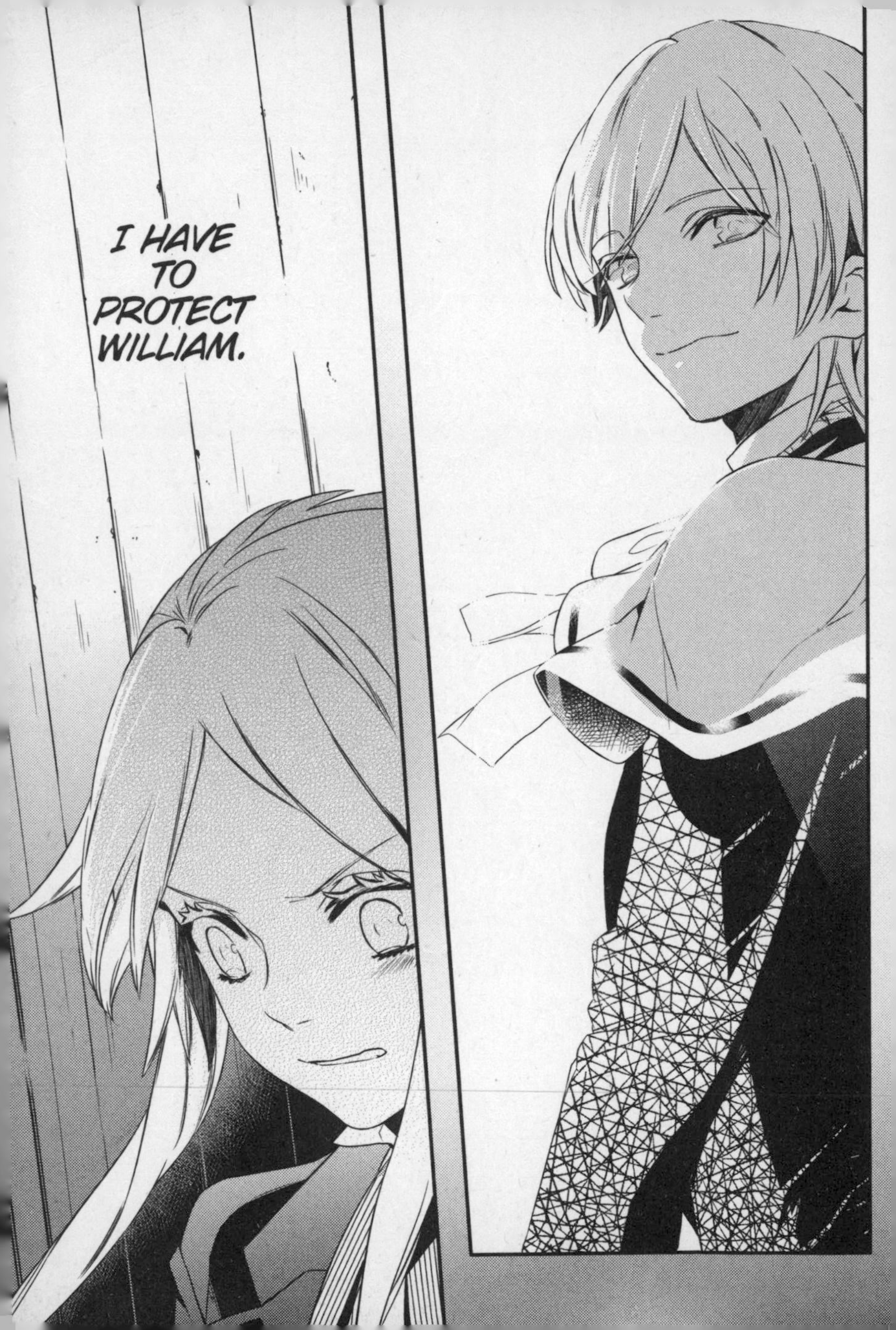
I HAVE TO PROTECT WILLIAM.

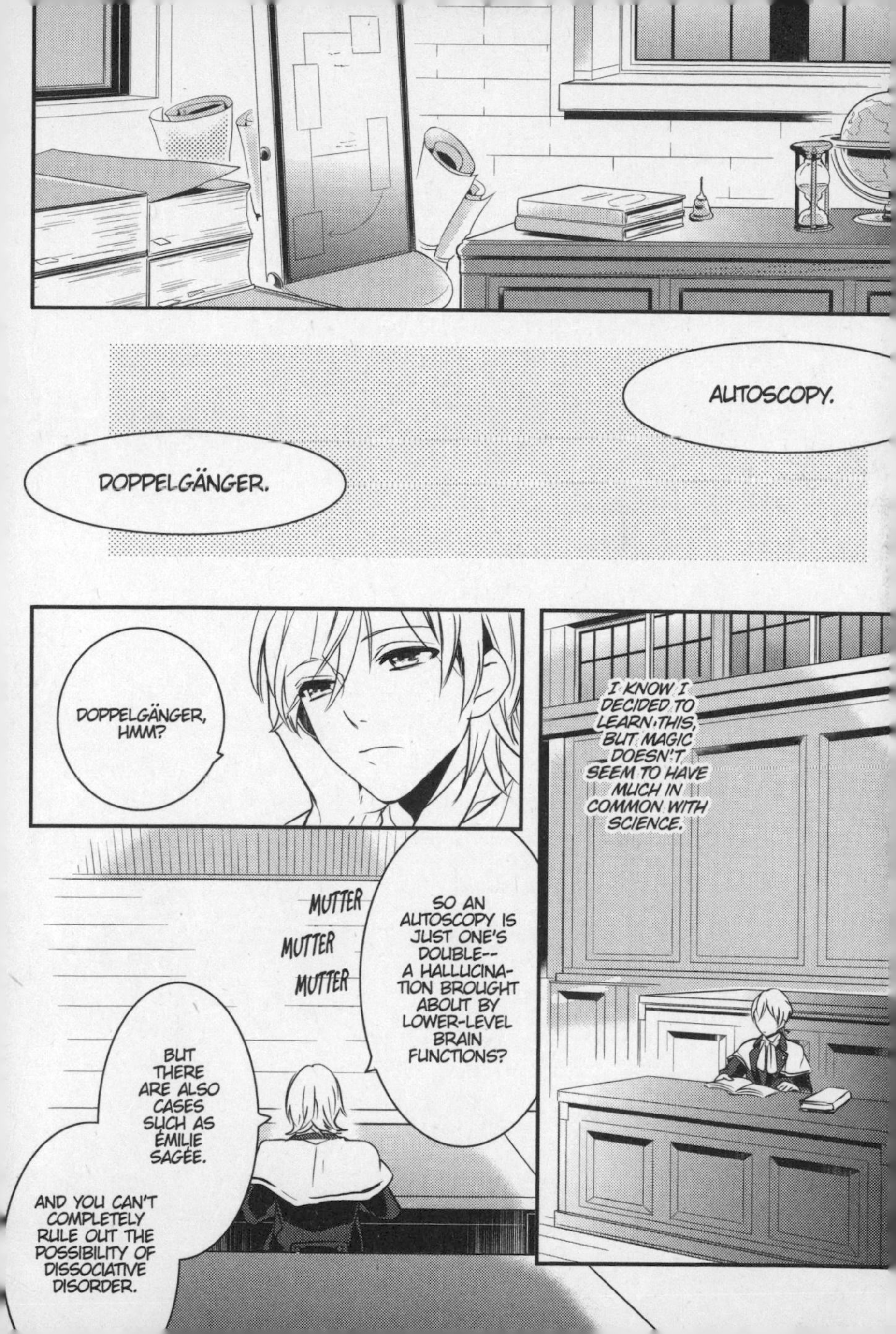
AUTOSCOPY.
DOPPELGÄNGER.
I KNOW I DECIDED TO LEARN THIS, BUT MAGIC DOESN'T SEEM TO HAVE MUCH IN COMMON WITH SCIENCE.
DOPPELGÄNGER, HMM?
SO AN AUTOSCOPY IS JUST ONE'S DOUBLE--A HALLUCINATION BROUGHT ABOUT BY LOWER-LEVEL BRAIN FUNCTIONS?
MUTTER
MUTTER
MUTTER
BUT THERE ARE ALSO CASES SUCH AS ÉMILIE SAGÉE.
AND YOU CAN'T COMPLETELY RULE OUT THE POSSIBILITY OF DISSOCIATIVE DISORDER.

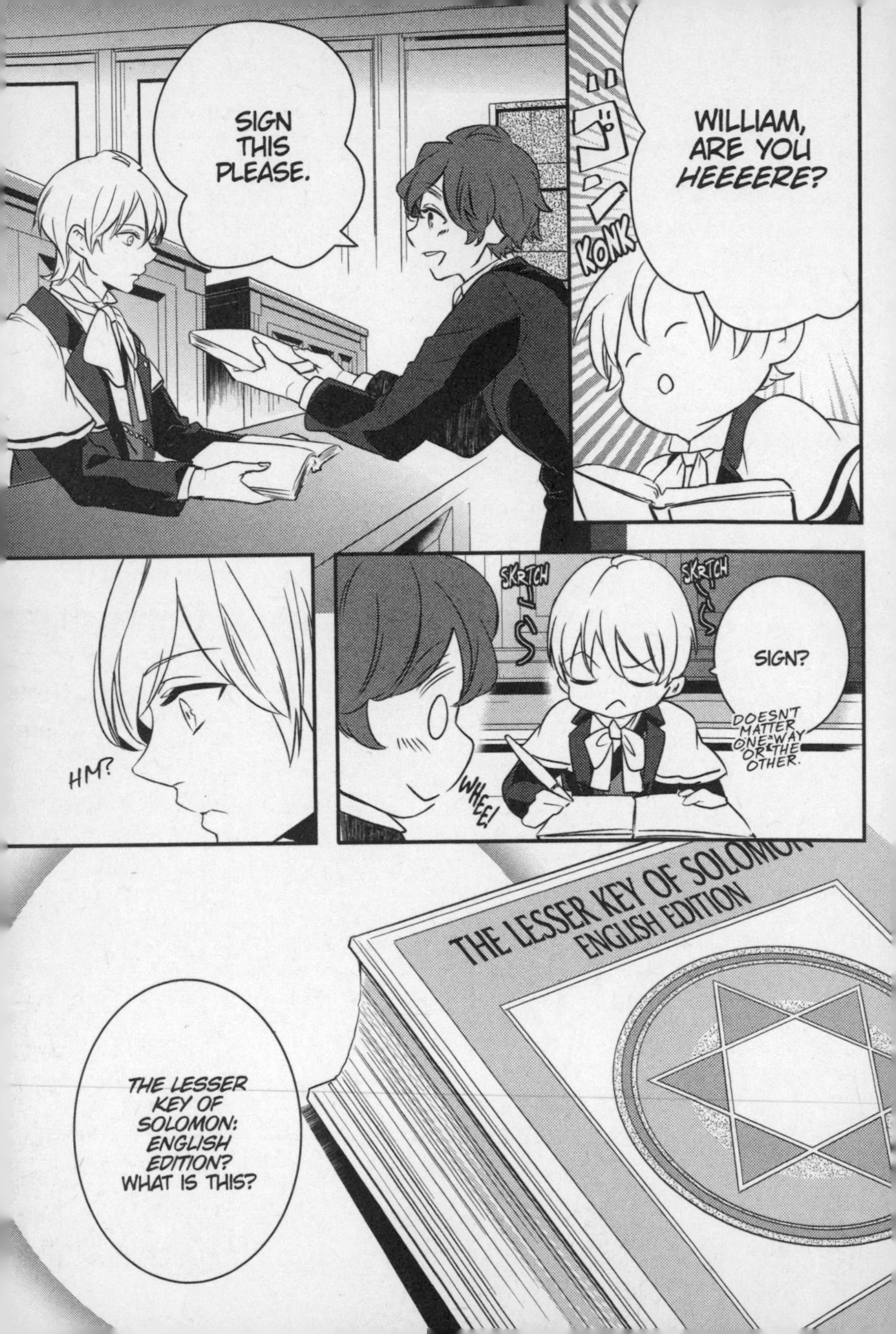
KONK
WILLIAM, ARE YOU HEEEERE?
SIGN THIS PLEASE.
SKRTCH
SKRTCH
SIGN?
DOESN'T MATTER ONE WAY OR THE OTHER.
WHEE!
HM?
THE LESSER KEY OF SOLOMON
ENGLISH EDITION
THE LESSER KEY OF SOLOMON: ENGLISH EDITION? WHAT IS THIS?

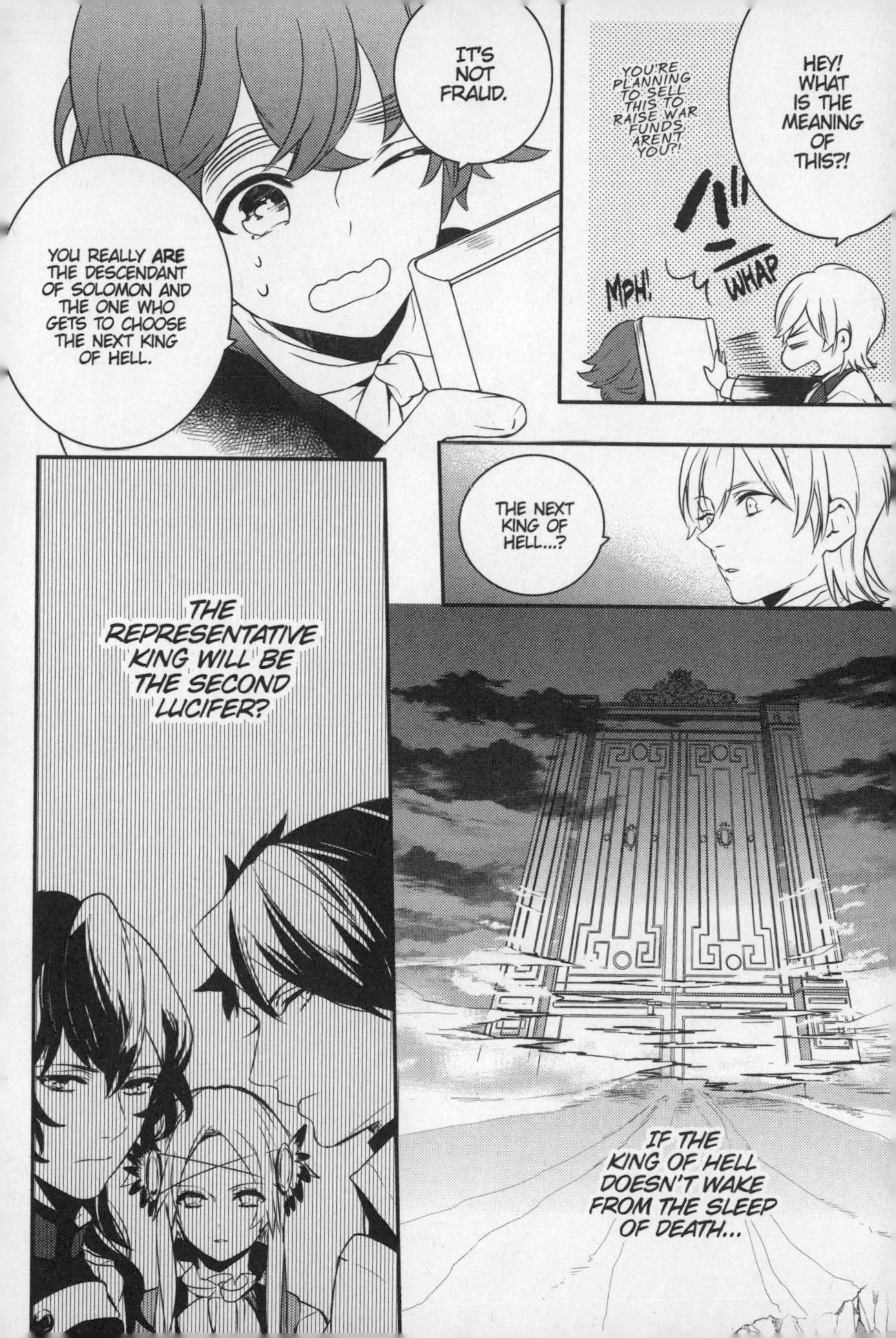
HEY! WHAT IS THE MEANING OF THIS?!
YOU'RE PLANNING TO SELL THIS TO RAISE WAR FUNDS, AREN'T YOU?!
MPH!
WHAP
IT'S NOT FRAUD.
YOU REALLY **ARE** THE DESCENDANT OF SOLOMON AND THE ONE WHO GETS TO CHOOSE THE NEXT KING OF HELL.
THE NEXT KING OF HELL...?
IF THE KING OF HELL DOESN'T WAKE FROM THE SLEEP OF DEATH...
THE REPRESENTATIVE KING WILL BE THE SECOND LUCIFER?

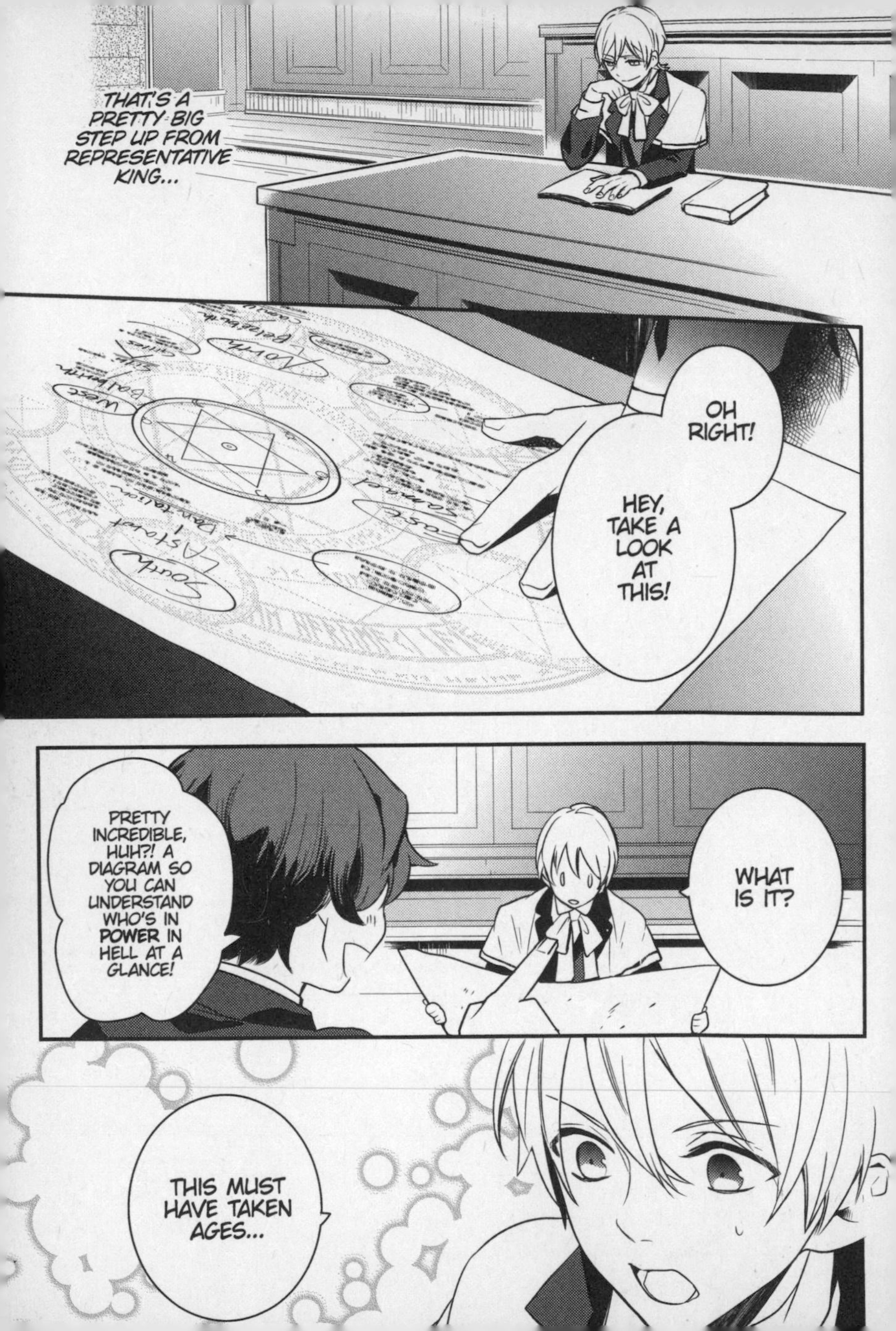
THAT'S A PRETTY BIG STEP UP FROM REPRESENTATIVE KING...
OH RIGHT!
HEY, TAKE A LOOK AT THIS!
WHAT IS IT?
PRETTY INCREDIBLE, HUH?! A DIAGRAM SO YOU CAN UNDERSTAND WHO'S IN POWER IN HELL AT A GLANCE!
THIS MUST HAVE TAKEN AGES...

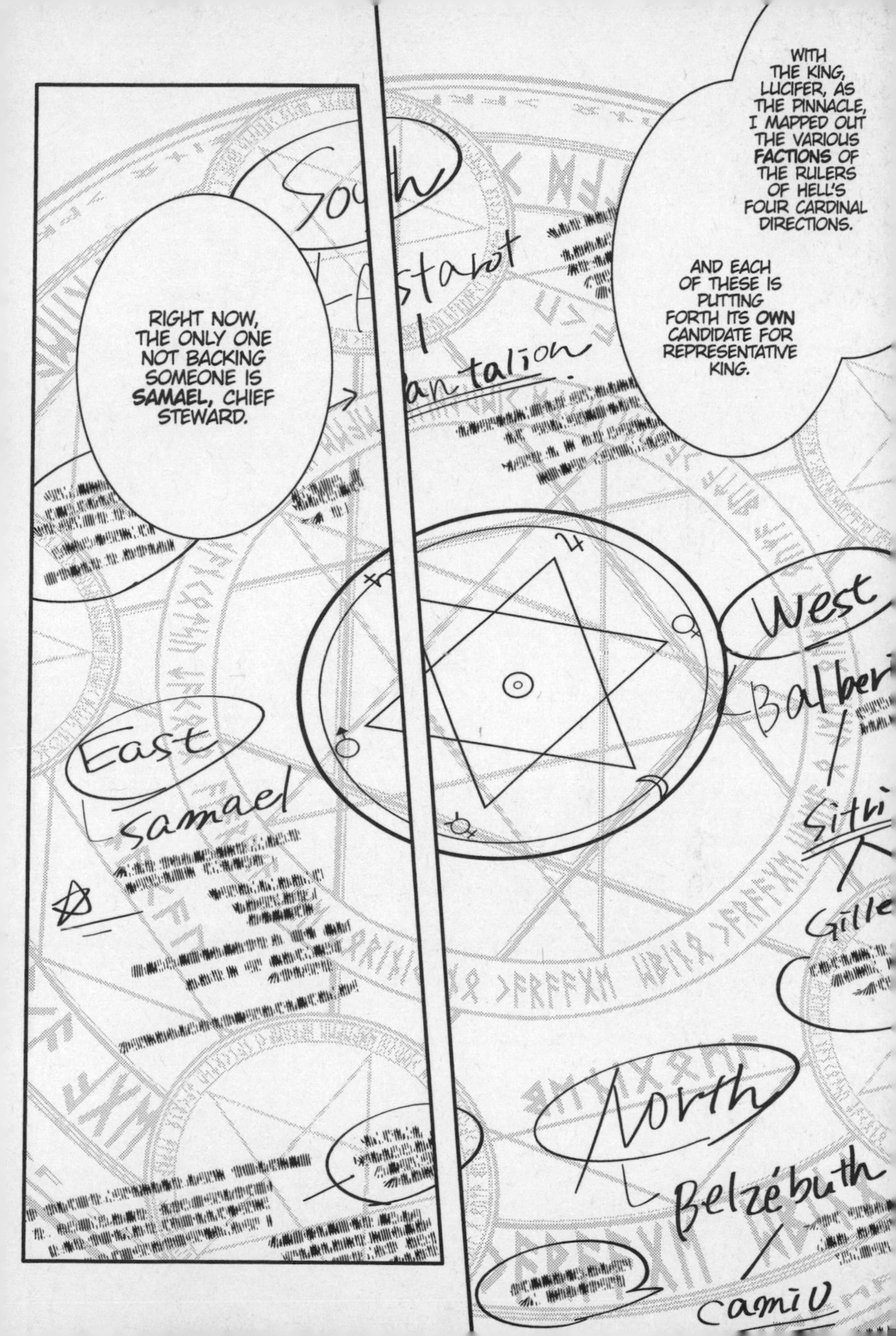
WITH THE KING, LUCIFER, AS THE PINNACLE, I MAPPED OUT THE VARIOUS **FACTIONS** OF THE RULERS OF HELL'S FOUR CARDINAL DIRECTIONS.
AND EACH OF THESE IS PUTTING FORTH ITS **OWN** CANDIDATE FOR REPRESENTATIVE KING.
South
Astarot
West
North
Belzébuth
RIGHT NOW, THE ONLY ONE NOT BACKING SOMEONE IS **SAMAEL**, CHIEF STEWARD.
East
samael

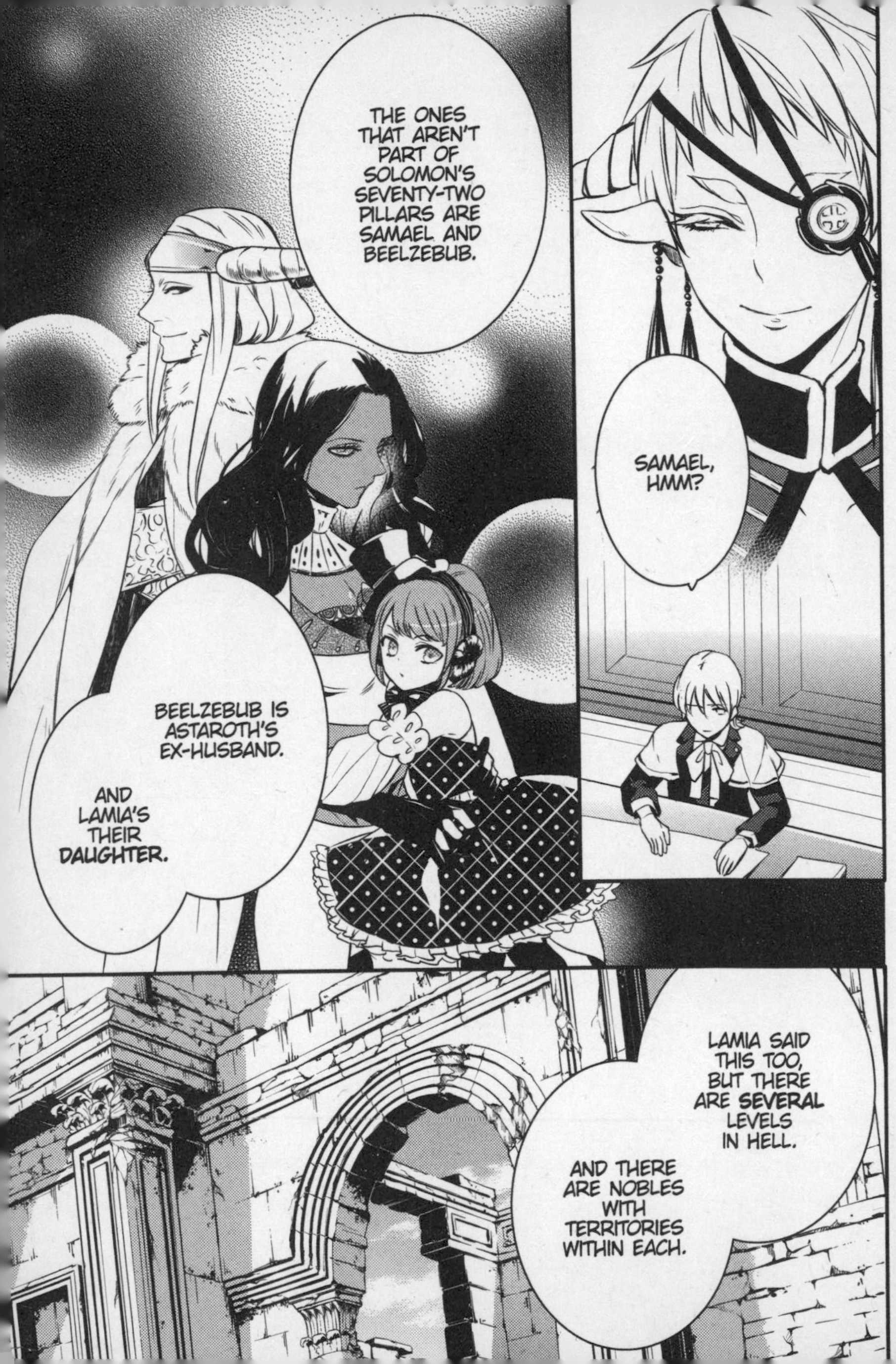
SAMAEL, HMM?
THE ONES THAT AREN'T PART OF SOLOMON'S SEVENTY-TWO PILLARS ARE SAMAEL AND BEELZEBUB.
BEELZEBUB IS ASTAROTH'S EX-HUSBAND.
AND LAMIA'S THEIR DAUGHTER.
LAMIA SAID THIS TOO, BUT THERE ARE SEVERAL LEVELS IN HELL.
AND THERE ARE NOBLES WITH TERRITORIES WITHIN EACH.

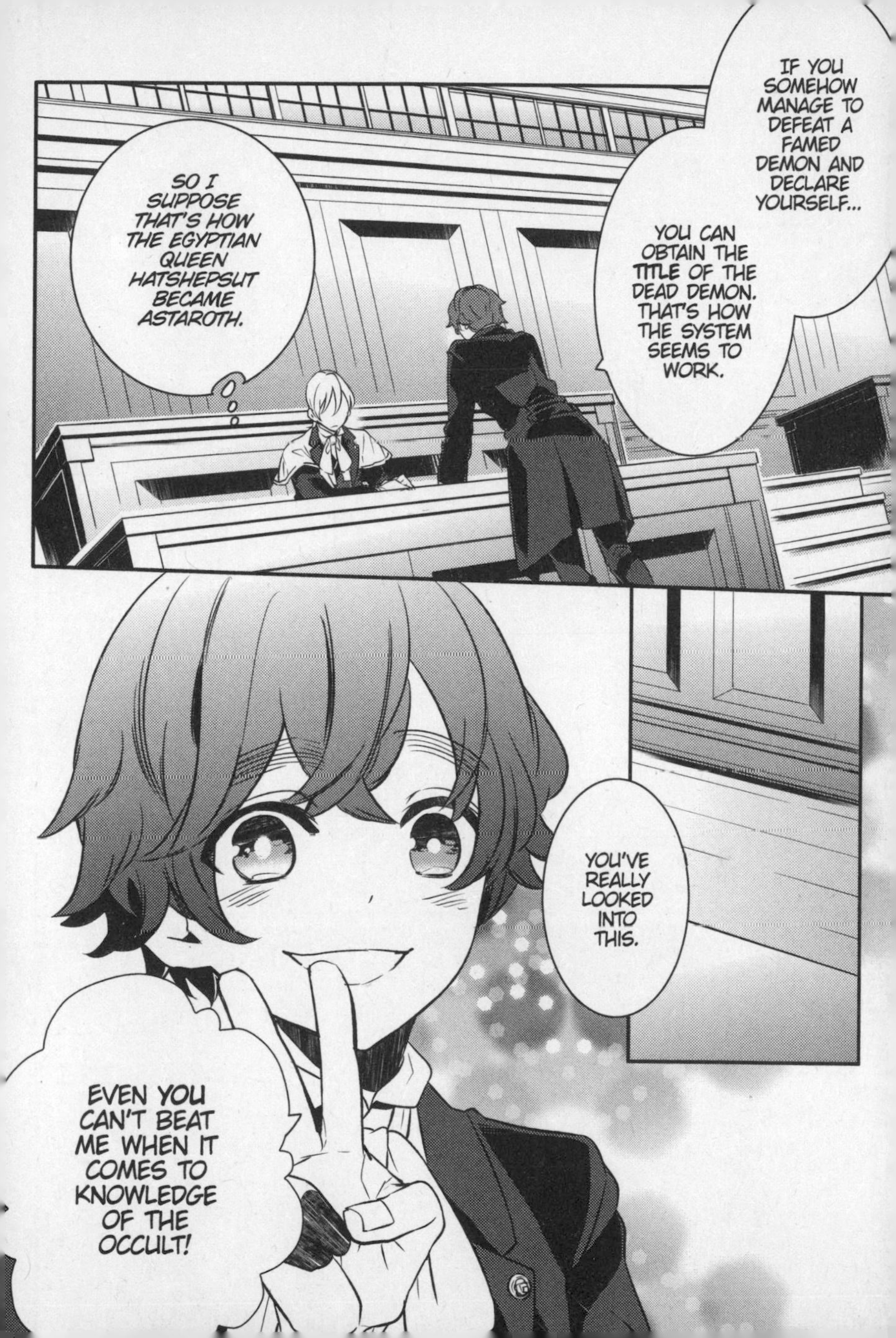
IF YOU SOMEHOW MANAGE TO DEFEAT A FAMED DEMON AND DECLARE YOURSELF...
YOU CAN OBTAIN THE TITLE OF THE DEAD DEMON. THAT'S HOW THE SYSTEM SEEMS TO WORK.
SO I SUPPOSE THAT'S HOW THE EGYPTIAN QUEEN HATSHEPSUT BECAME ASTAROTH.
YOU'VE REALLY LOOKED INTO THIS.
EVEN YOU CAN'T BEAT ME WHEN IT COMES TO KNOWLEDGE OF THE OCCULT!

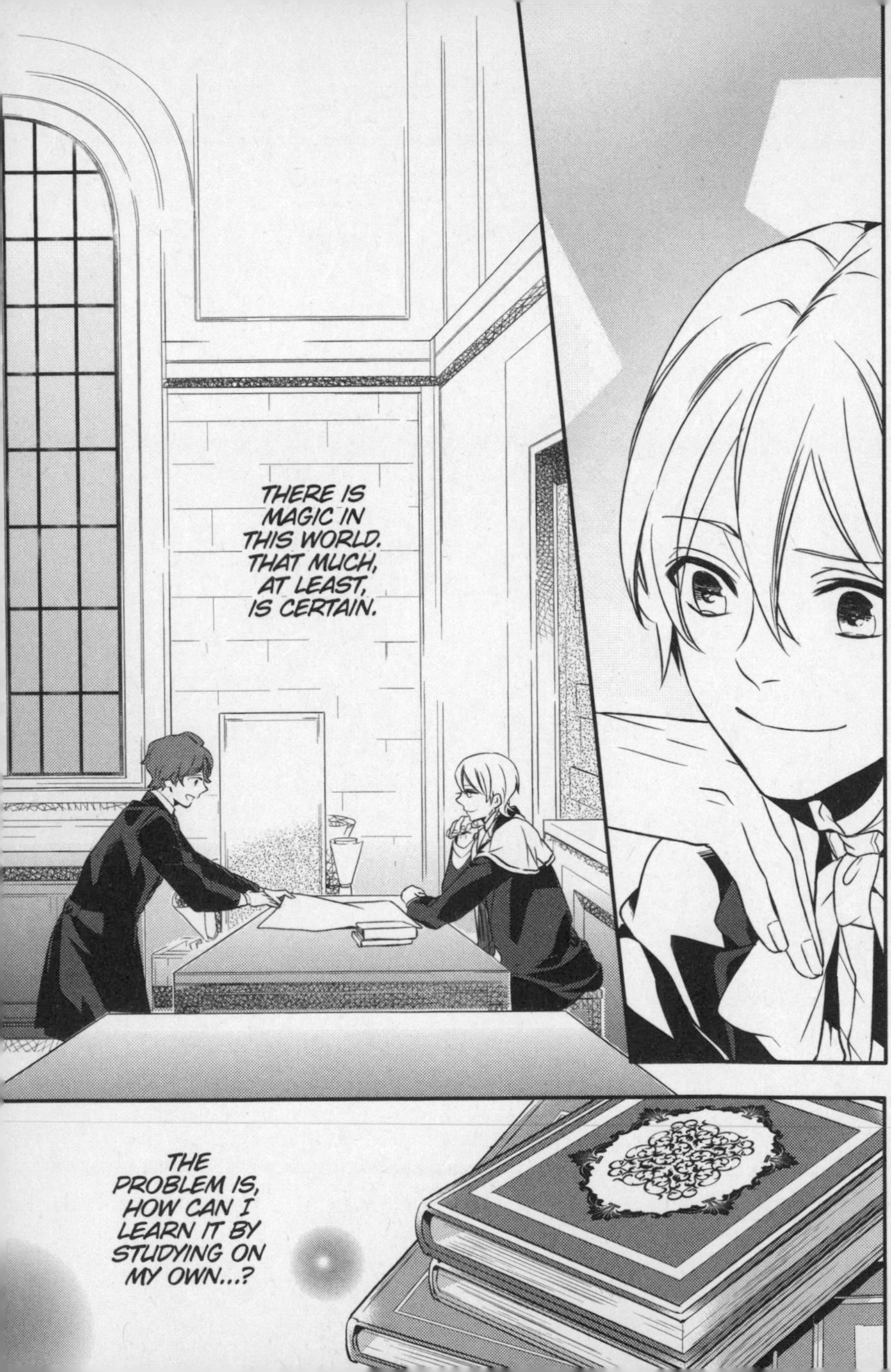
THERE IS MAGIC IN THIS WORLD. THAT MUCH, AT LEAST, IS CERTAIN.
THE PROBLEM IS, HOW CAN I LEARN IT BY STUDYING ON MY OWN...?

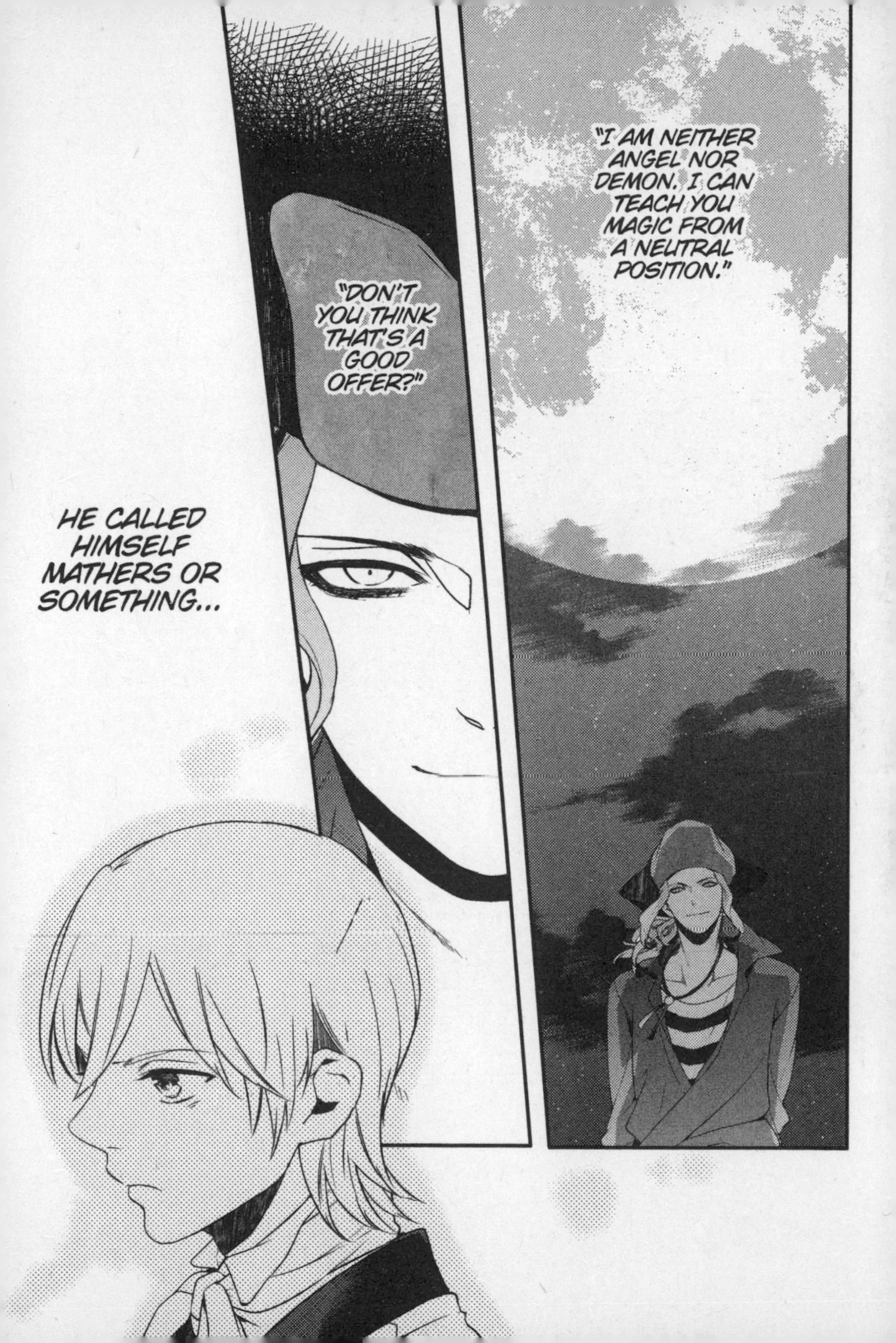
"I AM NEITHER ANGEL NOR DEMON. I CAN TEACH YOU MAGIC FROM A NEUTRAL POSITION."
"DON'T YOU THINK THAT'S A GOOD OFFER?"
HE CALLED HIMSELF MATHERS OR SOMETHING...

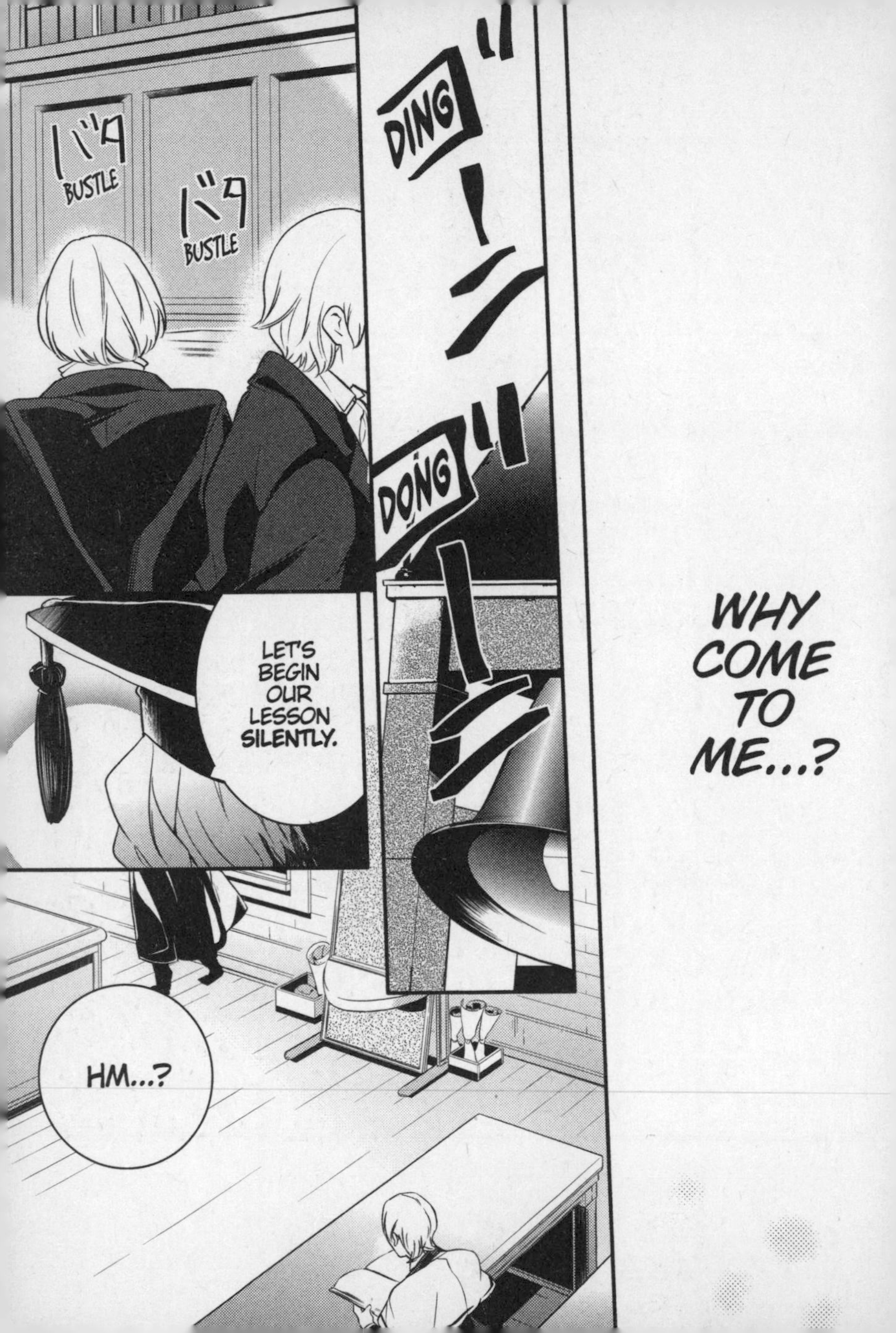
WHY COME TO ME...?
DING
DONG
バタ BUSTLE
バタ BUSTLE
LET'S BEGIN OUR LESSON SILENTLY.
HM...?

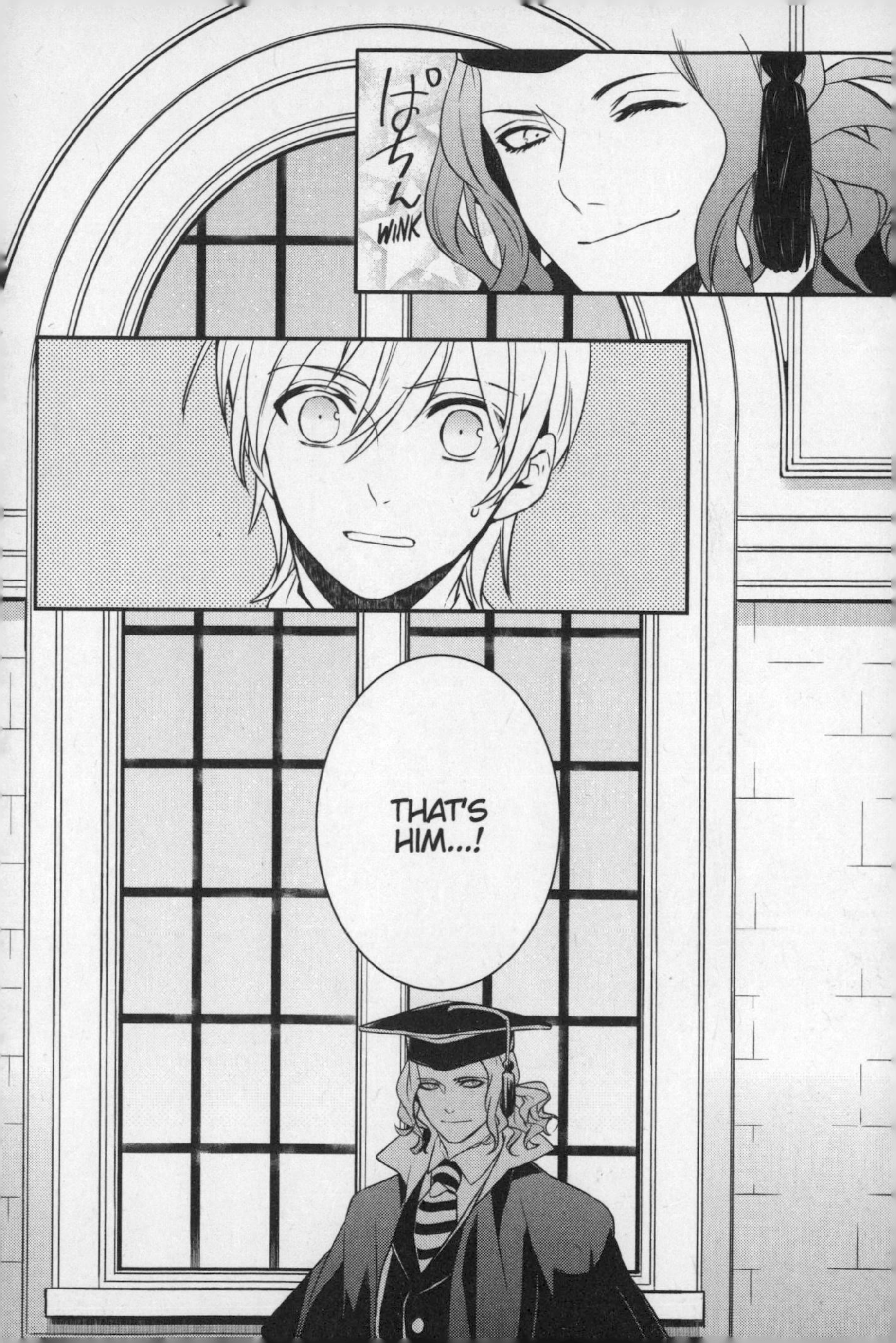
ぱちん
WINK
THAT'S HIM...!

Pillar 36

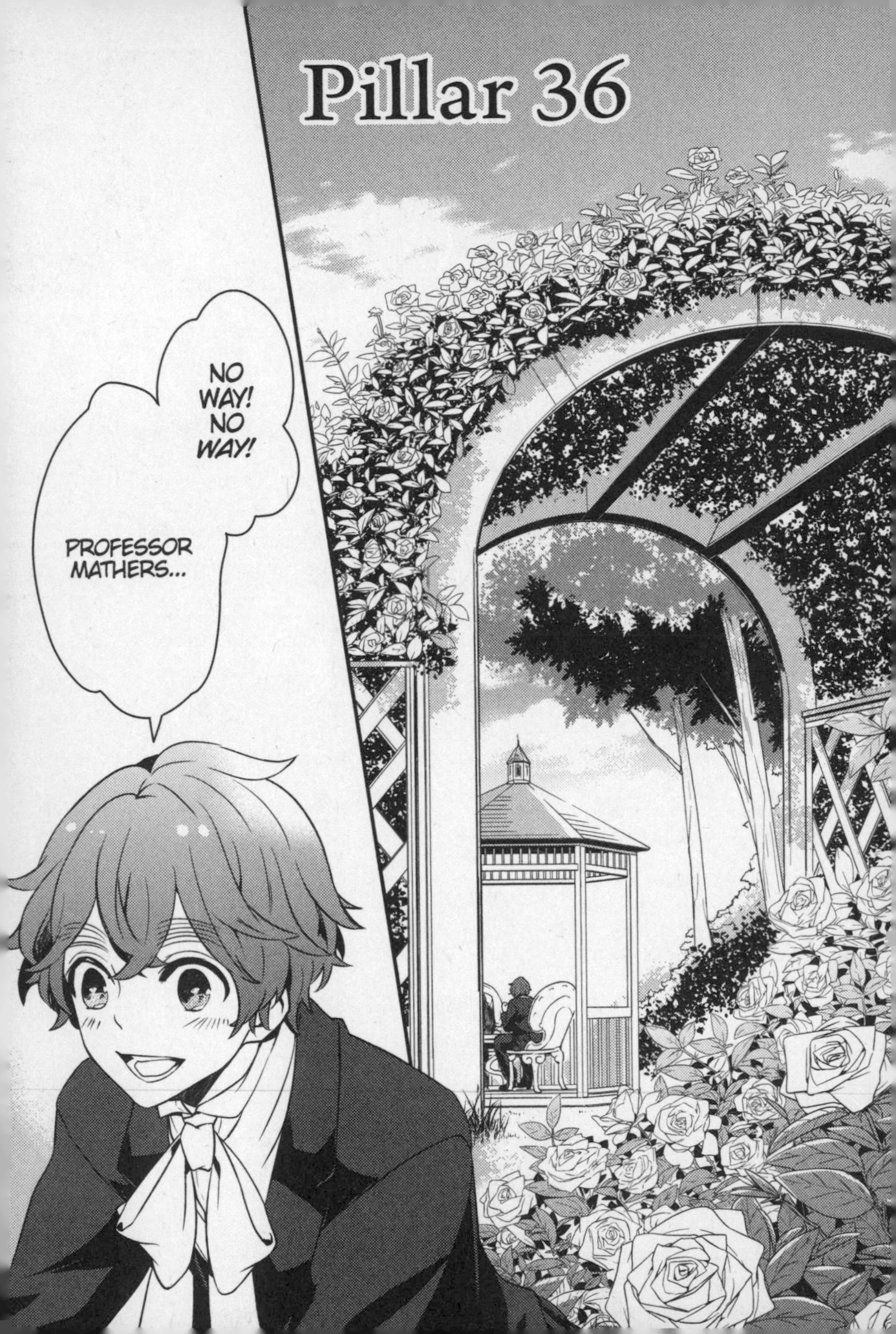
NO WAY! NO WAY!
PROFESSOR MATHERS...

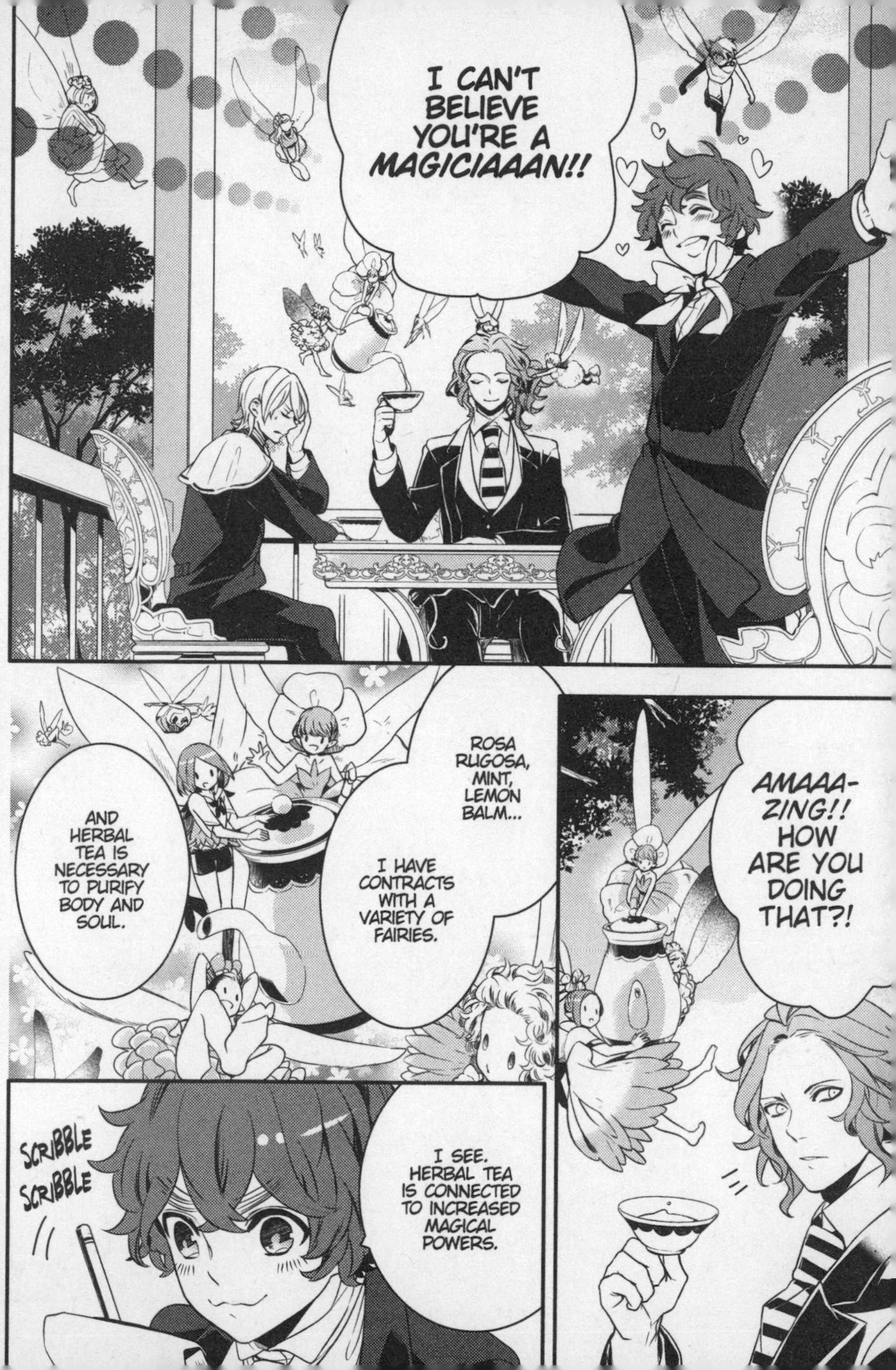
I CAN'T BELIEVE YOU'RE A MAGICIAAAN!!
AMAAA-ZING!! HOW ARE YOU DOING THAT?!
ROSA RUGOSA, MINT, LEMON BALM...
I HAVE CONTRACTS WITH A VARIETY OF FAIRIES.
AND HERBAL TEA IS NECESSARY TO PURIFY BODY AND SOUL.
I SEE. HERBAL TEA IS CONNECTED TO INCREASED MAGICAL POWERS.
SCRIBBLE SCRIBBLE

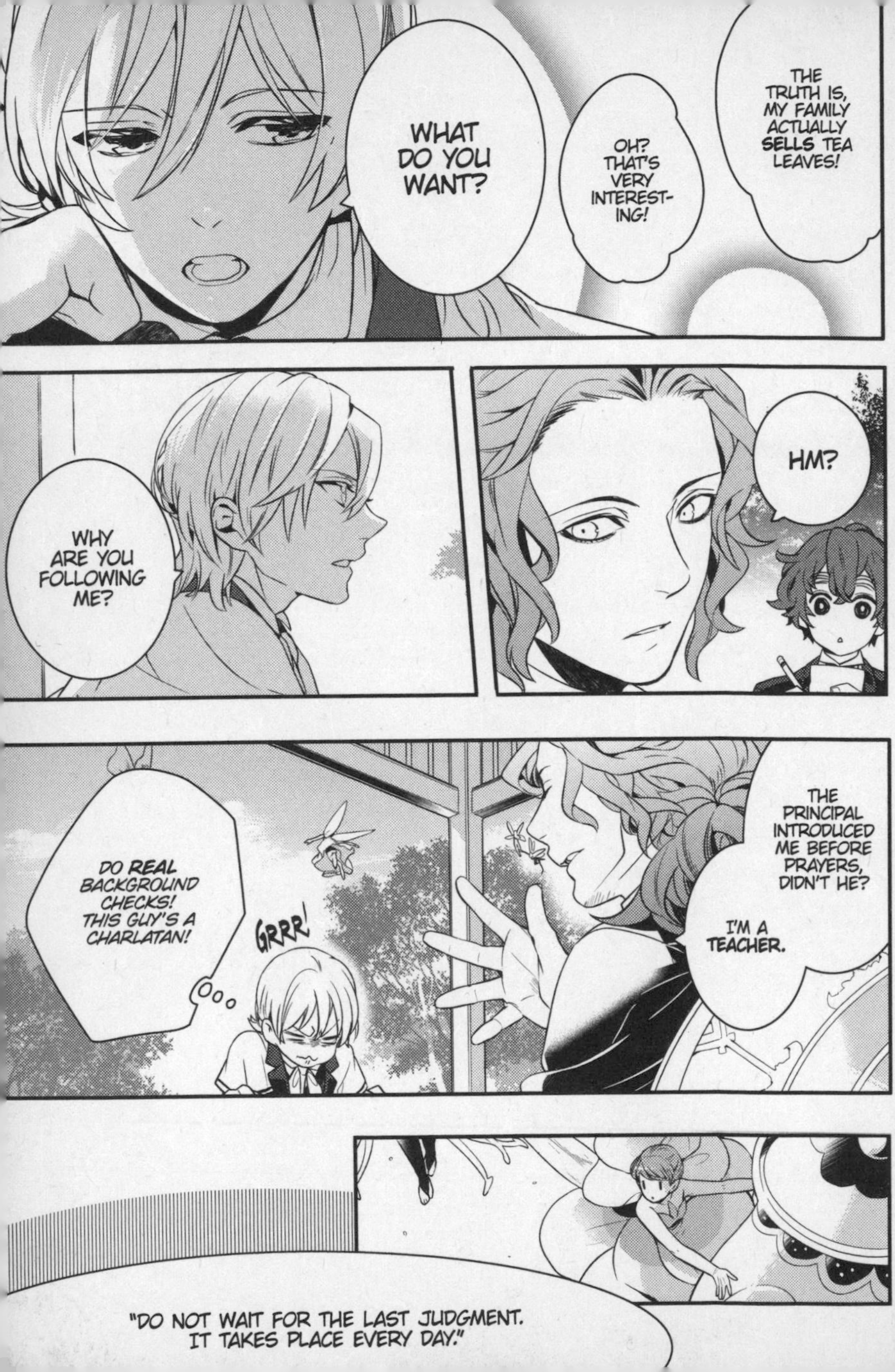
THE TRUTH IS, MY FAMILY ACTUALLY **SELLS** TEA LEAVES!
OH? THAT'S VERY INTEREST-ING!
WHAT DO YOU WANT?
HM?
WHY ARE YOU FOLLOWING ME?
THE PRINCIPAL INTRODUCED ME BEFORE PRAYERS, DIDN'T HE?
I'M A TEACHER.
GRRR!
DO **REAL** BACKGROUND CHECKS! THIS GUY'S A CHARLATAN!
"DO NOT WAIT FOR THE LAST JUDGMENT. IT TAKES PLACE EVERY DAY."

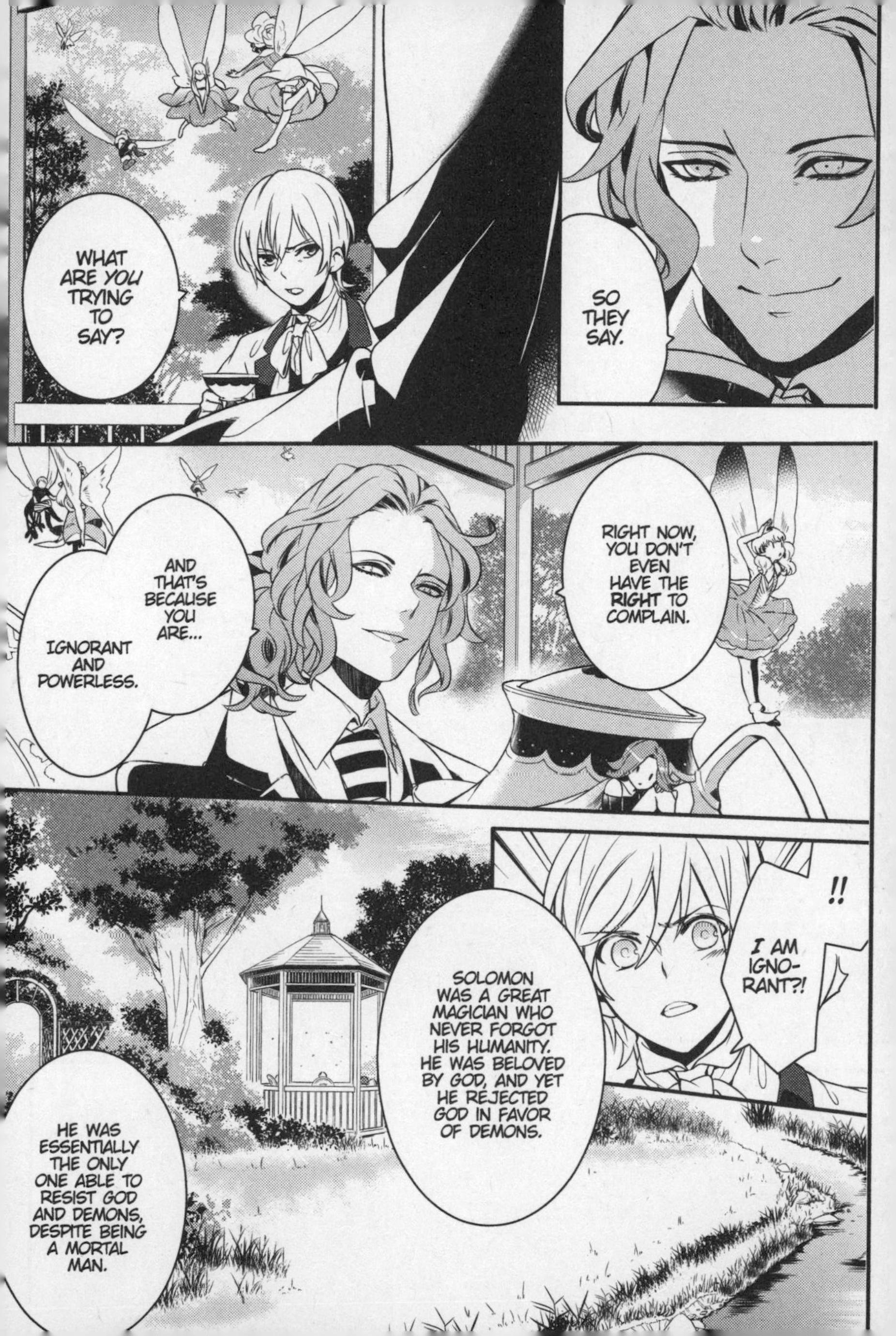
SO THEY SAY.
WHAT ARE YOU TRYING TO SAY?
RIGHT NOW, YOU DON'T EVEN HAVE THE RIGHT TO COMPLAIN.
AND THAT'S BECAUSE YOU ARE...
IGNORANT AND POWERLESS.
!!
I AM IGNO-RANT?!
SOLOMON WAS A GREAT MAGICIAN WHO NEVER FORGOT HIS HUMANITY. HE WAS BELOVED BY GOD, AND YET HE REJECTED GOD IN FAVOR OF DEMONS.
HE WAS ESSENTIALLY THE ONLY ONE ABLE TO RESIST GOD AND DEMONS, DESPITE BEING A MORTAL MAN.

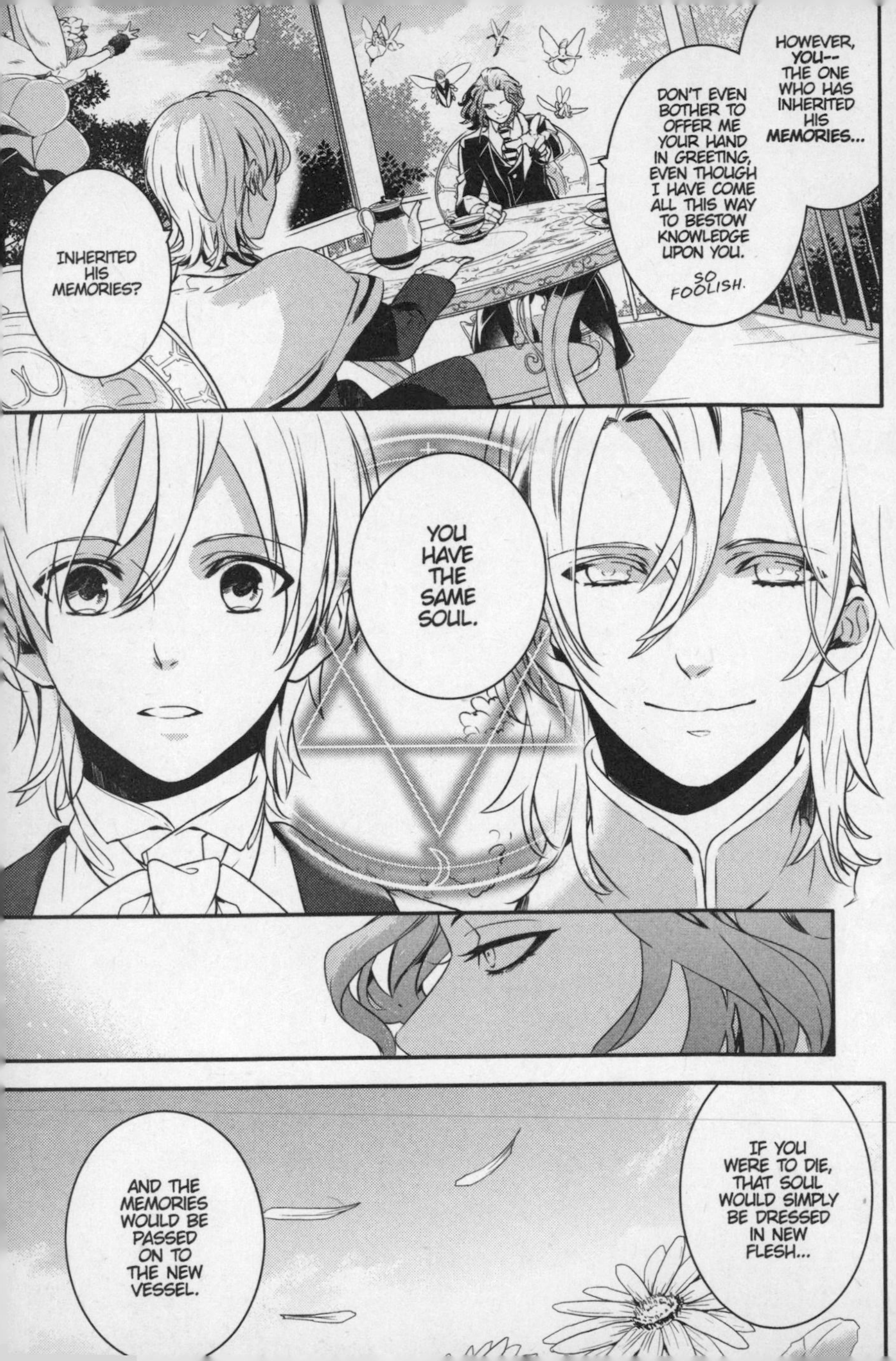
HOWEVER, YOU-- THE ONE WHO HAS INHERITED HIS MEMORIES...
DON'T EVEN BOTHER TO OFFER ME YOUR HAND IN GREETING, EVEN THOUGH I HAVE COME ALL THIS WAY TO BESTOW KNOWLEDGE UPON YOU.
SO FOOLISH.
INHERITED HIS MEMORIES?
YOU HAVE THE SAME SOUL.
IF YOU WERE TO DIE, THAT SOUL WOULD SIMPLY BE DRESSED IN NEW FLESH...
AND THE MEMORIES WOULD BE PASSED ON TO THE NEW VESSEL.

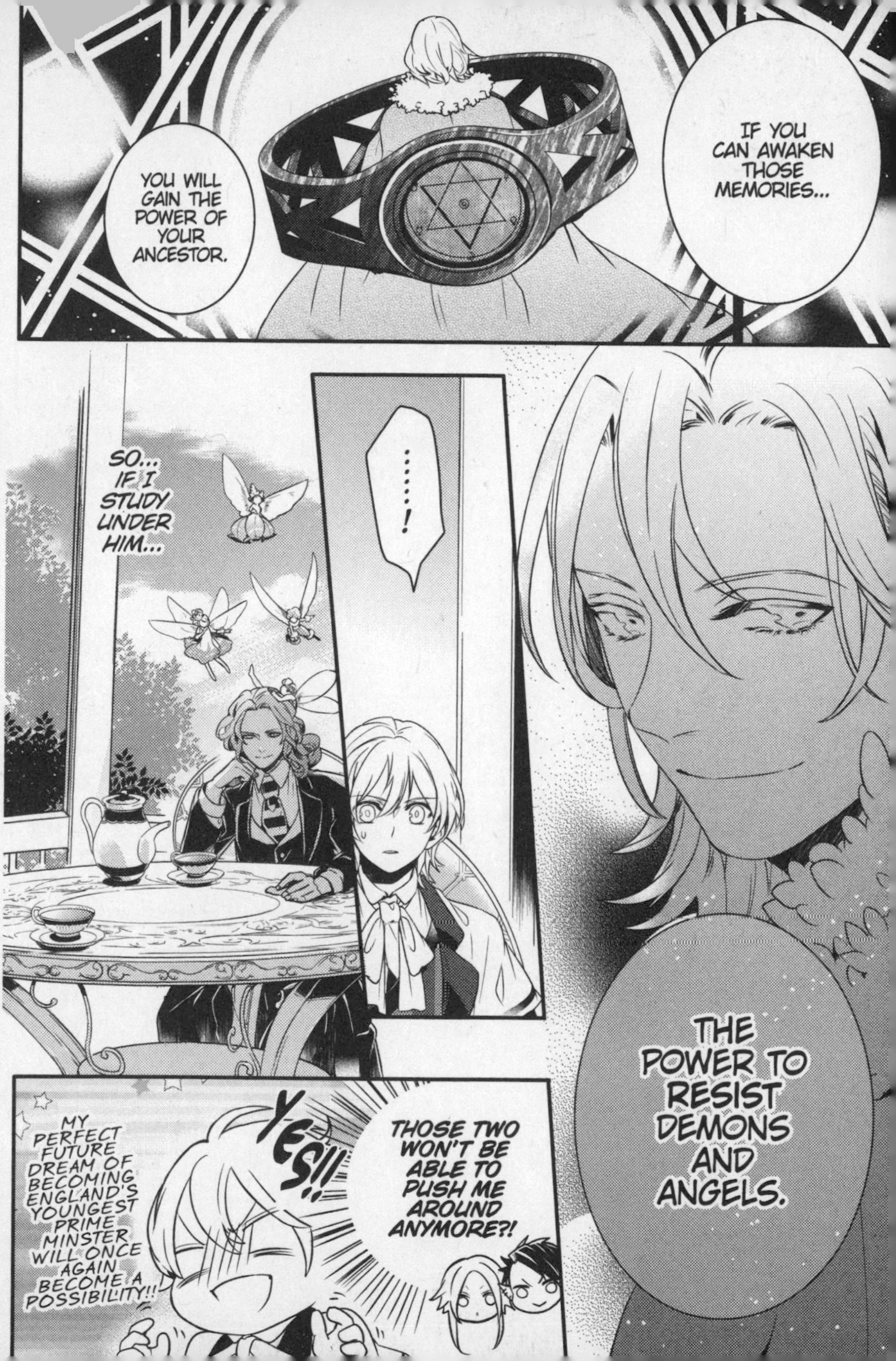
IF YOU CAN AWAKEN THOSE MEMORIES...
YOU WILL GAIN THE POWER OF YOUR ANCESTOR.
THE POWER TO RESIST DEMONS AND ANGELS.
......!
SO... IF I STUDY UNDER HIM...
THOSE TWO WON'T BE ABLE TO PUSH ME AROUND ANYMORE?!
YES!!
MY PERFECT FUTURE DREAM OF BECOMING ENGLAND'S YOUNGEST PRIME MINSTER WILL ONCE AGAIN BECOME A POSSIBILITY!!

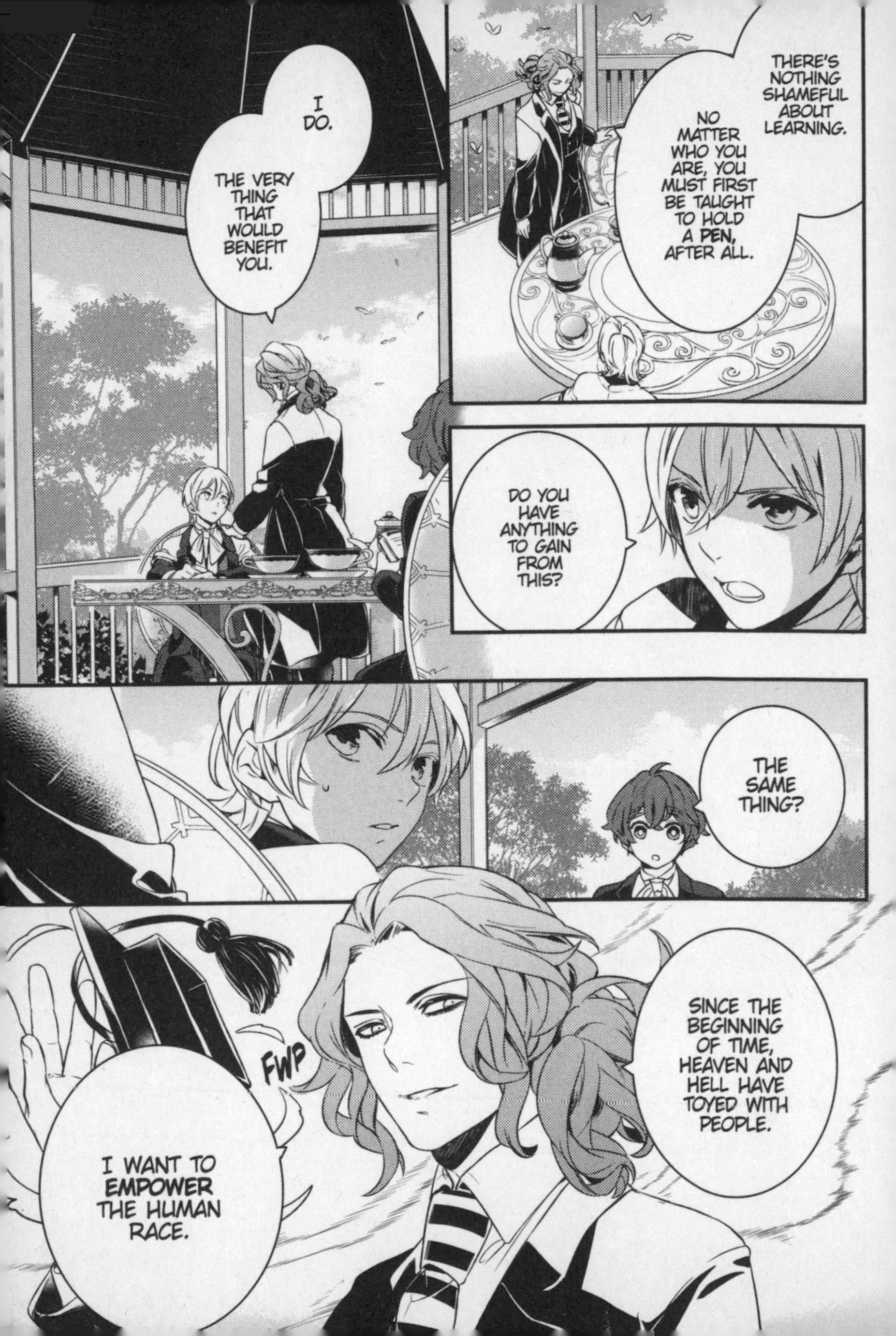

THERE'S NOTHING SHAMEFUL ABOUT LEARNING.
NO MATTER WHO YOU ARE, YOU MUST FIRST BE TAUGHT TO HOLD A PEN, AFTER ALL.
DO YOU HAVE ANYTHING TO GAIN FROM THIS?
I DO.
THE VERY THING THAT WOULD BENEFIT YOU.
THE SAME THING?
SINCE THE BEGINNING OF TIME, HEAVEN AND HELL HAVE TOYED WITH PEOPLE.
FWP
I WANT TO EMPOWER THE HUMAN RACE.

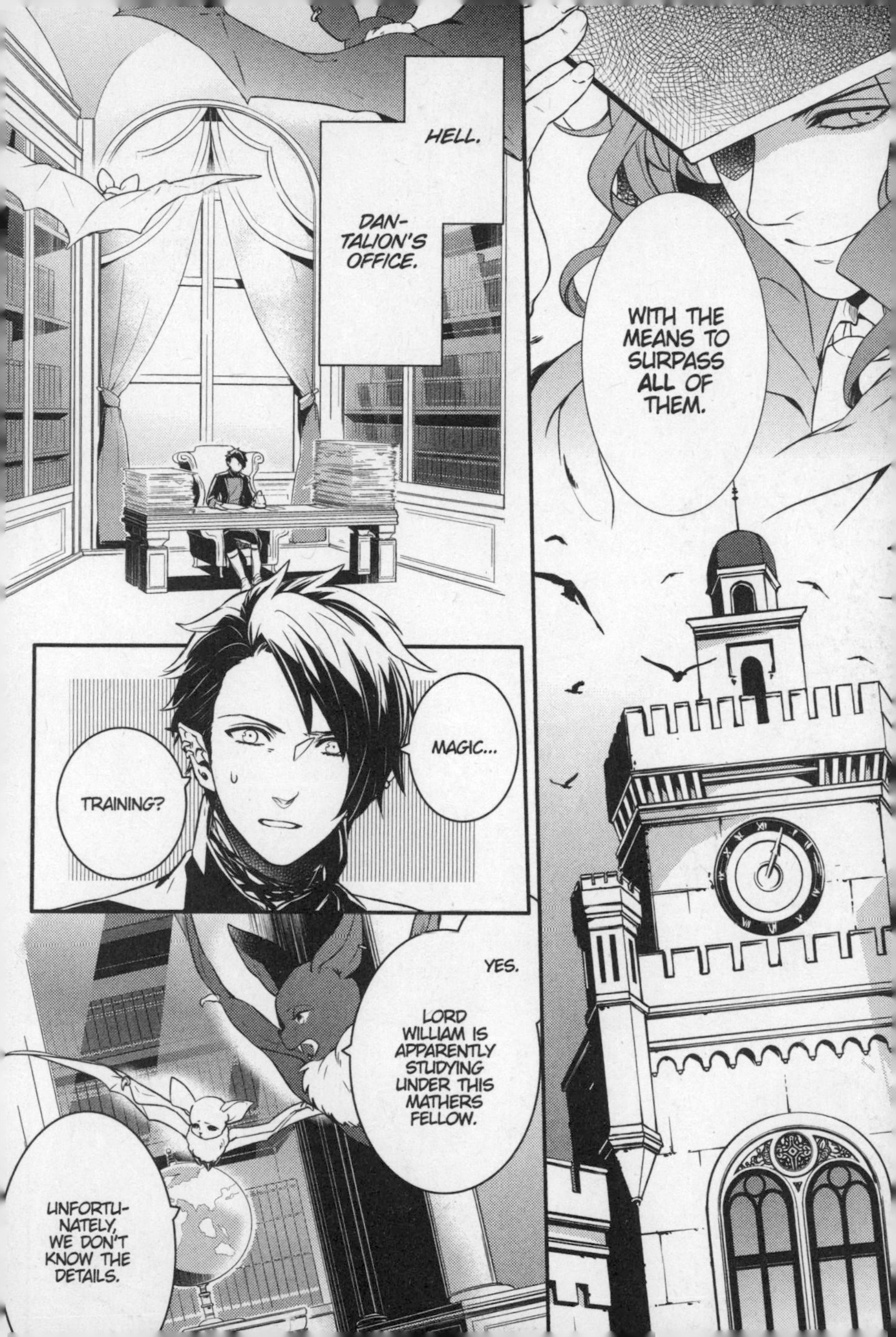
WITH THE MEANS TO SURPASS ALL OF THEM.
HELL.
DAN-TALION'S OFFICE.
MAGIC...
TRAINING?
YES.
LORD WILLIAM IS APPARENTLY STUDYING UNDER THIS MATHERS FELLOW.
UNFORTU-NATELY, WE DON'T KNOW THE DETAILS.

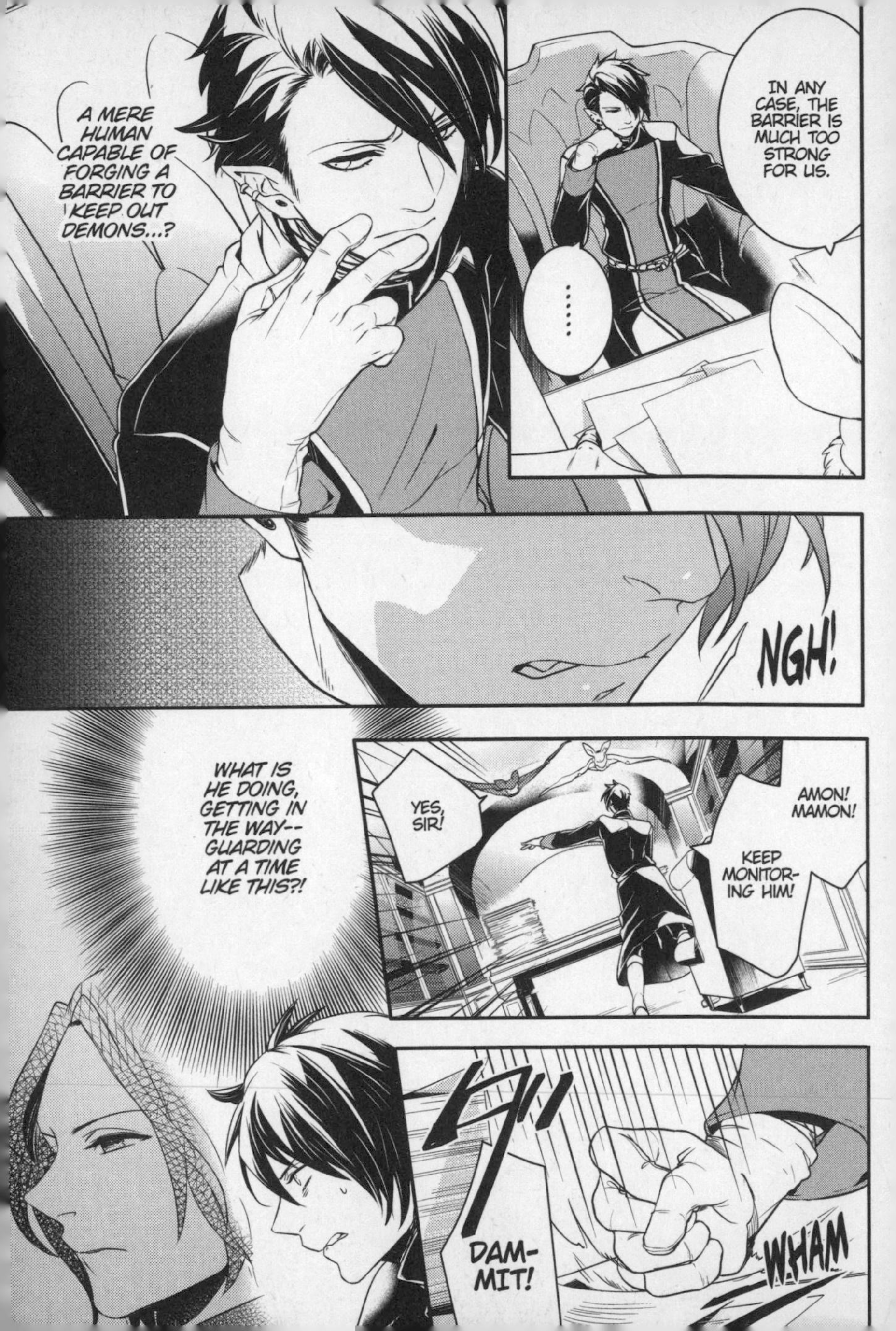
IN ANY CASE, THE BARRIER IS MUCH TOO STRONG FOR US.
......
A MERE HUMAN CAPABLE OF FORGING A BARRIER TO KEEP OUT DEMONS...?
NGH!
AMON! MAMON!
KEEP MONITORING HIM!
YES, SIR!
WHAT IS HE DOING, GETTING IN THE WAY-- GUARDING AT A TIME LIKE THIS?!
WHAM
DAM-MIT!

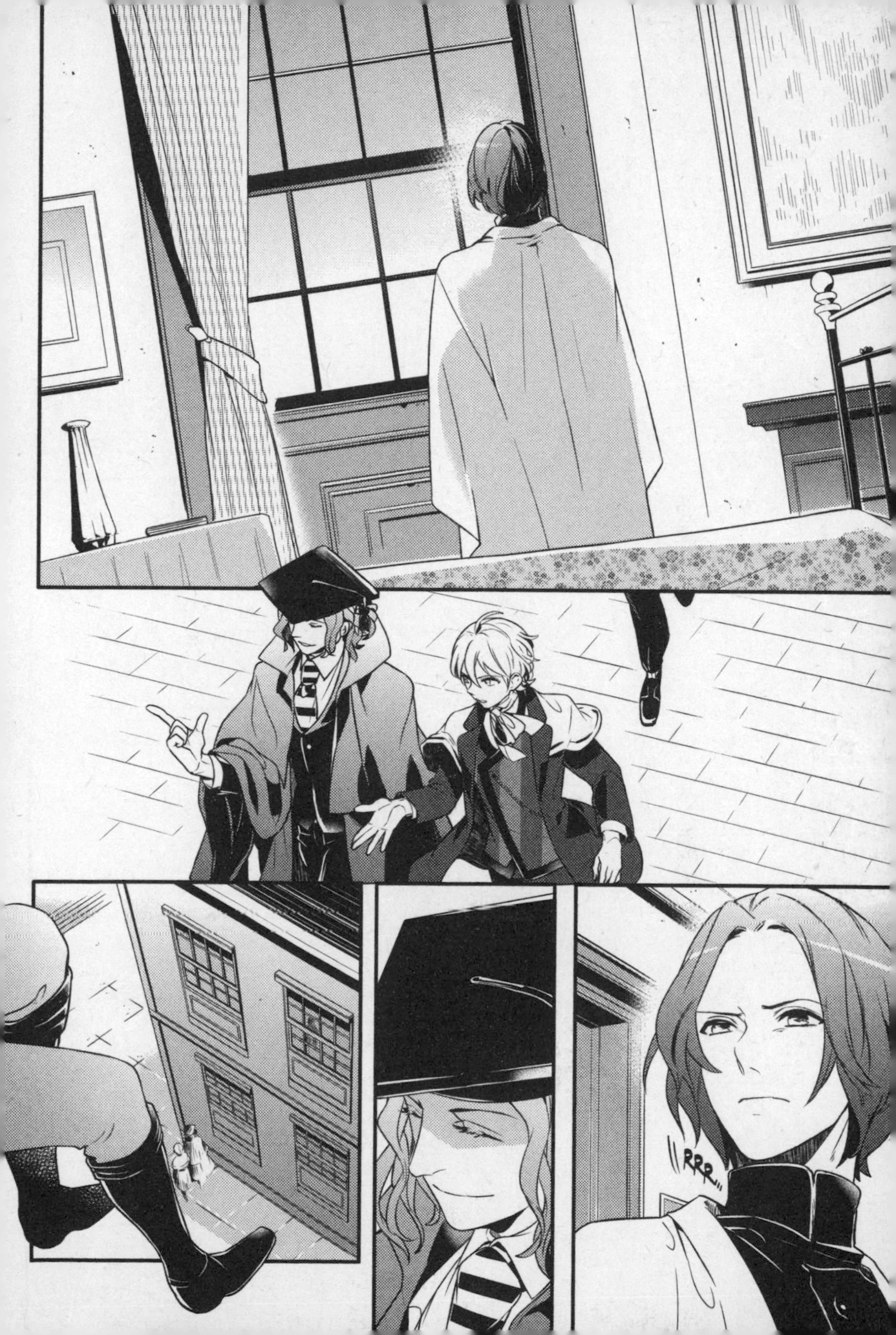
RRR...

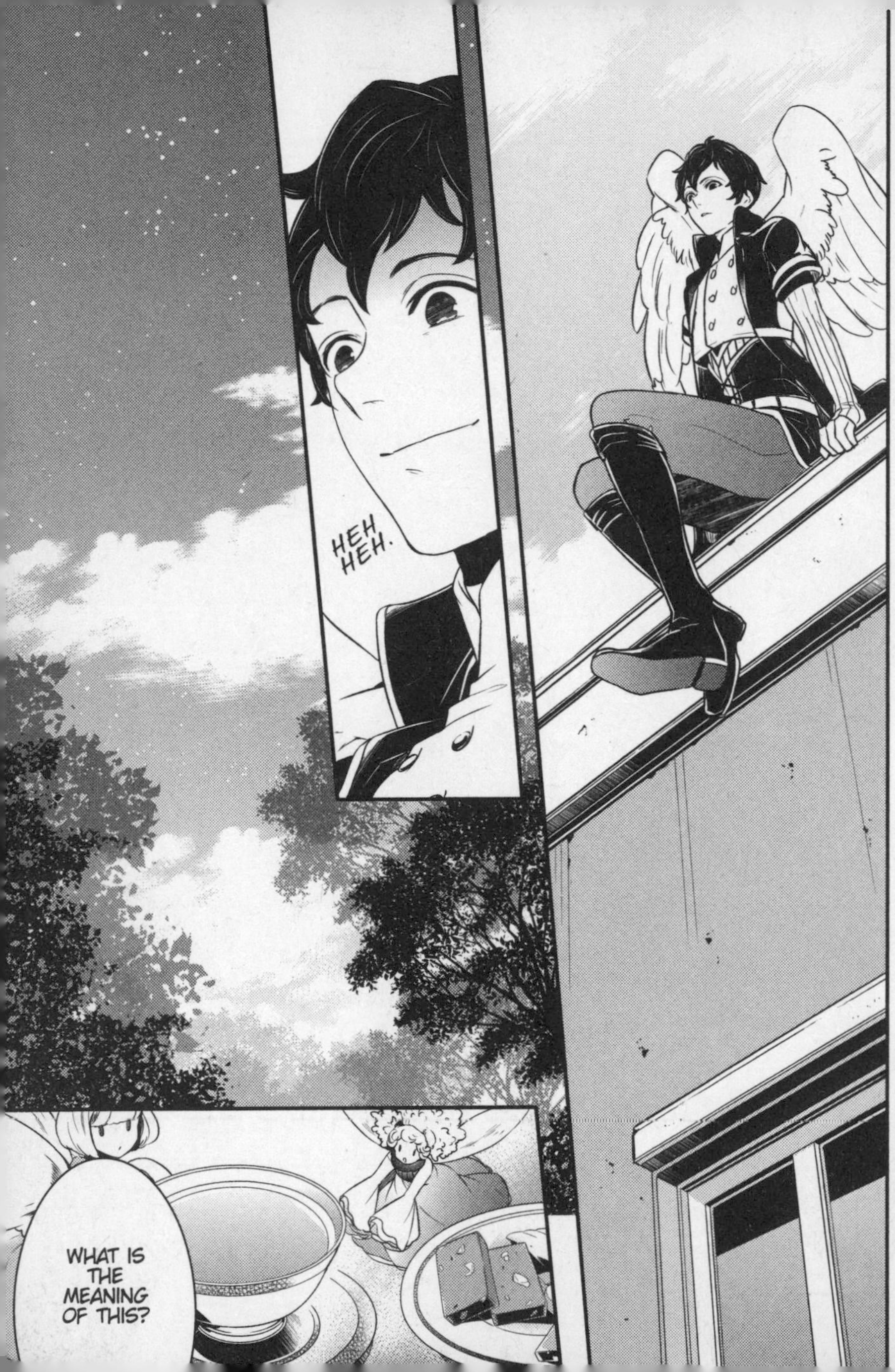
HEH HEH.
WHAT IS THE MEANING OF THIS?

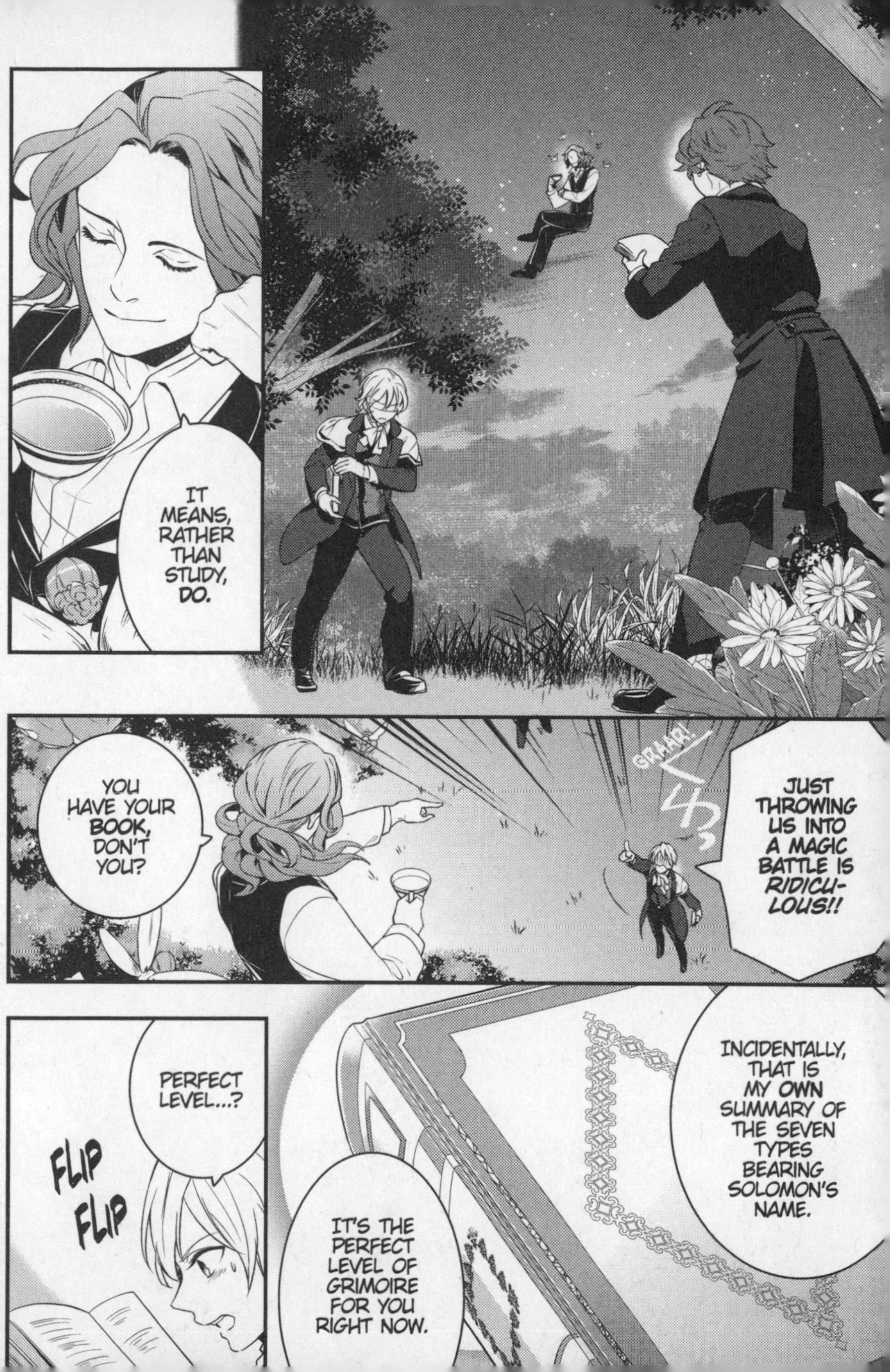
IT MEANS, RATHER THAN STUDY, DO.
JUST THROWING US INTO A MAGIC BATTLE IS *RIDICULOUS!!*
GRAAH!
YOU HAVE YOUR BOOK, DON'T YOU?
INCIDENTALLY, THAT IS MY OWN SUMMARY OF THE SEVEN TYPES BEARING SOLOMON'S NAME.
IT'S THE PERFECT LEVEL OF GRIMOIRE FOR YOU RIGHT NOW.
PERFECT LEVEL...?
FLIP FLIP

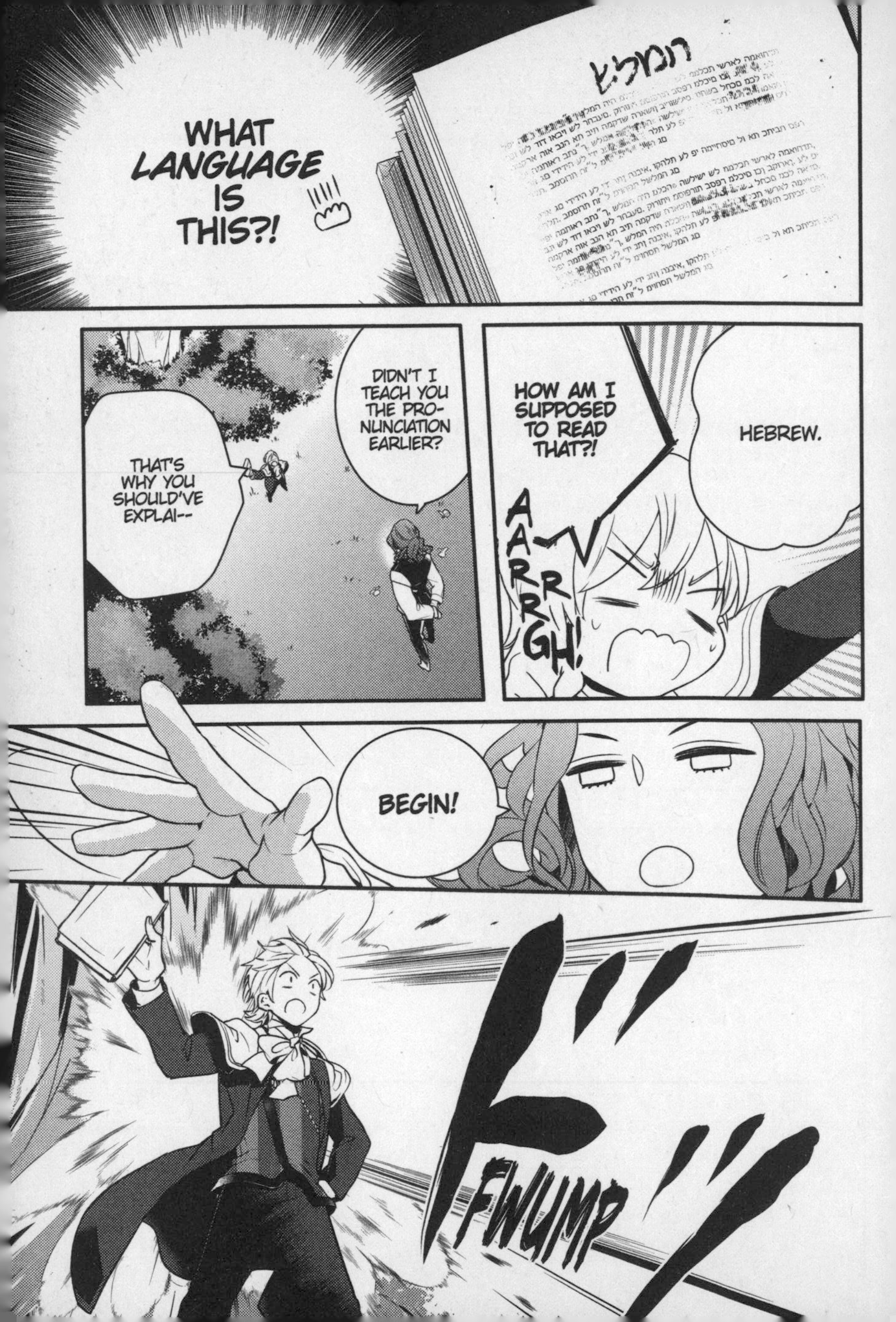
WHAT LANGUAGE IS THIS?!
HEBREW.
HOW AM I SUPPOSED TO READ THAT?!
AARRRGH!
DIDN'T I TEACH YOU THE PRO-NUNCIATION EARLIER?
THAT'S WHY YOU SHOULD'VE EXPLAI--
BEGIN!
FWUMP

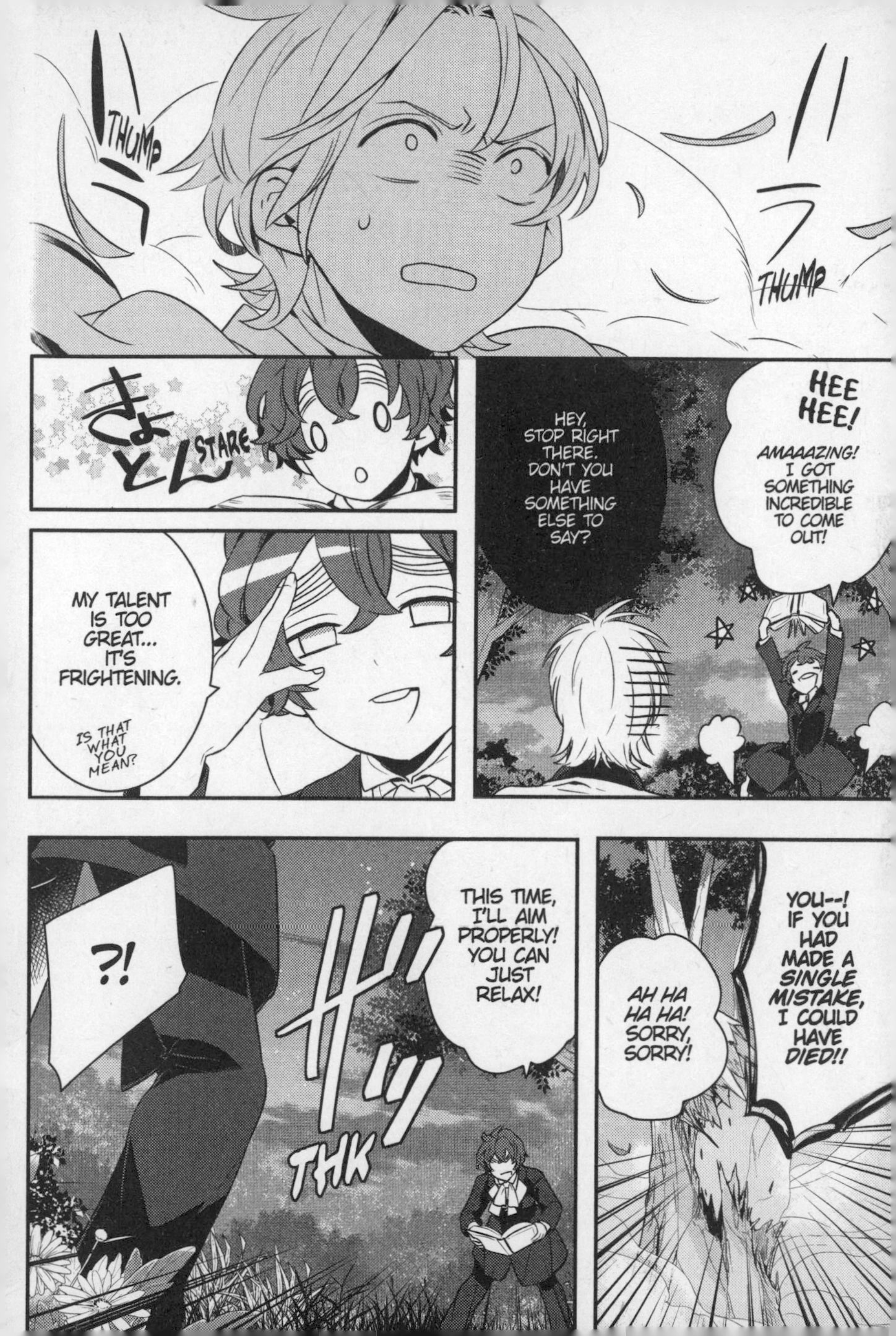
THUMP
THUMP
HEE HEE!
AMAAAZING! I GOT SOMETHING INCREDIBLE TO COME OUT!
HEY, STOP RIGHT THERE. DON'T YOU HAVE SOMETHING ELSE TO SAY?
きょとん
STARE
MY TALENT IS TOO GREAT... IT'S FRIGHTENING.
IS THAT WHAT YOU MEAN?
YOU--! IF YOU HAD MADE A SINGLE MISTAKE, I COULD HAVE DIED!!
AH HA HA HA! SORRY, SORRY!
THIS TIME, I'LL AIM PROPERLY! YOU CAN JUST RELAX!
?!
THK

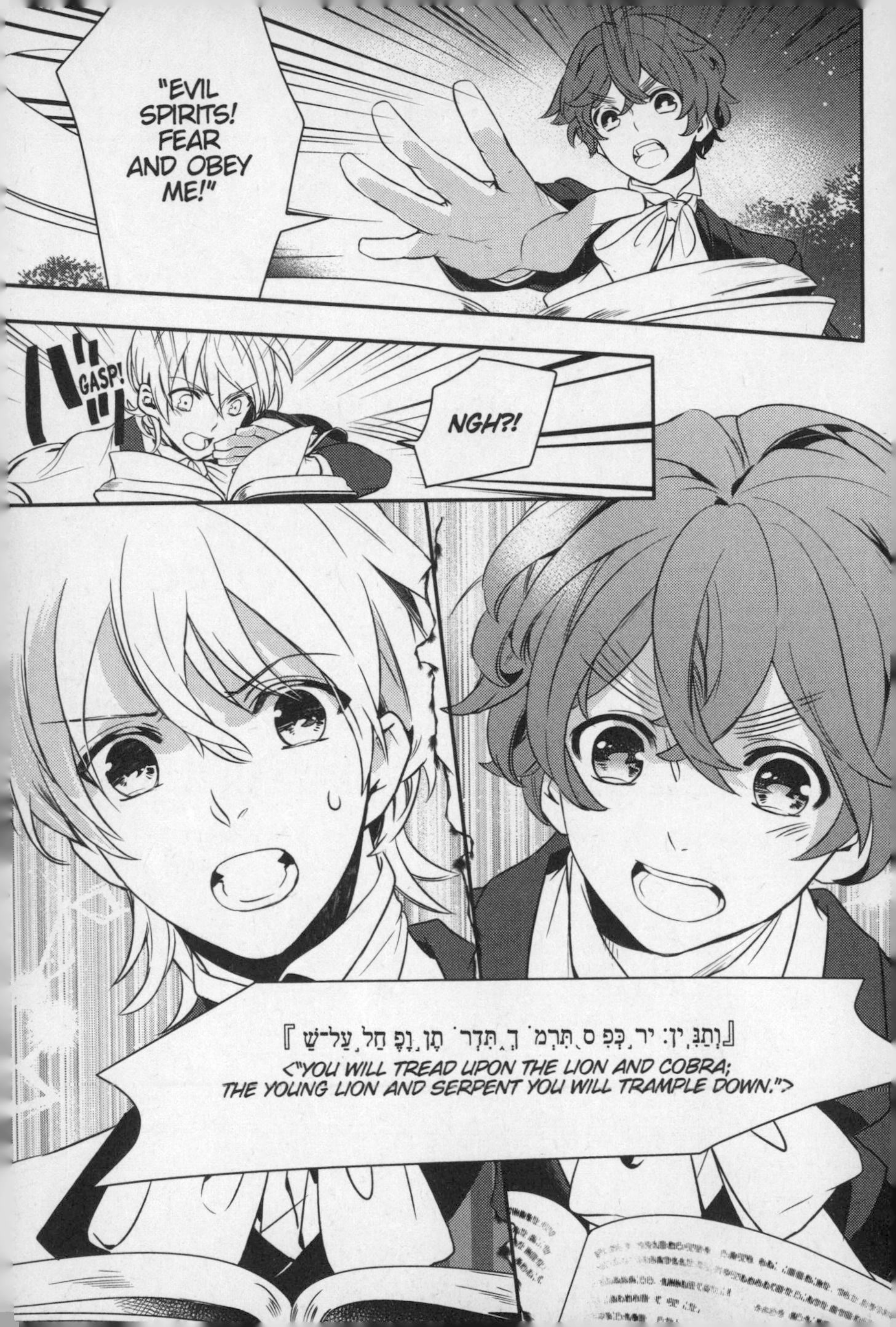
"EVIL SPIRITS! FEAR AND OBEY ME!"
NGH?!
GASP!
『וְתַנִּין: יר כְּפִ ס תִּרְמ דְ תִּדְר תֶּן וָפֶ חַל עַל־שַׁ』
<"YOU WILL TREAD UPON THE LION AND COBRA; THE YOUNG LION AND SERPENT YOU WILL TRAMPLE DOWN.">

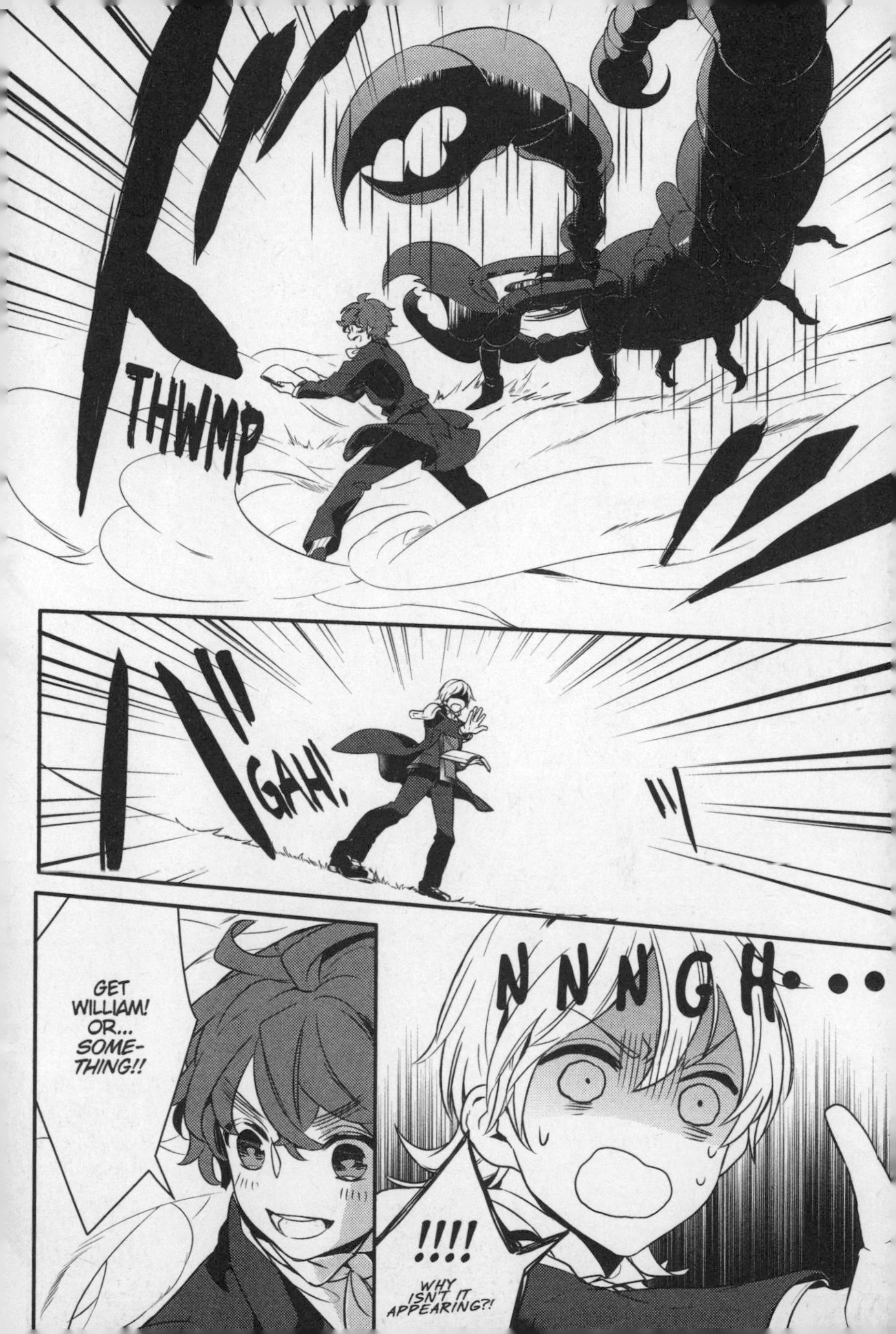
THWMP
GAH!
NNNGH...
!!!!
WHY ISN'T IT APPEARING?!
GET WILLIAM! OR... SOME-THING!!

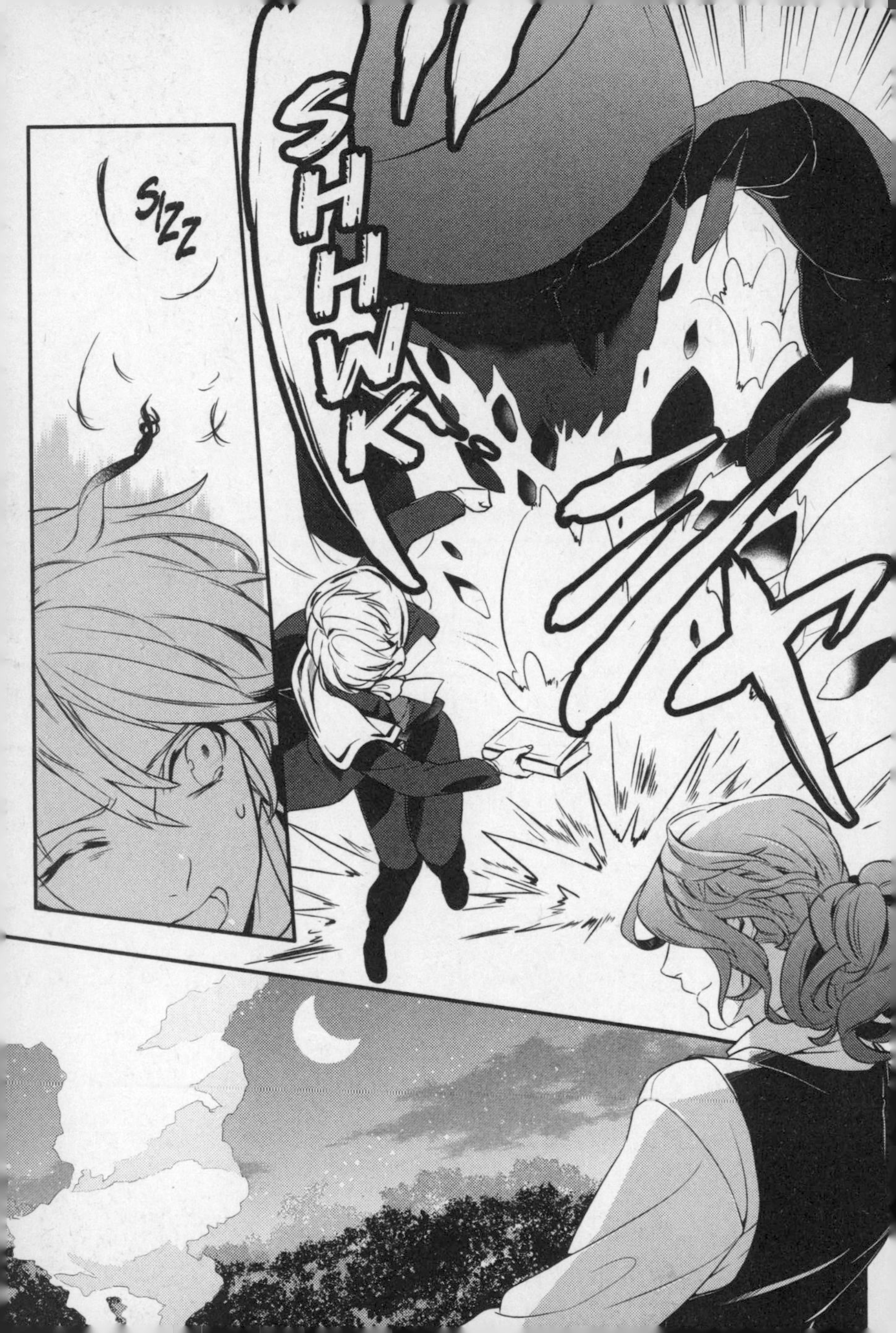
SHHWK
SIZZ

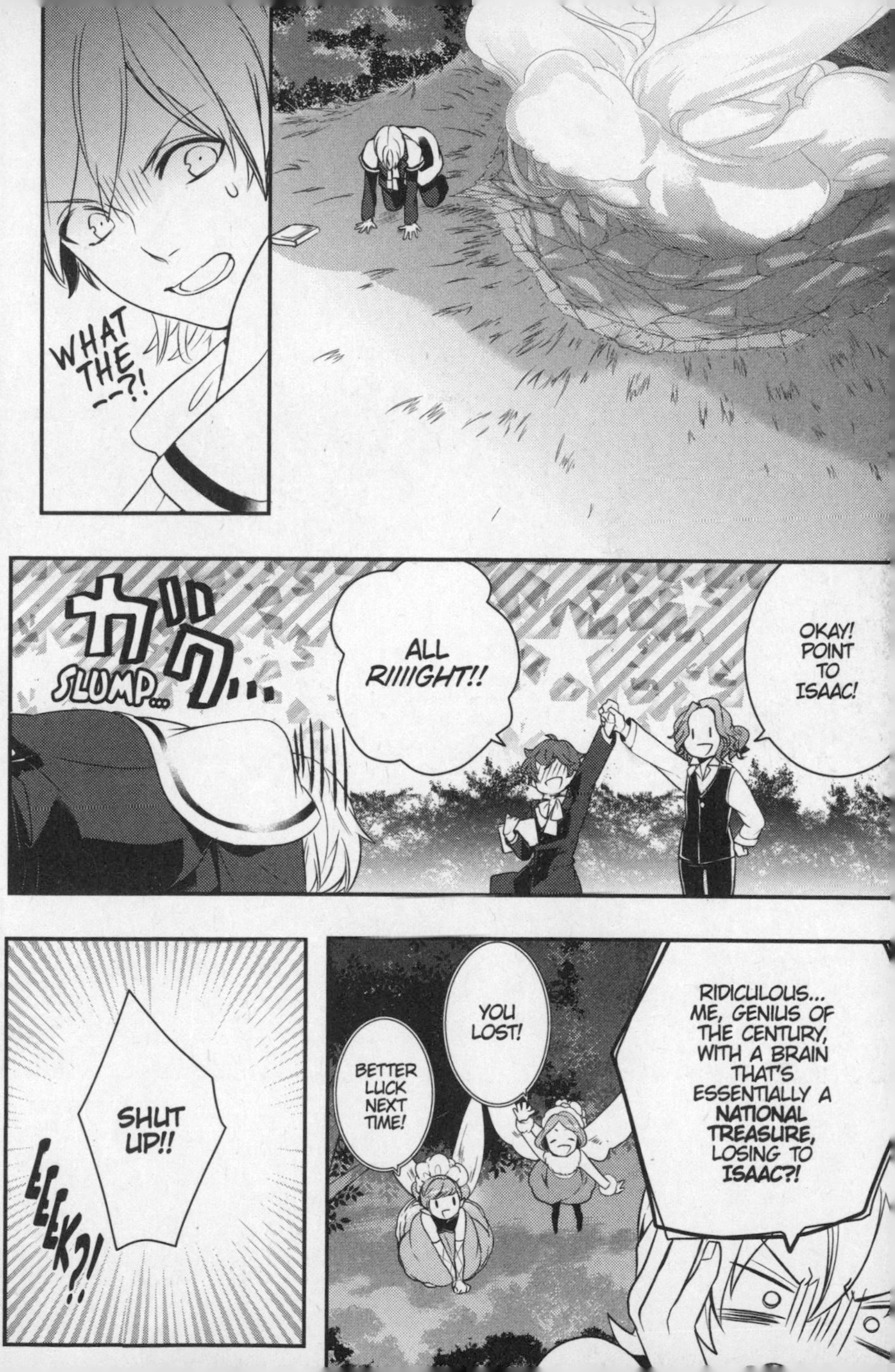
WHAT THE --?!
OKAY! POINT TO ISAAC!
ALL RIIIIGHT!!
ガク…
SLUMP...
RIDICULOUS... ME, GENIUS OF THE CENTURY, WITH A BRAIN THAT'S ESSENTIALLY A **NATIONAL TREASURE**, LOSING TO **ISAAC?!**
YOU LOST!
BETTER LUCK NEXT TIME!
SHUT UP!!
EEEK?!

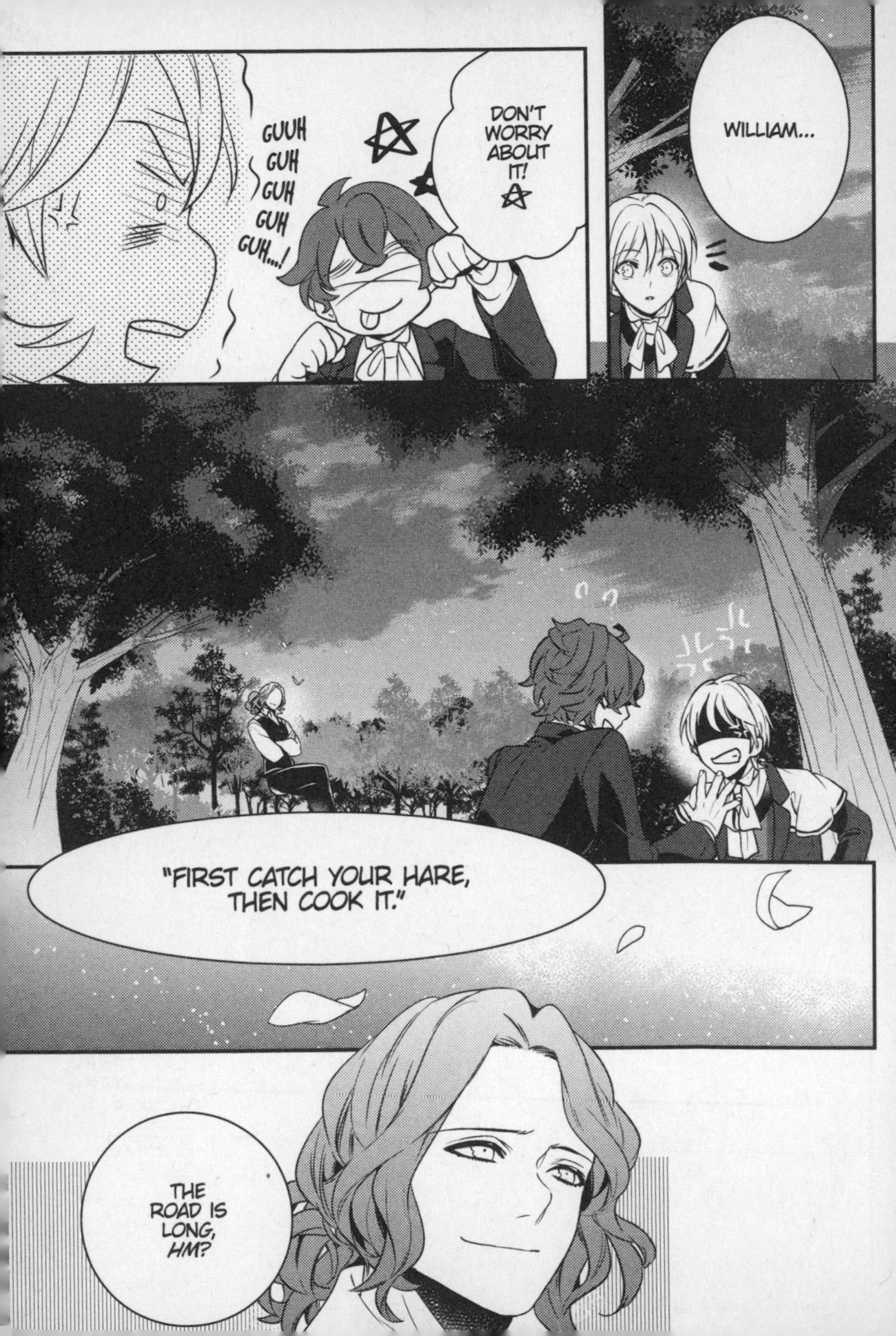
WILLIAM...
DON'T WORRY ABOUT IT!
GUUH GUH GUH GUH GUH...!
"FIRST CATCH YOUR HARE, THEN COOK IT."
THE ROAD IS LONG, HM?

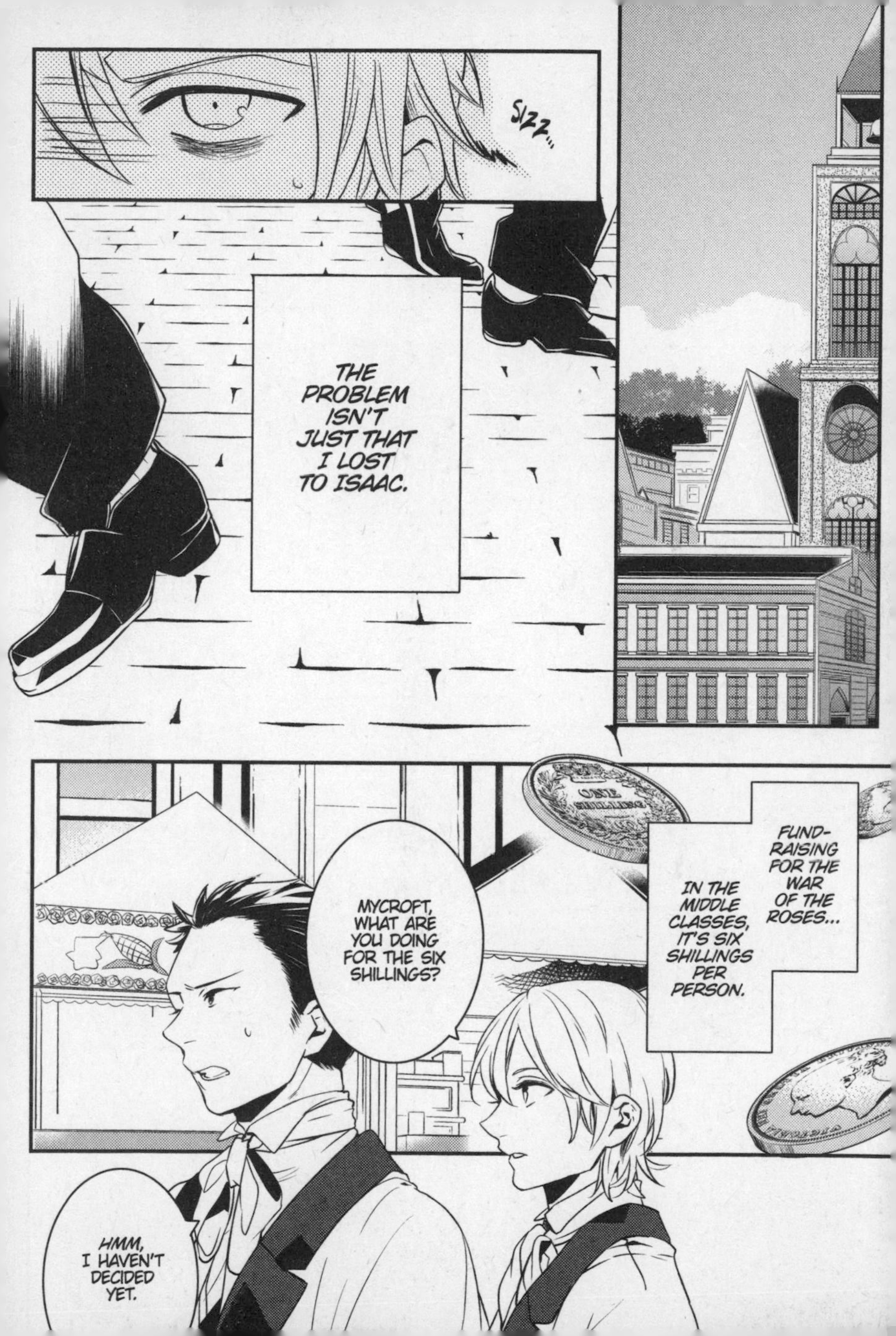
SIZZ...
THE PROBLEM ISN'T JUST THAT I LOST TO ISAAC.
ONE SHILLING
FUND-RAISING FOR THE WAR OF THE ROSES...
IN THE MIDDLE CLASSES, IT'S SIX SHILLINGS PER PERSON.
MYCROFT, WHAT ARE YOU DOING FOR THE SIX SHILLINGS?
HMM, I HAVEN'T DECIDED YET.

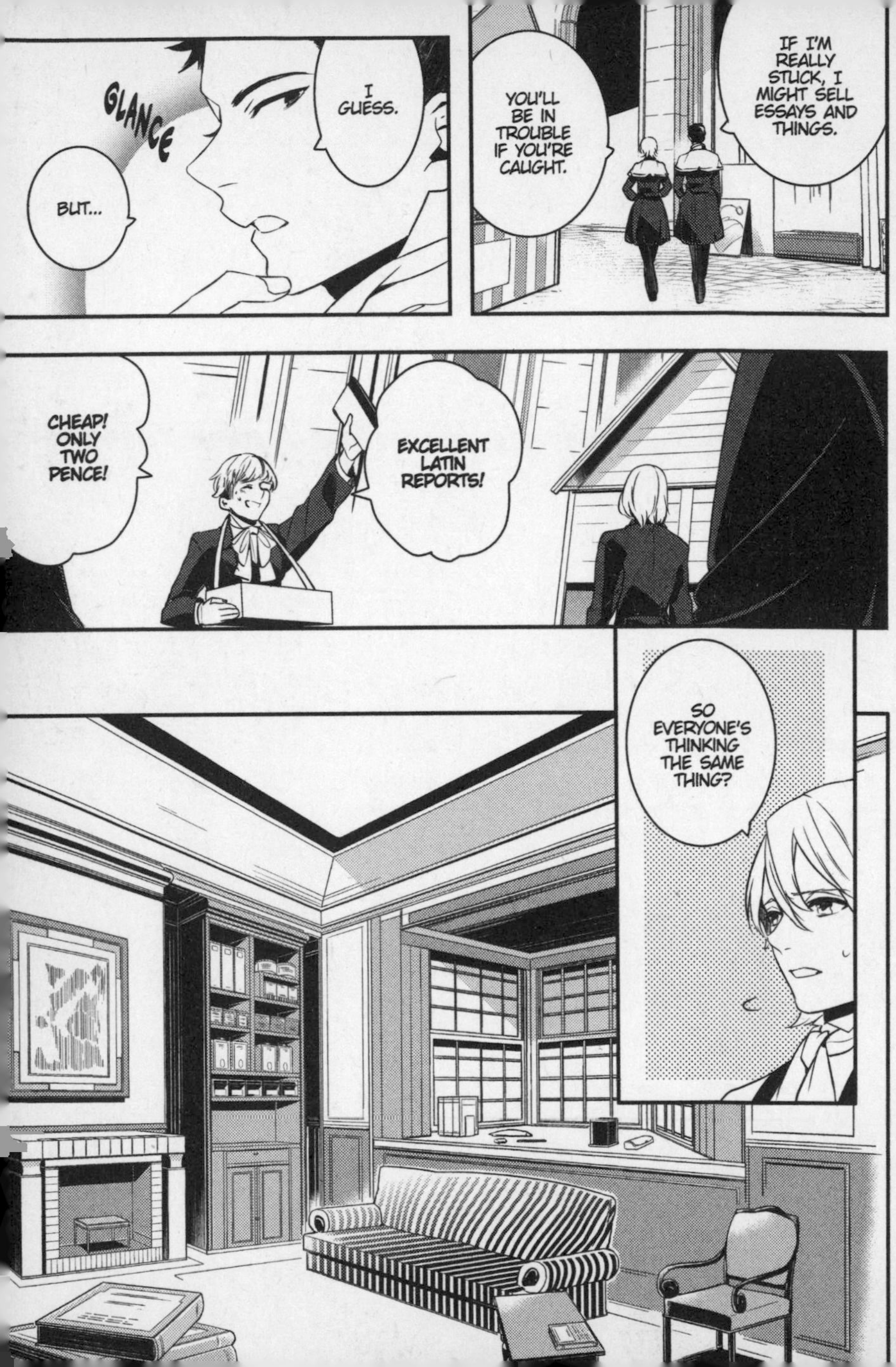
IF I'M REALLY STUCK, I MIGHT SELL ESSAYS AND THINGS.
YOU'LL BE IN TROUBLE IF YOU'RE CAUGHT.
I GUESS.
GLANCE
BUT...
EXCELLENT LATIN REPORTS!
CHEAP! ONLY TWO PENCE!
SO EVERYONE'S THINKING THE SAME THING?

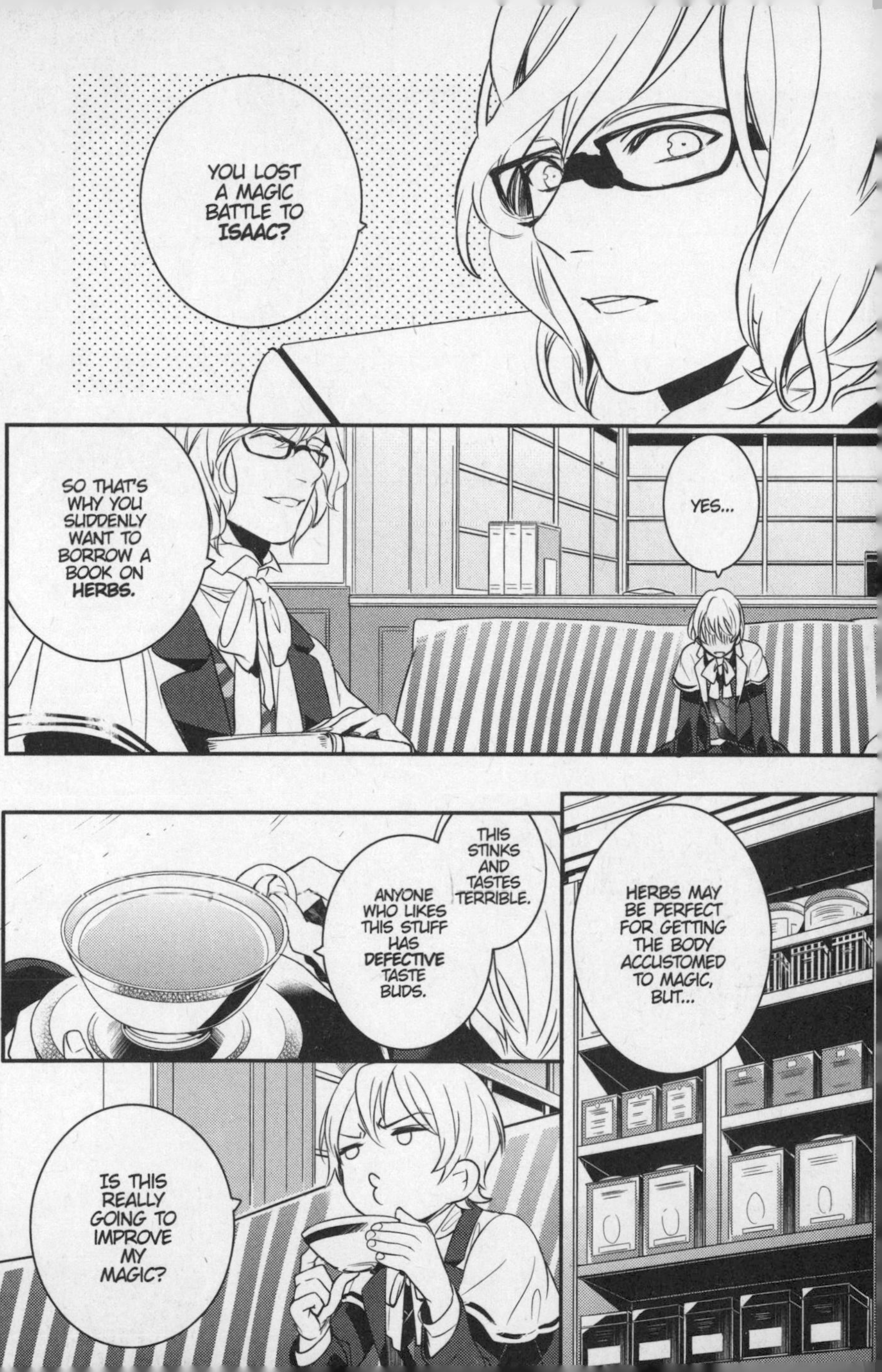
YOU LOST A MAGIC BATTLE TO ISAAC?
YES...
SO THAT'S WHY YOU SUDDENLY WANT TO BORROW A BOOK ON HERBS.
HERBS MAY BE PERFECT FOR GETTING THE BODY ACCUSTOMED TO MAGIC, BUT...
THIS STINKS AND TASTES TERRIBLE.
ANYONE WHO LIKES THIS STUFF HAS DEFECTIVE TASTE BUDS.
IS THIS REALLY GOING TO IMPROVE MY MAGIC?

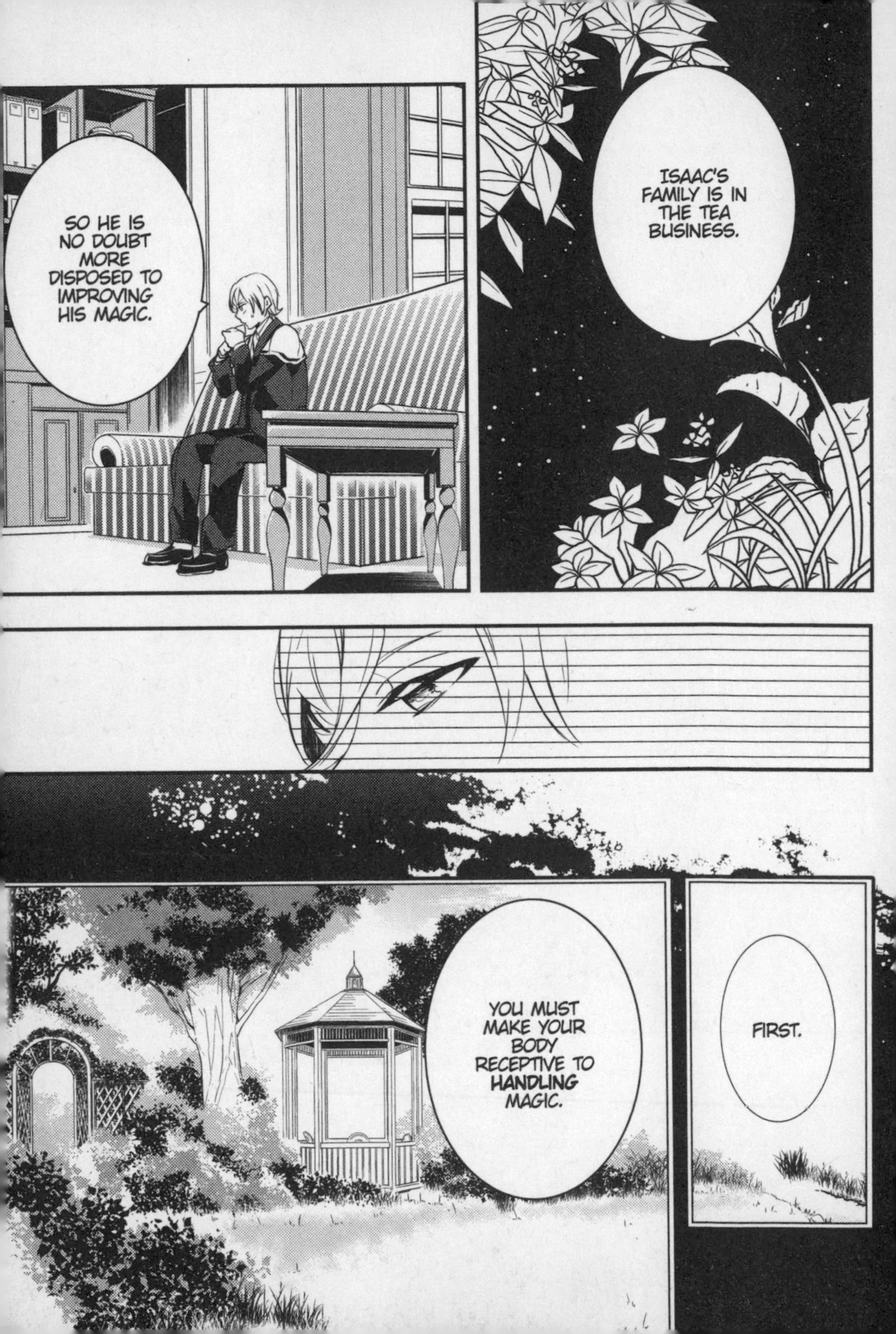
ISAAC'S FAMILY IS IN THE TEA BUSINESS.
SO HE IS NO DOUBT MORE DISPOSED TO IMPROVING HIS MAGIC.
FIRST.
YOU MUST MAKE YOUR BODY RECEPTIVE TO HANDLING MAGIC.

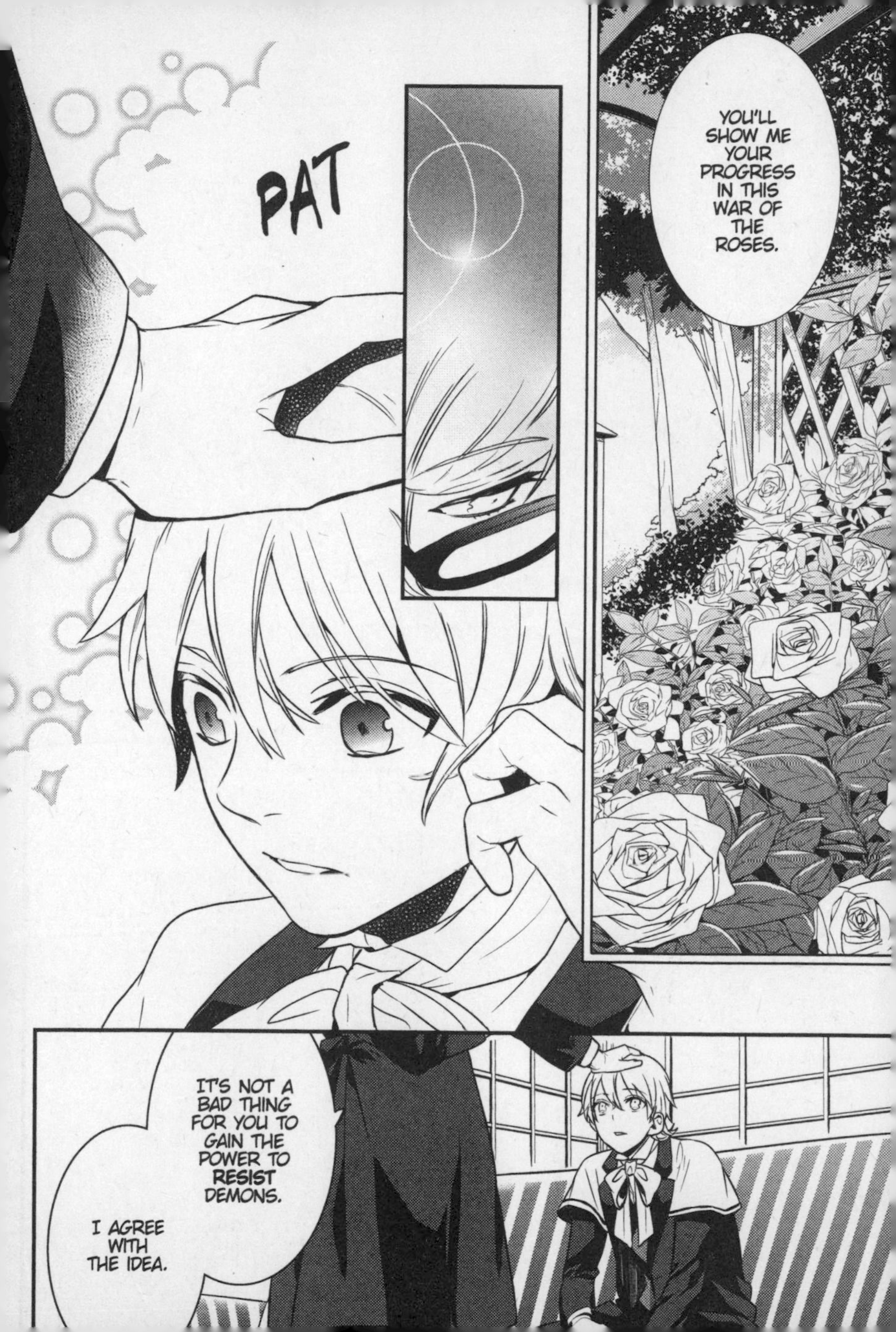
YOU'LL SHOW ME YOUR PROGRESS IN THIS WAR OF THE ROSES.
PAT
IT'S NOT A BAD THING FOR YOU TO GAIN THE POWER TO RESIST DEMONS.
I AGREE WITH THE IDEA.

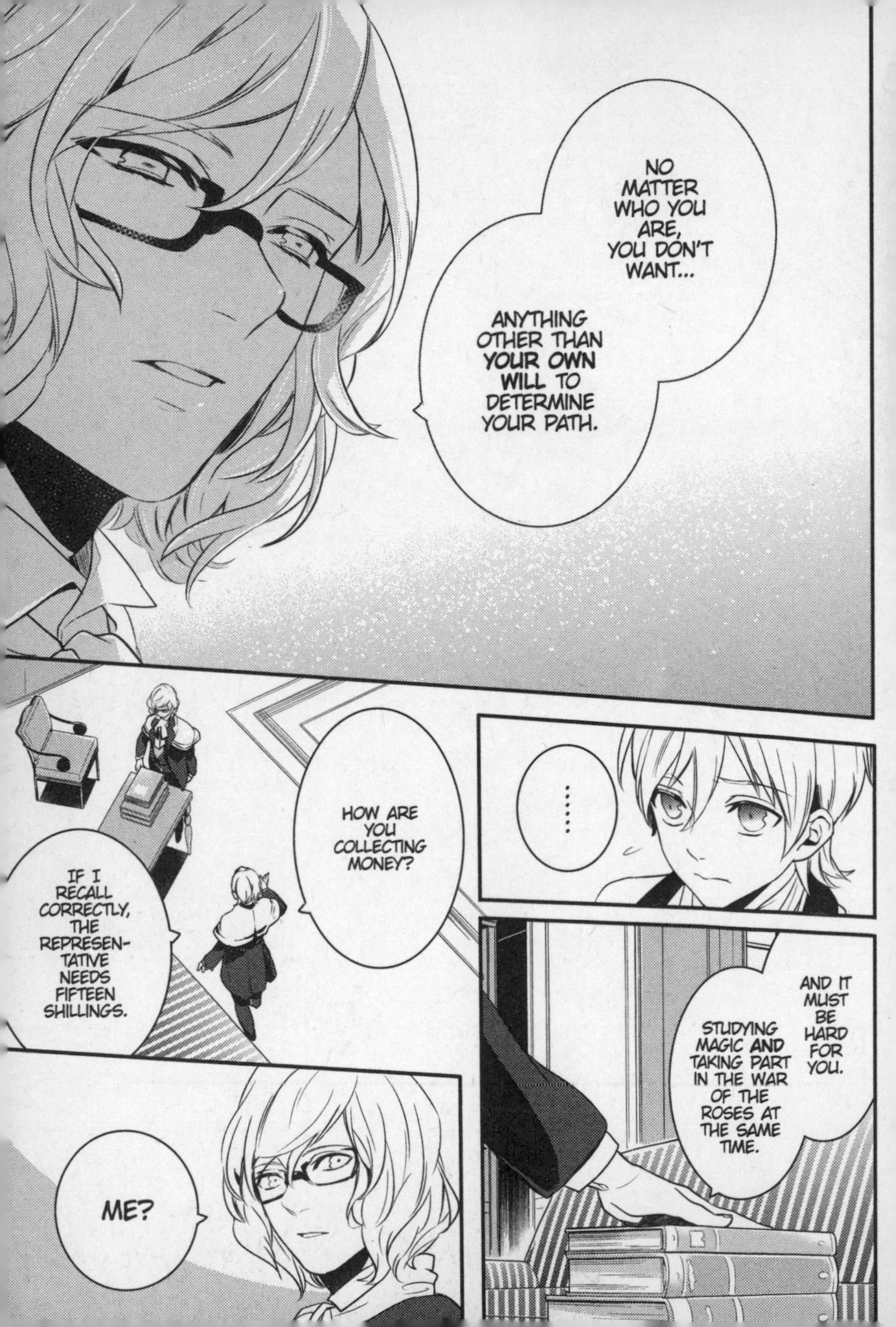
NO MATTER WHO YOU ARE, YOU DON'T WANT...
ANYTHING OTHER THAN YOUR OWN WILL TO DETERMINE YOUR PATH.
......
HOW ARE YOU COLLECTING MONEY?
IF I RECALL CORRECTLY, THE REPRESEN-TATIVE NEEDS FIFTEEN SHILLINGS.
ME?
AND IT MUST BE HARD FOR YOU.
STUDYING MAGIC AND TAKING PART IN THE WAR OF THE ROSES AT THE SAME TIME.

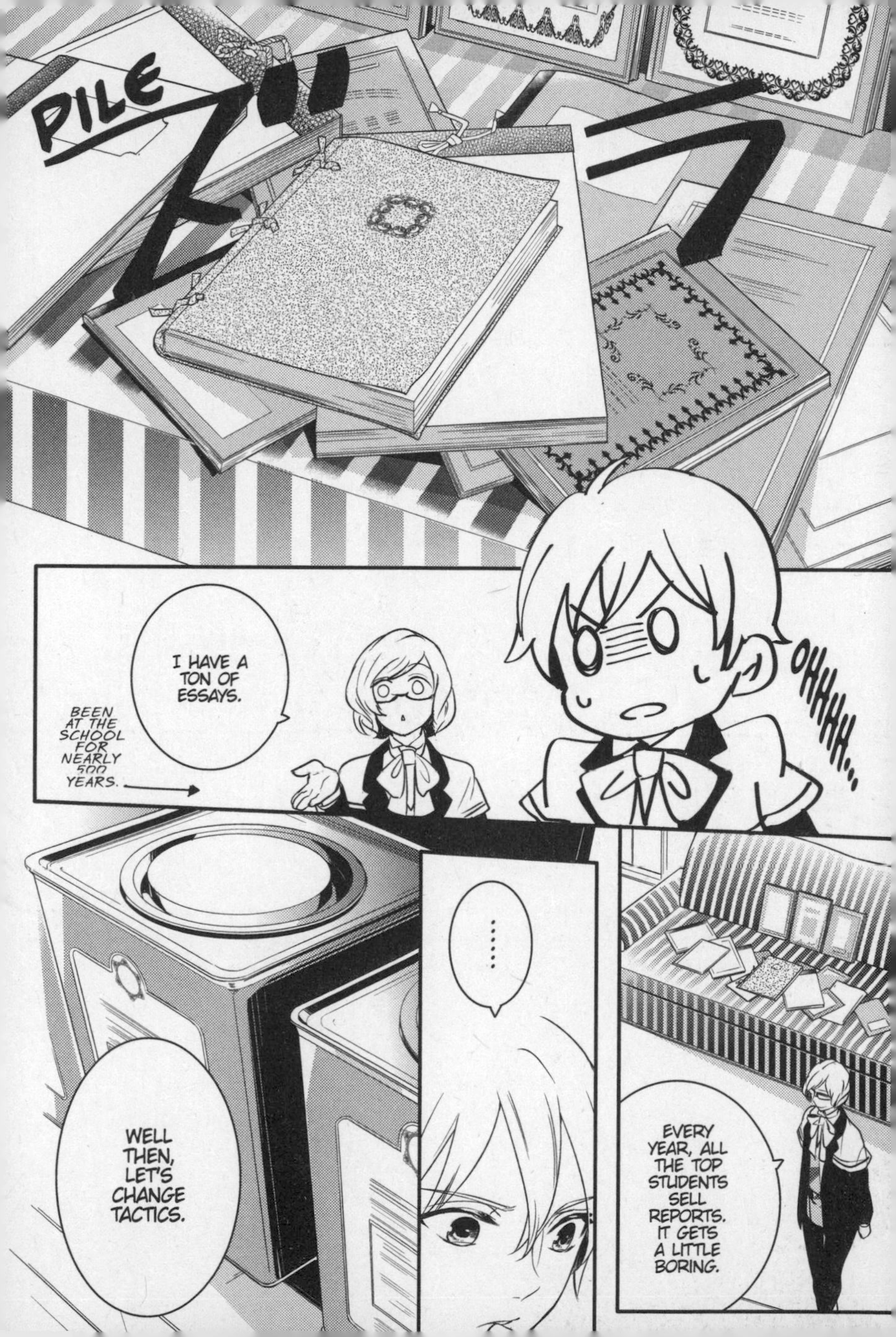
PILE
I HAVE A TON OF ESSAYS.
BEEN AT THE SCHOOL FOR NEARLY 500 YEARS.
OHHHH...
EVERY YEAR, ALL THE TOP STUDENTS SELL REPORTS. IT GETS A LITTLE BORING.
......
WELL THEN, LET'S CHANGE TACTICS.

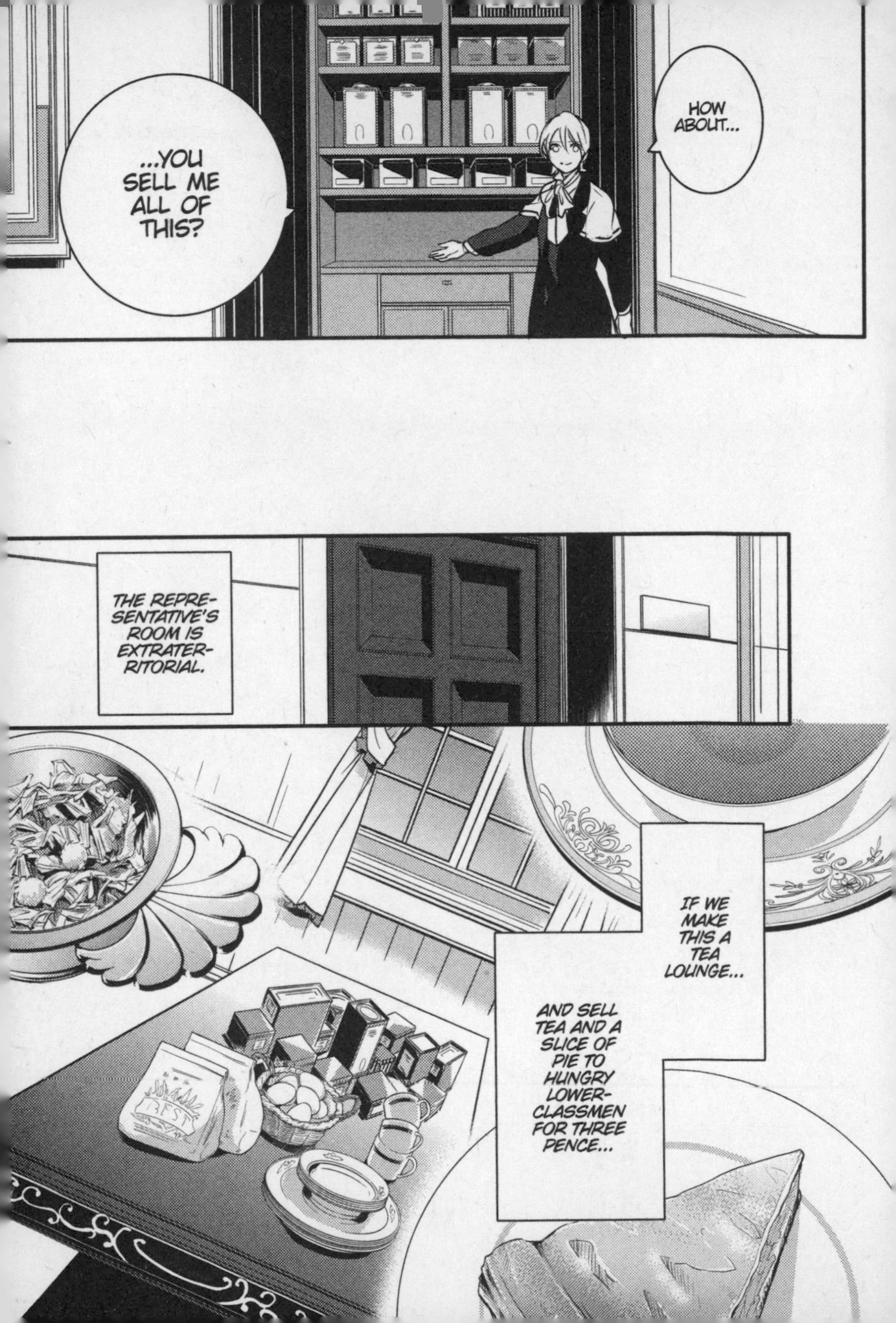
HOW ABOUT...
...YOU SELL ME ALL OF THIS?
THE REPRESENTATIVE'S ROOM IS EXTRATERRITORIAL.
IF WE MAKE THIS A TEA LOUNGE...
AND SELL TEA AND A SLICE OF PIE TO HUNGRY LOWER-CLASSMEN FOR THREE PENCE...

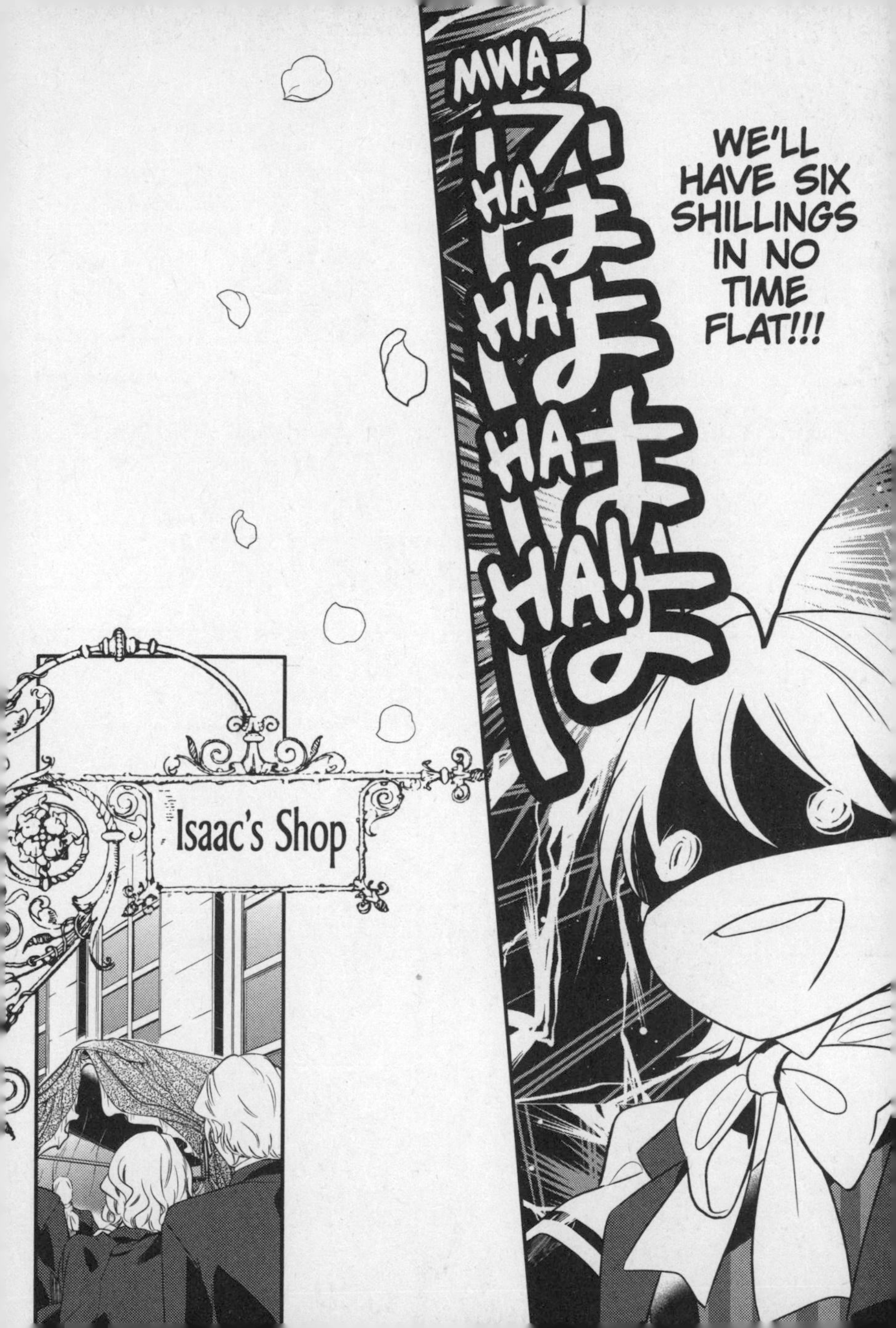
MWA HA HA HA HA!
WE'LL HAVE SIX SHILLINGS IN NO TIME FLAT!!!
Isaac's Shop

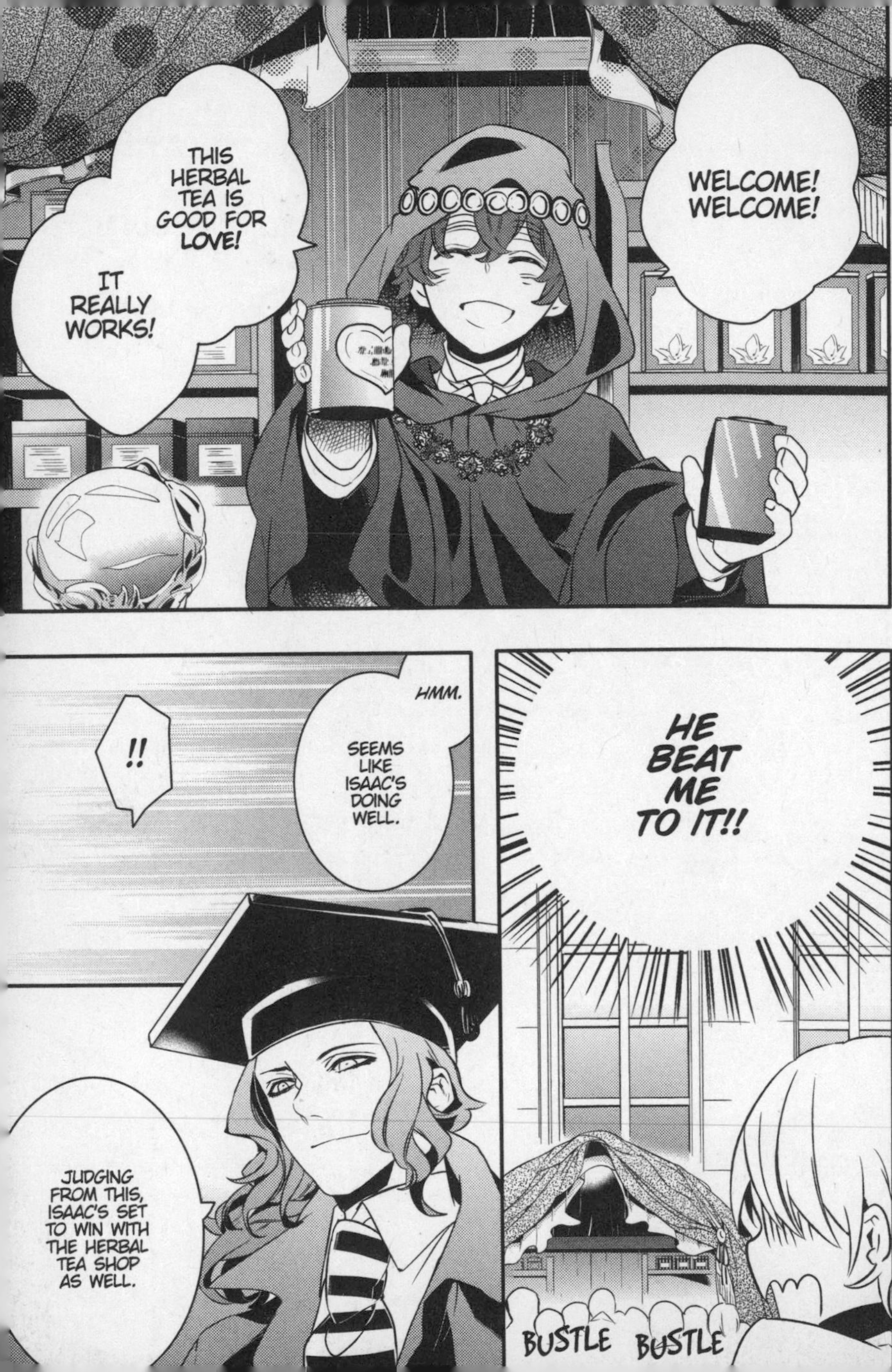
WELCOME! WELCOME!
THIS HERBAL TEA IS GOOD FOR LOVE!
IT REALLY WORKS!
HE BEAT ME TO IT!!
BUSTLE BUSTLE
HMM.
SEEMS LIKE ISAAC'S DOING WELL.
!!
JUDGING FROM THIS, ISAAC'S SET TO WIN WITH THE HERBAL TEA SHOP AS WELL.

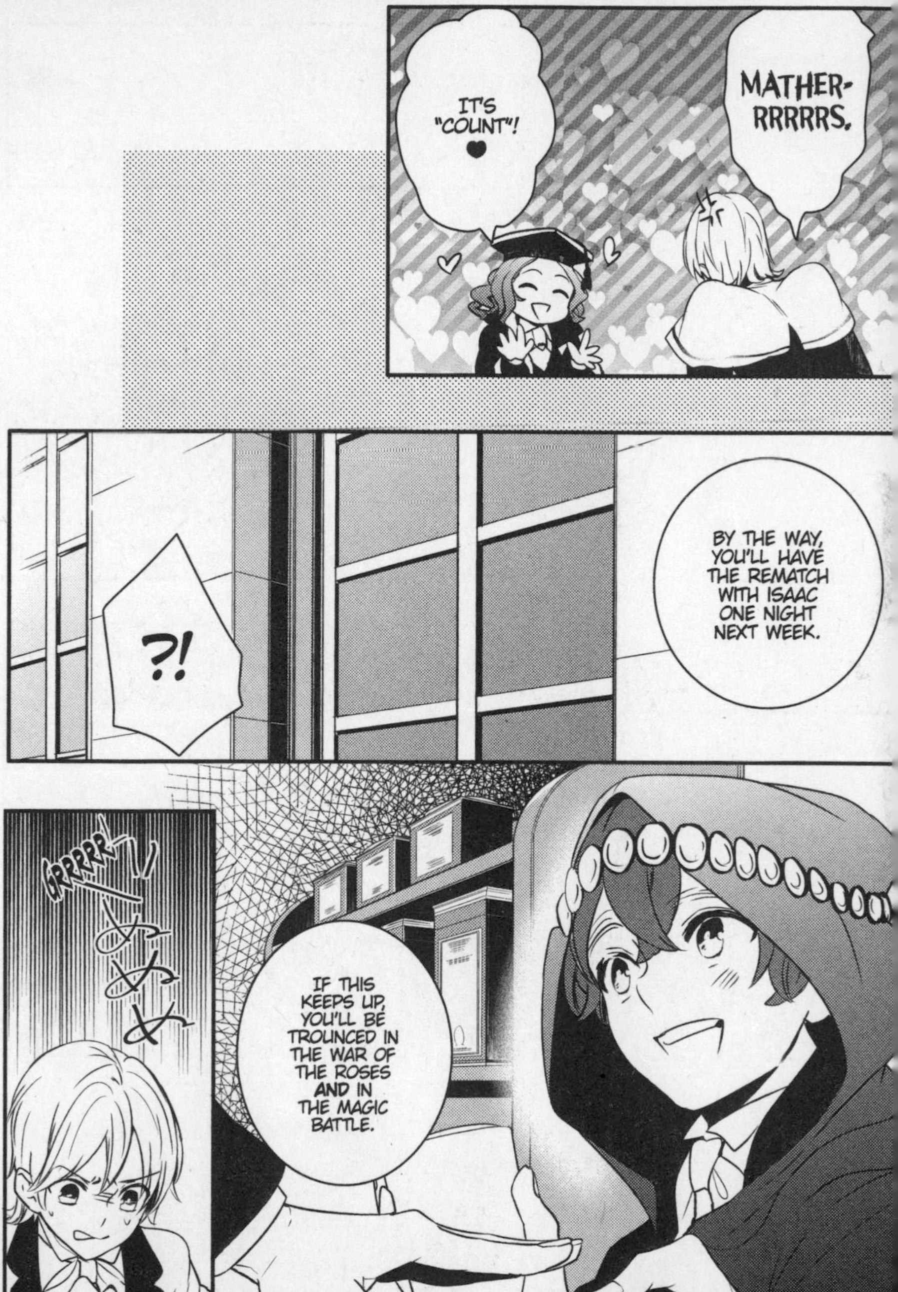
MATHER-RRRRRS.
IT'S "COUNT"! ♥
BY THE WAY, YOU'LL HAVE THE REMATCH WITH ISAAC ONE NIGHT NEXT WEEK.
?!
IF THIS KEEPS UP, YOU'LL BE TROUNCED IN THE WAR OF THE ROSES AND IN THE MAGIC BATTLE.
GRRRRR

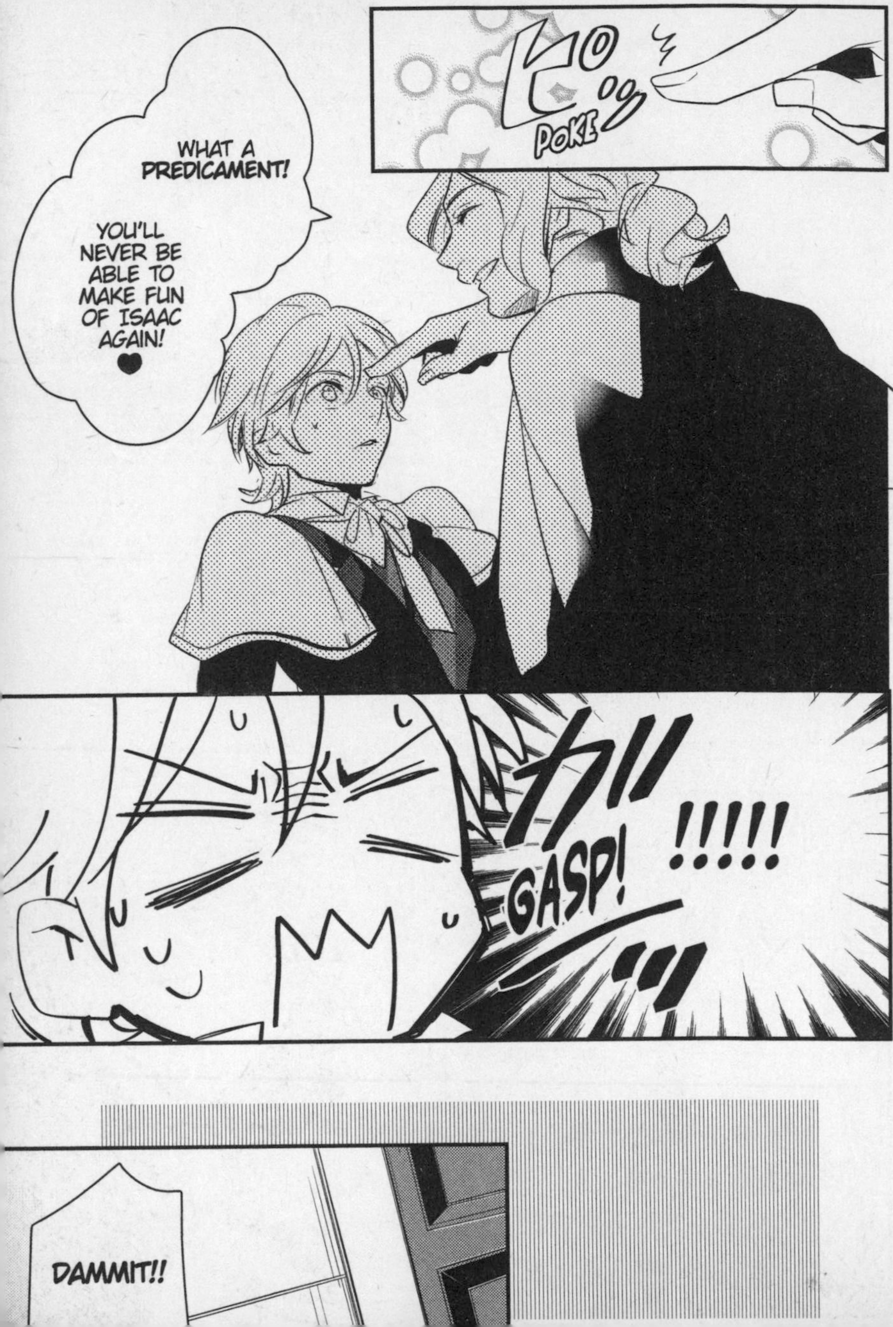
POKE
WHAT A PREDICAMENT!
YOU'LL NEVER BE ABLE TO MAKE FUN OF ISAAC AGAIN! ♥
GASP! !!!!!
DAMMIT!!

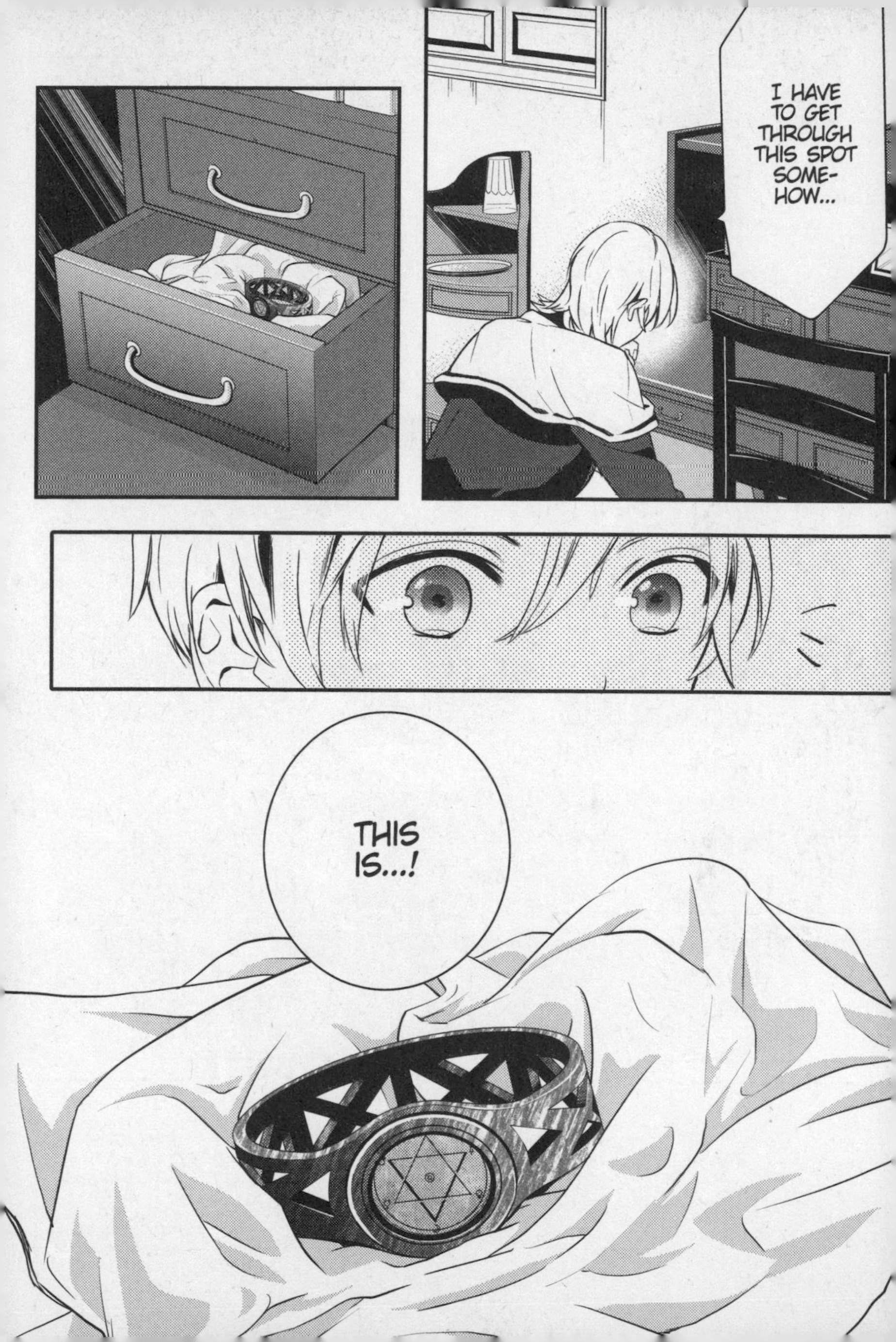
I HAVE TO GET THROUGH THIS SPOT SOME-HOW...
THIS IS...!

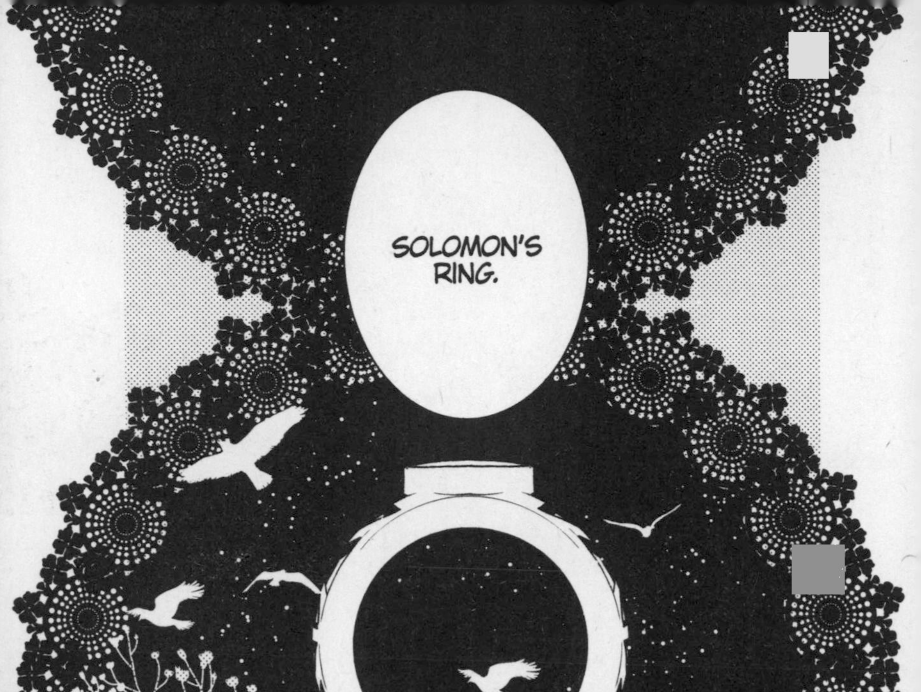
SOLOMON'S RING.
Pillar 37
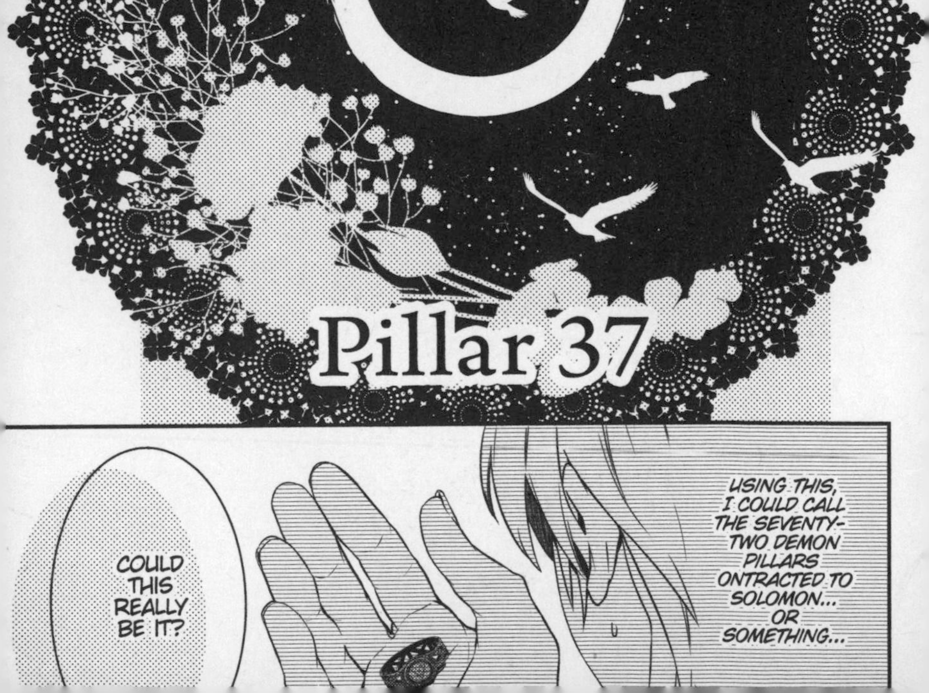
USING THIS, I COULD CALL THE SEVENTY-TWO DEMON PILLARS ONTRACTED TO SOLOMON... OR SOMETHING...
COULD THIS REALLY BE IT?

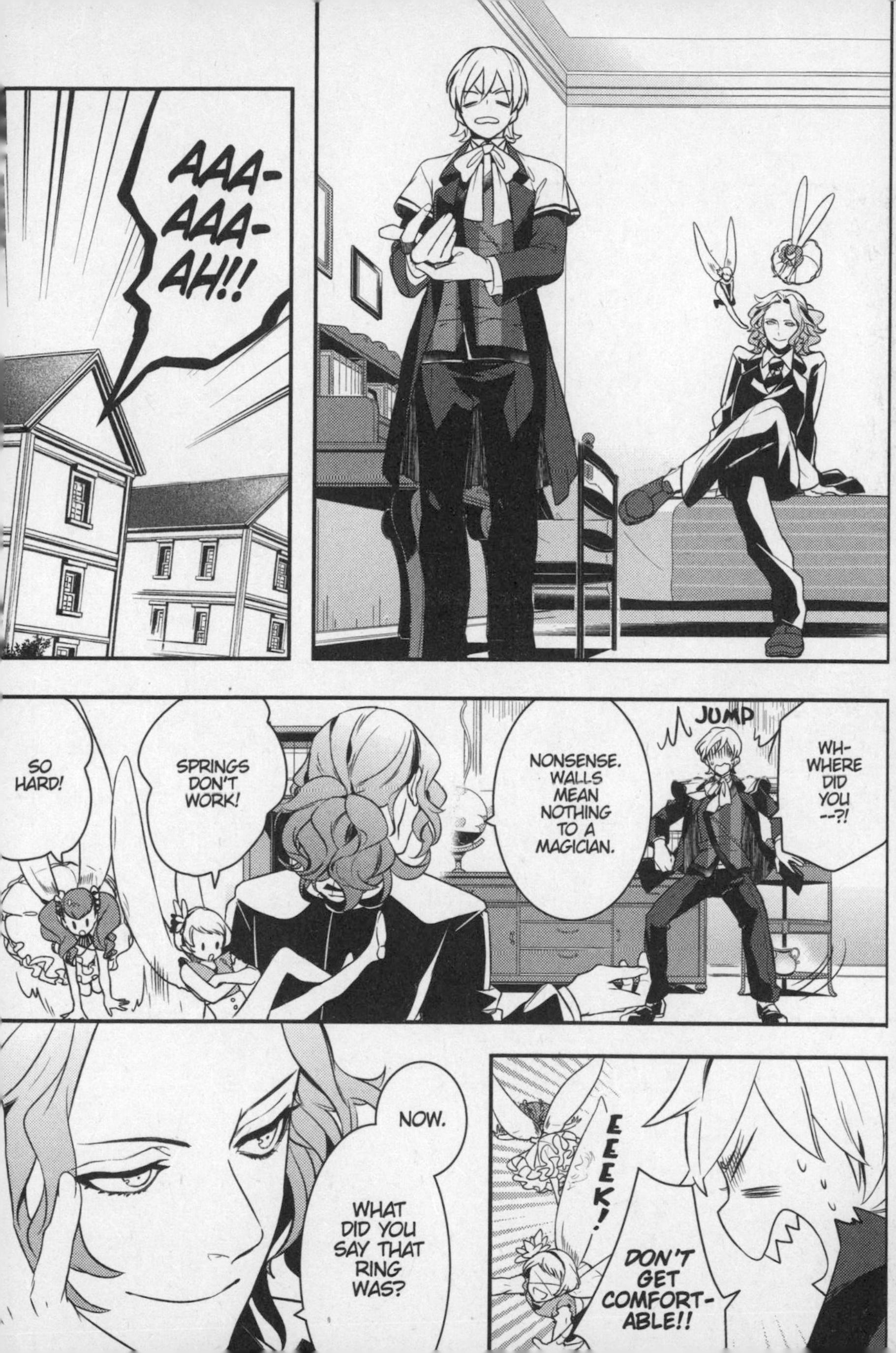
AAA-AAA-AH!!
WH-WHERE DID YOU--?!
JUMP
NONSENSE. WALLS MEAN NOTHING TO A MAGICIAN.
SPRINGS DON'T WORK!
SO HARD!
EEEK!
DON'T GET COMFORT-ABLE!!
NOW.
WHAT DID YOU SAY THAT RING WAS?

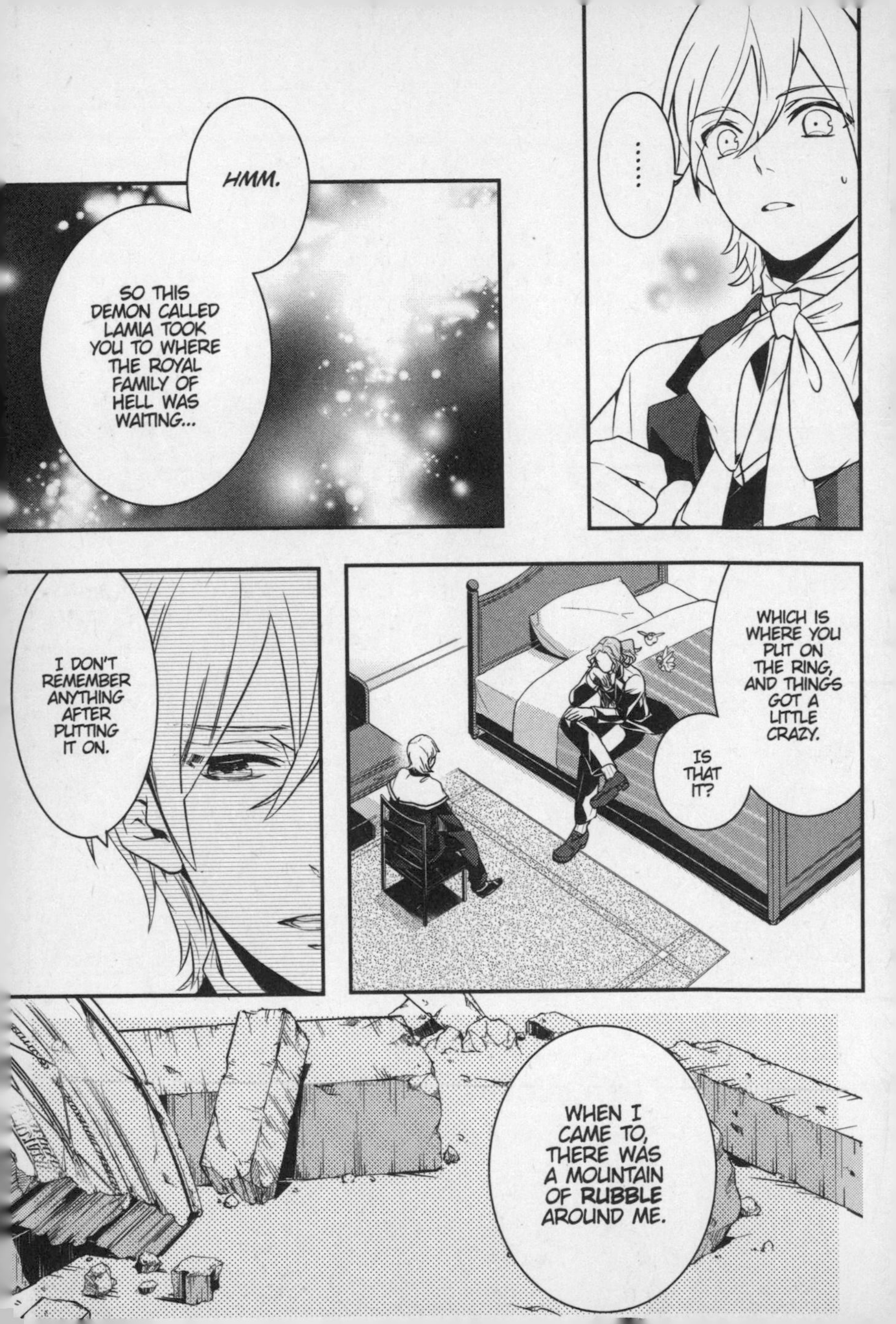
......
HMM.
SO THIS DEMON CALLED LAMIA TOOK YOU TO WHERE THE ROYAL FAMILY OF HELL WAS WAITING...
WHICH IS WHERE YOU PUT ON THE RING, AND THINGS GOT A LITTLE CRAZY.
IS THAT IT?
I DON'T REMEMBER ANYTHING AFTER PUTTING IT ON.
WHEN I CAME TO, THERE WAS A MOUNTAIN OF RUBBLE AROUND ME.

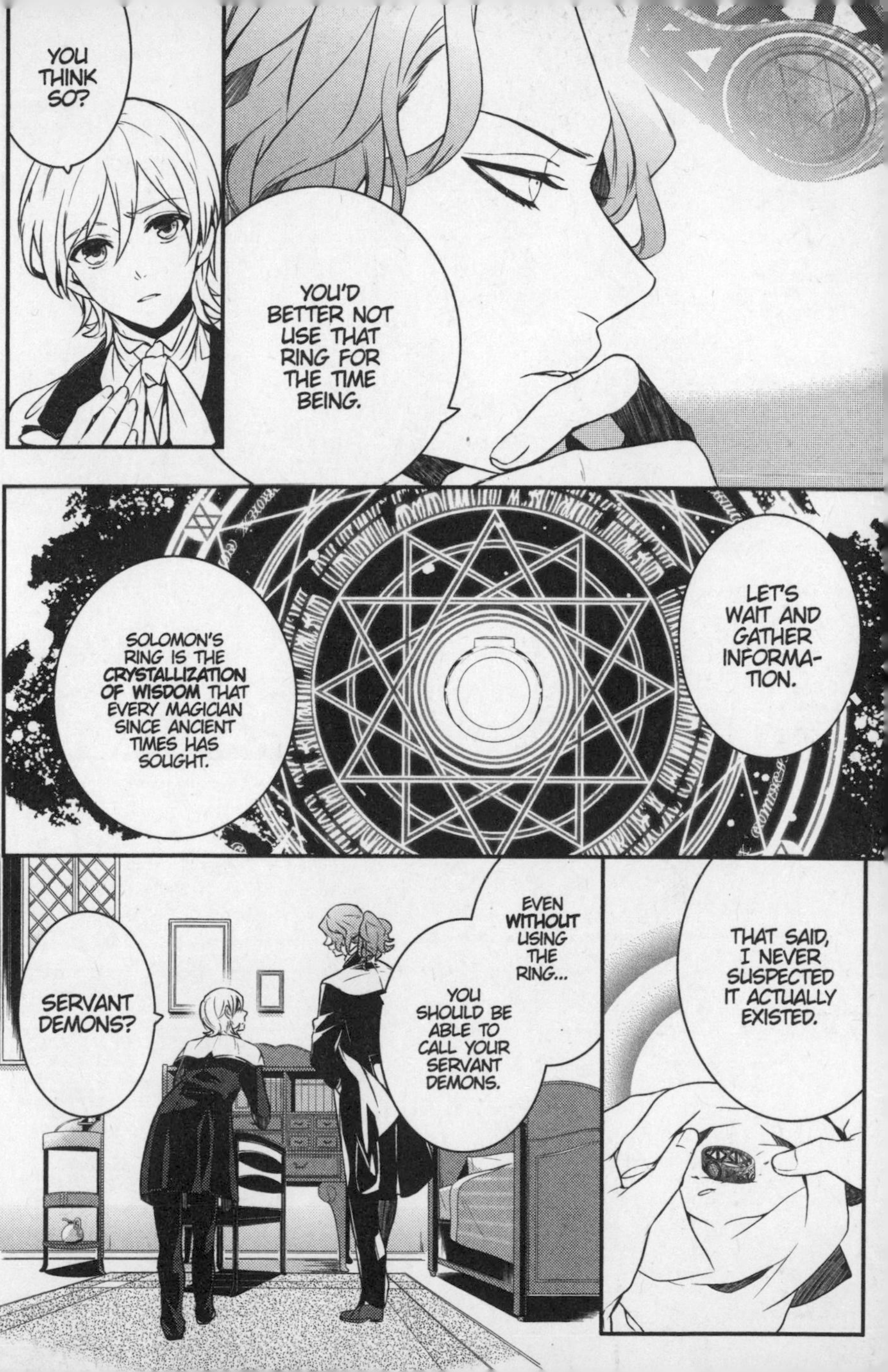
YOU'D BETTER NOT USE THAT RING FOR THE TIME BEING.
YOU THINK SO?
LET'S WAIT AND GATHER INFORMATION.
SOLOMON'S RING IS THE **CRYSTALLIZATION OF WISDOM** THAT EVERY MAGICIAN SINCE ANCIENT TIMES HAS SOUGHT.
THAT SAID, I NEVER SUSPECTED IT ACTUALLY EXISTED.
EVEN **WITHOUT** USING THE RING...
YOU SHOULD BE ABLE TO CALL YOUR SERVANT DEMONS.
SERVANT DEMONS?

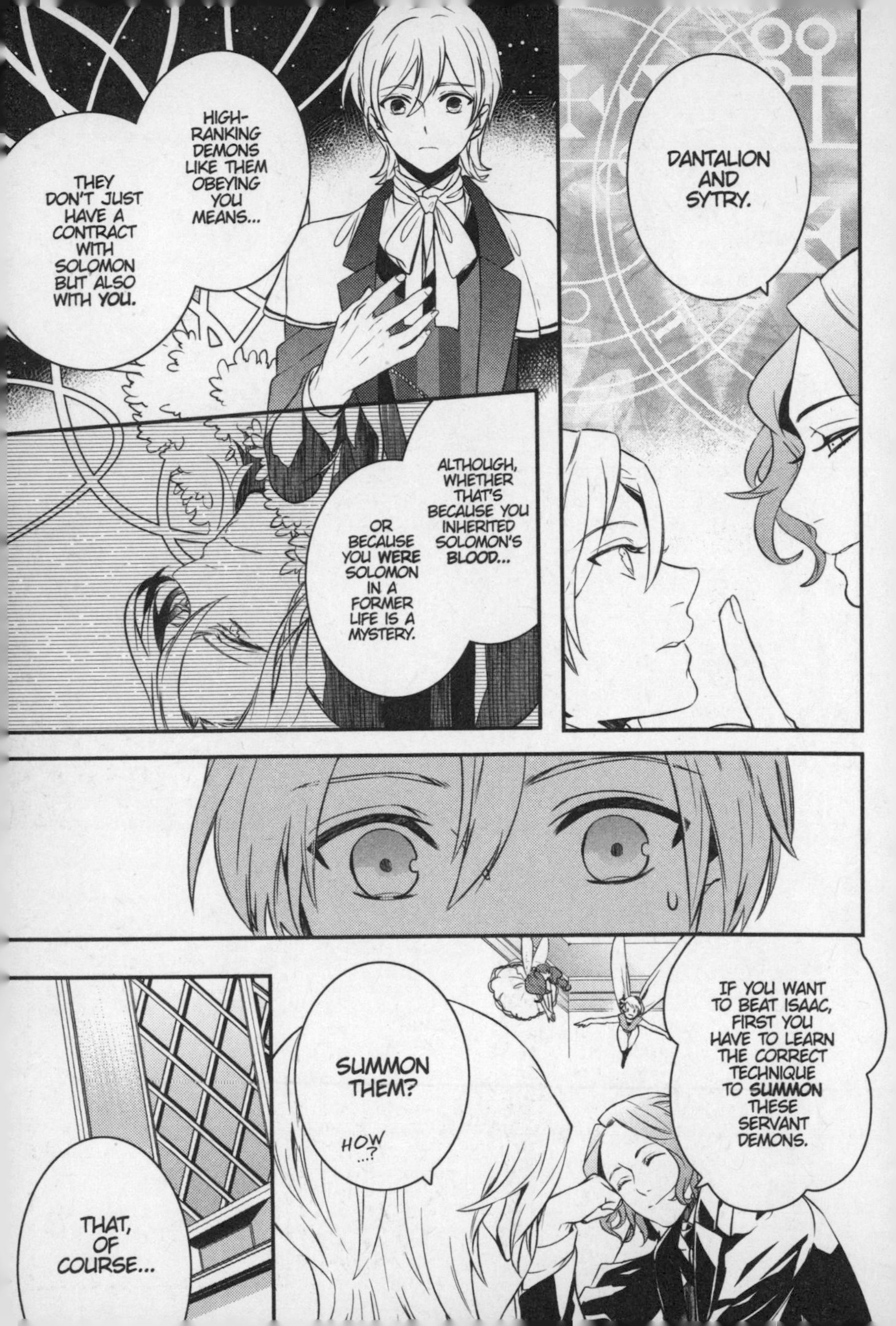
DANTALION AND SYTRY.
HIGH-RANKING DEMONS LIKE THEM OBEYING YOU MEANS...
THEY DON'T JUST HAVE A CONTRACT WITH SOLOMON BUT ALSO WITH **YOU**.
ALTHOUGH, WHETHER THAT'S BECAUSE YOU INHERITED SOLOMON'S BLOOD...
OR BECAUSE YOU WERE SOLOMON IN A FORMER LIFE IS A MYSTERY.
IF YOU WANT TO BEAT ISAAC, FIRST YOU HAVE TO LEARN THE CORRECT TECHNIQUE TO **SUMMON** THESE SERVANT DEMONS.
SUMMON THEM?
HOW...?
THAT, OF COURSE...

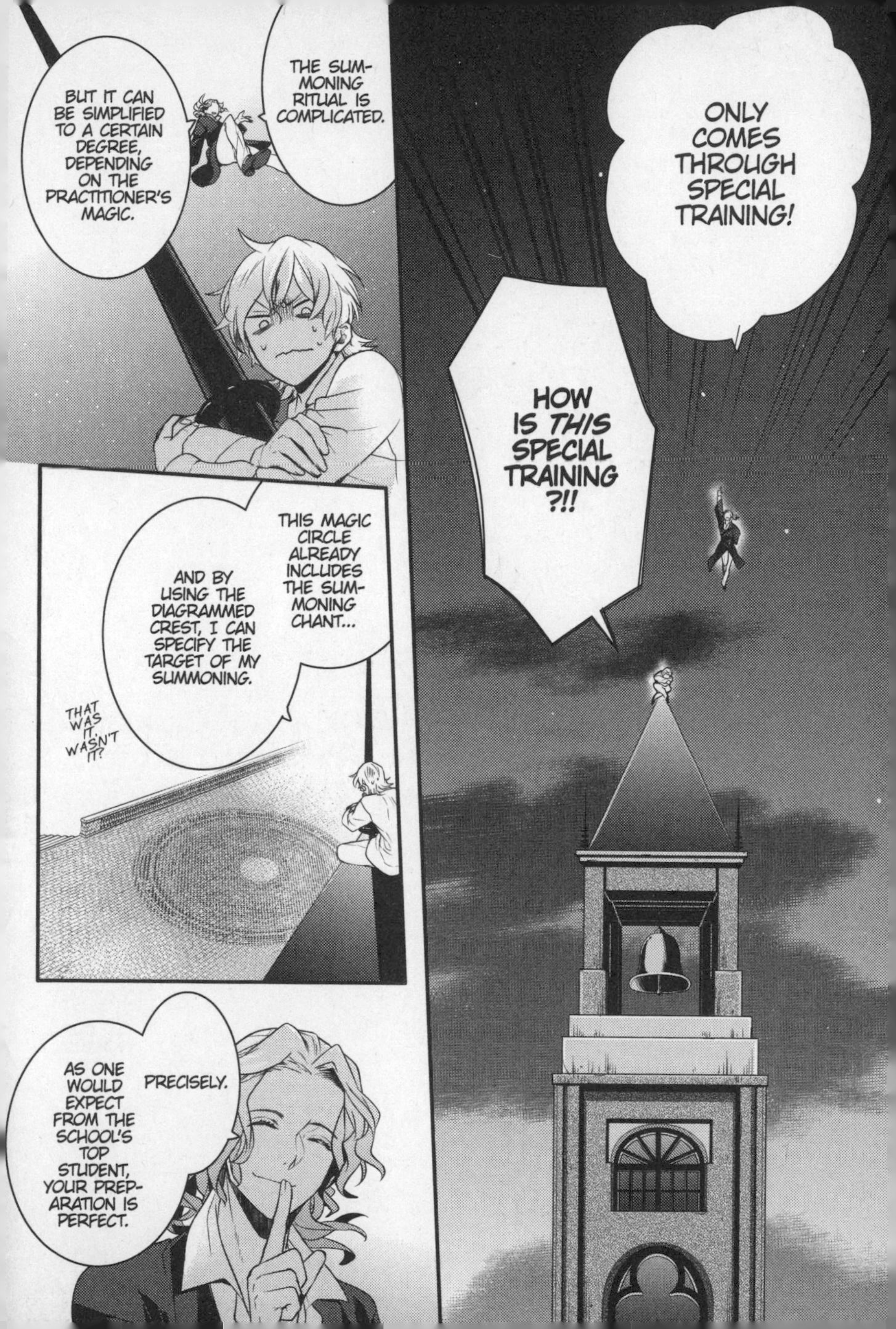
ONLY COMES THROUGH SPECIAL TRAINING!
HOW IS *THIS* SPECIAL TRAINING?!!
THE SUMMONING RITUAL IS COMPLICATED.
BUT IT CAN BE SIMPLIFIED TO A CERTAIN DEGREE, DEPENDING ON THE PRACTITIONER'S MAGIC.
THIS MAGIC CIRCLE ALREADY INCLUDES THE SUMMONING CHANT...
AND BY USING THE DIAGRAMMED CREST, I CAN SPECIFY THE TARGET OF MY SUMMONING.
THAT WAS IT, WASN'T IT?
PRECISELY.
AS ONE WOULD EXPECT FROM THE SCHOOL'S TOP STUDENT, YOUR PREPARATION IS PERFECT.

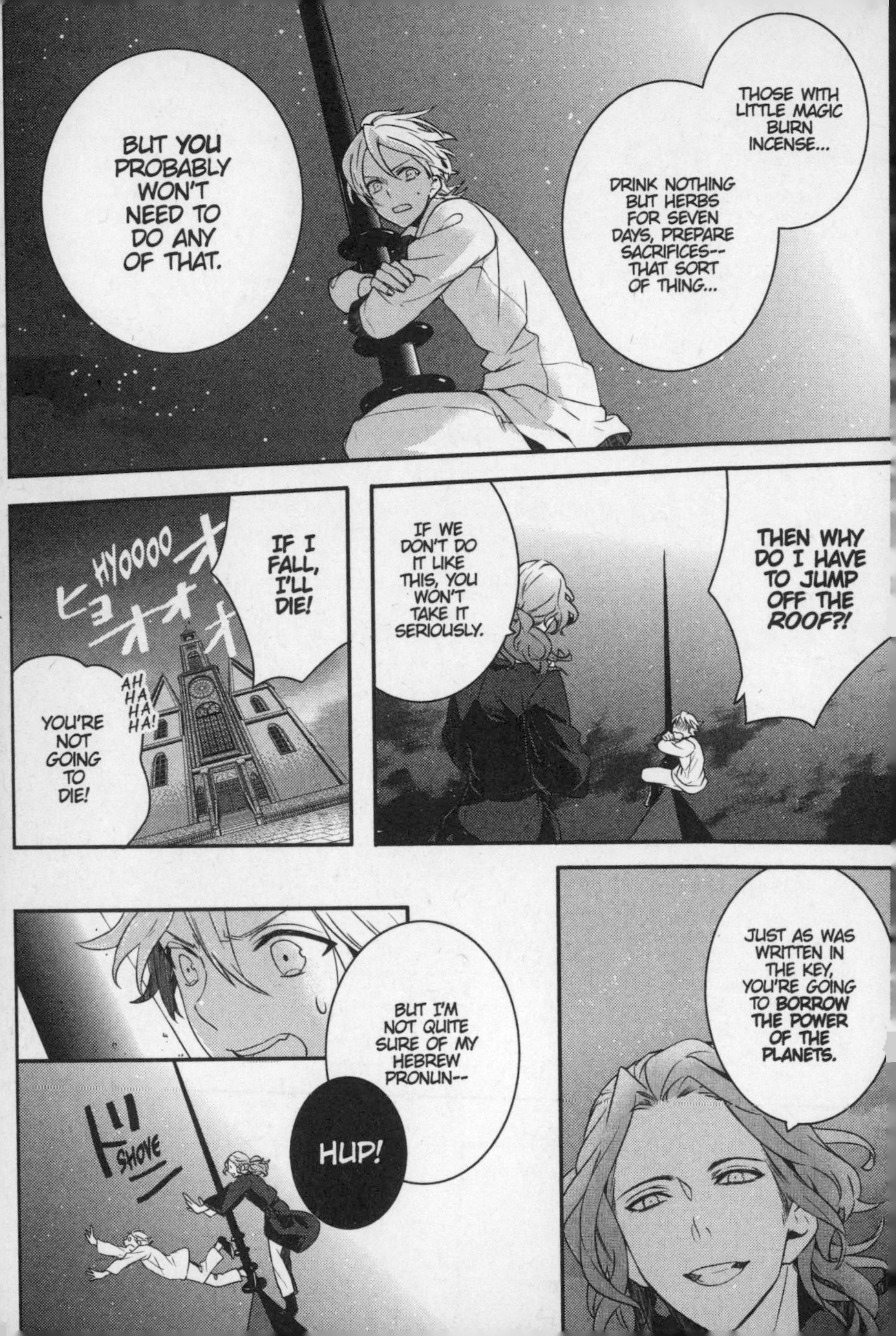
THOSE WITH LITTLE MAGIC BURN INCENSE...
DRINK NOTHING BUT HERBS FOR SEVEN DAYS, PREPARE SACRIFICES-- THAT SORT OF THING...
BUT YOU PROBABLY WON'T NEED TO DO ANY OF THAT.
THEN WHY DO I HAVE TO JUMP OFF THE *ROOF?!*
IF WE DON'T DO IT LIKE THIS, YOU WON'T TAKE IT SERIOUSLY.
IF I FALL, I'LL DIE!
HYOOOO
ヒョオオオオ
AH HA HA HA!
YOU'RE NOT GOING TO DIE!
JUST AS WAS WRITTEN IN THE KEY, YOU'RE GOING TO BORROW THE POWER OF THE PLANETS.
BUT I'M NOT QUITE SURE OF MY HEBREW PRONUN--
HUP!
ドン
SHOVE

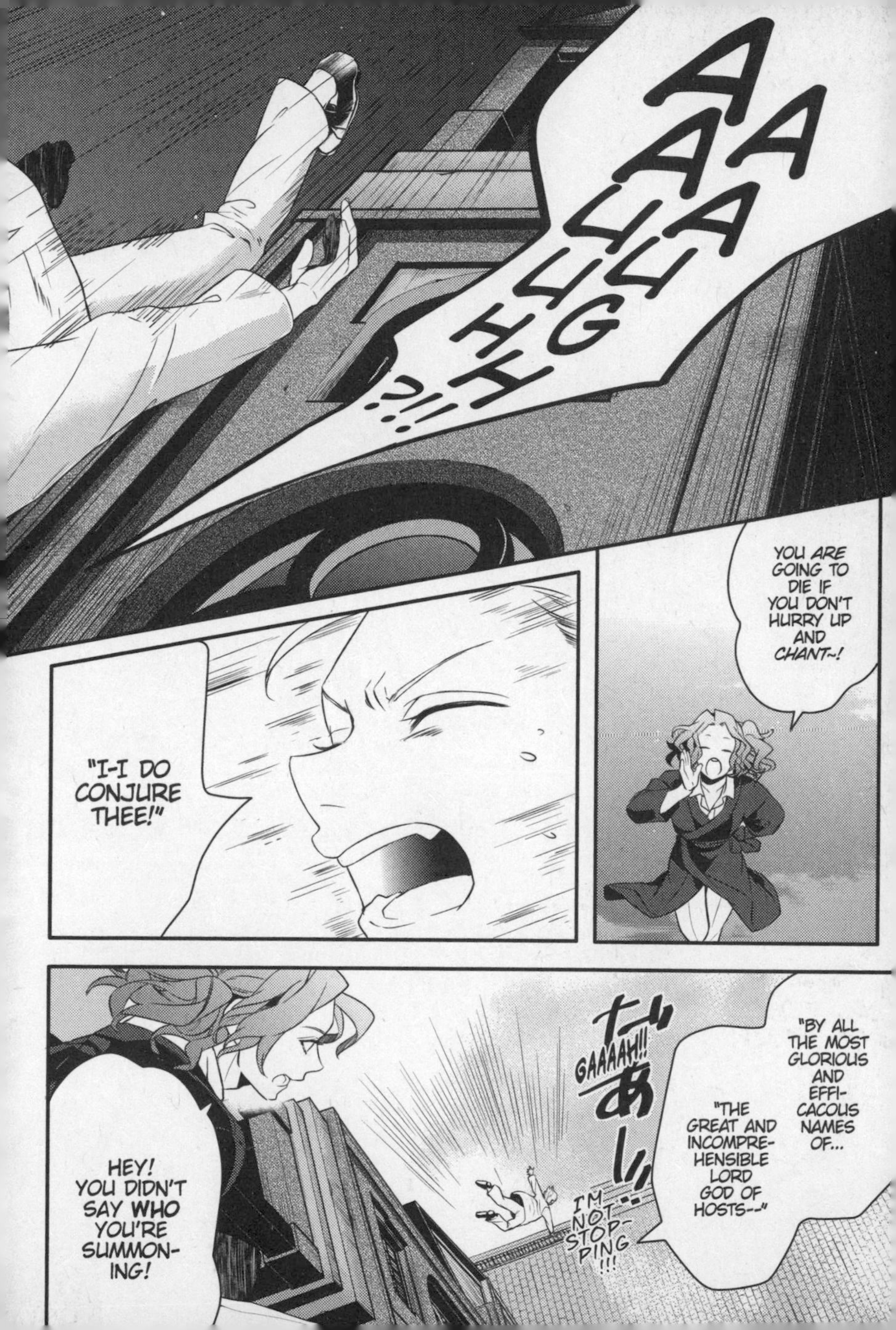
AAAAAUUUGHH?!!
YOU ARE GOING TO DIE IF YOU DON'T HURRY UP AND CHANT~!
"I-I DO CONJURE THEE!"
"BY ALL THE MOST GLORIOUS AND EFFICACIOUS NAMES OF...
"THE GREAT AND INCOMPREHENSIBLE LORD GOD OF HOSTS--"
GAAAAH!!
I'M NOT STOPPING!!!
HEY! YOU DIDN'T SAY WHO YOU'RE SUMMONING!

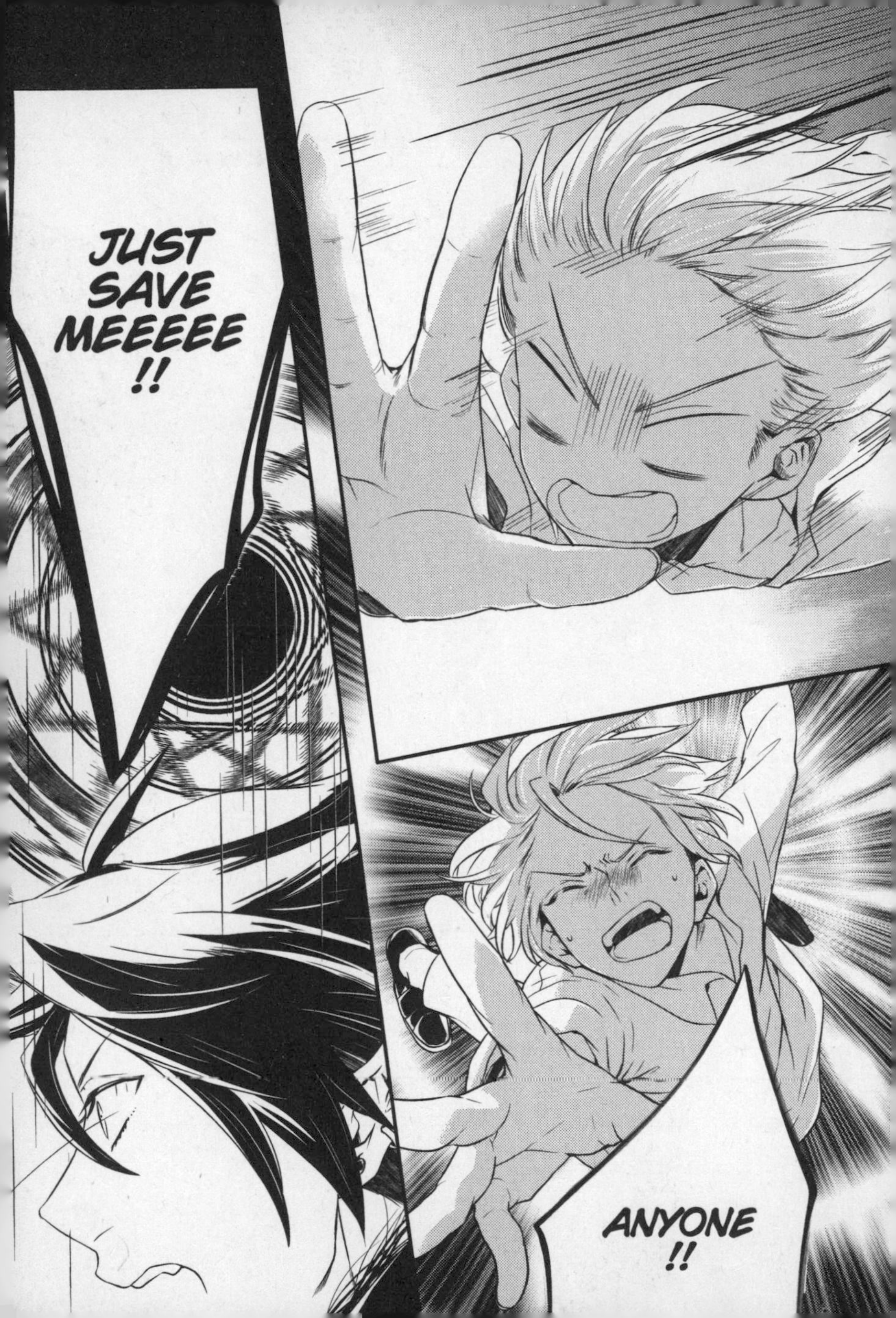
JUST SAVE MEEEEEE !!
ANYONE !!

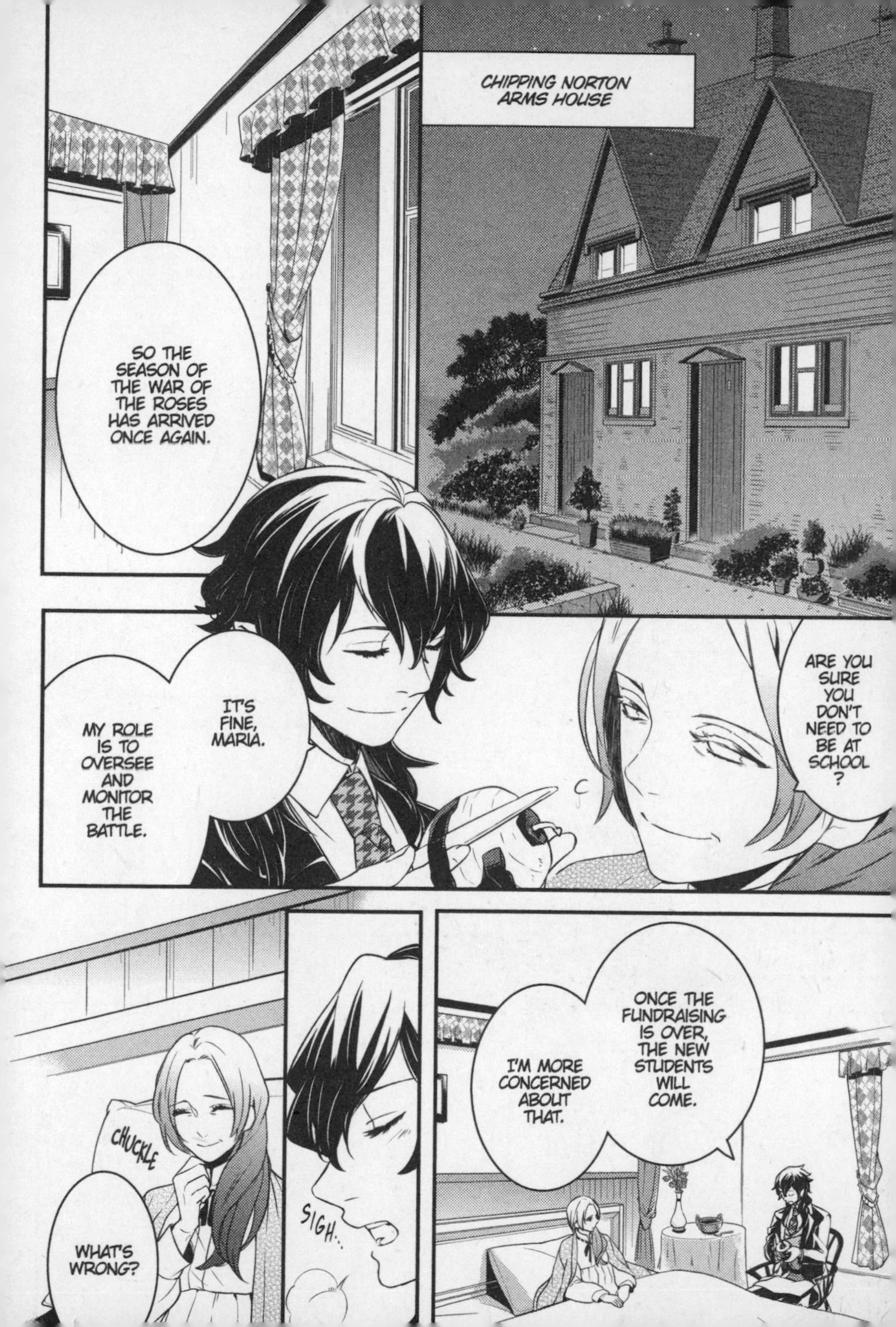
CHIPPING NORTON ARMS HOUSE
SO THE SEASON OF THE WAR OF THE ROSES HAS ARRIVED ONCE AGAIN.
ARE YOU SURE YOU DON'T NEED TO BE AT SCHOOL?
IT'S FINE, MARIA.
MY ROLE IS TO OVERSEE AND MONITOR THE BATTLE.
ONCE THE FUNDRAISING IS OVER, THE NEW STUDENTS WILL COME.
I'M MORE CONCERNED ABOUT THAT.
SIGH...
CHUCKLE
WHAT'S WRONG?

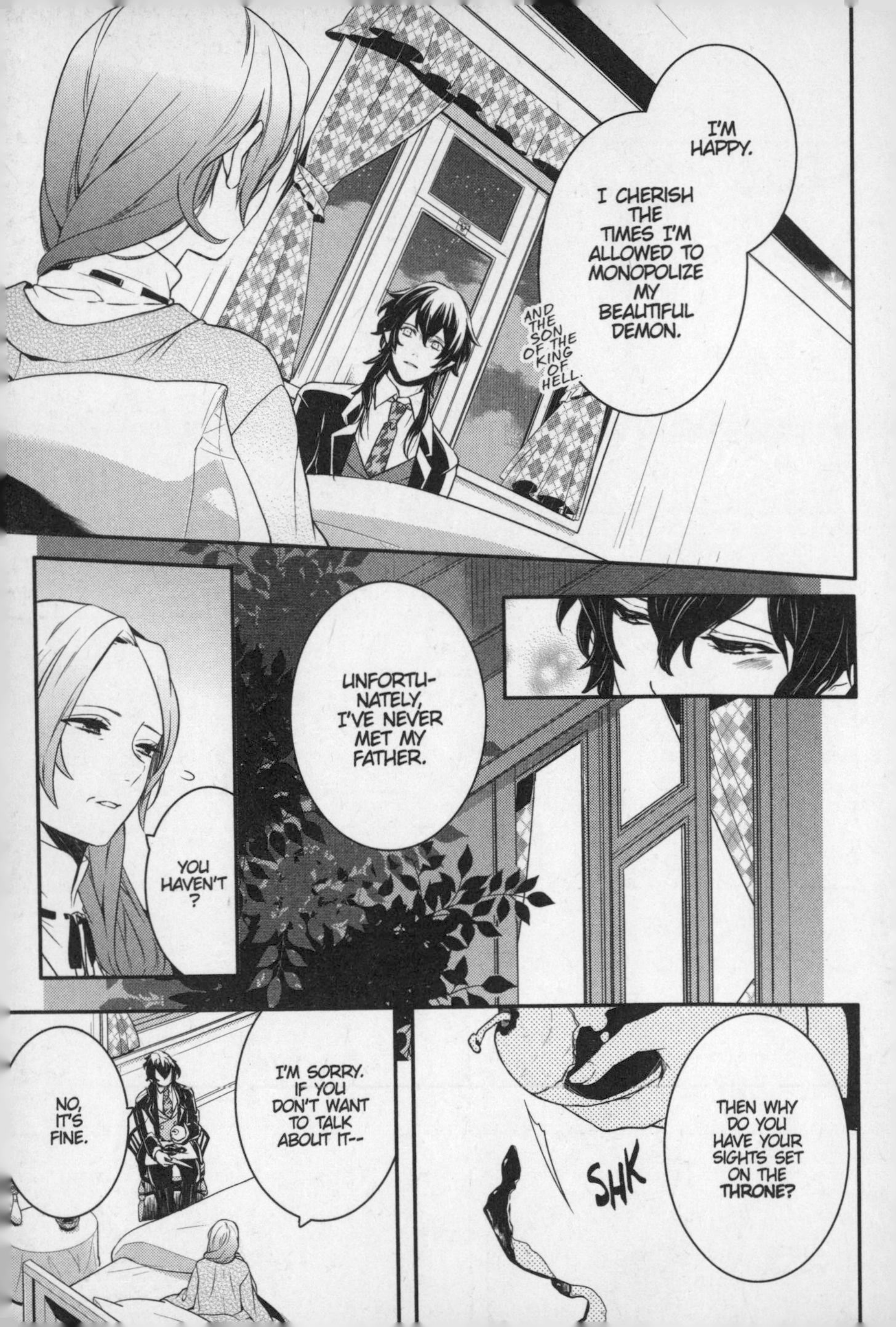
I'M HAPPY.
I CHERISH THE TIMES I'M ALLOWED TO MONOPOLIZE MY BEAUTIFUL DEMON.
AND THE SON OF THE KING OF HELL.
UNFORTU-NATELY, I'VE NEVER MET MY FATHER.
YOU HAVEN'T?
THEN WHY DO YOU HAVE YOUR SIGHTS SET ON THE THRONE?
SHK
I'M SORRY. IF YOU DON'T WANT TO TALK ABOUT IT--
NO, IT'S FINE.

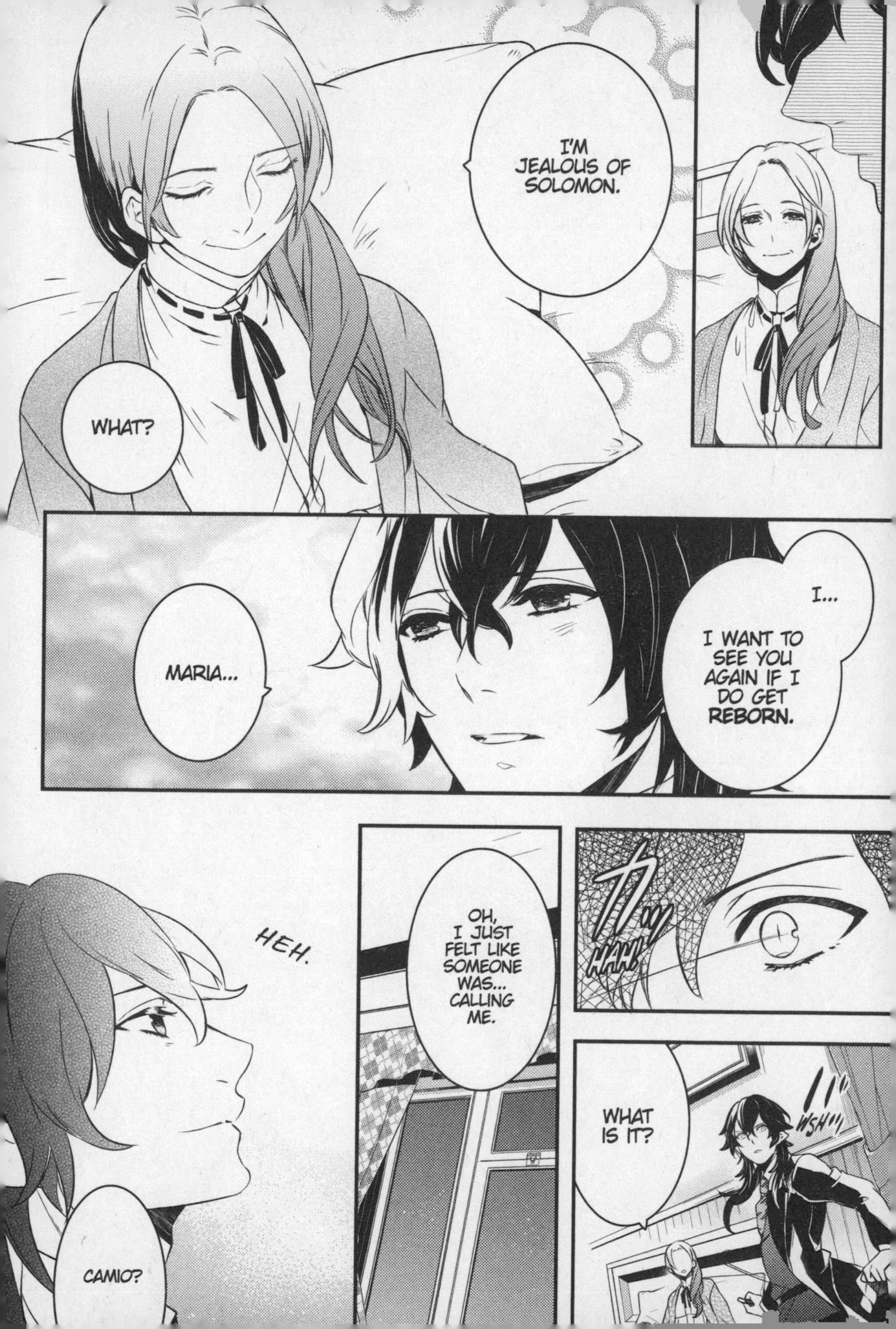
I'M JEALOUS OF SOLOMON.
WHAT?
I...
I WANT TO SEE YOU AGAIN IF I DO GET REBORN.
MARIA...
HAH!
WSH!!
WHAT IS IT?
OH, I JUST FELT LIKE SOMEONE WAS... CALLING ME.
HEH.
CAMIO?

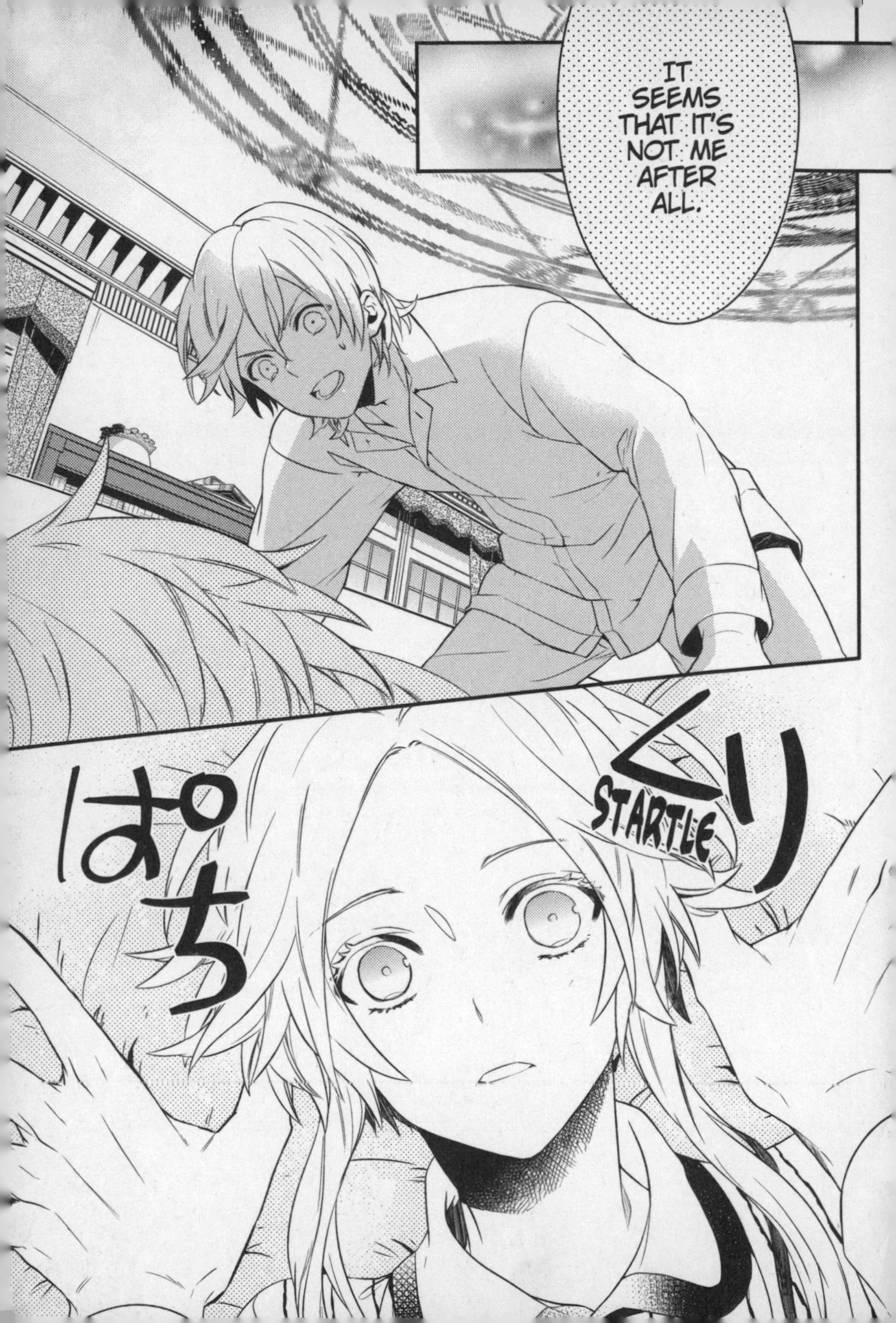
IT SEEMS THAT IT'S NOT ME AFTER ALL.
くり
STARTLE
ぱち

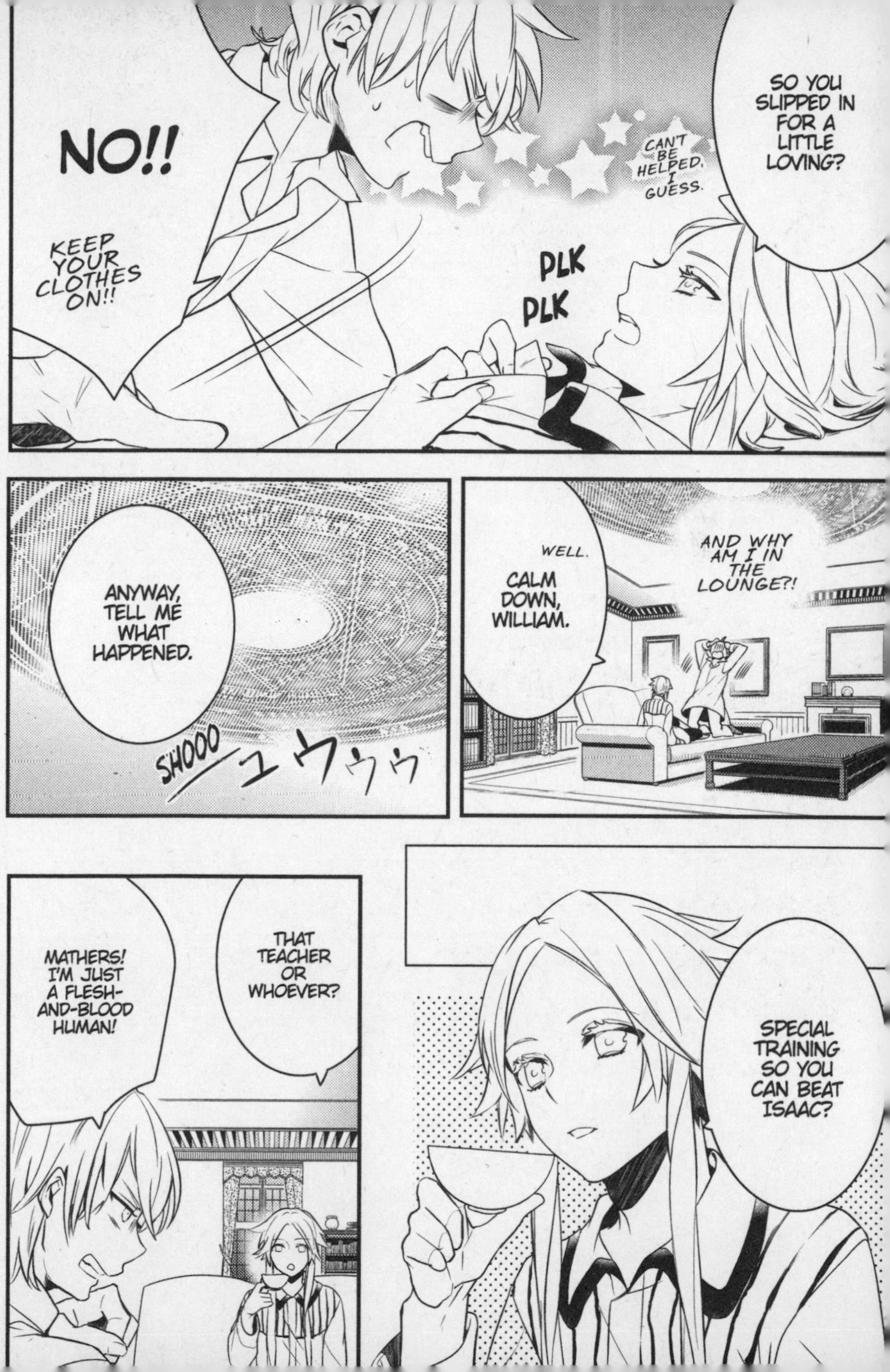
SO YOU SLIPPED IN FOR A LITTLE LOVING?
CAN'T BE HELPED, I GUESS.
PLK
PLK
NO!!
KEEP YOUR CLOTHES ON!!
AND WHY AM I IN THE LOUNGE?!
WELL.
CALM DOWN, WILLIAM.
ANYWAY, TELL ME WHAT HAPPENED.
SHOOO
ユウウウ
SPECIAL TRAINING SO YOU CAN BEAT ISAAC?
THAT TEACHER OR WHOEVER?
MATHERS! I'M JUST A FLESH-AND-BLOOD HUMAN!

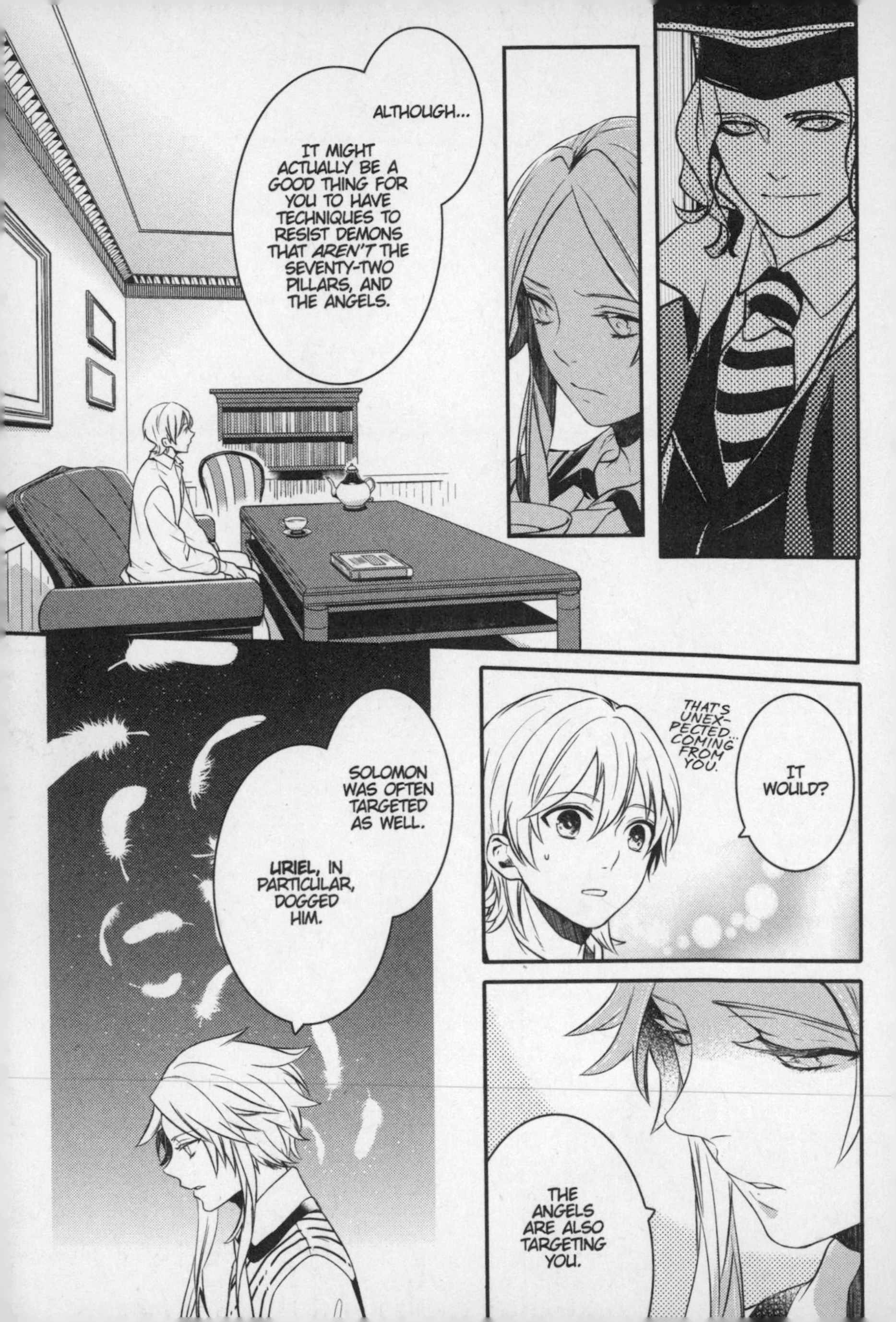
ALTHOUGH...
IT MIGHT ACTUALLY BE A GOOD THING FOR YOU TO HAVE TECHNIQUES TO RESIST DEMONS THAT *AREN'T* THE SEVENTY-TWO PILLARS, AND THE ANGELS.
IT WOULD?
THAT'S UNEXPECTED... COMING FROM YOU.
THE ANGELS ARE ALSO TARGETING YOU.
SOLOMON WAS OFTEN TARGETED AS WELL.
URIEL, IN PARTICULAR, DOGGED HIM.

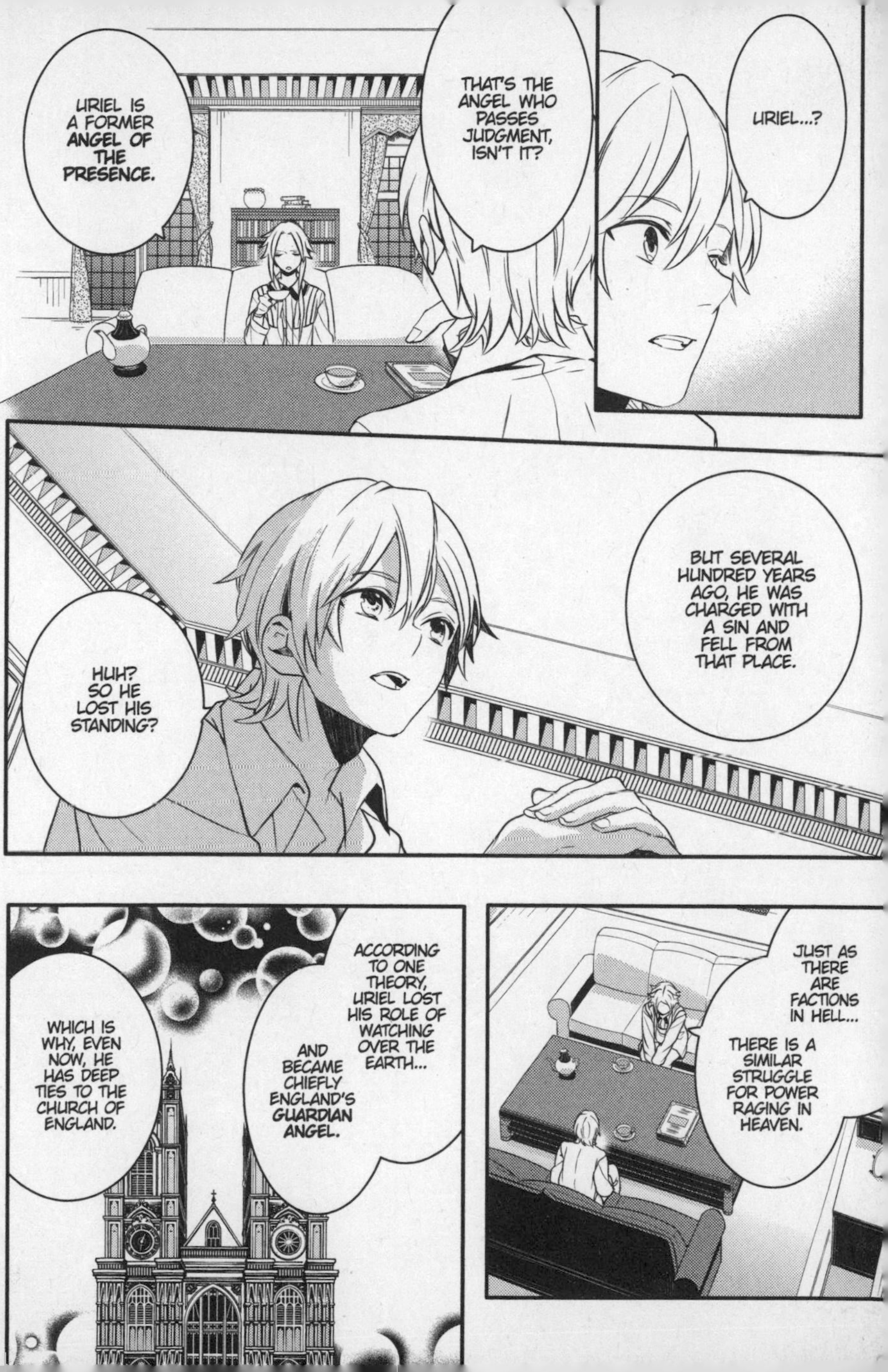
URIEL...?
THAT'S THE ANGEL WHO PASSES JUDGMENT, ISN'T IT?
URIEL IS A FORMER **ANGEL OF THE PRESENCE.**
BUT SEVERAL HUNDRED YEARS AGO, HE WAS CHARGED WITH A SIN AND FELL FROM THAT PLACE.
HUH? SO HE LOST HIS STANDING?
JUST AS THERE ARE FACTIONS IN HELL...
THERE IS A SIMILAR STRUGGLE FOR POWER RAGING IN HEAVEN.
ACCORDING TO ONE THEORY, URIEL LOST HIS ROLE OF WATCHING OVER THE EARTH...
AND BECAME CHIEFLY ENGLAND'S **GUARDIAN ANGEL.**
WHICH IS WHY, EVEN NOW, HE HAS DEEP TIES TO THE CHURCH OF ENGLAND.

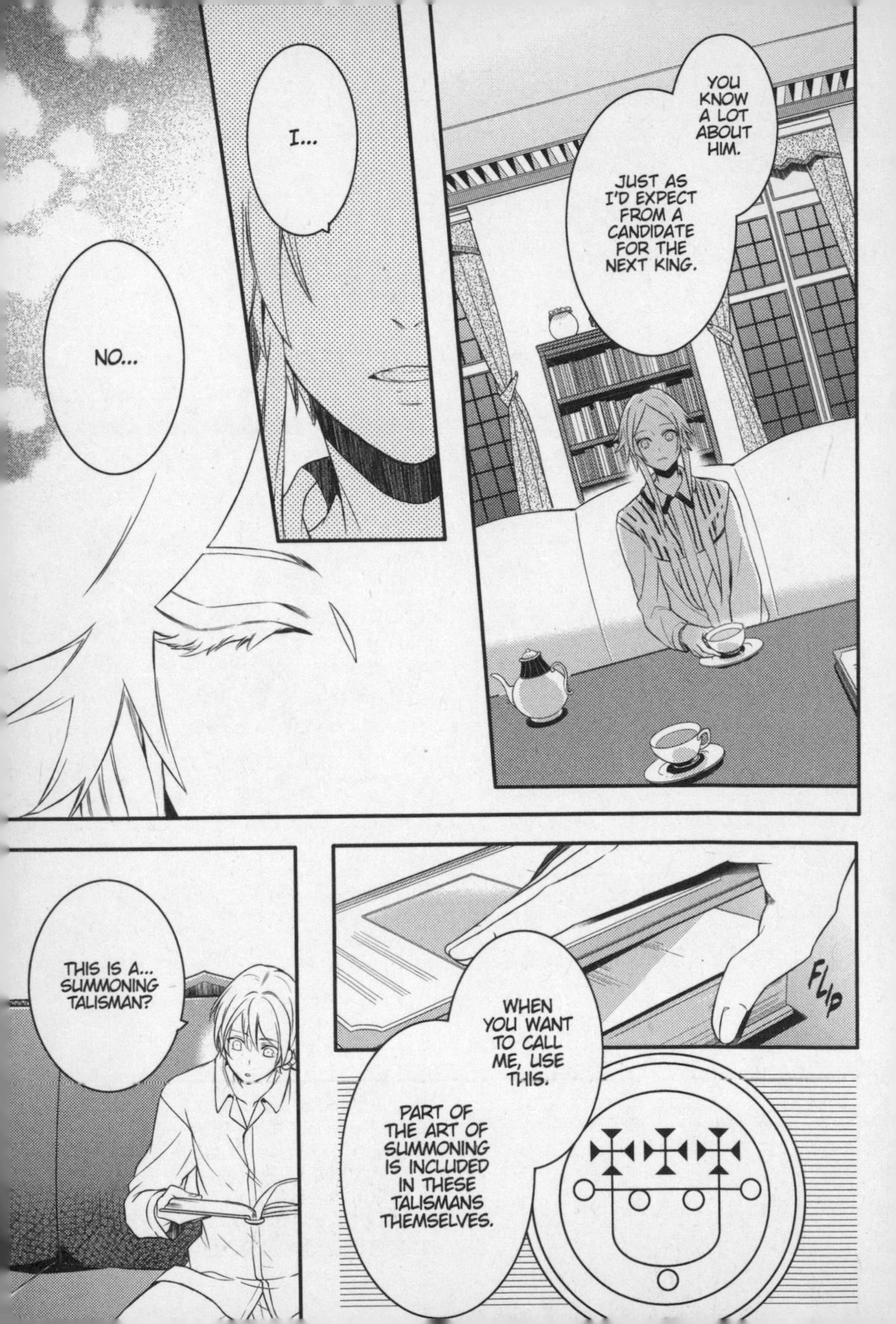
YOU KNOW A LOT ABOUT HIM.
JUST AS I'D EXPECT FROM A CANDIDATE FOR THE NEXT KING.
I...
NO...
FLIP
WHEN YOU WANT TO CALL ME, USE THIS.
PART OF THE ART OF SUMMONING IS INCLUDED IN THESE TALISMANS THEMSELVES.
THIS IS A... SUMMONING TALISMAN?

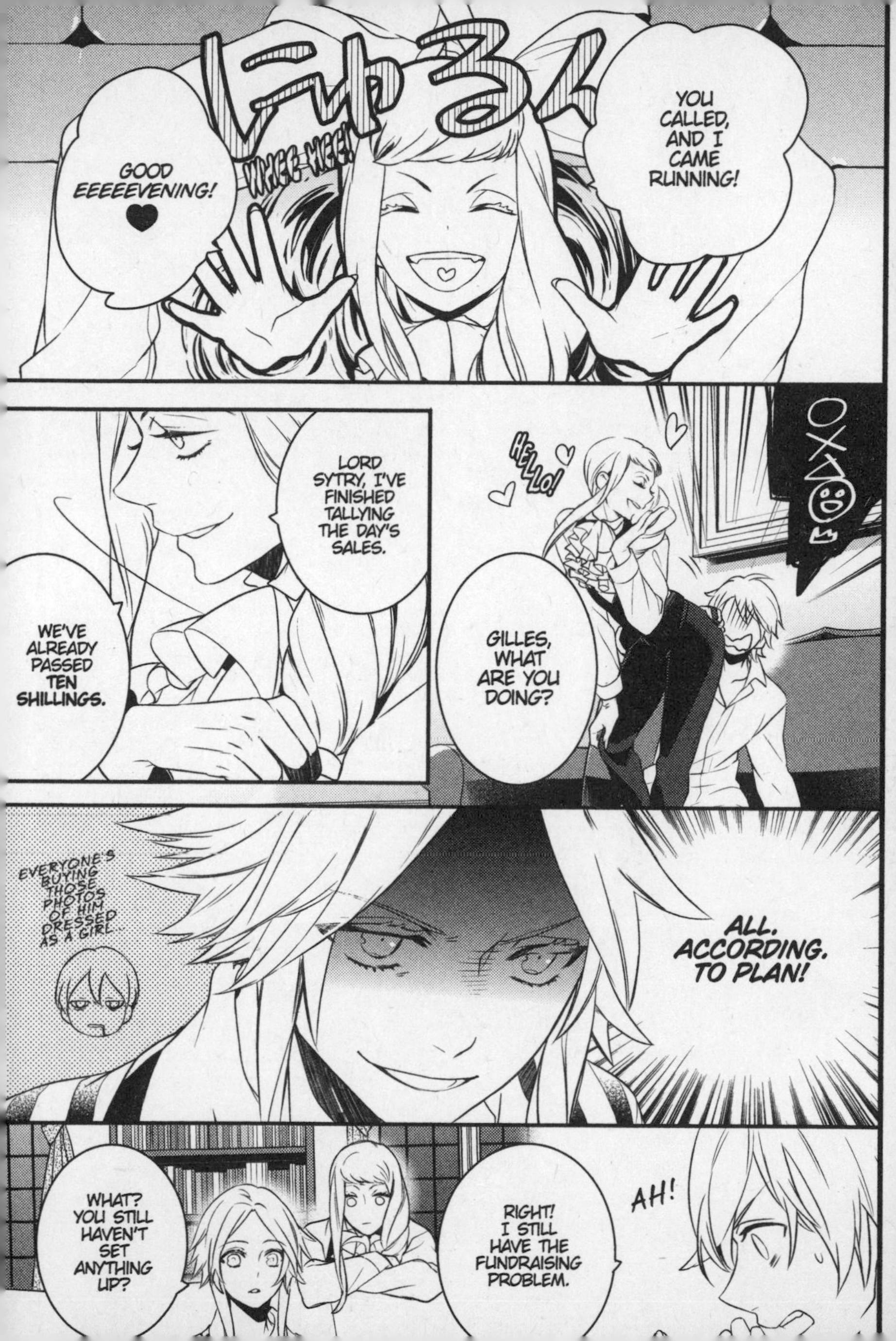
YOU CALLED, AND I CAME RUNNING!
WHEE HEE!
GOOD EEEEEVENING! ♥
HELLO!
GILLES, WHAT ARE YOU DOING?
LORD SYTRY, I'VE FINISHED TALLYING THE DAY'S SALES.
WE'VE ALREADY PASSED TEN SHILLINGS.
ALL. ACCORDING. TO PLAN!
EVERYONE'S BUYING THOSE PHOTOS OF HIM DRESSED AS A GIRL.
AH!
RIGHT! I STILL HAVE THE FUNDRAISING PROBLEM.
WHAT? YOU STILL HAVEN'T SET ANYTHING UP?

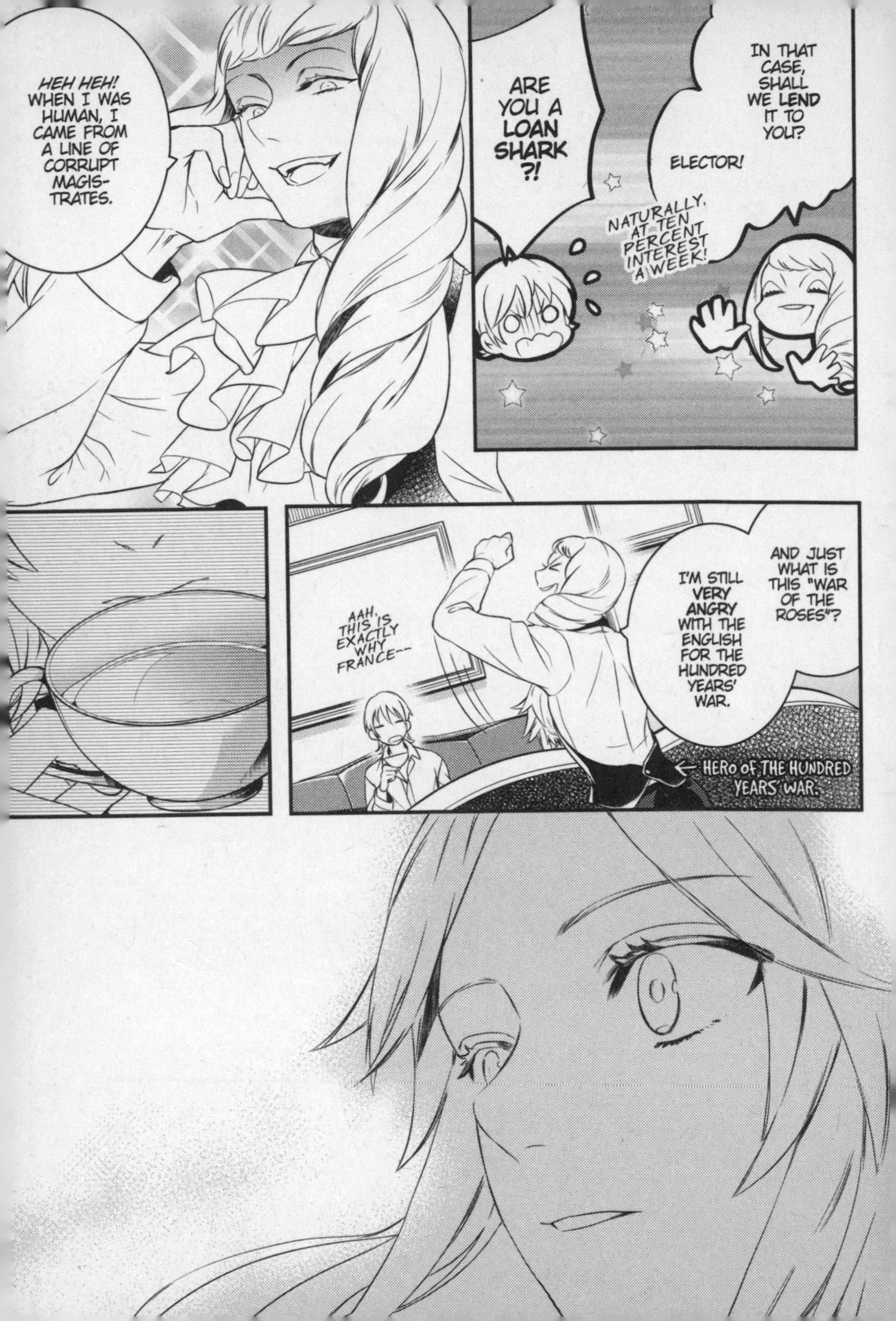
IN THAT CASE, SHALL WE LEND IT TO YOU?
ELECTOR!
ARE YOU A LOAN SHARK?!
NATURALLY, AT TEN PERCENT INTEREST A WEEK!
HEH HEH! WHEN I WAS HUMAN, I CAME FROM A LINE OF CORRUPT MAGIS-TRATES.
AND JUST WHAT IS THIS "WAR OF THE ROSES"?
I'M STILL VERY ANGRY WITH THE ENGLISH FOR THE HUNDRED YEARS' WAR.
AAH, THIS IS EXACTLY WHY FRANCE--
HERO OF THE HUNDRED YEARS' WAR.

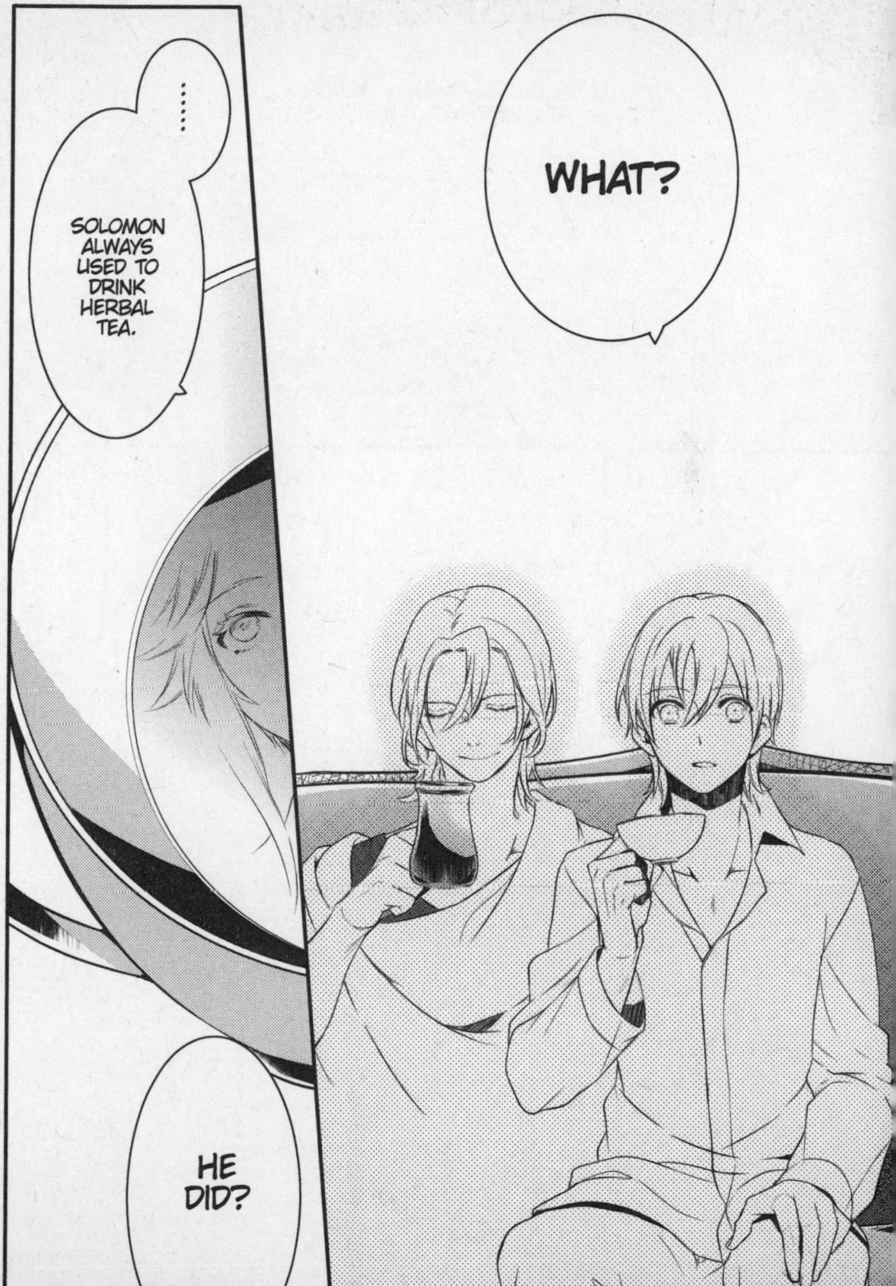
WHAT?
......
SOLOMON ALWAYS USED TO DRINK HERBAL TEA.
HE DID?

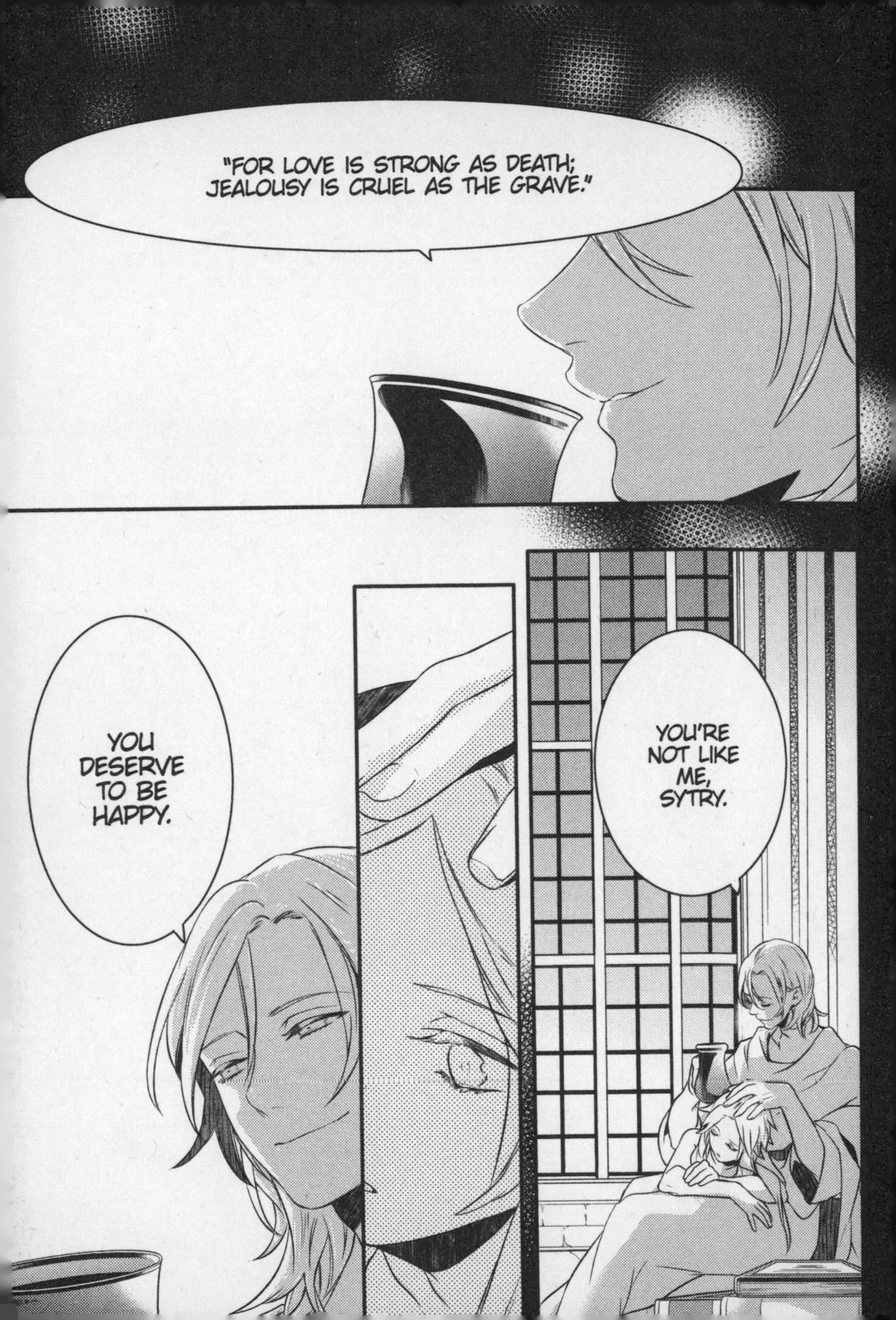
"FOR LOVE IS STRONG AS DEATH; JEALOUSY IS CRUEL AS THE GRAVE."
YOU'RE NOT LIKE ME, SYTRY.
YOU DESERVE TO BE HAPPY.

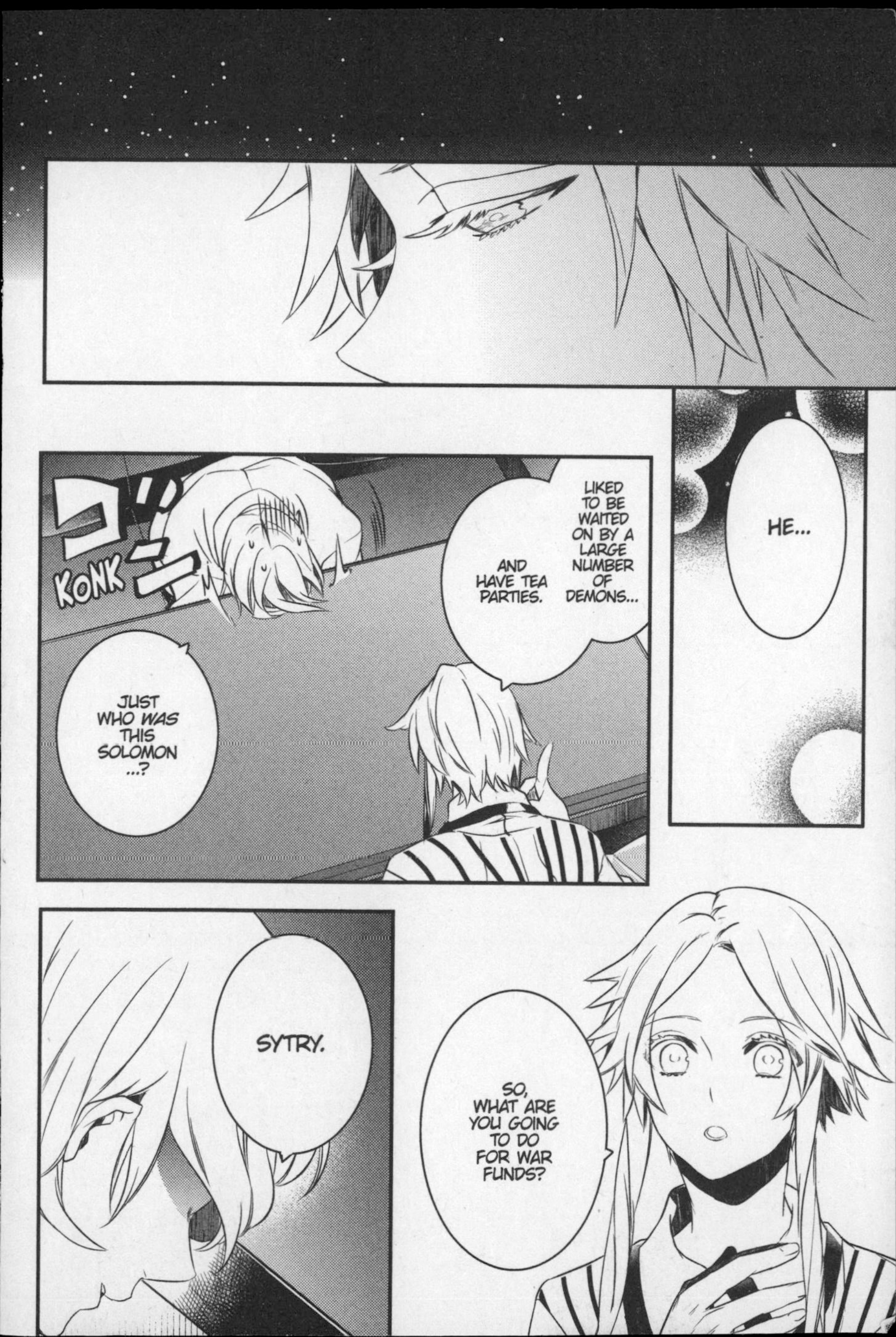
HE...
LIKED TO BE WAITED ON BY A LARGE NUMBER OF DEMONS...
AND HAVE TEA PARTIES.
KONK
JUST WHO WAS THIS SOLOMON ...?
SO, WHAT ARE YOU GOING TO DO FOR WAR FUNDS?
SYTRY.

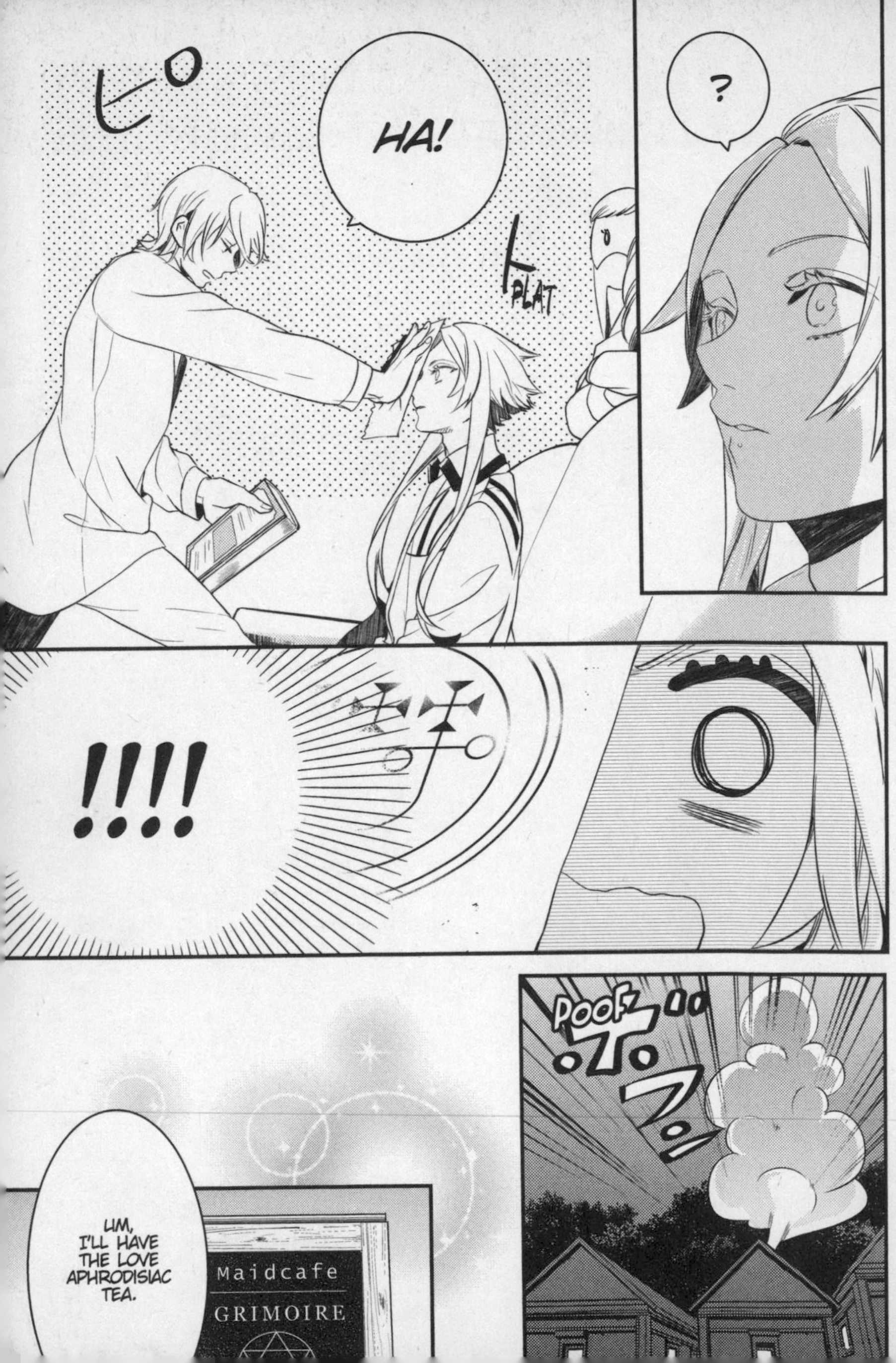
?
HA!
PLAT
!!!!
POOF
UM, I'LL HAVE THE LOVE APHRODISIAC TEA.
Maidcafe
GRIMOIRE

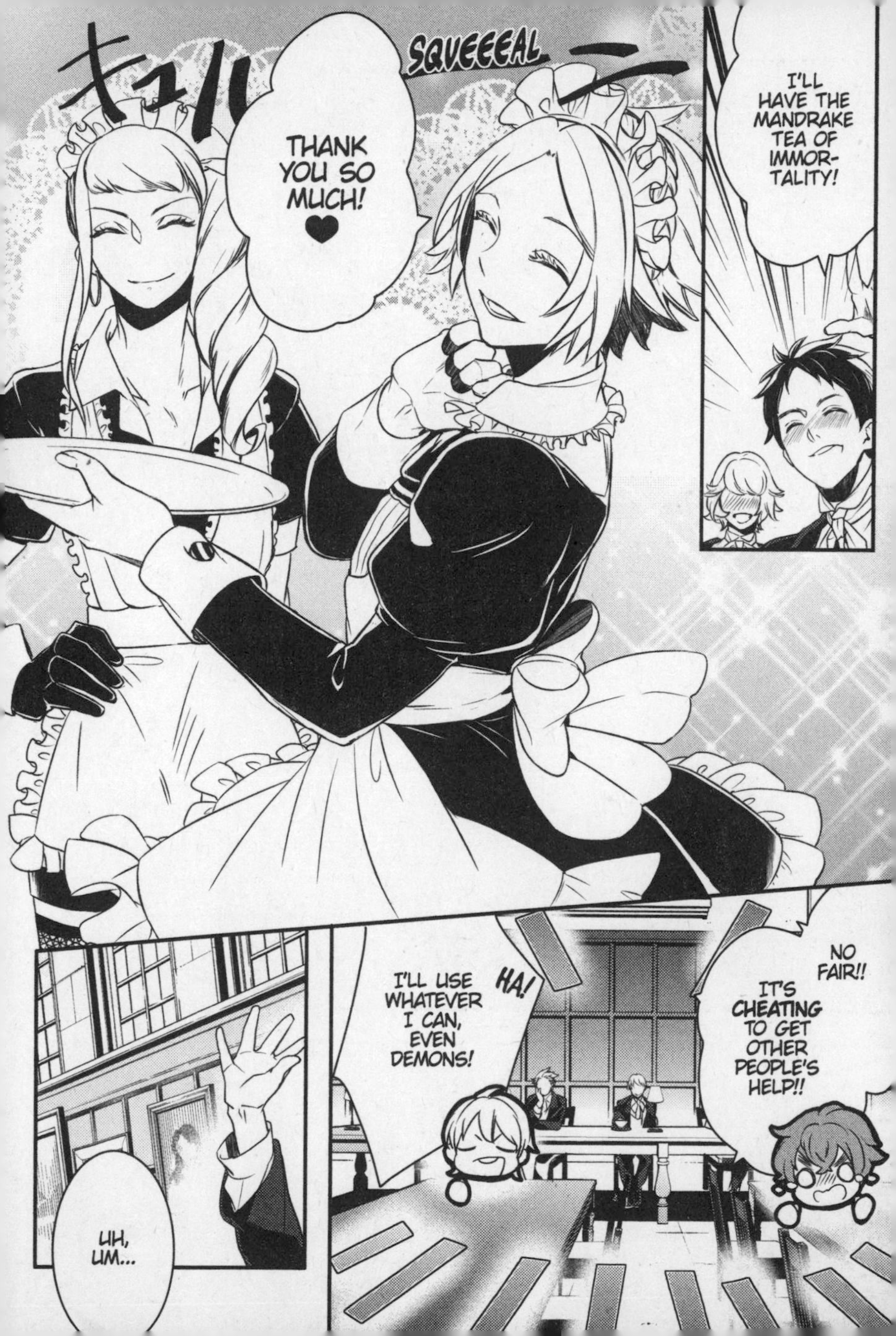
I'LL HAVE THE MANDRAKE TEA OF IMMORTALITY!
キュル
SQUEEEAL
THANK YOU SO MUCH! ♥
NO FAIR!!
IT'S CHEATING TO GET OTHER PEOPLE'S HELP!!
HA!
I'LL USE WHATEVER I CAN, EVEN DEMONS!
UH, UM...

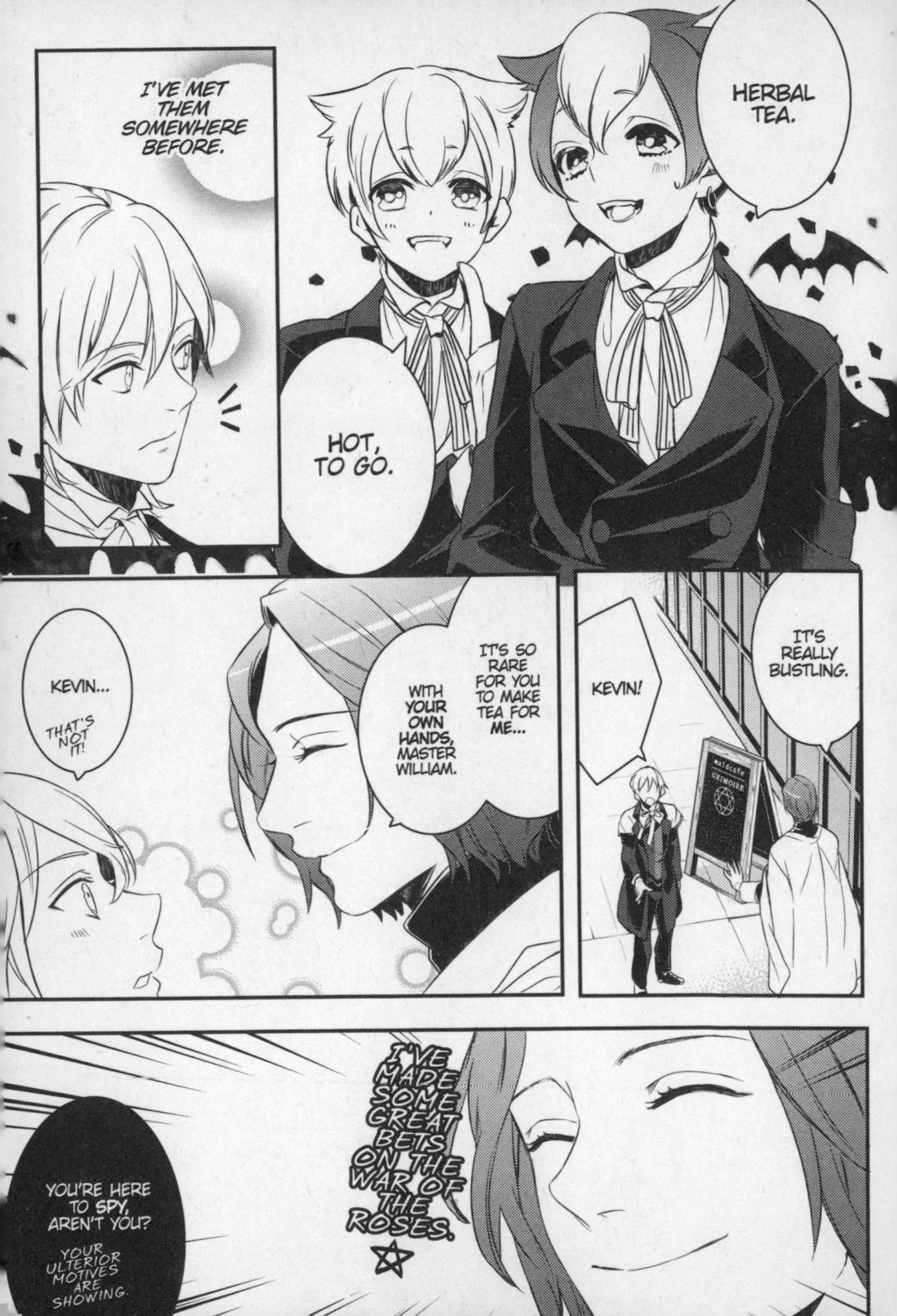
HERBAL TEA.
HOT, TO GO.
I'VE MET THEM SOMEWHERE BEFORE.
IT'S REALLY BUSTLING.
KEVIN!
Maidcafe GRIMOIRE
IT'S SO RARE FOR YOU TO MAKE TEA FOR ME...
WITH YOUR OWN HANDS, MASTER WILLIAM.
KEVIN...
THAT'S NOT IT!
I'VE MADE SOME GREAT BETS ON THE WAR OF THE ROSES.
YOU'RE HERE TO SPY, AREN'T YOU?
YOUR ULTERIOR MOTIVES ARE SHOWING.

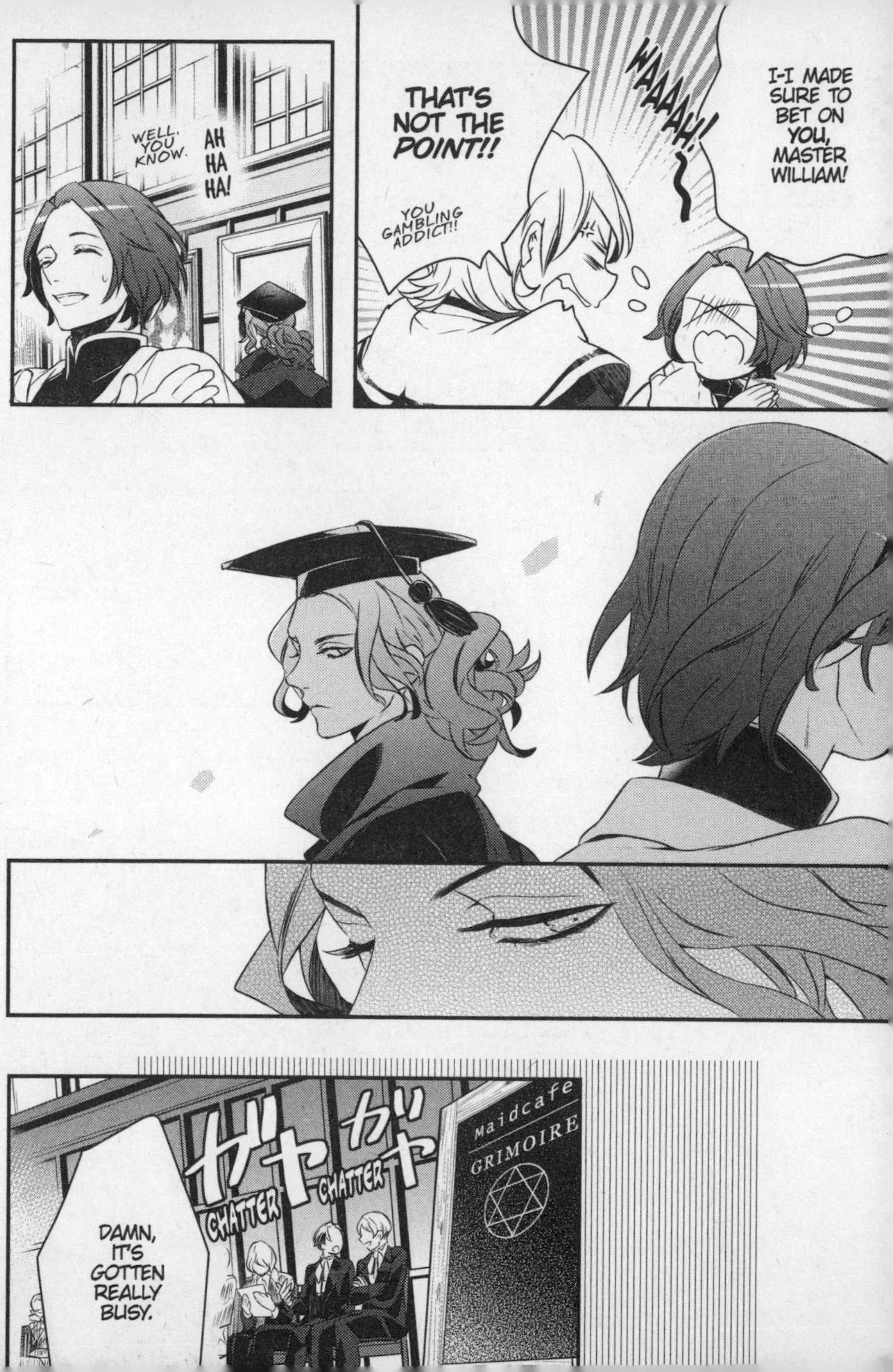
I-I MADE SURE TO BET ON YOU, MASTER WILLIAM!
WAAAAH!! ~
THAT'S NOT THE POINT!!
YOU GAMBLING ADDICT!!
AH HA HA!
WELL, YOU KNOW.
Maidcafe GRIMOIRE
ガヤ ガヤ
CHATTER CHATTER
DAMN, IT'S GOTTEN REALLY BUSY.

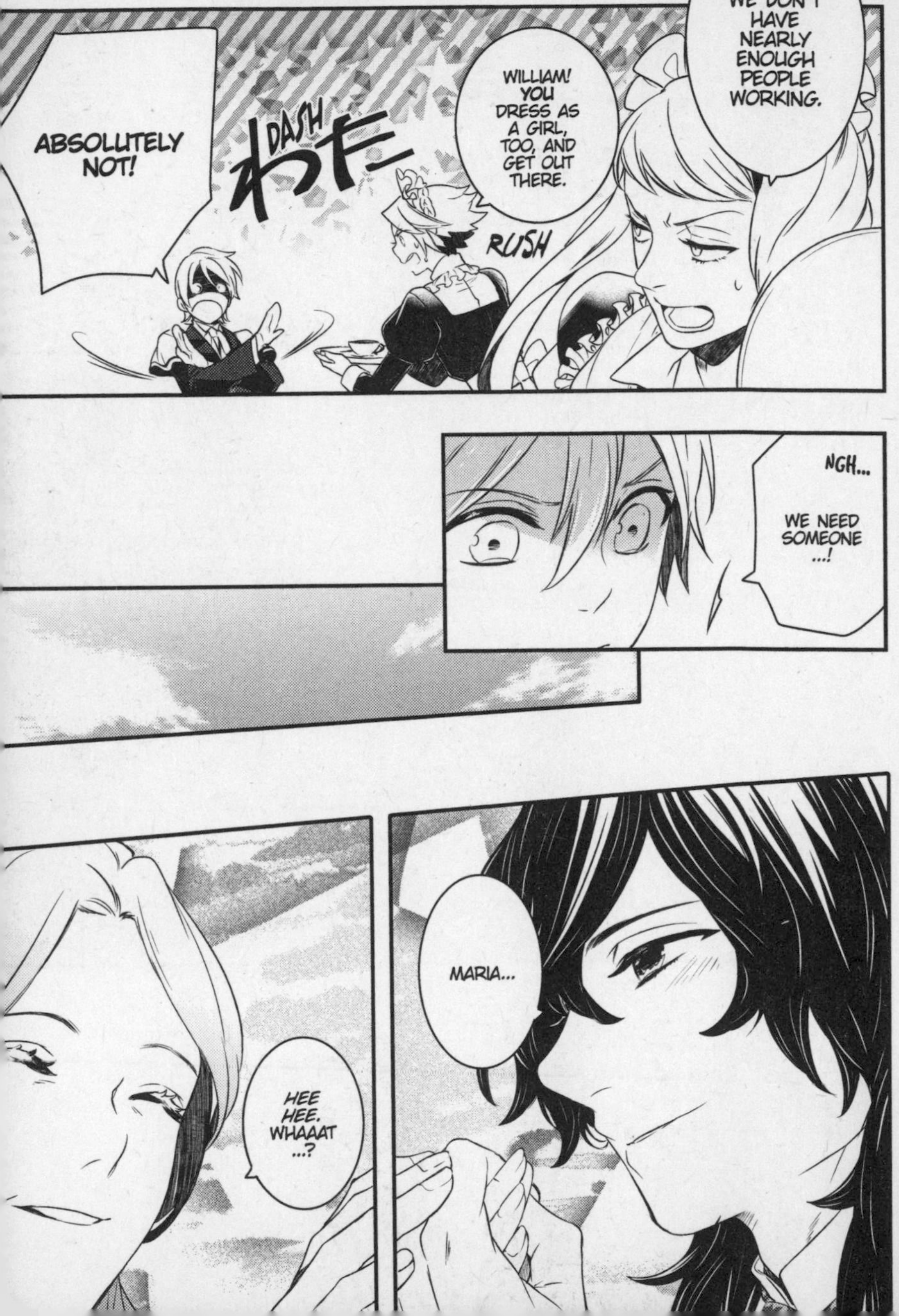
WE DON'T HAVE NEARLY ENOUGH PEOPLE WORKING.
WILLIAM! YOU DRESS AS A GIRL, TOO, AND GET OUT THERE.
RUSH
DASH
わー
ABSOLUTELY NOT!
NGH...
WE NEED SOMEONE ...!
MARIA...
HEE HEE. WHAAAT ...?

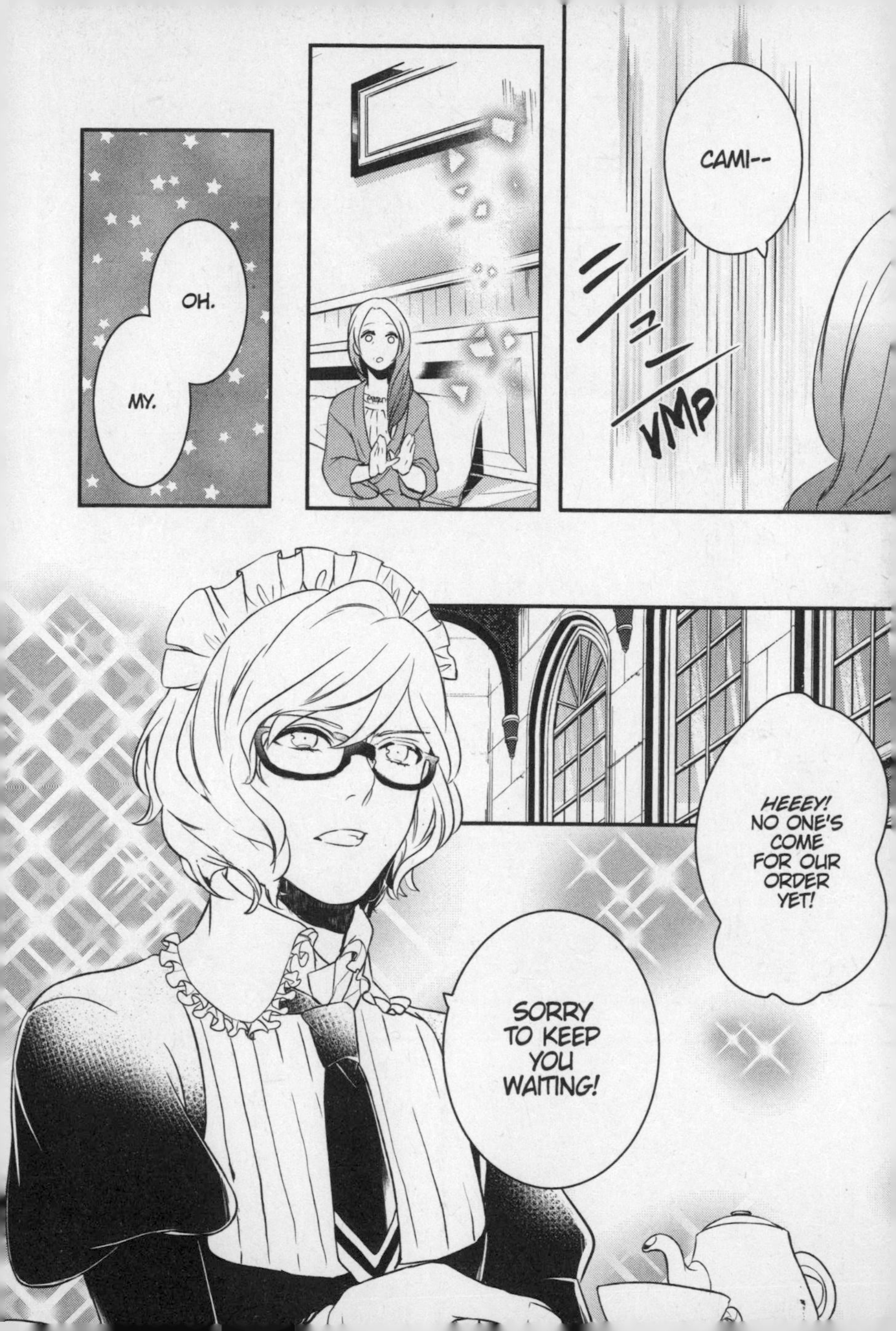
CAMI--
VMP
OH.
MY.
HEEEY! NO ONE'S COME FOR OUR ORDER YET!
SORRY TO KEEP YOU WAITING!

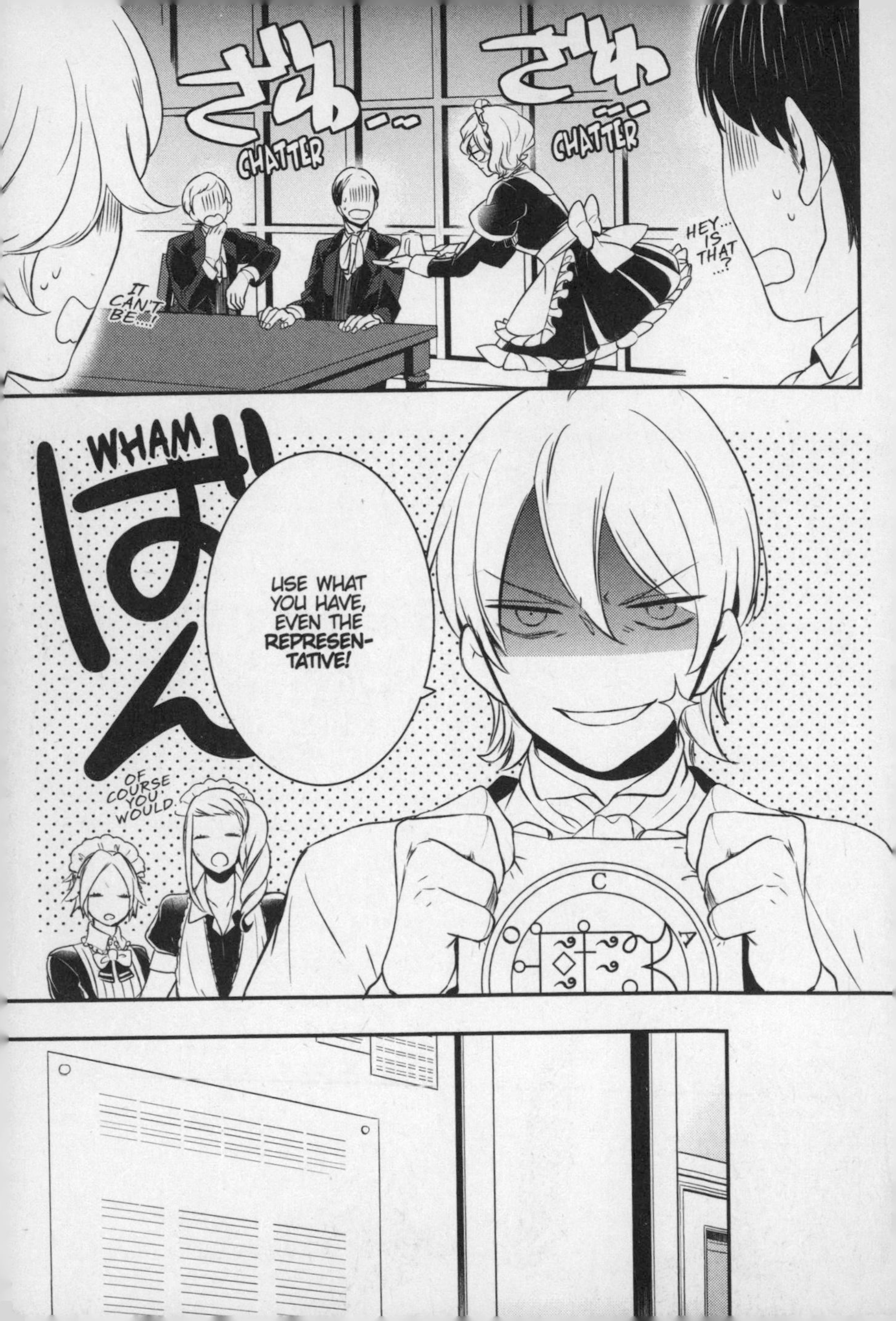
ざわ
CHATTER
HEY... IS THAT...?
ざわ
CHATTER
IT CAN'T BE...!
ばん
WHAM
USE WHAT YOU HAVE, EVEN THE REPRESENTATIVE!
OF COURSE YOU WOULD.

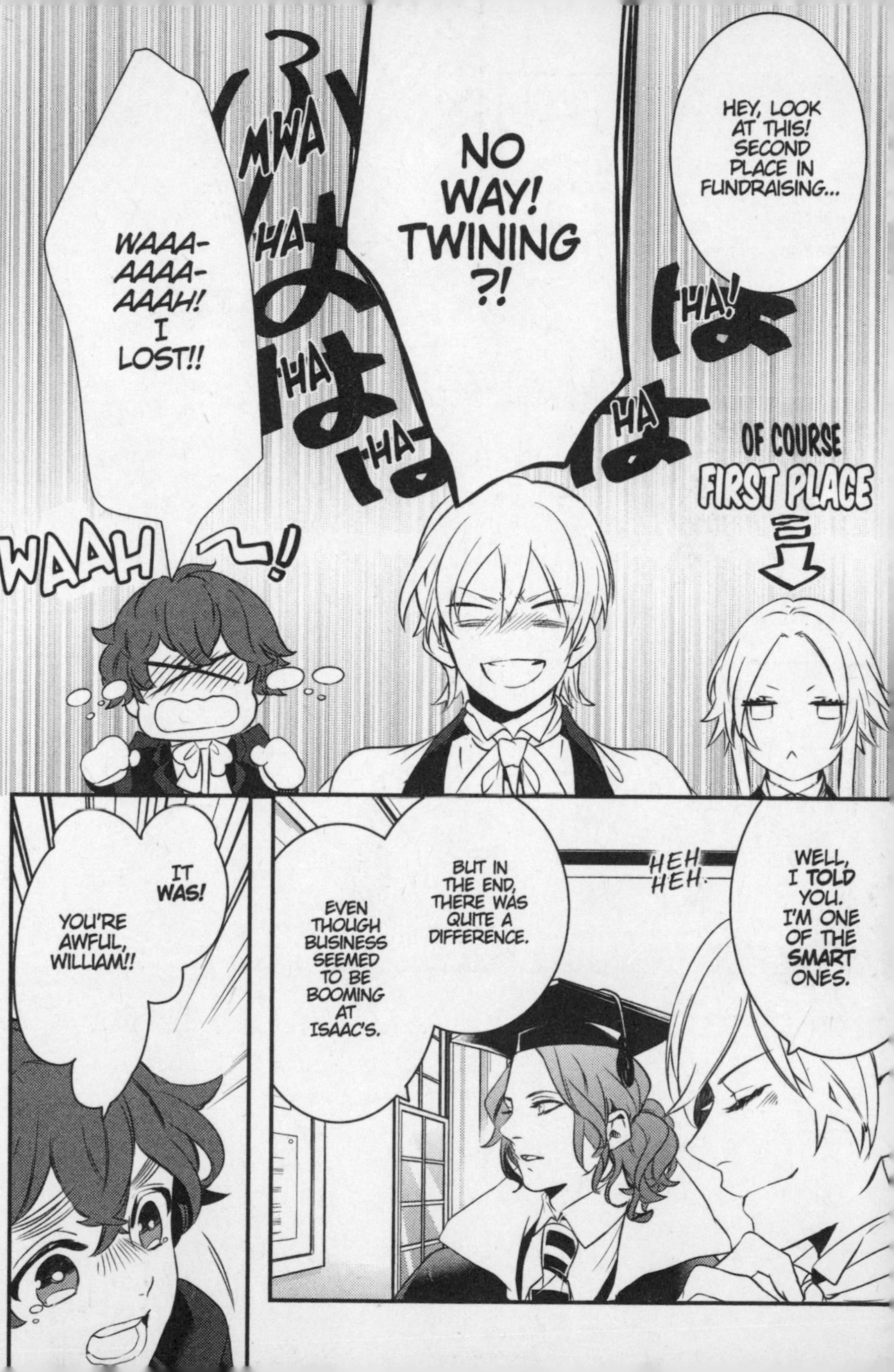
HEY, LOOK AT THIS! SECOND PLACE IN FUNDRAISING...
HA! HA
NO WAY! TWINING?!
MWA HA HA HA
WAAA-AAAA-AAAH! I LOST!!
OF COURSE FIRST PLACE
WAAH~!
WELL, I TOLD YOU. I'M ONE OF THE SMART ONES.
HEH HEH.
BUT IN THE END, THERE WAS QUITE A DIFFERENCE.
EVEN THOUGH BUSINESS SEEMED TO BE BOOMING AT ISAAC'S.
IT WAS!
YOU'RE AWFUL, WILLIAM!!

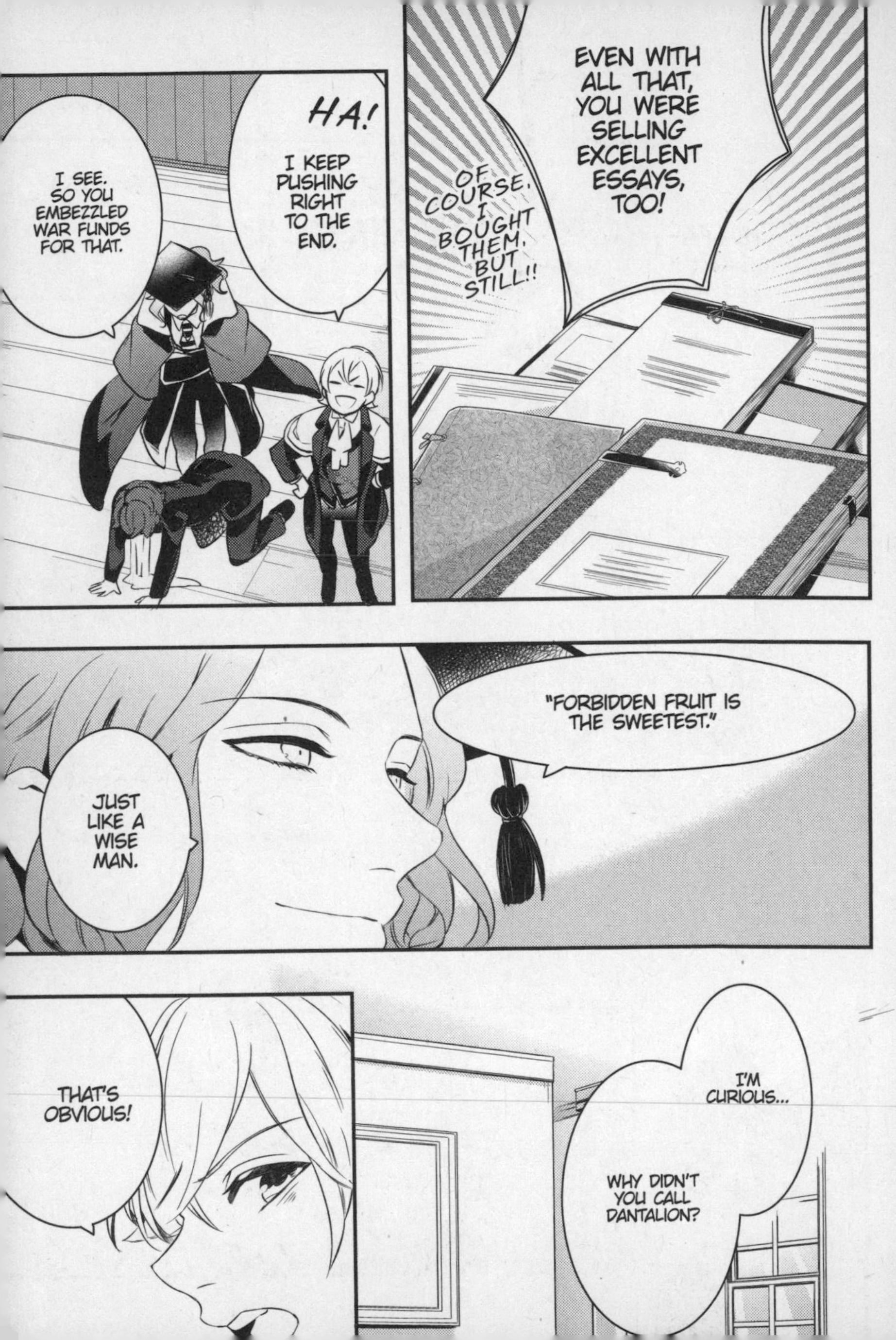
EVEN WITH ALL THAT, YOU WERE SELLING EXCELLENT ESSAYS, TOO!
OF COURSE, I BOUGHT THEM. BUT STILL!!
HA!
I KEEP PUSHING RIGHT TO THE END.
I SEE. SO YOU EMBEZZLED WAR FUNDS FOR THAT.
"FORBIDDEN FRUIT IS THE SWEETEST."
JUST LIKE A WISE MAN.
I'M CURIOUS...
WHY DIDN'T YOU CALL DANTALION?
THAT'S OBVIOUS!

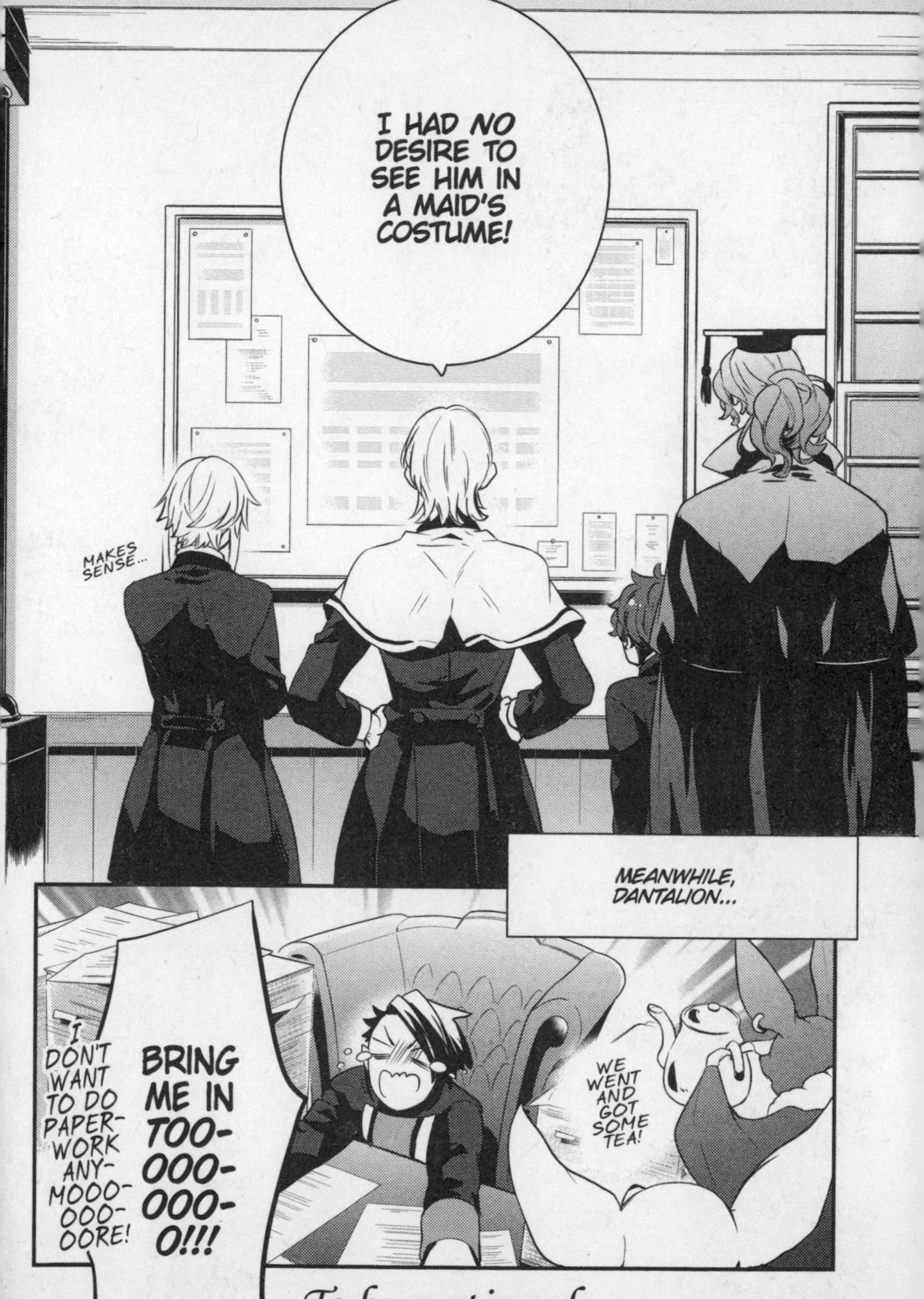
I HAD NO DESIRE TO SEE HIM IN A MAID'S COSTUME!
MAKES SENSE...
MEANWHILE, DANTALION...
WE WENT AND GOT SOME TEA!
BRING ME IN TOO-OOO-OOO-OOO-O!!!
I DON'T WANT TO DO PAPER-WORK ANY-MOOO-OOO-OORE!

To be continued...

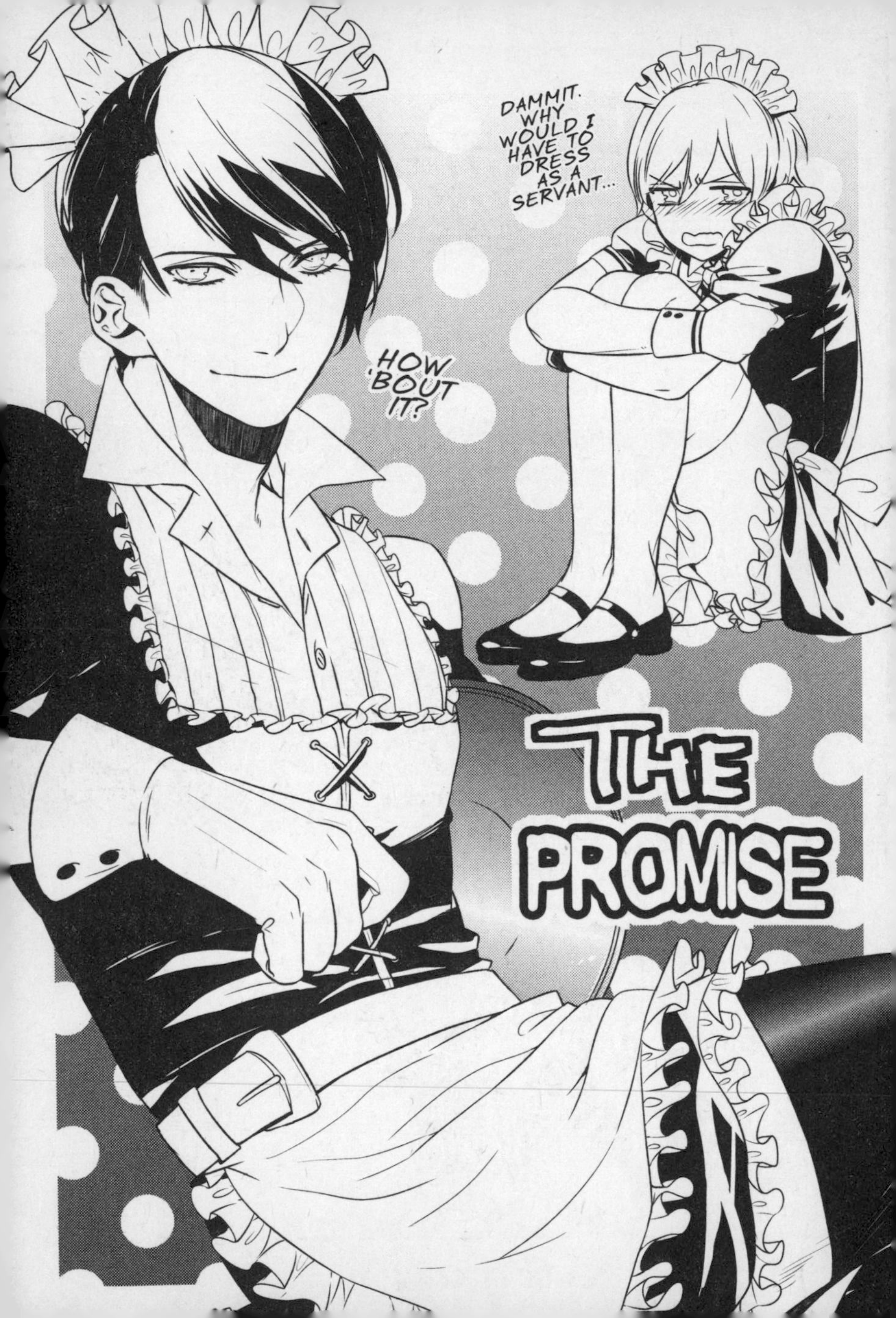
DAMMIT. WHY WOULD I HAVE TO DRESS AS A SERVANT...
HOW 'BOUT IT?
THE PROMISE

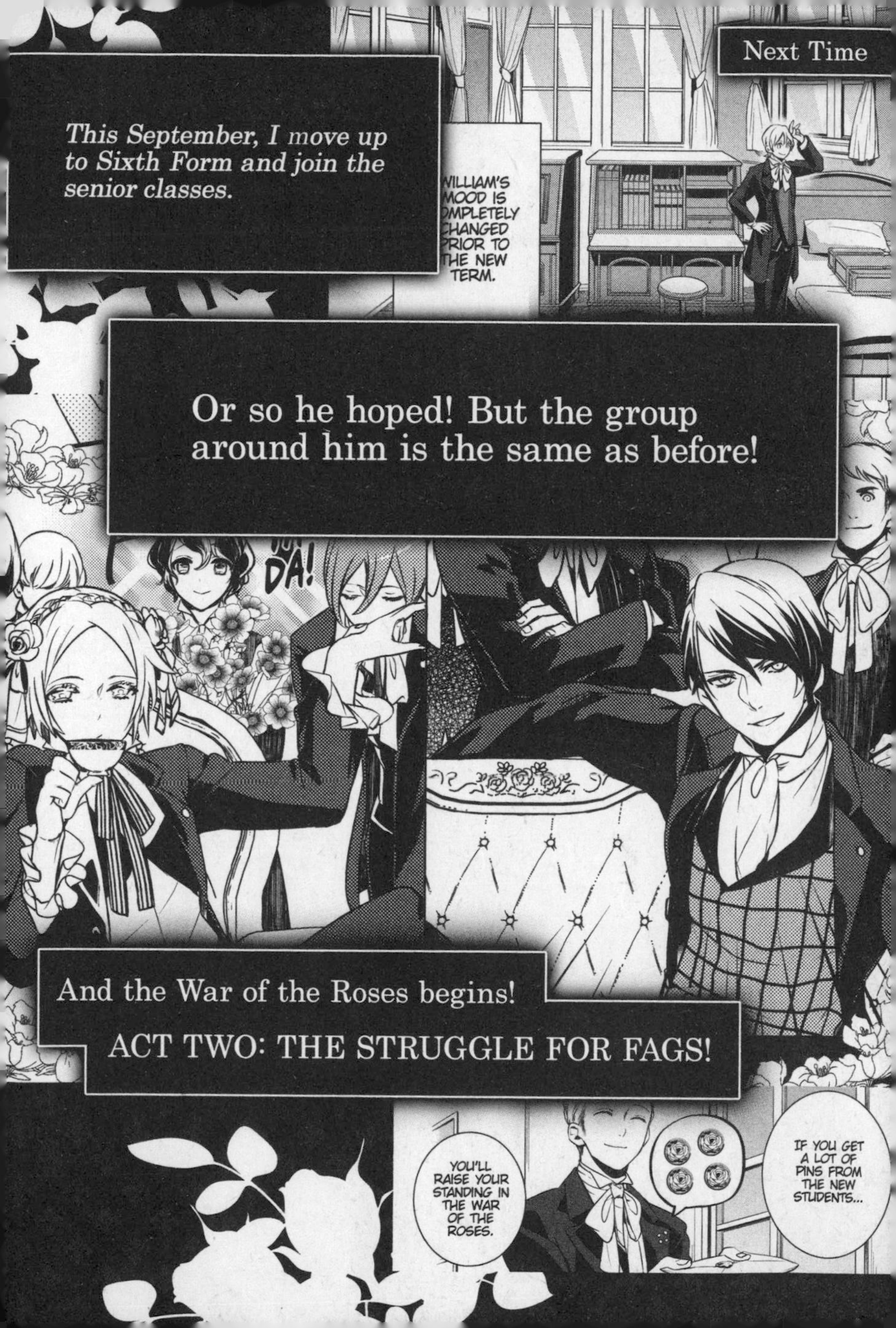
Next Time
WILLIAM'S MOOD IS COMPLETELY CHANGED PRIOR TO THE NEW TERM.
This September, I move up to Sixth Form and join the senior classes.
Or so he hoped! But the group around him is the same as before!
DA!
And the War of the Roses begins!
ACT TWO: THE STRUGGLE FOR FAGS!
IF YOU GET A LOT OF PINS FROM THE NEW STUDENTS...
YOU'LL RAISE YOUR STANDING IN THE WAR OF THE ROSES.